NETWORK MORPHOLOGY

Morphology is particularly challenging, because it is pervaded by irregularity and idiosyncrasy. This book is a study of word structure using a specific theoretical framework known as 'Network Morphology'. It describes the systems of rules which determine the structure of words by construing irregularity as a matter of degree, using examples from a diverse range of languages and phenomena to illustrate. Many languages share common word-building strategies, and many diverge in interesting ways. These strategies can be understood by distinguishing different notions of 'default'. The Network Morphology philosophy promotes the use of computational implementation to check theories. The accompanying website provides the computer-coded version of the Network Morphology model of word structure for readers to test, customize and develop. This book will be a valuable contribution to the fields of linguistic typology and morphology and will be welcomed by researchers and graduate students in these areas.

DUNSTAN BROWN is Senior Lecturer in Linguistics in the Surrey Morphology Group at the University of Surrey.

ANDREW HIPPISLEY is Associate Professor of Linguistics in the Department of English at the University of Kentucky.

In this series

101. DONKA MINKOVA: *Alliteration and sound change in early English*
102. MARK C. BAKER: *Lexical categories: verbs, nouns and adjectives*
103. CARLOTA S. SMITH: *Modes of discourse: the local structure of texts*
104. ROCHELLE LIEBER: *Morphology and lexical semantics*
105. HOLGER DIESSEL: *The acquisition of complex sentences*
106. SHARON INKELAS and CHERYL ZOLL: *Reduplication: doubling in morphology*
107. SUSAN EDWARDS: *Fluent aphasia*
108. BARBARA DANCYGIER and EVE SWEETSER: *Mental spaces in grammar: conditional constructions*
109. MATTHEW BAERMAN, DUNSTAN BROWN and GREVILLE G. CORBETT: *The syntax–morphology interface: a study of syncretism*
110. MARCUS TOMALIN: *Linguistics and the formal sciences: the origins of generative grammar*
111. SAMUEL D. EPSTEIN and T. DANIEL SEELY: *Derivations in minimalism*
112. PAUL DE LACY: *Markedness: reduction and preservation in phonology*
113. YEHUDA N. FALK: *Subjects and their properties*
114. P. H. MATTHEWS: *Syntactic relations: a critical survey*
115. MARK C. BAKER: *The syntax of agreement and concord*
116. GILLIAN CATRIONA RAMCHAND: *Verb meaning and the lexicon: a first phase syntax*
117. PIETER MUYSKEN: *Functional categories*
118. JUAN URIAGEREKA: *Syntactic anchors: on semantic structuring*
119. D. ROBERT LADD: *Intonational phonology second edition*
120. LEONARD H. BABBY: *The syntax of argument structure*
121. B. ELAN DRESHER: *The contrastive hierarchy in phonology*
122. DAVID ADGER, DANIEL HARBOUR and LAUREL J. WATKINS: *Mirrors and microparameters: phrase structure beyond free word order*
123. NIINA NING ZHANG: *Coordination in syntax*
124. NEIL SMITH: *Acquiring phonology*
125. NINA TOPINTZI: *Onsets: suprasegmental and prosodic behaviour*
126. CEDRIC BOECKX, NORBERT HORNSTEIN and JAIRO NUNES: *Control as movement*
127. MICHAEL ISRAEL: *The grammar of polarity: pragmatics, sensitivity, and the logic of scales*
128. M. RITA MANZINI and LEONARDO M. SAVOIA: *Grammatical categories: variation in romance languages*
129. BARBARA CITKO: *Symmetry in syntax: merge, move and labels*
130. RACHEL WALKER: *Vowel patterns in language*
131. MARY DALRYMPLE and IRINA NIKOLAEVA: *Objects and information structure*

Earlier issues not listed are also available

CAMBRIDGE STUDIES IN LINGUISTICS

Network Morphology: A Defaults-based Theory of Word Structure

NETWORK MORPHOLOGY

A DEFAULTS-BASED THEORY OF WORD STRUCTURE

DUNSTAN BROWN
University of Surrey

ANDREW HIPPISLEY
University of Kentucky

CAMBRIDGE UNIVERSITY PRESS
Cambridge, New York, Melbourne, Madrid, Cape Town,
Singapore, São Paulo, Delhi, Tokyo, Mexico City

Cambridge University Press
The Edinburgh Building, Cambridge CB2 8RU, UK

Published in the United States of America by Cambridge University Press, New York

www.cambridge.org
Information on this title: www.cambridge.org/9781107005747

First published 2012

Printed in the United Kingdom at the University Press, Cambridge

A catalogue record for this publication is available from the British Library

Library of Congress Cataloguing in Publication data
Brown, Dunstan.
Network morphology : a defaults-based theory of word structure /
Dunstan Brown, Andrew Hippisley.
p. cm. – (Cambridge studies in linguistics ; 133)
Includes bibliographical references and indexes.
ISBN 978-1-107-00574-7
1. Grammar, Comparative and general–Morphology. 2. Grammar, Comparative and general–Word formation. I. Hippisley, Andrew. II. Title.
P241.B76 2012
415′.9–dc23 2011040522

ISBN 978-1-107-00574-7 Hardback

Additional resources for this publication at www.cambridge.org/Brown-Hippisley

For Rachel and Shirley

Contents

List of tables *page* xiii
List of figures xiv
Preface xv
Abbreviations and Russian transcription system used xviii

1 Options in constructing a morphological framework 1
1.0 Locating generalizations 1
1.0.1 Paradigmatic relations 4
1.0.2 Semi-regularity 5
1.0.3 Options and chapter outline 6
1.1 Object of inquiry: lexeme rather than morpheme 6
1.1.1 Radical agglutination 7
1.1.2 Morphemes and word syntax 10
1.1.3 Summary of object-of-inquiry option 12
1.2 Morphological domain: autonomous rather than part of a seamless web 13
1.2.1 Autonomous morphology and function/form dissociations 13
1.2.2 Seamless-web morphology and Distributed Morphology 19
1.2.3 Some challenges for Distributed Morphology's seamless web 25
1.2.4 Concluding autonomous over seamless-web morphology 29
1.3 Generalization as default inheritance 30
1.3.1 Default rather than mandatory inheritance 33
1.3.2 Multiple inheritance and orthogonality rather than single inheritance 35
1.3.3 Inflection versus derivation and submodularity 37
1.4 Morphological formalization 41
1.5 Summary of Network Morphology options and book outline 41

2 A framework for morphological defaults 44
2.0 Introduction 44
2.1 Models and analyses of lexemes 45
2.2 Lexemes as part of a network 51

	2.2.1 Inheritance relations	52
	2.2.2 Hierarchy relations	54
	2.2.3 Attribute ordering	57
	2.2.4 Flexible paradigm signatures	64
	2.2.5 Network relations	69
	2.2.6 Morphology as a network	70
	2.2.7 Local and global context	80
	2.2.8 Evaluable paths	82
2.3	Defaults	83
	2.3.1 Path extension and underspecification	84
	2.3.2 Exceptional and normal case defaults	86
	2.3.3 Defaults and productivity	106
2.4	The default relationship between syntax and morphology	107
	2.4.1 Non-autonomy	107
	2.4.2 Morphosyntactic feature slippages	108
	2.4.3 Autonomous morphological features	109
2.5	Conclusion	110
3	**Inflectional classes**	111
3.0	Introduction	111
3.1	Inflectional classes within the wider typological space	113
	3.1.1 Example 1: No morphological hierarchy required	118
	3.1.2 Example 2: Morphological hierarchy required	122
	3.1.3 Inheritance between the lexemic and morphological hierarchies	139
3.2	Justifying morphological hierarchies	145
3.3	Conclusion	149
4	**Syncretism**	151
4.0	Introduction	151
4.1	Definitions	152
4.2	Syncretism by default inference	156
4.3	Syncretism by referral	167
4.4	Case study for generalized referrals: Dalabon verbal morphology	170
	4.4.1 The Dalabon paradigm without referrals	175
	4.4.2 Relating prefixes and clitics	177
	4.4.3 Adding referrals	178
	4.4.4 Summary	180
4.5	Combining stem indexing and default inference	180
4.6	Conclusion	184
5	**Morphological mismatch and extended deponency**	186
5.0	Introduction	186

5.1 Extended deponency as defaults-based rule interaction 188
5.1.1 The hierarchical characterization of deponency 189
5.2 The Network Morphology account of Latin verb inflection 194
5.2.1 Non-regulars excluding deponents 199
5.3 Classical deponency 201
5.3.1 Mismatch, Property 1: overriding the first-order default 202
5.3.2 Lack of full participation, Property 2: overriding the second-order default 203
5.3.3 Semi-deponents, Property 3: overriding the second- and third-order defaults 205
5.3.4 'Form' defaults and defectiveness, Properties 4 and 5 208
5.4 Extended deponency and Archi nouns 209
5.4.1 The Network Morphology account of Archi nouns 209
5.4.2 Integrating deponent lexical entries 213
5.5 Is Latin deponency really morphological mismatch? 217
5.6 Concluding remarks 219

6 Defaults and paradigmatic restructuring: diachronic deponency 221
6.0 Introduction 221
6.1 Diachronic deponency as paradigmatic restructuring 222
6.2 Virtual paradigms and inheritance from the morphological hierarchy 226
6.3 The Network Morphology account of diachronic deponency 231
6.3.1 Activation of deponents 234
6.3.2 Passivation of deponents 238
6.4 Questions about virtual paradigms 243
6.4.1 Neo-deponents and virtual paradigms 244
6.4.2 Variation and virtual paradigms 245
6.4.3 Deponency in Greek 245
6.4.4 Before deponency 246
6.5 Concluding remarks 247

7 Derivation 249
7.0 Introduction 249
7.1 Derivation as lexeme-formation 251
7.2 Inheritance-based derivational relatedness 258
7.2.1 Conversion 262
7.2.2 Transposition 263
7.2.3 Category-preserving derivation 265
7.3 Resolving affix competition 269
7.3.1 Syntactic conditions 271
7.3.2 Formal conditions 272
7.3.3 Semantic conditions 275

7.4	Productivity	277
7.5	Concluding remarks on derivational morphology in Network Morphology	281
8	**Conclusion**	283
8.0	Taking stock	283
8.1	Autonomous morphology	283
8.2	Rules and defaults in morphology	285
8.3	Consequences	286
8.4	Importance of implementation for morphological theory	287
	Notes	289
	References	299
	Index of languages	314
	Index of names	316
	Index of subjects	319

Tables

4.1	Paradigm of Dalabon subject/object combinations	*page* 171
5.1	Deponency viewed as levels of default	193
5.2	Latin present indicative of verbs of the four conjugations	194

Figures

1.1	A morphological hierarchy for Russian nouns	*page* 31
1.2	The lexeme *zakon 'law'* inherits its morphology from Declension I	32
2.1	The lexeme `Stol` 'table'	48
2.2	The lexemic hierarchy with example lexical entry for the noun *stol* 'table'	56
2.3	The lexical entry for the noun *stol* 'table' inherits inflectional information from an orthogonal source	70
2.4	A partial stress hierarchy for Russian	75
2.5	The hierarchy and network relations associated with Russian Declension I morphology and stress	79
3.1	A fragment of Kokota morphology	120
3.2	The lexemic hierarchy with unstructured inflectional classes	125
3.3	Morphological hierarchy for Russian (version 1)	126
3.4	The hierarchical structure of Russian declensional classes	135
3.5	Isomorphic hierarchies	146
4.1	Web of nominal categories and syncretism from a thirty-language sample	166
6.1	Paradigm linkage and Latin deponents	230
7.1	A base and its derivative in Network Morphology	249

Preface

The name Network Morphology denotes a way of conceptualizing a language's morphological system as the assemblage of facts gathered at nodes that are themselves linked together with other nodes all inhabiting the same network, as we will see in the following chapters. Network Morphology is also suggestive of the highly collaborative nature of this framework's origins and ongoing development. How this network of linguists and computational linguists took shape is the story behind the story of this book. On a day in February 1988 at the University of Sussex, Gerald Gazdar demonstrated to Grev Corbett the workings of DATR, a lexical knowledge representation language invented by Roger Evans and Gerald, which was later adopted as the formalism that underpins Network Morphology theories. Immediately Grev recognized DATR's expressiveness for describing distinctly morphological issues. The collaborative network had just begun to form, but what proved to be a crucial addition had to wait a further three years, when Grev met Norman Fraser, both a linguist and computational linguist with near native fluency in DATR. A series of DATR sessions yielded the first proto-Network Morphology paper which was read at the First International DATR conference in August 1991, and was on Russian nominal inflection. The theme of the paper was syncretism, one of several major areas of word structure which Network Morphology has been so extensively engaged in. Through this early work on Russian inflectional morphology, two other themes were to emerge: parsimonious representation of inflectional classes and gender assignment. An early paper on these topics is Corbett and Fraser (1993). Russian morphology seemed a good place to start to play with some of these ideas, and in September 1992 Dunstan Brown and Andrew Hippisley joined Grev and Norman as research fellows on two major grants, sponsored by the Economic and Social Research Council (ESRC) and Leverhulme Trust to develop a DATR-representation of fragments of Russian's inflectional and derivational systems. Alan Timberlake became involved to advise on morphophonological aspects; he also collaborated on one of the first morphophonological Network Morphology papers, Brown, Corbett,

Fraser, Hippisley and Timberlake (1996). Soon after Dunstan and Andrew's arrival the name Network Morphology was given to the default inheritance and DATR-represented approach to word structure. The development of Network Morphology was supported by a further major grant from the ESRC in 1995, and the emergent framework started to yield analyses of other languages besides Russian such as Arapesh (Fraser and Corbett 1997), Polish (Brown 1998a) and Bininj Gun-wok (Evans, Brown and Corbett 1998). It also brought in Nick Evans, Marianne Mithun and Greg Stump, consultants on the project and wonderful support ever since.

It is to the members of this network that we wish to express our gratitude, without whom the Network Morphology book would not have been possible. We would also like to thank the following for their careful reading of draft chapters, and whose insightful comments we have attempted to assimilate: Matthew Baerman, Patricia Cabredo Hofherr, Grev Corbett, Roger Evans and Greg Stump. Thanks are also due to Andrew Spencer for discussion of clitics and edge features, among many other things. We owe an intellectual debt to the champions of the lexeme-based approach to morphology, which Network Morphology unswervingly takes: Mark Aronoff, Stephen Anderson, Peter Matthews, Gregory Stump and Arnold Zwicky. We would like to thank the Cambridge Studies in Linguistics series editorial board both for their excellent comments and for their encouragement for the project; these have unquestionably improved the final product. For material support we would like to thank the ESRC (R000233633) and the Leverhulme Trust (F.242M) for bringing us to Grev and Norman, and for bringing us together, the ESRC (R000236063) for supporting the development of the theory, the British Council and German Academic Exchange Service (DAAD) for supporting work on Russian verbal morphology, the British Council and Research Council of Norway who supported work on case exceptions in Russian, and the ESRC (R000237939) for supporting work on syncretism, which brought Matthew Baerman into the Network Morphology enterprise. The ESRC also supported projects on paradigms in use (RES-000–23–0082), deponency (RES-000–23–0375) and periphrasis (RES-062–23–0696) from which elements of the book have benefited. The Arts and Humanities Research Council is to be thanked for supporting projects on defectiveness (AH/D001579/1) and on languages of the Bougainville region (B/RG/AN4375/APN19365) on which Bill Palmer was the researcher. We thank Bill for answering our questions on Kokota during the writing of this monograph. The European Research Council is to be thanked for providing funding for the project on morphological complexity (ERC-2008-AdG-230268 MORPHOLOGY) during which part of the research for the book was carried out. We are grateful to the University of Kentucky's College of Arts & Sciences for a summer fellowship to employ our excellent proof reader, Amanda Barie, and to support Andrew Hippisley's visit to Surrey in May 2010. Thanks go to Penny Everson and Claire Turner for further editorial assistance. For their help with seeing the book through to publication we would like to thank Andrew Winnard and colleagues at Cambridge University Press, Sarah Green, Tom O'Reilly, and Kay McKechnie for copy-editing. We would also like to express our gratitude to Marina Chumakina for discussion of Archi-related issues. She and Alexander Krasovitsky also helped us with judgments on Russian-related matters, and Magda Fiałkowska is to be thanked for her intuitions on some of the Polish examples.

Brown is responsible for the writing of Chapters 2, 3, 4 and 8 and Hippisley for the writing of Chapters 1, 5, 6 and 7, but the ideas presented throughout the book and the theoretical underpinnings they share result from our joint thinking on these topics. Some chapters are developments from earlier published work. Much of Chapter 2 is new, but it draws on work from Brown (1998a, b), Brown's contribution to Evans, Brown and Corbett (2002) and Brown (2007). Chapter 3 draws in part on work carried out in Brown (1998b), but the presentation is new and the theoretical basis substantively revised in the light of recent developments. Sections of Chapter 4 are based on parts of Brown's contribution to Baerman, Brown and Corbett (2005), particularly the discussion of Dalabon and Dhaasanac. Parts of Chapter 5 were first published as Hippisley (2007), parts of Chapter 6 as Hippisley (2010a, b), and the ideas presented in Chapter 7 originate in Hippisley (1997, 1998, 2001). A full bibliography of Network Morphology style analyses can be found at www2.surrey.ac.uk/english/research/smg/webresources/network_morphology_bibliography.htm

Full Network Morphology theories of the various morphological analyses presented in the following chapters can be downloaded and tested using the book's accompanying website www.cambridge.org/Brown-Hippisley

Our final and deepest acknowledgement is to our wives, Rachel Hippisley and Shirley Kennedy. Thank you for your tireless, unending support.

Abbreviations and Russian transcription system used

1. Abbreviations

1	first person
2	second person
3	third person
A	agent
ABL	ablative
ABS	absolutive
ACC	accusative
ACT	active
ADIT	aditive
ADJ	adjective
ADV	adverb
AGR	agreement
ALL	allative
AN	animate
ANTIP	antipassive
APPL	applicative
ART	article
AUG	augmentative
AUX	auxiliary
BEN	benefactive
CAUS	causative
CISLOC	cislocative
COMP	complementizer
COMPAR	comparative degree
CONPOSS	consumable possession
CONT	continutive
COP	copula

DAT	dative
DEF	definite
DEM	demonstrative
DES	designative
DIS	disharmonic
DU	dual
EP	epenthetic
ERG	ergative
EXCL	exclusive
EXPR	expressive
F	feminine
(F)	inherent feminine
FUT	future
GEN	genitive
GENPOSS	general possession
IMP	imperative
IMPF	imperfect
INAN	inanimate
INCL	inclusive
INDF	indefinite
INF	infinitive
INS	instrumental
INTENS	intensifier
INTR	intransitive
IPFV	imperfective
LOC	locative
M	masculine
MEDIOPASS	mediopassive
N	neuter
(N)	inherent neuter
NARR	narrative
NEG	negation
NMLZ	nominalizer, nominalization
NMP	non-masculine-personal
NOM	nominative
NUM	number
OBJ	object
OBL	oblique
P	patient

PASS	passive
PAUC	paucal
PER	person
PERS	personal
PIE	Proto-Indo-European
PF	perfect
PFV	perfective
PL	plural
POSS	possessive
PPLE	participle
PRED	predicative
PRF	perfect
PREP	prepositional case (Russian)
pro	pronoun
PRS	present
PST	Past
PTCP	participle
REFL	reflexive
SBJ	subject
SBJV	subjunctive
SG	singular
ST	stative
SUFF	suffix
TAM	tense, aspect, mood
THEME	theme vowel
TRANS	translative
TR	transitive
VOC	vocative

2. Russian transcription

Many of our language examples are taken from Russian; it is therefore important to be clear on the transcription standard that we adopt, which differs significantly from the transliteration used in many expositions of Russian linguistics. We are grateful to Alan Timberlake for his guidance on this issue in the early years of the Network Morphology enterprise. What follows is based on our discussions with Alan and his comments published in Timberlake (1993: 828–32; 2004: ch. 2).

Consonants

In Russian the set of paired palatalized (soft) and unpalatalized (hard) consonants are distinguished by the diacritic ′ (acute) which marks the soft member of the pair. For example in the minimal pair *l′uk* 'hatchway' and *luk* 'onion' the first example is in the soft consonant. The diacritic is used for phonemic contrast.

However, Russian has a rule of palatalization before /e/:

(1) C → C′ before /e/ (where C is not an affricate or palatoalveolar).

Any C palatalized by this rule is not marked with a diacritic. For example, *zakon* 'law' has prepositional singular in /e/, which is transcribed as *zakone*.

Russian has another rule that palatalizes all velars occurring before the high front vowel /i/.

(2) K → K′ before /i/ (where K is a velar).

The velars /k/, /g/ and /x/ are hard unless they feed the rule in (2). Softened velars are therefore *not* transcribed with the diacritic ′. For example the noun *ručka* 'handle' forms its genitive singular with the exponent /i/, transcribed as *ručki* with no diacritic.

Finally, the glide /j/, a soft consonant with no hard counterpart, is never marked with the acute; and the unvoiced alveopalatal affricate /č/, also soft without hard counterpart, is always (redundantly) transcribed with the acute. Consonants preceding the glide /j/ assimilate in softening automatically, and so they do not carry the diacritic in this context.

Vowels

Russian has five vowel phonemes, if we ignore reduced vowels not under stress. These are /a/, /e/, /i/, /o/ and /u/, and are transcribed as such. The /i/ phoneme has the centralized allophone /ɨ/ which is standardly transliterated as *y*, as in *Bratja Karamazovy* 'The Brothers Karamazov'. Centralization is due to the rule in (3).

(3) [i] → [ɨ] after a hard consonant.

The /i/ is used for the non-centralized allophone as the basic alternant. No symbol is made available for the centralized allophone, since it would be redundant due to (3). The acute used to denote soft consonants implies the [i] allophone, and lack of acute the [ɨ]. So *sir* 'cheese' is with [ɨ] but *s′irij* 'orphaned' is sequentially with [i] and [ɨ]. In transliteration the two words would be respectively *syr* and *siryj*.

Examples

Cyrillic	Gloss	Transliteration	Transcription	Rationale
играть	'play'	igrat´	igrat´	[i] is default for /i/
книги	'books'	knigi	kn´igi	/n´/ underlyingly soft; rule (2) applies to /g/
комнате	'room' (prep sg)	komnate	komnate	rule (1)
лиса	'fox'	lisa	l´isa	first C underlyingly soft
пью	'drink' (first sg)	p´ju	p´ju	/j/ indicated by ь grapheme in Cyrillic; preceding C underlyingly soft, e.g. infinitive p´it´
сыграть	'play' (perf)	sygrat´	sigrat´	rule (3)

Example sentences taken from works of literature, or other standard sources, are transliterated rather than transcribed. So (4) is an extract from Leskov's *Zaxudalyj rod* 'A Family in Decline', used in Chapter 1.

(4) knjažn-a reši-l-a ostavi-t´ mater-in dom
princess(F)-SG decide-PST-SG.F leave-INF mother-ADJ.SG.M house
'The princess decided to leave her mother's house'

1 *Options in constructing a morphological framework*

1.0 Locating generalizations

Morphology is pervaded by varying degrees of exceptionality, and any morphological framework must be able to accommodate morphology's highly non-systematic nature while defining in precise terms the systematic facts. Success in meeting this aim depends partly on finding the right generalizations. And that in turn depends on where we decide to 'pitch' generalizations. For instance, suppose we wanted to get a better understanding of an under-documented language's verbal system. As more data become available, we can begin to generalize over patterns of form and meaning. For example, in Shughni, a threatened Eastern Iranian language spoken mostly in the mountainous Badakhshan region of Tajikistan, the following sentences and their analyses would lead to several initial generalizations.[1]

(1) a. Present intransitive

wuz	wirāfc-um.
I	stand-1SG

'I stand.'

b. Present transitive

wuz	kud	win-um.
I	dog	see-1SG

'I see a dog.'

(2) a. Present intransitive

tu	wirāfc-i.
you (sg)	stand-2SG

'You stand.'

b. Present transitive

tu	kud	win-i.
you (sg)	dog	see-2SG

'You see a dog.'

(3) a. Present intransitive

yu/ya	wirofs-t.
he/she	stand-3SG

'She stands.'

b. Present transitive

yu/ya	kud	wīn-t.
he/she	dog	see-3SG

'She sees a dog.'

As the examples above indicate, the language has agreement, specifically head marking where formatives expressing person and number agreement with the subject argument are aligned to the right of a verbal root. One way of generalizing over these data is to view both verb stem and (agreement) formative as lexical entries. So, for example, *-um* is a lexical entry with the meaning 'first-person singular agreement', *-i* is a separate entry with 'second-person singular agreement', and *-t* yet another lexical entry. The formative lexical pieces would be distinguished from free morpheme lexical entries such as *kud* 'dog' and the first-person personal pronoun *wuz*, and have to carry instructions about combinability to capture the fact they are bound, and more specifically bound to the right edge of verb pieces. Something akin to a subcategorization frame could be employed to account for agreement formative morphotactics (e.g. Lieber 1992).

When an attempt at analysis assumes that the basic object of enquiry in morphology is the morpheme, then the morphological generalizations being sought are akin to those that hold for phrase structure. By placing phrase structure and word structure in the same (or nearly the same) problem space, the natural expectation is that they also occupy the same (or nearly the same) solution space. In other words, if word structure is viewed as a kind of phrase structure, then principles that apply to the latter may also apply to the former. In such an approach, generalization is located at a relatively high level and holds over different types of structure, including word structure. For example, subcategorization frames used to constrain possible *syntactic* configurations could also be used to express configurations of lexical pieces below the word level. Generalization at this level carries a number of expectations. Returning to Shughni, we expect that if plural subjects trigger plural agreement, this will be manifested by a formally differentiated set of affixes that can be treated as counterparts to singular lexical entries. In other words, there is a bias in our expectations towards affixation, i.e. that the plural exponents will also be affixes; and there is symmetry in function and form, i.e. one affix type is for singular and another for plural. Another expectation will be about linearization: if singular affixes are right-aligned with respect to the verbal head, the plural affixes will be too. That is, the expectation is not just affixation but suffixation. If linearization plays a role in phrase structure where syntactic constituents of the same type are distributed in the same way, lexical entries of the same type (root type, functional type, functional involving agreement subtype, etc.) should share similar positions in a complex word.

Another approach to the Shughni data is to try to pitch generalization at a lower level. Namely, a verb's *paradigm* of word forms is the starting point for generalization. The present-tense subparadigms of 'stand' and 'see' are given in (4).

(4)

	'stand'		'see'		*pattern*	
	SG	PL	SG	PL	SG	PL
1st	wirāfc-um	wirāfc-ām	win-um	win-ām	-um	-ām
2nd	wirāfc-i	wirāfc-et	win-i	win-et	-i	-et
3rd	wirofs-t	wirāfc-en	wīn-t	win-en	-t	-t

Association of meaning and form occurs through a stem's place in a paradigm of *cells*, groupings of any number of morphosyntactic feature values, including a single feature value. So *wirāfc-um* in (4) occupies the cell which is the grouping of {NUM:SG} and {PER:1}.[2] In this approach, the suffix *-um* is not a lexical entry that pairs form and meaning; rather it is an exponent of a particular morphosyntactic grouping. The generalization being made is found in the third column: a pattern of exponence of morphosyntactic groupings shared by two verbs. In paradigm-based approaches, it is this abstracted pattern to which *paradigm* refers (Spencer 2004: 7).[3] Just as in the first approach, meaning–form association as well morphotactics are being encoded in the generalization (exponents are identified as suffixes in the third column). But because the formatives are not lexical entries the paradigm-based approach does not entail a syntax of words, hence generalizations are at a 'lower' level. Word structure is not similar to phrase structure and thus should not be expected to have syntactic correlates. For example, in the paradigm of 'see', the exponence of {PER:3, NUM:SG} is complex, consisting of the affix *-t* together with a change in the feature of the stem's vowel from [- long] to [+ long]. Multiple exponence of a single function is not the expected situation in syntax,[4] and non-concatenative operations seem to be the reserve of morphology. At the same time, the special character of morphology is itself subject to generalization. Vowel lengthening in the stem used for the third-person singular present is found elsewhere in this verb's paradigm, namely in the past tense, as shown in (5).

(5) wuz=um kud wīn-t.
I=1.SG dog see-PST
'I saw a dog.'

Using the paradigm of 'see' as the location of generalization allows us to capture the fact that any process that operates over the stem in the {PER:3, NUM:SG, TENSE:PRS} (3) does the same in a subset of cells elsewhere in the paradigm, namely those containing {TENSE:PST} (5). This is a special kind of word-structure behaviour found in a particular Shughni verb that could itself be generalizable across all verbs in the language, or at least a subclass of verbs.

1.0.1 Paradigmatic relations

The {PER:3, NUM:SG, TENSE:PRS} = {TENSE:PST} generalization has the paradigm as its starting point. A paradigm-based approach to word structure attempts to discover generalizations about paradigmatic organization. To illustrate, consider the paradigms of four Russian nouns *zakon* 'law', *karta* 'map', *rukop´is´* 'manuscript' and *boloto* 'marsh'.[5]

(6)

	I	II	III	IV
Singular				
NOMINATIVE	zakon	kart-a	rukop´is´	bolot-o
ACCUSATIVE	zakon	kart-u	rukop´is´	bolot-o
GENITIVE	zakon-a	kart-i	rukop´is´-i	bolot-a
DATIVE	zakon-u	kart-e	rukop´is´-i	bolot-u
INSTRUMENTAL	zakon-om	kart-oj	rukop´is´-ju	bolot-om
PREPOSITIONAL[6]	zakon-e	kart-e	rukop´is´-i	bolot-e
Plural				
NOMINATIVE	zakon-i	kart-i	rukop´is´-i	bolot-a
ACCUSATIVE	zakon-i	kart-i	rukop´is´-i	bolot-a
GENITIVE	zakon-ov	kart	rukop´is´-ej	bolot
DATIVE	zakon-am	kart-am	rukop´is-am	bolot-am
INSTRUMENTAL	zakon-am´i	kart-am´i	rukop´is´-am´i	bolot-am´i
PREPOSITIONAL	zakon-ax	kart-ax	rukop´is´-ax	bolot-ax

A characteristic of the Russian noun morphology system is that there are different patterns of exponence, expressed as four major declensional classes, which partition the noun lexicon.[7] In such a system the simplest organizing principle would be that each class has a unique set of forms to set it apart from the other classes: a 'canonical' system of inflectional classes (Corbett 2009). So looking horizontally across a particular cell pausing at, for instance, {NUM:SG, CASE:INS} there would be four different values because there are four different patterns of exponence. Rather surprisingly this does not happen here: for Declension I the suffix *-om* is used; for Declension II *-oj*; for Declension III *-ju*; and Declension IV uses the same *-om* as Declension I. Even more surprising is that there is not a single cell where a four-way distinction is made. Another expectation is that within a class each cell would be different from the other, so for example forming a nominative singular is different from a nominative plural. While there is a tendency for *vertical* distinctions across cells, it is only a tendency. So for Declension II, dative singular is in *-e*, but so is prepositional singular. In fact, in the world's languages that have inflectional classes fully horizontal and fully vertical distinctions are rare (Corbett 2009). The paradigm-based approach addresses departures from the canonical inflectional class situation in terms of special *horizontal* or *vertical* relations. For instance, lack of distinction in vertical relations is expressed in terms of syncretism, a topic explored in Chapter 4.

1.0.2 Semi-regularity

We began with the observation that morphological facts may be the products of a system or may fall outside it. Another way of putting this is that a fact may or may not be subject to a given generalization. In the paradigm-based approach, the pattern of inflections is a generalization holding for a given subclass of lexical entries, as illustrated with the facts about Russian noun morphology. But there are items in Russian, as in many languages, whose pattern of exponence deviates in one way or another from what is included in the generalization. We can consider three different situations. The word for 'soldier' *soldat* has nominative singular *soldat* and genitive plural *soldat*. Such a pattern falls outside Declensions I to IV in (6). As a second instance, the word for 'person' is *čelovek* in the nominative singular but *l′ud′i* in the nominative plural. Here the stem that is used in the singular is exchanged for a wholly distinct stem in the plural. And third, the word for 'sledge' *san′i* has no singular morphology; rather it uses plural word-forms in both plural and singular contexts. In one view each instance is non-systematic, since there is a break with the noun inflection generalization given in (6). Alternatively we could think of them as *partially* systematic, since they are not completely disengaged from the inflectional system. So *soldat* behaves like a Declension I noun except for the genitive plural cell, and *san′i* is a perfectly regular Declension I noun with respect to plural forms. In terms of pattern of exponence, *čelovek* does whatever Declension I nouns do. Not shown in (6) is the genitive/accusative syncretism characteristic of animate nouns (we see this later in Chapter 2, Section 2.3.7); *čelovek* as an animate shows this syncretism.[8] Much of morphological irregularity is like this and is therefore better treated as *semi-regularity*. The paradigmatic system is still relevant, but it is the non-standard way in which it is engaged that makes an item look as though it is excluded from the generalization. If the generalization is pitched at the level of the paradigm, then accommodation can be made for semi-regularity.

1.0.3 Options and chapter outline

Network Morphology is a paradigm-based framework: morphological generalizations are gathered at the level of the paradigm. In this chapter we create a profile of Network Morphology by outlining options available to a morphological framework and showing which ones are taken. We can think of where to locate generalization – at the morpheme level or at the paradigm – as the first set of options. Other options largely follow from the choice made here. In Section 1.1 we consider options in what is taken to be the fundamental object of enquiry in morphology. A paradigm-based approach entails that this is the lexeme rather than the morpheme. Choosing the lexeme entails other options; for example, that the approach is also *inferential* rather than *lexical*. In Section 1.2 we look at options in how to conceive morphology in relation to the rest of the grammar. We contrast the notion of an autonomous component for morphology, adopted by Network Morphology, with the alternative that the grammar is more like a seamless web where there are no boundaries between syntax and morphology. The alternative naturally follows from the option that generalization is at the morpheme level, such that principles of word structure could in theory be principles of phrase structure. A good representative alternative is Distributed Morphology, and this theory therefore receives most of our attention. The nature of generalization is explored in Section 1.3, where we discuss the concepts of *inheritance hierarchy* and *network* that are fundamental to Network Morphology's way of capturing generalizations, as well as accommodating semi-regular cases. Exactly how inheritance is interpreted provides further options: mandatory or default inheritance, single or multiple inheritance. Network Morphology is a *formal* framework: it is computer interpretable due to the lexical knowledge representation language in which its theories are expressed, the DATR language. Formalization as an option for morphological frameworks is briefly discussed in Section 1.4. A summary of the options taken (and not taken) by Network Morphology is presented in Section 1.5, a character profile of the framework. How this profile is projected into the chapters of the book is briefly outlined, too.

1.1 Object of inquiry: lexeme rather than morpheme

All paradigm-based frameworks adopt the *lexeme* rather than the morpheme as minimal sign, for example A-morphous Morphology (Anderson 1992) and

Paradigm Function Morphology (Stump 2001). The lexeme is a unity of syntactic, semantic, phonological and (if relevant) morphological class properties that makes one word distinct from another. We could view the lexical entry for the Declension I noun *zakon* 'law' schematically as in (7).

(7) ZAKON
syntactic level
syn cat = Noun
semantic level
'law'
phonological level
stem = /zakon-/
morphological level
mor class = Class_I

Levels of lexical representation play different roles (Aronoff 1994). The syntactic level determines what phrase-level configurations the item can appear in; the semantic level indicates its broad meaning as well as any features that can be used to express selectional restrictions; the phonological level defines its basic sound form as a *stem*; and finally the morphological level flags its inflectional class.

The morphological level of representation determines the shape of the lexeme within a given syntactic context because it serves to locate the pattern of correspondences that hold between a cell's *content*, morphosyntactic feature combination, and *form*, exponent. Generalization at the paradigmatic level assumes that the correspondences are rule-based. A rule of exponence is triggered by the morphosyntactic feature combination of the cell that the stem occupies. So, for example, a stem occupying a cell whose content is {NUM:SG, CASE:DAT} triggers a *-u* suffix exponent if the lexeme carries Declension I at its morphological level (6). Therefore, generalization at the level of the paradigm entails lexemes instead of morphemes as the basic morphological units and an *inferential* rather than a *lexical* approach to word structure (Stump 2001). The approach is inferential since the exponents of the content are introduced by rule, rather than being lexical objects or vocabulary items. Thus, the complex word is *inferred* from the lexeme's stem.

1.1.1 Radical agglutination

In (6) above there are a number of cells lacking an exponent. Exponentless cells are in fact found in all four classes. For Declension I these are {NUM:SG, CASE:NOM} and {NUM:SG, CASE:ACC}, for Declension II {NUM:PL, CASE:GEN}, for Declension III {NUM:SG, CASE:NOM} and {NUM:SG, CASE:ACC}, and finally for Declension IV {NUM:PL, CASE:GEN}. A paradigm-based framework has no stake in pervasive exponence since exponence serves a contrastive end rather than constituting the phonological part of a morpheme lexical sign item. But in a lexical entries as morphemes approach, word structure is assumed to be compounding, entailing what Spencer (2004: 76) calls *radical agglutination*, a prerequisite to the compositionality of the complex unit. Just as syntactic compositionality requires consistency in the function:form mapping of words filling terminal nodes in phrase structure trees, so a one-meaning:one-form mapping has to be assumed for the affixes and stems making up a complex word. The reality is that deviations from radical agglutination abound in just about every way possible. Spencer (2004) provides the following deviation taxonomy.

(8)

Meaning		Form	Term
Radical agglutination			
0.	one	one	–
Radical agglutination deviations			
1.	one	zero	zero morphs
2.	zero	one	meaningless morphs
3.	> one	one	cumulation
4.	one	> one	extended exponence

We have already come across type 1 deviation, zero morphs, in the course of our discussion about Russian nouns where the meaning 'singular nominative/ accusative' lacks an exponent for Declension I and III nouns, and 'plural genitive' is exponentless for Declension II and IV. We can also see the Shughni and Russian data as examples of type 3, cumulation, since more than one feature maps onto a single form. In the Shughni verb examples, these are number and person features, and for the Russian data number and case features. Spencer is careful to point out that systems that are predominantly agglutinative do not escape deviation. Past-tense forms of the Finnish verb 'to be' are shown in (9) (Haspelmath 2002: 33).

(9) Finnish past tense 'to be'

ol-i-n	'I was'
ol-i-t	'you (sg) were'
ol-i	's/he was'
ol-i-mme	'we were'
ol-i-tte	'you (pl) were'
ol-i-vat	'they were'

The stem *ol-* lines up with verb lexical semantics, the formative /i/ maps to 'past', leaving the remainder of the complex word to be interpreted as person/ number feature values. In the third-person singular, we clearly have an example of a zero morph (type 1 deviation). But throughout the paradigm, we also have type 3 deviation (cumulation) going on where more than one feature maps onto a single form. There are no dedicated 'pieces' for number and person values. Rather values are fused onto one suffix: number is contrasted when we compare formatives /n/ and /mme/, but person is contrasted when we compare /n/ with /t/.

A kind of reverse situation is type 4, extended exponence. In (4) we saw the third-person singular of the Shughni verb *win-* 'to see' as an example of this where, in addition to the *-t* suffix, the verb stem's vowel is lengthened. In other words, the meaning has two different phonological reflexes, albeit of different kinds: a suffix and an alternation of the vowel. Stump (1990, 2001) provides an example of extended exponence where the two segments are not only of the same kind – both affixes – but are actually identical. In Breton 'boat' is *bag* and its plural *bagou*. However, in the diminutive formed in *-ig*, the *-ou* suffix shows up twice: *bagouigou* meaning 'little boats' as opposed to *bagig* 'little boat'. Examples of this type are counterexamples to what Lieber terms Redundancy Restriction (Lieber 2004: 161–5), a constraint preventing more than one affix lexical entry from introducing the same meaning in a given word. Lieber gives the derivational example *dramatical*, which if compared to analogous *theatric* suggests the *-al* formative is redundant. In fact the form *dramatic* could be viewed as the redundant free co-variant, except even here there is no meaning for the /t/ formative to map to if the base is *drama*. This is an example of type 2 deviation where /t/ and /al/ are meaningless morphs.

Spencer (2004) notes that it is not a breakdown in isomorphism per se that calls into question the affixes-as-words approach. Cases of allomorphy, as found in inflectional classes like those in Russian nouns, are affixal analogues of synonymy; affix syncretism is akin to lexical homonymy or polysemy (systematized homonymy). Even zero morphs have a parallel life in the stem world, albeit marginally. In Basque the copula *ezan* has a 'zero' stem in the third-person singular (10). This example has been described as a special instance of stem suppletion (Hippisley, Chumakina, Corbett and Brown 2004: 414).

(10) Basque copula *ezan* (see Hualde and Ortiz de Urbina 2003)

	SG	PL
1st	n-**in**-tzen	g-**in**-en
2nd	h-**in**-tzen (informal)	z-**in**-eten
3rd	z-**Ø**-en	z-**ir**-en[9]

However, when stems are collocated within a compound (or within a phrase as syntactic words) the meaning:form deviations of types 2, 3 and 4 do not occur.

Because in the paradigm-based approach the meaning–form association is computed by a stem's place in a particular cell of features and the exponence of that particular situation, Spencer (2004) argues that deviation type 2, meaningless morphs, is entailed by this approach. In other words, exponents do not carry meaning in the same way as words do; they are, as we have said, a mechanism for making a contrast amongst different feature combinations. So provided their contrasting service can be characterized, they can be multiple (deviation 4), zero (deviation 1) or double-duty (deviation 3).

1.1.2 Morphemes and word syntax

When morphemes are the basic object of morphological enquiry, generalizations about phrase structure could be expanded to cover word structure, as has been proposed in word-syntax approaches to morphology, for example Williams (1981), Selkirk (1982) and Lieber (1992). As noted in Lieber (2000: 408), morphotactics in early versions of phrase structure grammar were defined by a special set of rewrite rules. The apparatus used in modern generative grammar could also be pressed into the service of morphological description. For example, in the morpheme-based theory of Lieber (1992) word constituency is subjected to an X-bar treatment with typing of word constituents as heads, complements and specifiers.[10] So in the compound *cat lover* the first element is the complement of *lover* (the head) evidenced by the phrasal equivalent 'lover of cats'. In the compound *filing cabinet*, on the other hand, the first element is a modifier. Turning to a derivational example, in *happiness* the head is the suffix and the base neither complement nor modifier, so therefore must belong to the functionally 'heterogeneous' specifier class (Lieber 1992: 55).[11] Just as lexical heads assign theta roles to their complements in phrase structure, so does the head of a word piece to its complement piece. In examples like *debug* and *encase* the category-changing prefix is the head and the noun root its complement. The theta role assigned to the complement is Theme in the first example, i.e. 'remove the bug [+Theme] from X', and Location in the second, i.e. 'put X in a case [+Loc]' (Lieber 1992: 57). Semanticosyntactic interpretation is simply a matter of computing the semanticosyntax of each morpheme lexical entry. Since all word structure (compounding, derivation, inflection) is endocentric like phrase structure, heads such as *lover* in *cat lover*, *-ness* in *happiness* and *de-* in *debug* determine the category of the word as a whole through feature percolation to the word's top node, where priority is given to head features: *lover* is + Noun, *-ness* + Noun, and *de-* is +Verb. In more recent work, coindexation plays a key role in interpretation where affixes and stems are assumed to have an argument structure, and upon composition of a stem and affix, lexical entries (stem or affix) and their arguments are coindexed (Lieber 2004). Because affixes have the same status in the grammar as stems, their semantics is constrained by what we see in stems. The consequence is that there is no such thing as distinct derivational semantics. Lexical semantics and derivational semantics are one and the same.

This word-structure-as-phrase-structure approach is beset by problems. Before summarizing the object-of-enquiry option which Network Morphology takes, the theme of this section, it is instructive to consider some of the concerns, first raised in Spencer (1993) and Stump (1993), two reviews received very shortly after Lieber's proposals were published. The first major concern deals with allotting X-bar categories to word pieces. Between elements in certain types of compound there does seem to be something analogous to the head–complement and head–modifier relation. Unlike with phrase structure, however, it is claimed that X-bar rules at the word level do not introduce lower levels – there is no X^{-1}, X^{-2} etc. This means we cannot pick out the specifier, complement or head through their place on a hierarchy; we have to rely on a semantic motivation. This can work with modifier, complement and head, but for specifier we really do need hierarchical information: 'sister of X´ and daughter of XP'. But heads are also problematic. In phrase structure, head-alignment is an essential factor in determining word order, and Lieber's claim is that, by default, below-the-word heads will determine parallel word order amongst word constituents. So if a language lines up complements to the right of the head in phrase structure, we should see the head piece to the left of the word piece in a complex word. The verbs *debug* and *encase* (again) are evidence of this, where the prefixes *de-* and *en-* contribute the V elements. But there is a host of 'counterexamples' (e.g. *happiness*, *cat lover*) where phrase structure and word structure have opposite head ordering. Spencer makes the important point that languages with free head ordering in phrase structure should have freedom below the word level, too. So if Chukchi is claimed to be a free-word-order language (e.g. Skorik 1977), it is surprising that compounds which are the result of incorporation of an argument by a verb and compounds where nouns have incorporated modifiers (and specifiers) are all right-headed (Spencer 1993: 584). Then there is the associated problem of equating a head element in an endocentric compound with an affix in a derived word. Both head types percolate their features, a major criterion for head-hood. But in inflectionally complex words, though the affix is the head, features can be percolated from the non-head ('back-up percolation'). Zwicky (1985a, 1993), Bauer (1990) and Beard (1998) provide lists of differences between word heads and syntactic heads, calling into question parallels between morphological heads and syntactic heads. The alternative is to view the *stem* as the head, which is where the core semantics of the complex word comes from in derivation and inflection, a position argued by Zwicky (1993) and Beard (1998) and more recently by Stump (2001).

1.1.3 Summary of object-of-inquiry option

Generalization at the level of the paradigm entails the lexeme as the minimal sign, rather than the morpheme. Lexemes are multilayered representations that include form, semantic and syntactic features, and in addition, morphological class features which link a lexeme's paradigm of word-forms to a generalizable pattern of exponence that holds over other lexemes. The form:meaning correspondence is captured through rules of exponence operating over the lexeme's stem within a given cell of morphosyntactic features. This paradigm-based *inferential* approach contrasts with the morpheme-based *lexical* approach, where the pieces of words are lexical entries rather than rule outputs, and all word structure is therefore compounding. When the morpheme is the basic object of enquiry, we run into the problem of deviations from the radical agglutination that word structure as compounding assumes. Furthermore, the breakdown in parallels between morphology and syntax suggests that word structure as phrase structure, possible where the morpheme is the minimal sign, is pitching morphological generalization at too high a level. Network Morphology is lexeme-based, taking an inferential approach to morphology where paradigms are central. Network Morphology is also *realizational* because the content that is part of a complex word is not a consequence of gathering together pieces of content that are part of morphemes to yield an aggregate content, as in Lieber's *incremental* syntax of words theory; rather the content is 'already there', features from the syntax demanding phonological expression at the level of the paradigm. In other words, the content is a precondition of form rather than a consequence of it (Ackerman and Stump 2004).[12]

In the next section we explore another set of options. These touch on the place of morphology in the broader grammatical context, and are partly determined by a decision on the broadest level of morphological generalization. As we have discussed, the choice is between situating generalization at the level of the paradigm, or in combinatory principles that obtain for both phrase structure and word structure alike. We will argue for an autonomous treatment of morphology, where word structure is viewed as a component in its own right.

We contrast this approach with one where morphology is seen as an aspect of syntax.

1.2 Morphological domain: autonomous rather than part of a seamless web

A lexeme-based approach where generalization is anchored in the paradigm carries no expectation that morphology should be anything other than distinct from other grammatical components; for one thing, no other component has anything that resembles paradigms.[13] The alternative to autonomous morphology is a logical extension of morphemes as lexical entries, that a single component is responsible for both phrase structure and word structure. The grammatical system could feasibly be one where phrase-structure and word-structure (as well as sound-structure) phenomena reference and feed each other within a 'seamless web' (Zwicky 1996: 301). In this section we present the autonomous morphology option that Network Morphology takes, which allows it to account for the various *dissociations* between morphosyntax and its expression. Such dissociations are frequently encountered across the world's languages. We also consider the alternative, seamless web morphology, as exemplified by Distributed Morphology's approach to word structure as phrase structure.

1.2.1 Autonomous morphology and function/form dissociations

Inflectional class systems such as the one presented in (6) point to a dissociation between syntactic function and morphological form since one function has multiple formal expressions. The dissociation can be handled by housing the system in a separate grammatical component which contains its own generalizations about how the function:form mapping is regulated. The type and nature of these generalizations are explored in Chapter 3, Section 3.1.3. A different kind of dissociation is where multiple functions can map onto a single form, which we discussed in Section 1.0.1 as removing the vertical distinction that holds between two cells in a given class. For the Declension II lexeme KARTA two syntactic words with the features {NUM:SG, CASE:DAT} and {NUM:SG, CASE:PREP} converge on the single form *karte*. Generalizations about paradigmatic relations regulate cases of *syncretism*, a topic explored in Chapter 4. There is a third kind of dissociation that points to morphological autonomy. At issue here is not multiple mappings between function and form but rather a function:form *mismatch*. Latin deponent verbs are a classic example. The Latin verb for 'encourage' uses passive morphology in syntactically active contexts, illustrating a mismatch between function and form in the context of voice. (11) is an example from Plautus.

(11) sed coqu-os… horta-batur
but cook-PL.ACC… encourage-3SG.PASS (=ACT)
'but he encouraged the cooks' (Plantus, *Mercator* Act IV, Lines 695–7)

The form *hortabatur* is passive but its meaning is active. Mismatch phenomena suggest that there must be purely morphological features as distinct from morphosyntactic features, and though the two types of feature line up in most cases, they do not in all cases. Chapter 5 treats morphological mismatch as an upset in the *default* link between two different feature sets used in different parts of the grammar. Purely morphological features suggest an autonomous component. We briefly consider instances of features that have relevance only to the morphological component, yet more evidence of an autonomous morphological component.

We start with the idea of inflectional class membership as a feature. Recall that such a feature type is implied by our representation of the lexeme in (7), which includes a purely morphological level of description. Evidence of such a feature is found in Russian expressive morphology, the mechanism for realizing diminutive, augmentative, pejorative and affectionate shades of meaning on a given noun.[14] The system is characterized by a number of rival affixes whose selection depends on the inflectional class of the base noun. The correspondence between inflectional class and diminutive affix is shown in (12).

(12)

Declension I	Declension II, III	Declension IV
-´ik	*-k*	*-(e)c*
dom 'house' > *dom-´ik*	*rabot-a* 'work' > *rabot-k-a*	*zolot-o* 'gold' > *zolot-ec-o*

There is a default association between inflectional class and gender in Russian such that gender can be deduced from class, where Declension I implies masculine, Declension IV neuter and Declensions II and III feminine gender (Corbett 1982). But what we have here is not a case of gender determining choice of affix, since there are masculine nouns that belong to Declension II and that do not take the Declension I suffix but the Declension II/III suffix. So *d´ad´a* 'uncle' controls masculine agreement and derives the diminutive *d´adka*. Russian possessive adjective derivation behaves in a similar way, where the *-ov* affix is selected for Declension I nouns and the *-´in* affix for Declension II and III nouns. (13) is an example where Declension III *mat´* 'mother' derives the possessive adjective *mater´-in-* 'mother's'.[15]

(13) knjažn-a reši-l-a ostavi-t´ mater-in dom
princess(F)-SG decide-PST-SG.F leave-INF mother-ADJ.SG.M house
'The princess decided to leave her mother's house' (Leskov, *Zaxudalyj rod*)

When *d´ad´a* derives a possessive adjective, it selects the *-in* affix in accordance with its inflectional class membership. It is an inflectional class feature that acts to determine the correct affix.

(14) d´ad´-in-o pourč´en´ij-o
uncle-ADJ-SG.N sermon(N)-SG
'Uncle's sermon'

In some inflectional class systems the class feature has formal expression. For example, Latin verb classes are associated with different *theme* vowels. (15) shows the present infinitive of the verbs belonging to Latin's four major verb conjugations.

(15)

Conj I		Conj II		Conj III		Conj IV	
amō 'love'		*moneō* 'advise'		*regō* 'rule'		*audiō* 'hear'	
ACTIVE	PASSIVE	ACTIVE	PASSIVE	ACTIVE	PASSIVE	ACTIVE	PASSIVE
am-ā-re	*am-ā-rī*	*mon-ē-re*	*mon-ē-rī*	*reg-e-re*	*regī*	*aud-ī-re*	*aud-ī-rī*

The formatives /ā/, /ē/, /e/ and /ī/ have no function beyond that of regulating inflectional classes, hence are expressions of something purely morphological. A stem formative may also act to characterize a set of cells in a lexeme's paradigm, where the content of the cells does not necessarily form a natural class. The verb *amō* has three stems distinguished by stem formatives, as shown in (16).

(16) stem 1 stem 2 stem 3
amā- *amāv-* *amāt-*

The first stem occurs in imperfect (present and past) cells and the second stem in perfect cells. But the third stem includes in its set of cells perfect aspect, past tense, future tense and supine. It is also the form used for different types of derivative including agent nouns, desiderative, intensive and iterative verbs (Aronoff 1994: 38). The mixed content associated with a single stem form shows that morphology can have a solely organizational role. Indexing the stems as in (16) expresses best the *morphomic* role played by the stem formative (Aronoff 1994).

The distribution of stem types within a paradigm has been claimed to constrain paradigmatic restructuring in Romance (Maiden 2002, 2004), as well as regulate cases of full suppletion. Stem distribution is also one of three factors that work together to constrain suppletive paradigms from being levelled (Hippisley *et al.* 2004). For example, Latin *ferre* 'to bear' has three suppletive stems *fer-o*, *tul-i* and *lat-um*, and they are associated with the same three sets of morphosyntactic features as the first, second and third stems of Latin regular verbs. A more interesting example that Hippisley *et al.* (2004) give is Archi (Nakh-Daghestanian), whose stem distribution follows absolutive singular, ergative singular (and all cases based on the ergative singular) and plural.

(17)

		SINGULAR	PLURAL
a. 'ram'	ABS	baIk'	baIk'-ur
	ERG	baIk'-li	baIk'-ur-čaj
b. 'dress'	ABS	k'onc'ol	k'onc'ol-um
	ERG	k'onc'ol-a	k'onc'ol-um-čaj

The word for 'father' is suppletive but only has singular forms. Its stem alternation partitions the paradigm in the same way that stems of regular nouns do in the singular: absolutive versus ergative and other cases. The word for 'man' has two suppletive stems and has plural forms; its distribution is also constrained by the stem distribution of regulars: singular cells versus plural cells.

(18)

		SINGULAR	PLURAL
a. 'father'	ABS	abt̄u	–
	ERG	um-mu	–
b. 'man'	ABS	bošor	Lele
	ERG	bošor-mu	Lele-maj

The morphomic level of description is taken up in our discussion of inflectional classes in Chapter 3.

A partitioned grammar with an autonomous morphological component entails two kinds of morphology-relevant features, those used in the interface with the syntactic component and those that apply to the morphological component only. Included in the latter would be theme vowels, inflectional class membership features, and morphomes. Corbett and Baerman (2006) term these *morphological* features and distinguish them from *morphosyntactic* features that apply at the morphology/syntax interface. Network Morphology as a realizational framework assumes a featural interface with syntax. This is in contrast to incremental approaches, such as those proposed by Lieber (1992) and Williams (1981), where the information exchanged at the interface is filtered through the information contained in the constituent morphemes, in other words where the interface is *formative*.[16] We have seen that radical agglutination is not always maintained in word structure, with the consequence that forms may be empty of (syntactically relevant) content. Theme vowels and stem formatives are good examples of empty form. The structure of a word in incremental theories really amounts to an embarrassment of riches in the sense that there may be plenty of internal structure on display that serves no real purpose in the grammar. A featural interface also accounts for the other dissociations noted above. In the syncretism example, in a given situation it is the features {NUM:SG, CASE:DAT} that are associated with an instance of *karte* that syntax cares about, not the features {NUM:SG, CASE:PREP} that are associated in another syntactic situation. In a case of morphological mismatch such as the Latin verb form in (11), syntax is blind to the passive morphological structure and sees only the active morphosyntactic labelling of the object. So a word's morphosyntactic representation, not its formal structure, is 'the only aspect of it that is visible to syntax' (Anderson 1992: 90). As Kuhn (2007: 623) puts it, 'details irrelevant outside a module [=component] should not be part of the interface representation'.

The autonomous morphological component serves the syntactic component by generating objects that are inserted into syntax. These objects are *encapsulated*, to borrow a term from object-oriented systems analysis, i.e. they are treated as black boxes (Kuhn 2007: 617; Williams 2007: 335). From this option in the design of the syntax and morphology interface follow two principles, the principle of morphology-free syntax and the principle of syntax-free morphology (Zwicky 1992: 354–5; 1996: 30). By virtue of opting for autonomous morphology, Network Morphology adopts these two principles. The principle of morphology-free syntax is a constraint on the nature of syntactic rules: no rule of syntax can make reference to the internal structure of a word or to purely morphological features. Conversely, the principle of syntax-free morphology is a constraint on morphological rules paying attention to syntactic context or purely syntactic features. So, for example, the selection of pattern of exponence given a choice of patterns, i.e. affiliation to a given inflectional class, should not take into consideration the syntactic context: selection of Declension III should not depend on whether or not the syntactic context is one of subject–auxiliary inversion.

Cases where these principles do not appear to hold require an explanation. Corbett and Baerman (2006) discuss a potential counterexample to the principle of morphology-free syntax. Serbian/Croatian/Bosnian (SCB) is a South Slavonic language that has masculine, feminine and neuter genders (Browne 1993). When two NPs are conjoined and each conjunct is headed by nouns of different gender or both are neuter, the agreement on the target is resolved in favour of masculine gender. If, on the other hand, both conjuncts are feminine then the agreement will be feminine. There is one situation, however, where we do not necessarily get feminine agreement despite feminine nouns in each NP, specifically if one conjunct is headed by a feminine noun belonging to a less common inflectional class, the so-called Feminine *i*-stem class. Corbett and Baerman (2006) illustrate with an example from the renowned author Andric´ (originally cited and discussed in Corbett 1991: 301).

(19)	vređa-l-i	su	ga	nebrig-a	i
	offend-PST-PL.M	AUX-3PL	3SG.ACC	carelessness(F)-SG	and
	lakomislenost				
	capriciousness(F)				
	'(Tahir-beg's) carelessness and capriciousness offended him'				

Here *nebriga* 'carelessness' belongs to the default Feminine *a*-stem class, but *lakomislenost* 'capriciousness' to the less productive class. This appears to be a case where a rule belonging to the syntactic world is sensitive to inflectional class membership, a fact that surely belongs solely to the morphological world. An alternative analysis that preserves the principle of morphology-free syntax suggests itself when semantics is factored in. Feminine agreement in resolution contexts is only obligatory if females are actually being denoted. Nouns in *-ost* are inanimate since *-ost* is the most productive deadjectival abstract noun suffix (Browne 1993: 340), hence feminine agreement is not obligatory. Instead, masculine agreement is the resolved agreement (Corbett and Baerman 2006: 234).

The principle of syntax-free morphology ensures that no rule of morphology has access to syntactic properties of the word it applies to, other than syntactic category information. So, for example, a rule cannot access the syntactic configuration the word is a part of. As an example, the choice of plural exponent, including lack of exponent for a given lexeme, cannot rest on information about the syntactic construction it finds itself in (Zwicky 1993: 36). But Ackema and Neeleman (2004: 192; 2007: 341) present a case where this seems to be precisely what is happening. In Dutch present-tense verbs, the second-person singular is realized either with suffix *-t* or simply with no exponent at all. As Dutch is a V2 language, the subject does not necessarily precede the verb. In situations where the verb precedes the subject, including yes–no questions, the verb is exponentless. The examples they give in (2007: 341) are repeated here in (20).

(20) a. *Subject–Aux order*
jij lees-t het boek
you read-2SG the book

b. *Aux–Subject order*
lees jij het boek?
read.2SG you the book?

One solution is to think of this as a case of ‘reduced agreement’ (Corbett 2006: ch. 6; personal communication). Corbett shows how the size of the set of agreement features relevant in a given situation may depend on various factors. These include how canonical the controller is: a subject controller is most canonical if it is an agent, the topic of the clause and in the default order with respect to the verb. A slip from canonicity in any of these categories can result in a reduction in the agreement features carried by the predicate. So in Somali agreement is reduced when the controller is the focus (2006: 203–4). In Modern Standard Arabic, gender and number are relevant when the controlling subject precedes the verb, but only gender when subject and verb are inverted (2006: 154). The Dutch example can then be analysed as an instance of reduced agreement due to a non-canonical subject, which is non-topical. An alternative analysis by Ackema and Neeleman (2004) is that in the inverted situation the VP joins the same prosodic domain as the DP subject; once defined, the domain itself can then be viewed as the condition on the size of the agreement feature set used.

The alternative to viewing morphology as autonomous is to handle it in the same space as phrase structure, so that morphology and syntax are part of a seamless web of linguistics knowledge. The major proponent of this view is the theory of Distributed Morphology.

1.2.2 Seamless-web morphology and Distributed Morphology

With a word-syntax approach to morphology we have the possibility of the simplest ontology of rule types (Zwicky 1992: 347), where phrase structure and word structure rules are essentially the same. Generalizations are sought that hold over both structure types.

We can find a number of phenomena that are suggestive of syntax and morphology forming a seamless web. Zwicky (1992: 355) presents the following. First, there is function sharing between syntax and morphology in that a single function can find expression in either syntax or morphology. For example, the comparative is expressed morphologically in *kinder* and syntactically in *more handsome*. In Shughni the present tense has morphological expression (it is synthetic), but the past involves combining an agreement clitic with a special form of the verb stem, two syntactic atoms, as shown in (5) above. If one were to accept the argument that periphrasis is syntactic, the TAM system of Latin alternates between syntactic and morphological expression. A second type of phenomenon that seems to indicate a kind of transparency between syntax and morphology is the maintenance of a verb's argument requirements after it has undergone morphological modification. In Russian the verb 'to govern' requires an internal instrumental case-marked argument, as shown in (21).[17]

(21) Nekotory-e glagol-y uprvalja-jut tvoritel´n-ym
some-PL.NOM verb-PL.NOM govern-3PL instrumental-SG.INS
padež-om
case-SG.INS
'Some verbs govern the instrumental case'

This same requirement is 'inherited' by its morphologically derived noun.

(22) V russk-om jazyk-e vstreča-et-sja
In Russian-SG.PREP language-SG.PREP meet-3SG-REFL
upravl-eni-e tvoritel´n-ym padež-om
govern-NMLZ-SG.NOM instrumental-SG.INS case-SG.INS
'In Russian you get government of the instrumental case'

English synthetic compounds represent a third phenomenon, where head and argument in phrase structure are identifiable in word structure, as in the example *cat lover* discussed in the previous section. Finally, incorporation suggests parallels between the two levels since it appears that the incorporated element which is word internal still plays the role of an argument and carries a grammatical relation such as object. (23a, b) are phrasal and incorporated variants of 'I eat (the) flesh' in the Aztec language Nahuatl (Sapir 1911, discussed in Gerdts 1998: 84–5).

(23) a. ni-c-qua in nacatl
I-it-eat the flesh
'I eat the flesh'

b. ni-naca-qua
I-flesh-eat
'I eat flesh'

Incorporation examples of this kind are, in Mithun's words, 'the most nearly syntactic of all morphological processes' (1984).

Distributed Morphology (Halle and Marantz 1993) is a morpheme-based framework that takes syntactic-looking word-structure phenomena such as these as its starting point and pushes the seamless-web option (as opposed to the autonomous-component option) to it logical extreme. The framework is an attempt to locate generalizations at the highest level where word structure is really phrase structure, representing a kind of null hypothesis where sentences are built directly out of morphemes (Williams 2007: 359). As Embick and Noyer (2007: 290) put it:

> In the default case…the principles that govern the composition of 'words' are the same as those that govern the composition of larger syntactic units.

So in the context of grammar as a whole, one assumes 'syntactic hierarchical structure all the way down' (Harley and Noyer 1999: 3). What is inserted in phrase structure terminal nodes are pieces of words, drawn from the lexicon. This makes it a *lexical* theory of word structure. One node provides for the root, and the other carries a set of features, which is satisfied by a vocabulary item carrying a subset of the same features. This makes it a *realizational* theory, like paradigm-based theories. In Stump's (2001) taxonomy of morphological approaches, Distributional Morphology is representative of the lexical-realizational approach. In the incremental morpheme-based frameworks of Lieber, Scalise, Williams and others, bound morpheme lexical entries bring their features with them. In Distributed Morphology, the features are already there, in the syntactic nodes, so that what is inserted are really *exponents* of these features. A terminal node with morphosyntactic features to be realized through lexical insertion is (rather confusingly) called a *morpheme* in Distributed Morphology. We will use the term DM-morpheme to avoid confusion.

We illustrate syntactic hierarchy and feature realization through lexical insertion by the treatment of the Mansi (Uralic) expression for 'by means of two kettles' in (24), from Embick and Noyer (2001: 559).

(24) pūt-əɣ-təl
kettle-DU-INS
'by means of two kettles'

Lexical entries are of two types: root and functional. A single complex word is analysed as a constituent containing a root node plus DM-morpheme node, such that both types of lexical entry are inserted into their respective nodes. Functional lexical entries carry information about form along with a set of features that is a subset of those found on the DM-morpheme node, serving to license their insertion. Functional lexical entries are, therefore, really exponents of combinations of morphosyntactic features. The constituent structure of words is represented schematically in (25), from Embick and Noyer (2001: 559).

(25)

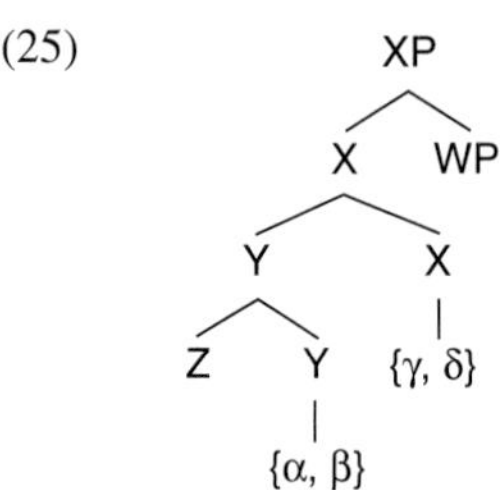

Given (25), the Mansi example in (24) has the following treatment. If Z represents a Noun, then the root *pūt-* is inserted there. Y heads a NUMBER functional projection furnished with the value DUAL. The functional lexical entry /-əɣ/ is assumed to carry the feature {NUM:DU} so is inserted into Y, satisfying its feature value. Finally X heads another functional projection, CASE, and is furnished with {CASE:INS}; here the functional lexical entry /-təl/ carrying the appropriate case feature value is inserted into the X syntactic node.

An advantage of this realizational morpheme-based approach over the incremental (e.g. Lieber's, see discussion in Sections 1.1.2 and 1.1.3) is less reliance on a one-to-one mapping of meaning to form. For a single DM-morpheme there could be a number of competing lexical entries that carry a subset of the features on the morpheme. Competition can be resolved *Pāṇini* style, where lexical entries with more specific feature sets beat those with less specific ones. Another advantage is that the DM-morpheme nodes that contain the features can be involved in movement rules in the same way as other nodes, and in this way explain the dissociation between head alignment due to generative rules of phrase structure and surface head alignment. The assumption is that the DM-morpheme nodes head their constituent. Distributed Morphology follows Baker's line of argument that all morphological structure involving grammatical change is a reflex of phrase structure combined with movement, enshrined in the Mirror Principle (Baker 1985; 1988). So passive morphology, a reflex of change of valency, involves movement such that the head of VP ends up adjacent to the passive morpheme node. The analysis of 'My car was stolen' is given in (26) (based on Roberts 2007: 116).

(26)

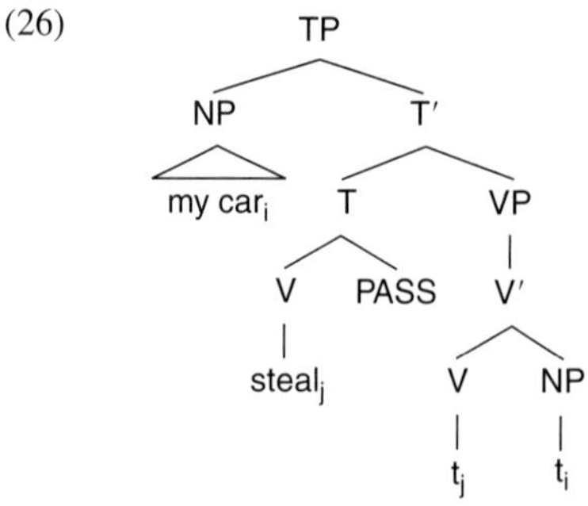

Here the verb that heads VP has moved into the head of TP; the VP complement moves to specifier of TP for the usual reasons (Case assignment and satisfying the EPP).[18] The dissociation between the alignment of *-en* in *stolen* and its phrase structure analysis is explained by head-to-head movement. Thus, word complexity is due to syntactic *head* complexity, in this case head of TP.

Complex heads and head-to-head movement are used in Distributed Morphology to capture the function sharing between morphology and syntax for English comparatives, one of the phenomena that is suggestive of syntax and morphology forming a seamless web, as mentioned above. The complementary distribution of the periphrastic expression of the comparative as in *more handsome* and the synthetic expression as in *kinder* is used as evidence that the complex word *kinder* has the same underlying phrase structure representation as *more handsome*. Embick and Marantz's (2008: 45–7) Distributed Morphology analysis is given here in (27).[19]

(27)

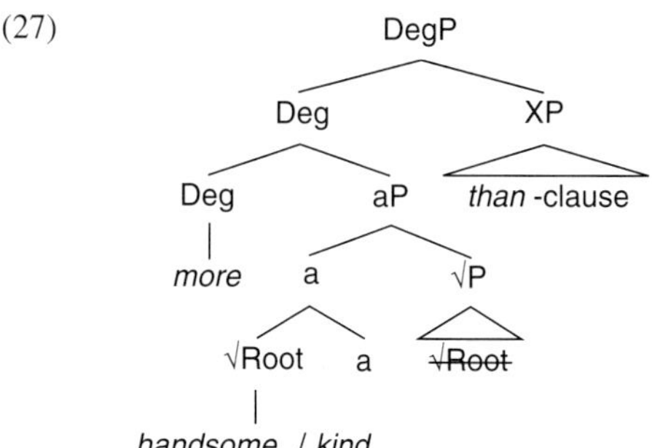

Syntax derives an underlying representation where *more* heads the functional category DegP (Degree Phrase). When the lexical entry *kind* is inserted as an adjectival root it satisfies particular phonological properties (monosyllabic or disyllabic with light second syllable), the consequence of which is that Deg will move and be incorporated into aP forming a complex head. The realization of this complex head will be the root *kind* combined with *-er*. Otherwise Deg stays where it is and is filled by *more*.

Distributed Morphology attempts to capture a high-level default – that the complexity of words is due to the same principles used for the complexity of phrases, as we said at the beginning of this section. But as noted by Embick and Noyer, there are 'deviations from the default case' (2007: 104). The Mirror Principle and head movement are invoked to account for *ordering* deviations, a dissociation between syntax-driven head alignment and head alignment in the surface representation, e .g. *kind-er* as opposed to **er-kind* (see (27)). A second kind of deviation is where the tree structure supplied for realization as word structure is too short: too much morphology. And a third kind of deviation is, conversely, where the tree structure supplied for realization as word structure is too long: not enough morphology.

This last kind, where syntax generates a structure that oversells morphology as it were, is briefly discussed in Halle and Marantz (1993: 117) with reference to *fusion*, an operation that combines, or fuses, nodes and their features. An example requiring a fusion treatment is Russian nouns. In one formative two feature values are conflated. Recall that we gave this as an example of cumulative exponence (radical agglutination type 3 deviation) in (8). For Russian *kartu* (6), a DM-morpheme node with {CASE:ACC} is fused with another node carrying {NUM:SG}. This approach is motivated by languages such as Turkish which would require two separate nodes to insert two separate functional lexical entries. Looking top-down we have agglutination and looking bottom-up fusional morphology.

With the second kind of deviation, the syntax undersells the morphology. As a deviation from radical agglutination, it is type 1, zero morphs. Theme vowels in Latin were used above as an illustration of this deviation, one of the dissociations between function and form that we used to build a case for autonomous morphology. Distributed Morphology uses the quaint term *ornamental morphology* to refer to features such as Theme (Embick and Marantz 2008: 30). To illustrate, the gloss of Latin *laudābāmus* 'we were praising' is given in (28), following the account in Embick and Marantz.

(28) laud-ā-bā-mus
praise-THEME-IPFV-1.PL

Neither Theme nor agreement features are *interpretable* so are not needed for logical form (LF) (Embick and Noyer 2007: 305). Within the Minimalist model which Distributed Morphology assumes, functional projections for theme vowels and agreement morphology are actually created *after* the syntactic derivation has diverged along the phonetic form (PF) and LF branches; in other words, agreement and theme vowel morphology are treated differently from *syntactic* morphology. The heads of these functional projections are moved into the head of TP, forming a complex head, and into the root head, forming another complex head. This is shown in (29).

(29)

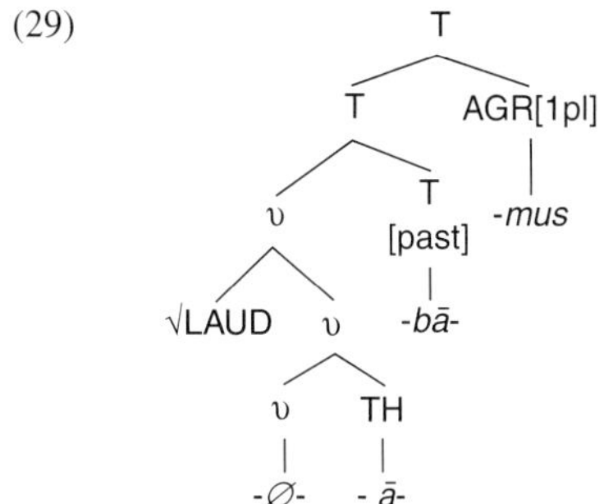

In sum, an alternative to treating morphology as a component in the grammar that is autonomous and contains principles exclusive to the morphological system is to subsume principles of word structure under principles of phrase structure, a move that captures what appears to be a shared behaviour. Dissociations between phrase structure and word structure can be handled in various ways. Head-to-head movement accounts for situations where syntax-generated constituent order does not line up with (surface) word-constituent order. DM-morpheme nodes merge, accounting for cases where syntax generates more nodes than there are word pieces. For converse cases where there are more word pieces than DM-morpheme nodes, adding nodes post-syntactically in PF allows DM-morphemes to maintain the meaning–form symmetry. The need to account for such dissociations is real when the option is taken to generalize word structure as phrase structure. Unfortunately Distributed Morphology's approach to these dissociations is highly problematic, as we now discuss.

1.2.3 Some challenges for Distributed Morphology's seamless web

Seamless web morphology is a rejection of the lexicalist hypothesis, which is broadly a claim that although syntax and morphology may share some vocabulary (for example, 'noun', 'verb' and 'head'), they differ fundamentally both in contribution to the overall grammar and in the principles that govern them. A separate grammatical component, a structured lexicon, captures the differences in terms of the design of the grammar. And indeed the number and degree of differences found between phrase structure and word structure leave a morphological framework no option but to accept the lexical hypothesis. Williams (2007: 358) observes that the only item in Distributed Morphology's list of distinguishing properties that is actually distinguishing is its rejection of the lexicalist hypothesis.[20] Opting out isolates Distributed Morphology somewhat from the community of word-structure frameworks since the vast majority adopts the lexicalist hypothesis to a greater or lesser degree.

Yet even in Distributed Morphology, the notion of a separate morphological domain is implied in its taxonomy of word pieces. As well as exponents of DM-morpheme nodes generated in syntax, we have just seen that some word pieces are exponents of a class of PF-generated morpheme nodes, cases of 'ornamental' morphology. Their generation happens in a reserved space in the grammar, along the PF branch. Another class of word pieces is the expression of part of speech. In Distributed Morphology, root lexical entries are neutral with respect to part of speech. They end up as a particular part of speech by being inserted into a node which is in a particular configuration. For example, the neutral root √CONSTRUCT may be inserted into an N configuration or a V configuration. The correlation between the root √CONSTRUCT and the noun word-form *construction* results from a readjustment rule triggered by N. So *-ion* is not an exponent of a DM-morpheme but is instead part of the structural description of a readjustment rule.[21] The distinction DM makes between word structure behaving like phrase structure and behaving like something else is tacit acknowledgement of something like the lexical hypothesis, albeit a weaker version which effects a 'split' in the morphology.

There are also problems with the class of word pieces that are exponents of DM-morpheme nodes generated in syntax. Within the solid word-structure-as-phrase-structure cases, there is evidence to suggest that we are dealing with something other than syntax. Complex words can have syntactic paraphrases, such as 'more X' as the phrase structure equivalent to X-*er*. But the parallels between the phrase-structure and word-structure expressions are not as clear as they first appear. An example from Williams (2007: 355) is the sentences 'John again washed the dishes on Tuesday' and 'John re-washed the dishes on Tuesday.' At first blush the word piece *re-* is functionally equivalent to the adjunct *again*. But they differ in scope properties: *re-* is restricted in scope to the argument of the verb to which it attaches. In other words, it does not have as a possible interpretation that dish-washing occurred twice on Tuesday: the only interpretation is that it happened to be a Tuesday when John decided to do a better job at getting the dishes clean. However, this is a possible interpretation with the *again* sentence, since here the scope of *again* could extend to the time adverb.

Mithun and Corbett (1999) show how incorporation examples that motivate the Mirror Principle cannot in fact be the products of syntax as they display a number of characteristics that play no part in syntactic description. The illustrative example they give is taken from Mohawk and is presented here in (30a) and (30b). The incorporated element is the root *tsi'tsi* 'flower'.

(30)	a. *Incorporated expression*	b. *Syntactic counterpart*	
	wak-tsi'tsi-a-ientho-on	o-tsi'tsi-a'	wak-ientho-on
	1SG.P-flower-EP-plant-ST	N-flower-NOUN.SUFF	1SG.P-plant-ST
	'I've planted flowers'	'I've planted flowers'	

First, the word pieces in (30a), including *tsi'tsi*, do not have any meaning in isolation. In other words, (30a) displays lexical integrity, or atomicity, a defining property of the lexicalist hypothesis. Second, (30a) and (30b) do not operate in free variation: the syntactic counterpart is preferred when the argument is new information, hence functionally (30a) and (30b) are not real equivalents. Third, incorporated expressions lack the full productivity of their syntactic counterparts. Not all NPs have a corresponding incorporating expression, for example you cannot incorporate expressions for domestic animals. (A kind of generic root *-nahskw-* is used in such cases, Mithun and Corbett: 1999: 54.) At the same time, not all transitive verbs incorporate. And there is a productivity cline for those that do. Related to this is the lack of transparency of the incorporated item relative to the syntactic counterpart. (30a) displays full transparency, but this is not the case with all expressions. One of the examples Mithun and Corbett give is *atekhwà:ra* 'it has food set on it', meaning 'table', for which speakers appear to be unable to parse out the item for 'food', *-khw*. Fourth, reference to the incorporated argument is only apparent and not actual, as predicted by lexical integrity. The incorporated element plays some role in getting the inference right, but that is all it does. In this way incorporated elements behave like other compound elements. So in the English example 'I have a headache; it really hurts' the element *head* assists in resolving the antecedent of the pronoun but is not actually the antecedent (1999: 57). Finally, there is evidence that the incorporated element is not analogous to a verb's core argument since the object agreement prefix marking the head of VP is not present in the incorporated equivalent. (31b) shows how Mohawk marks agreement of third masculine singular acting on third plural [+animate], namely through the pronominal prefix *hshako-*. This element is missing in the incorporated expression 'he hunts people', where the root *onkwe't* 'people' is the incorporated element (31a).

(31)	a. ra-at-onkwe't-isak-s	b. ta-hshako-hser-e'
	M.A-MIDDLE-person-seek-IPFV	CISLOC-M.A/3PL.P-chase-IPFV
	'he hunts people'	'he was chasing them'

A different kind of evidence that suggests word formation does not take place in syntax is an inconsistency in the effects of pure syntactic movement and movement that is morphologically motivated, i.e. head-to-head movement. Ackema and Neeleman (2007) cite stranding effects and the nature of the constituent from which a head can be extracted.[22] When syntax derives complex words as complex heads, the derivation can be generalized as in (32), where the moved item is the head of a complement that is moved into the head of the phrase taking that complement (Ackema and Neeleman 2007: 331).

(32)

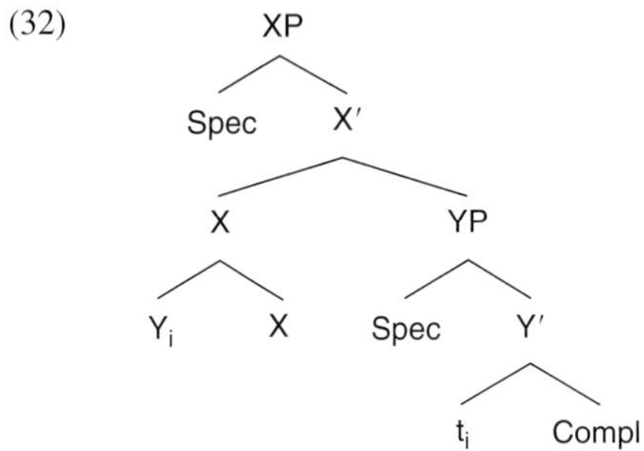

Ackema and Neeleman's argument against word formation in syntax is that the trace of Y should be able to license whatever Y licenses before movement, so that complement material should be able to remain after movement as stranded material. But complex words do not allow this stranded material to remain. One of the examples they give is the Dutch compound noun *probeer papier*, where the first element is the root of the verb 'try out', so the full expression means something like 'try-out paper', the kind of paper one might use to test paints or the quality of a pen. Pre-movement it would require an external agent argument and a patient argument that is its complement:

(33) dat [de dichter [niewe ganzeveren probeert]]
that the poet new quills tries.out
'that the poet tries out new quills'

But both arguments are omitted if the *probeer* root occupying Y is moved to form a complex head with *papier*, occupying X.

(34) *dit is het [probeer$_i$ papier] [[(door) de dichter]] [nieuwe ganzeveren t$_i$]]
this is the try.out paper (by) the poet new quills
'this is the paper on which the poet tries out new quills'

Stranding is also predicted in derivationally complex expressions but is equally ruled out. The sentence 'more central to our arguments' cannot derive:

(35) *[central$_i$ize] [more [t$_i$ [to our arguments]]

Note that the suffix *-ize* is analysed as the head, so occupies X; *central* has its origins in Y with the PP 'to our arguments' as its complement.

Another way in which morphological movement would be inconsistent with conventional syntactic movement is in the restrictions on extraction. It is claimed that adjuncts are islands for extraction, explaining (36), and that adjuncts themselves cannot be moved, as discussed in Baltin and Collins (2007: 5).[23]

(36) *Who$_i$ does John visit Sally [because he likes t$_i$]?

So incorporation instances should exclude any element of an adjunct phrase. Yet such elements can be incorporated. Spencer (2000b: 315) gives the following example from Chukchi.

(37)

a. *Incorporated expression*	b. *Syntactic equivalent*	
jəq-amecat-gʔe	nə-jeq-ʔew	amecat-gʔe
quick-hide-2SG	ADV-quick-ADV	hide-2SG
'you hid quickly'	'you hid quickly'	

1.2.4 Concluding autonomous over seamless-web morphology

Network Morphology opts for a modular grammar where principles and rules of word structure are housed in their own component. Throughout this book we will attempt to motivate this choice by addressing cases of function/form dissociation. The first type represented by inflectional classes is where one function is associated with multiple forms. A second type is where several functions map onto one form, syncretism. Another type is where there is a mismatch between function and form, deponency. A final type of dissociation is where morphological features have no relevance to syntax.

At the same time there are phenomena that suggest a much more direct link between syntax and morphology, and this directness is after all what a seamless-web approach tries to capture. A legitimate reservation about autonomous morphology is that in the case where morphology is a direct expression of syntax, this generalization may be lost. In the next section we look at an option specific to the *nature* of generalization. Because Network Morphology allows for a *default* relationship between syntax and morphology which is direct, autonomous morphology arises where this higher-level default generalization is overridden.

1.3 Generalization as default inheritance

We began with the thought that there are generalizations at the level of the paradigm – paradigmatic relations (Section 1.0.1) – that are worth capturing. Such generalizations are a property of the autonomous morphological component. Illustrating with the inflectional classes of Russian nouns, we mentioned two kinds of relations, horizontal and vertical. Network Morphology captures these relations as a system within a system by borrowing a concept from artificial intelligence to represent knowledge about classes, the *inheritance hierarchy*.[24] The four inflectional classes presented in (6) are, for convenience, repeated here in (38).

(38)

	I	II	III	IV
Singular				
NOMINATIVE	zakon	kart-a	rukop´is´	bolot-o
ACCUSATIVE	zakon	kart-u	rukop´is´	bolot-o
GENITIVE	zakon-a	kart-i	rukop´is´-i	bolot-a
DATIVE	zakon-u	kart-e	rukop´is´-i	bolot-u
INSTRUMENTAL	zakon-om	kart-oj	rukop´is´-ju	bolot-om
PREPOSITIONAL	zakon-e	kart-e	rukop´is´-i	bolot-e
Plural				
NOMINATIVE	zakon-i	kart-i	rukop´is´-i	bolot-a
ACCUSATIVE	zakon-i	kart-i	rukop´is´-i	bolot-a
GENITIVE	zakon-ov	kart	rukop´is-ej	bolot
DATIVE	zakon-am	kart-am	rukop´is´-am	bolot-am
INSTRUMENTAL	zakon-am´i	kart-am´i	rukop´is´-am´i	bolot-am´i
PREPOSITIONAL	zakon-ax	kart-ax	rukop´is´-ax	bolot-ax

The rather monolithic view of inflectional facts given in (38) could be replaced by a hierarchical one where facts collected at nodes are linked to facts at other nodes by a relation of inheritance: facts belonging to nodes situated at a higher place on the hierarchy are inherited by a node lower down. To understand how an inheritance hierarchy represents the same set of facts given in (38), consider Figure 1.1, which is a representational alternative to (38).

A generalization over two or more entities denotes the sharing of one or more facts among entities. In Figure 1.1 fact sharing is expressed as fact inheritance. For example, in the Russian noun inflectional system, one horizontal relation that holds is for the realization of the dative, instrumental and prepositional plural. From (38) we see that these facts are the same across

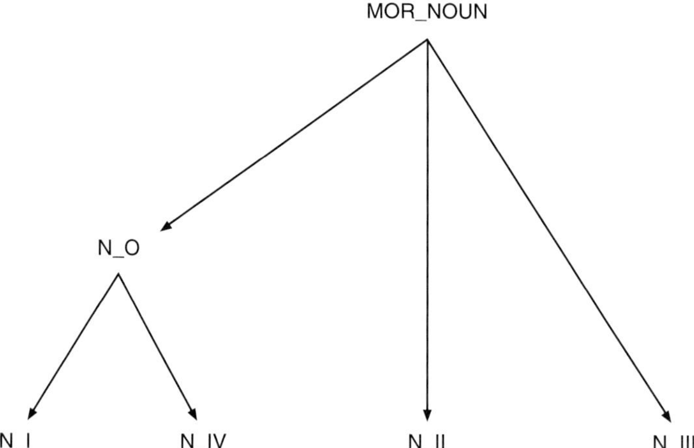

Figure 1.1 *A morphological hierarchy for Russian nouns (based on Corbett and Fraser 1993)*

all four classes. This horizontal relation can be captured within the inheritance hierarchy representation of Russian noun inflection by situating the facts at the node MOR_NOUN or higher. As we will see later in Chapter 2, Section 2.3.1, these facts can be generalized over all nominal classes. They are then inherited by hierarchically lower nodes expressing the different inflectional classes. Horizontal relations are actually *hierarchical* relations in this approach, because the sharing between Declensions implied by these relations can be treated as defaults. Another horizontal relation concerns the facts shared between Declensions I and IV. From (38) we can pick out these facts as the genitive, dative, instrumental and prepositional singular. In Figure 1.1 we introduce the node N_O so that we can express this particular horizontal relation as a hierarchical relation. The node N_O is an abstraction of the properties common to N_I and N_IV. We explain this further in Chapter 3, Section 3.1.2.

Hierarchical relations can be thought of as inter-node inheritance. For vertical relations, inheritance is not between nodes but between facts belonging to a single node – intra-node inheritance. A vertical relation is not expressed as hierarchical inheritance since there is no sense in which facts belonging to the same node can be hierarchically related. For example, within Declension I the nominative and accusative singular share the same realization. One has to imagine lines of inheritance that are internal to the N_I node. The intra-node relation can denote cases of syncretism, a paradigmatic relation to which we

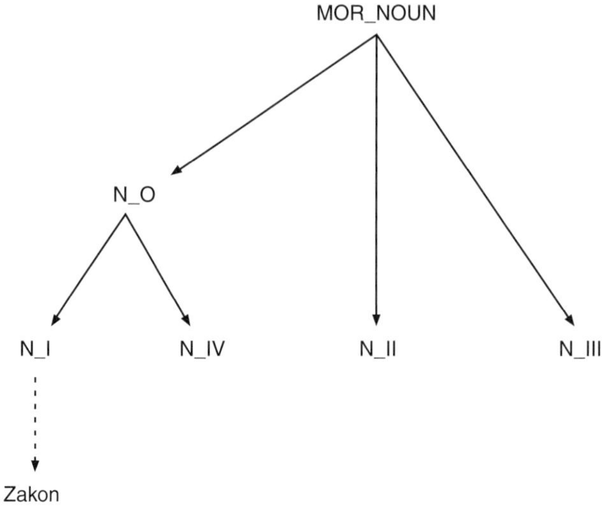

Figure 1.2 *The lexeme* zakon 'law' *inherits its morphology from Declension I*

devote the whole of Chapter 4. Interestingly, an intra-node relation can itself be shared between class nodes, so Declension IV shares with Declension I the fact that nominative and accusative singular have the same realization. This vertical relation can therefore be 'pushed up' the hierarchy to occupy a position in N_O. Unlike the other facts in N_O, this fact is itself a relation. There are other paradigmatic relations in (38) that can be captured by inheritance, and these are discussed fully in Chapter 3.

Inflectional classes are abstractions of paradigmatic possibilities found across Russian nouns (see Section 1.0.1). Each class is therefore a set of generalizations that holds for a subclass of nouns. Within an inheritance hierarchy treatment, individual nouns can be expressed as lexical entry nodes that inherit from appropriate inflectional class nodes. Figure 1.2 shows how the hierarchy has been augmented by plugging in a node at the bottom of the hierarchy, just under N_I, to capture the morphological behaviour of the Declension I lexeme *zakon* 'law'.

Its position in the hierarchy ensures that the node Zakon inherits all facts that are true for N_I. Some of these facts may be local to N_I while some, as we have seen, may be inherited from higher up the hierarchy. Lexical-entry nodes represent lexemes and thus will contain facts belonging to various levels of lexical description. Zakon as a lexeme was shown in (7), repeated here in (39).

(39) ZAKON
syntactic level
syn cat = N
semantic level
'law'
phonological level
stem = /zakon-/
morphological level
mor class = Class_I

The morphological level of description contains class-membership information. In hierarchical terms, we can think of this information as a hook to attach to the N_I node (see Corbett and Baerman 2006: 245). Lexemes sharing the same inflectional hierarchy information hook into the hierarchy in the same way.

1.3.1 Default rather than mandatory inheritance

Returning to (38) we see that most but not all classes share the way the prepositional singular is realized, with the exponent *-e*. Declension III is alone in maintaining uniqueness in this cell, where we find *-i* instead. An attempt at capturing the horizontal relation by placing the *-e* for prepositional case at the root node would mandate the inheritance of this fact at N_III. For an inheritance approach to generalization, there is the option of mandatory/monotonic inheritance or default/non-monotonic inheritance. To allow a generalization to hold for most cases rather than all cases, Network Morphology opts for a *default* interpretation of lines of inheritance, such that within a family of nodes inheriting from the same source node, a member may be able to *override* the inheritance of a fact. When this option in inheritance interpretation is taken, the prepositional singular in *-e* can be placed at the root node MOR_NOUN, from where it will be inherited by default by all daughter nodes. But the daughter node N_III can be made to override the default by carrying an alternative value for the prepositional singular.

Default inheritance not only provides a more elegant way of locating generalizations within the system, here the noun inflection system, but also captures what we called semi-regularity in Section 1.0.2. We gave *soldat* 'soldier' as an example of an irregular noun. But we were careful to point out that its irregularity lies in only one cell of its paradigm: in all respects it behaves like a regular Declension I noun except for its genitive plural, which is *soldat* rather than expected **soldatov*. To capture its irregularity as semi-regularity, we hook it into the hierarchy just like *zakon* but include a statement that it overrides the inheritance of the fact about the genitive plural in *-ov* with an alternative realization. In this way we express the fact that it behaves just like *zakon* except in one respect. The other examples we gave can be treated in similar fashion: inheritance expresses their similarity to regular cases, and their override pinpoints the precise manner of their irregularity. A hierarchical organization also allows us to draw together a class of irregulars that are irregular in the same way. In Section 1.0.2 we gave *san'i* 'sledge' as an example of a *plurale tantum* noun, but Russian has many other examples. We could situate a *plurale tantum* node under N_I to inherit all plural morphology and override singular morphology. Any *plurale tantum* lexical entry would be made to inherit from the semi-regular node, from where it would get both the regular and irregular facts.

Defaults are also useful for resolving rule competition. Pāṇini's principle, or the Elsewhere Condition, regulates the application of rival rules. The *scope* and *content* of the more general rule is inferred until there is another rule that is more specific in scope or content. As an illustration of scope, the featural make-up of the base is a determining factor in resolving affix competition in derivational morphology, as argued for by Plag (2002; 2003), Lieber (2004) and others, and statistically demonstrated by Plag and Baayen (2009).[25] For example, in Russian the affix *-sk* attaches to bases to form relational adjectives, as in *avtor* 'author' > *avtorsk-ij* 'author (adj)'. One of its rivals is *-ov*, found for example in the derivative *šumov-oj* 'sonic'. Whereas the *-sk* affix attaches to bases that denote people or geopolitical facts, the *-ov* affix is less fussy in its application. The rule of *-ov* affixation has broader scope and applies until the narrow *-sk* becomes relevant, i.e. when the base has the specific features that it requires. An example where the content of a general rule is inferred until it is superseded by a rule of more specific content is the realization of the prepositional case in Russian, elaborated in Chapter 2, Section 2.2.3. Some Declension I nouns can express a strictly locational prepositional case (second locative), as opposed to a case that is governed by prepositions that include location. The more general case has the *-e* exponent, as we have seen. The narrower, stricter case has *-ú*. So for *pol* 'floor' the form *pol-ú* is preferred when it is a location, leaving *pol-e* for all other prepositional contexts.

Network Morphology adopts default inference as the means of resolving rule competition in both the inflectional and derivational domain. In this way it subscribes to Stump's Pāṇinian Determinism Hypothesis.

(40) *Pāṇinian Determinism Hypothesis* (Stump 2001: 23)
Competition among members of the same rule block is in all cases resolved by Pāṇini's principle.

It should be noted that the Pāṇinian principle is also employed in Distributed Morphology through the Subset Principle (Harley and Noyer 1999: 4–5; Embick and Noyer 2007: 298–300), since lexical entries are featurally underspecified for the DM-morphemes that they realize. Williams (2007) observes that the Pāṇini principle follows directly from feature underspecification, which itself falls out from the realizational approach Distributed Morphology adopts. However, Distributed Morphology does not subscribe to the Pāṇinian Determinism Hypothesis since, in the case of no winner, competition is resolved by other means: extrinsic ordering (Embick and Marantz 2008: 5), a form of the Feature Hierarchy (Noyer 1997) or feature geometry (Harley 1994).

Pāṇini's principle is default inference: 'elsewhere' in the absence of more specific information. Defaults are suited to specifically lexical generalization due to the preponderance of irregularity and competition amongst rules. For example, HPSG makes use of monotonic inheritance to capture generalizations about syntactic constraints, but (in some versions) defaults for lexical information. Sag, Wasow and Bender (2003: 230) discuss default inheritance of constraints 'to express the idea that language embodies generalizations that have exceptions – subclasses with subregularities and individual elements with idiosyncrasies'. Bonami and Boyé (2006) assert, 'In the absence of an explicit alternative, we take it that the use of defaults is the only known way to model regularity in an HPSG implementation of the stem space.' A default interpretation is not enough, however, to flesh out all the lexical generalizations that can be made. Figures 1.1 and 1.2 show single inheritance hierarchies. But there is an alternative that Network Morphology adopts, and by so doing models morphological facts not as a hierarchy but rather as a *network* of hierarchies.

1.3.2 Multiple inheritance and orthogonality rather than single inheritance

Revisiting the irregular noun *soldat*, it is interesting that the cell of its paradigm that marks it as irregular is exactly what is predicted if it belonged to another inflectional class, namely Declension II. For this class of nouns the genitive plural is exponentless, e.g. *kart-Ø* 'of maps' (38). If the genitive plural of *soldat* were realized differently to all four classes of noun, then we would want to override the inheritance from Declension I and specify the alternative at the lexical entry for *soldat*. But to do that when the alternative is available as an inheritable fact would be to miss an important generalization. By allowing an item to inherit from more than one source, we can better capture the nature of *soldat*'s irregularity: it is a case of mild heteroclisis, where a single item belongs to more than one inflectional class, in this case Declensions I and II.

When *multiple inheritance* is supported, we can also capture more horizontal relations amongst inflectional classes themselves. Both Declension II and IV share the exponentless realization of the genitive plural. We can capture this by adding N_II as a secondary source of inheritance for the N_IV node, for the fact about the genitive plural only.

A problem with multiple inheritance is that the two sources of inheritance may hold the same feature combination but with different values, so that multiple inheritance will result in a conflict of evaluation. In the artificial intelligence literature, this is known as the 'Nixon diamond' scenario, where a node representing former US president Richard Nixon multiply inherits from the nodes REPUBLICAN and QUAKER. The two sources have different values for the attribute 'pacifist', so Nixon will be in conflict about pacifism (Touretzky 1986: 11). Multiple source conflicts necessitate a decision between two further inheritance-based options, prioritized multiple inheritance or orthogonal multiple inheritance. In the prioritized option, inheritance sources are labelled for which one takes priority over the other in case of conflict (Flickinger 1987: 60; Daelemans, de Smedt and Gazdar 1992: 209; Evans, Gazdar and Moser 1993: 38). Network Morphology opts for orthogonality where a network contains not only a taxonomy tree structure but hierarchy structures that lie orthogonal to one another.

It is through orthogonality that Network Morphology expresses the autonomy of morphology, since it distinguishes a hierarchy of lexemes from a morphological hierarchy with its own distinctly morphological generalizations. Through orthogonality, facts from the morphological hierarchy inform the lexemic hierarchy with appropriate function:form mappings needed by syntax. Separating out two hierarchies provides for cases where the morphology delivers a form that is not typical for a particular function. Such cases were discussed in Section 1.2.1 as various kinds of dissociation between syntax and morphology. Due to an interpretation of inheritance as default inheritance, Network Morphology, while providing for autonomous morphology, can also capture the normal situation where morphosyntax and its realization are aligned in the expected way. Overrides capture dissociations as misalignment. Orthogonal hierarchies belong to a single network and are linked in a default way. They are, therefore, subject to override, thereby capturing inflectional classes, syncretism and deponency as we show in the following chapters.

Network Morphology opts for a multiple inheritance network architecture rather than a single inheritance hierarchy architecture. This allows us to capture generalizations over inflectional classes as well as lexical entries that single inheritance would miss. Orthogonality, combined with the default interpretation of inheritance, allows for autonomous morphology while maintaining the more direct association between syntax and morphology as the default. Moreover, such a network architecture allows us to introduce submodularity to the morphological component in order to capture the major differences between inflectional and derivational morphology. In Chapter 7 we look at how morphological submodularity is expressed by a separate but orthogonally related derivational hierarchy. For the moment we briefly survey the familiar differences between inflection and derivation, which serve as motivation for modularizing the morphological component.

1.3.3 Inflection versus derivation and submodularity

Opting for an autonomous morphological component entails a further option: whether this component is 'unitary' or 'modular' (Zwicky 1992: 357–8; 1996: 302–3). Network Morphology opts for modularity in the morphological component to capture generalizations about inflectional morphology and distinguish them from generalizations about derivational morphology. Example (41) is the familiar list of parameters which taken together distinguish canonical inflection from canonical derivation. As Stump (1990: 99) notes, any morphological framework has to account for observed morphological behaviour that is due to such a list.[26]

(41)

	Parameter	Inflection	Derivation
1.	Purpose	build the form of a lexeme required by a given syntactic context	build a new lexeme from an existing lexeme
2.	Syntactic determinism	determined by syntax	not determined by syntax
3.	Obligatoriness	function is obligatory	function is not obligatory
4.	Productivity	fully productive	not fully productive
5.	Transparency	transparent	not always transparent
6.	Base inheritance	all base features are inherited	base features that are inherited are limited
7.	Exponence order	after derivational exponent; closes word	before inflectional exponent; need not close word

An account of the differences must surely be anchored in the difference in *purpose* between inflection and derivation, where inflection serves syntax by providing it with the appropriate form of a lexeme to express a given syntactic function, and derivation serves in the expansion of a language's lexical stock by building lexemes from already existing lexemes (Zwicky 1992: 357–8). Modularity captures the two distinct purposes of morphology. Similarly, the syntactic and phonological components lend themselves to modularity to capture different rule types and different principles. In phonology one would want to distinguish principles driving morphophonemic alternations from those handling allophonic variation (Zwicky 1996: 302). And in syntax rules that order heads and modifiers are distinguished from principles such as the EPP and other triggers of movement.

If inflection serves syntax and derivation does not, Parameters 2, 3, 4, 5 follow naturally. The Shughni verb lexeme 'see' contains the paradigm of present-tense forms in (4), but in a construction with a first-person plural subject it is only the *win-ām* member of the paradigm that is relevant, so the choice of this form over the others is determined by the syntactic construction. Conversely, there is no syntactic construction that requires specifically agent-derived nouns in English, so that in the sentence 'What kind of X are you looking for', X can be filled by the lexemes *employers* or *employees* (Stump 1990: 99). Since the functions which inflection realizes are syntactic, each member of the inflectional paradigm is obligatory, expressing a particular function and implying that some other function is not in play (Parameter 3). If a language, for instance Shughni, has number and person agreement for verbs, then every member of Shughni's 'see' paradigm is obligatorily saying *something* about person and number. Even when there is no exponent for a feature value, information about the feature is being conveyed at least by implication. So in English both *cat* and *cats* are saying something about number, because number is obligatory in all English count nouns; it is not possible to say 'on this occasion Number information is not relevant' (see Plank 1994: 1672). But in derivation the functions are not obligatory: a value for agentness does not have to be expressed in every noun, either using an exponent or implying a value with lack of an exponent.

Parameters 2 and 3 have a pressure effect on how lexemes interact with inflectional rules: lexemes need full paradigms, and the inflectional rules that generate them will be fully productive (Parameter 4). And lack of this same pressure for derivation means that a paradigmatic approach to derivation would inevitably show gaps. Again we return to purpose: there is no parallel pressure to extend the lexical stock in any one particular direction – agent lexemes, qualitative adjectives, etc. At best there are tendencies to build in a particular direction, so at best derivation displays semi-productivity. The product of an inflectional rule should be completely transparent (Parameter 5) given its syntactic function; the product of derivation should also be transparent, but because it is an independent member of the lexical stock, it is subject to the same processes of semantic change as any other lexical entry, such that its original meaning may cease to be its primary meaning. The Parameter 6 setting for inflection falls out from its purpose: building an array of syntactic atoms for a single lexeme. The variable is the form of the lexeme, not its syntacticosemantic features; they are preserved. Likewise the purpose of derivation is to create new lexemes; only part of the deriving lexeme is preserved in the new lexeme. In Chapter 7 we show how this is captured by different degrees of inheritance from the base lexeme depending on the type of derivation.

Parameter 7 provides a good argument for the logical directionality implied by a modular morphological component (Zwicky: 1992). If morphology is the input to syntax, then within morphology the derivational module sets up objects on which inflectional rules can operate. From this it follows naturally that markers of derivation will typically be found inside markers of inflection.

Through the various options taken, a framework should be able to neatly account for the parameter settings in (41). But these settings reflect the canonical situation. The framework must at the same time be able to provide for any apparent canonical departures. Inflectional non-canonical behaviour includes instances where the inflectional exponent is inside a derivational one, a departure from the Parameter 7 setting. A Shughni example involving an expressive derivative is given in (42).

(42)	čost	wam	gujbuc-en-ik=en	dis	maỹʒůnǰ-idi
	appear.PST	her.OBL	babygoat-PL-EXPR=3PL	very	hungry-INTENS

‘The dear little kids appeared very hungry to her’
(From the *Goat’s Tale*, narrated by Shahlo Nekushoeva)

Here the *-en* suffix closest to the root *gujbuc-* is the plural inflectional exponent; the clitic *=en* is hosted by *gujbuc-en-ik* and expresses subject agreement in past-tense contexts. Furthermore, expressive morphology in other languages such as Russian yields an instance of non-canonical derivation with regard to Parameter 6. The expressive examples in (12) inherit *all* features of their base: syntactic category, gender, semantics. In fact even when expressive derivation results in a change in inflectional class, the new lexeme takes the gender associated with the base rather than that associated with the new class, as this example from Chekhov’s *Svetlaja ličnost´* demonstrates:

(43)	gromadn-yj	ryž-ij	dom-išč-e
	huge-SG.M	rust-SG.M	house(CLASS 4)-AUG-SG

‘the huge rust-red house’

Here the base is Declension I *dom* and its derivative Declension IV, the class associated with neuter nouns. A way to account for some of these instances is to adopt Stump's (2001: 99–112) taxonomy of derivational rules: while many are category changing, some are category preserving. Of this latter type they may or may not be *head marking*, that is the inflection is marked on the head/root of the expression rather than on the expression as a whole. So *-en* in (42) is attached to the root *gujbuc* instead of the stem *gujbucik* when it appears in the plural cell of the derived lexeme's paradigm. We will return to head-marking and category-preserving derivation in Network Morphology's treatment of word formation in Chapter 7.

It has been observed that inflection can be unproductive and opaque, a departure from Parameters 4 and 5's canonical settings. Bybee (1985: 91) gives as an example the plural *clothes* which of course does not mean 'more than one *cloth*'. But if the product of inflection ends up being lexicalized, then this is simply an instance of semantic drift. So if the framework provides for lexicalization of inflected forms, then Parameter 5 non-canonical behaviour can be accounted for. The lack of a first-person singular for the Russian verb *pobed´it´* 'to conquer' is a well-known instance where inflection is unproductive (see Baerman 2008 for this and similar examples in Russian). This is a particularly serious example since it is actually a refusal by the lexeme to serve syntax (Parameter 1). As observed in Baerman and Corbett (2010: 2), 'Defectiveness represents an unwanted intrusion of morphological idiosyncrasy into syntax.' An account that can factor in defectiveness should, therefore, be able to handle non-canonical Parameter 4 instances.

Finally, the examples of partial agreement we alluded to in Section 1.2.1 could be viewed as non-canonical inflection with regard to Parameter 3. If number and person are agreement features in Dutch, then they are obligatory. Lexemes cannot deliver forms that say nothing about these features; but this is what appears to be implied by the partial agreement account. However, if the elements being reduced are the features themselves (in other words, a feature is taken out of action in a particular context), then the lack of value could be explained. In Chapter 2, Section 2.2.4 we will discuss verb paradigms where the agreement features relevant in one tense are not relevant in another. Network Morphology accounts for such behaviour through two types of principle. The first imposes a partial ordering on attributes. The other allows for flexible paradigm signatures, but requires the features which split the paradigm to be at its root.

1.4 Morphological formalization

We end our discussion with one final option in the construction of a morphological framework: whether to insist on a means of formalizing claims about word structure so that all the framework's theories are computer interpretable, or whether to rely utterly on the clarity of the practitioner's prose style. As Stump puts it, the option is between using 'an explicitly interpreted formalism' or 'an informal system of metaphors which helps the readers arrive at a purely intuitive conception of the theory' (Stump 2001: 29). Through Evans and Gazdar's (1996) lexical knowledge representation language DATR, the Network Morphology framework takes the first option. Details of Network Morphology formalism await Chapter 2 and its formal theories the subsequent chapters.

1.5 Summary of Network Morphology options and book outline

Network Morphology takes the paradigm of a lexeme's word-forms as a starting point for making generalizations about word structure. This way it captures paradigmatic relations and systemizes them to account for the possible ways meaning and form can be associated at the level of the word. This makes Network Morphology a paradigm-based framework, entailing a number of other options. First, the minimal sign is not the morpheme but the lexeme, a location of syntactic, semantic, phonological and morphological types of information. Second, because paradigmatic cells of content (combinations of morphosyntactic features) are associated with a lexeme's stem, the form and meaning association is both inferential and realizational. It is realizational because the content that is part of a complex word is not a consequence of gathering together morphemes to yield an aggregate content; rather the content is 'already there', features from the syntax demanding phonological expression. In other words, the content is a precondition of form rather than a consequence of it (Ackerman and Stump 2004). And it is inferential since the exponents of the content are introduced by rule, rather than being lexical objects or vocabulary items. Thus the complex word is inferred from the lexeme's stem. The paradigm-based approach allows Network Morphology to opt out of radical agglutination, a theorem of the word-structure-as-phrase-structure approach. Realizational rules can introduce one, many or no exponents; the cell licensing the rule can be defined as a combination of features, so many functions can have a single exponent.

Network Morphology does not opt for a seamless web of syntactic and morphological rules and principles, since there is no expectation that word structure is an analog to phrase structure. Rather Network Morphology opts for autonomous morphology to capture principles whose domain is strictly the word and to provide for the distinction between word-structure properties that contribute directly at the interface with a separate syntactic component and those that do not, such as inflectional class membership. The products of the syntactic component and the products of the morphological component are therefore different. The syntax operates over the morphological product, which is treated as an encapsulated object. This interaction between the components entails the principle of morphology-free syntax since syntactic rules and principles cannot refer to word-internal structure: the asymmetry of the syntax–morphology interaction means that a morphological rule responds to syntactic structure but cannot be an element in the rule that delivers syntactic properties. The principle of syntax-free morphology also follows since a morphological rule cannot take as part of its structural description a purely syntactic fact, such as information regarding the ordering of constituents to express a syntactic function.

To represent lexical knowledge and capture horizontal and vertical paradigmatic relations, Network Morphology imports a concept from artificial intelligence, the inheritance hierarchy. The further option of a default interpretation of inheritance allows irregularity to be recast as *non-regularity*. By replacing a single inheritance network with a multiple inheritance network, the framework is better positioned to locate paradigmatic generalizations and further distinguish degrees of non-regularity. Network Morphology invokes orthogonality to resolve multiple inheritance conflicts, and orthogonality combined with defaults allows the framework to capture the autonomous behaviour of morphology when it occurs. Orthogonality is also invoked to distinguish inflection from derivation, expressed as facts inhabiting two distinct hierarchies of information. In this way Network Morphology opts for further modularization of the morphological component to capture word-structure generalizations that directly follow from the two purposes of morphology, to create a lexeme's paradigm of word-forms for syntax and to create new lexemes. In sum, Network Morphology is an inferential-realization framework based on inheritance. Interactions of morphological rules occur through defaults and overrides. These interactions are regulated by their position in default-inheritance hierarchies.[27]

In what follows we show how the options outlined above are formalized so as to offer an account of word structure that captures morphological regularity as a scalar notion. We concentrate in this book on synthetic morphology, not least because it is required as basic for determining the analytic kind. We do, however, mention periphrasis at certain points, especially where it interacts with syncretism in Chapter 4, Section 4.4. By the same token we concentrate on stem-modification word-formation (Anderson 1985), rather than compounding. In Chapter 2 we build on the foundations of lexeme-based morphology using the default inheritance approach that lies at the heart of Network Morphology, and the DATR formalism. Chapter 3 lays out our approach to paradigmatic relations through a careful examination of inflectional class properties, resulting in a theory of 'possible inflectional class'. In an inflectional system, what we called a vertical paradigmatic relation may or may not be systematic. In Chapter 4 we discuss principles for identifying and classifying systematic relations, thereby providing a formal account of syncretism. With syncretism there is a dissociation between syntactic content associated with a lexeme and its formal expression, so for example a 'syntactic' accusative is expressed with genitive morphology. We fold such phenomena into a framework that keeps the syntactic and morphological worlds separate. A different kind of syntax–morphology dissociation is *mismatch* provided by deponency, the theme of Chapter 5. We represent deponency as a hierarchy of defaults that in theory can be overridden at any level, the highest level being the default that syntactic and morphological representations line up. Such a hierarchy yields the full range of mismatch cases corresponding to degrees of non-regularity. This way classical deponency (Latin and Greek) as well as 'extended' deponency (other languages) can be handled in the same problem and solution space. Framing non-regularity in this way is extended in Chapter 6 to the diachronic dimension by examining paradigmatic restructuring as a 'resetting' of one of the defaults in a hierarchy of defaults. The phenomenon that is accounted for is the regularization of Latin deponents.

Up to this point, the focus is on inflectional issues, captured in the context of an inflectional hierarchy of facts interacting with an orthogonal hierarchy of lexemic facts. In Chapter 7 we shift the focus to derivational morphology, expressed as a third hierarchy which completes the set of hierarchies in the network and represents the modular approach to morphology to which we adhere. A complex lexeme is characterized as inheriting multiply from the hierarchy of lexemes as well as a hierarchy of derivational rule statements; these in turn refer to the inflectional hierarchy. Thus we end with the full definition of the lexeme, a partially specified locus of parallel types of information inheritable from various subnetworks of lexical information. Conclusion and prospects are outlined in Chapter 8.

2 A framework for morphological defaults

2.0 Introduction

Exceptional or irregular behaviour comes in different flavours. As we shall argue, it can often be characterized in terms of the way that a rule is accessed, rather than as a matter of absolute exclusion from the system of rules. If we consider the English lexeme *go*, for example, it is exceptional in a number of different ways, but it can also be partially classified as following rules to which other lexemes are subject. On the one hand, its past participle *gone* fits with a group of strong verbs which have the N-participle. In contrast its suppletive preterite form *went*, it would appear, is entirely irregular because it has no connection with the root *go*. A more common kind of exceptionality does not involve the use of completely new material unrelated to the prevalent morphology of the language. Instead it involves an irregular or unusual *combination* of rules. If we consider the English verb *beat*, for instance, its preterite form is *beat* and its past participle is *beaten*. We can find other verbs where the present, preterite and past participle have the same form, such as *hit* (Huddleston and Pullum *et al.* 2002: 1601).[1] The verb *beat* differs from these by using for the past participle the *-en* suffix associated with other verb classes. While this suffix is not the most common one, we can see that what makes *beat* odd is the combination of realizations it makes use of, none of which, taken individually, are unique to it. This suggests that lexemes are part of a network where morphological information flows from different sources and with different types of default playing a role in morphology.

In this chapter we introduce some foundational distinctions of Network Morphology in Section 2.1 and show in Section 2.2 how Network Morphology treats the lexeme as a locus of parallel information, where semantic, syntactic, phonological and morphological information are combined. This also means that there is potential for slippage between morphological knowledge and other linguistic levels so that it can become autonomous. In Section 2.3 we consider the different types of default generalization which Network Morphology makes possible. We emphasize the ability to model cross-linguistic tendencies with attribute ordering, in particular in terms of the predictions they make about neutralization and syncretism. We also show that Network Morphology has a *flexible paradigm signature* which can account for apparently different types of phenomena: marginal features on the one hand, and splits in the paradigm on the other. We then explain the role of normal and exceptional case defaults. The former are used for the general case that normally applies, whereas the latter are used as the last resort. Having considered these different types of default within morphology we move on to look at the default relationship with syntax, which naturally leads to a typology for morphological autonomy in Section 2.4, starting from a non-autonomous situation where the morphological hierarchy is isomorphic with the lexemic hierarchy, and therefore eliminable, and moving to a situation where inflectional classes create structure which is not reflected in the lexemic hierarchy. The framework, therefore, allows for different degrees of morphological autonomy and imposes constraints on possible morphological systems. We illustrate how Network Morphology treats the relationship with syntax in Section 2.4 and summarize in Section 2.5.

2.1 Models and analyses of lexemes

Network Morphology embraces a philosophy of implementing analyses in order to achieve some degree of external validation. The analyses of morphological phenomena are expressed using the DATR language (Evans and Gazdar 1996), because it is a straightforward way to implement default inheritance. Our aim is to introduce some of the key ideas for understanding Network Morphology, and so we will concentrate on those concepts which are relevant.

The purpose of developing a framework for looking at morphology is to understand what shape morphological systems can take and to develop analyses which can make generalizations about those systems. This leads us to an important conceptual distinction – the distinction between a *full morphological model* for a given language and a *morphological analysis* of that language.

(1) *Full morphological model*
Complete sets of forms of lexemes and associated information relevant for syntax.

(2) *Morphological analysis*
A sufficiently minimal and optimal description of a language's morphological system such that, by applying the appropriate rules of inference, a full morphological model can be obtained.

Naturally, (2) should be of most interest to linguists, and when we refer to diagrams of different parts of the network in various parts of the book, these are associated with morphological analysis as understood in (2). The full morphological model in (1) can essentially be understood as a list of lexemes, associated forms and relevant morphosyntax. The way in which these forms are generated or accessed is of most interest, and this is the role of (2), of course.

It should be noted, however, that (1) is not entirely without interest, as it is possible to have constraints associated with (1) in addition to (2). The constraint we present in Section 2.2.3 is made in relation to the full morphological model, by specifying restrictions on the shape of complete paradigms for the morphosyntactic features case, number and gender. It naturally follows that the morphological analyses which are compatible with the complete morphological model are also restricted by this constraint. In Section 2.2.4 on the other hand, we present a constraint for *flexible paradigm signatures* in morphological analyses. Similarly, in Section 2.3.1 we present a constraint which determines where default information can be placed, and, as this is a constraint which refers to inheritance hierarchies, it is also a constraint on morphological analysis. When we refer to *theorems* at different stages in the book, we are referring to elements of the full morphological model which can be inferred from the morphological analysis.

Within the morphological analysis itself we should note another key characteristic of Network Morphology, as encapsulated in (3).

(3) *There are potentially many routes to a morphological rule.*

What we mean in (3) is that the very same rule can be general in its application for some items, being inherited as part of a larger class, or it can be accessed directly by a lexeme (as we argue in our discussion of *exceptional case defaults* in Section 2.3.2). Hence, a neat distinction between pure lexical listing on the one hand and rule on the other cannot be drawn, as summed up by the mantra in (4).

(4) *It's rules all the way down, and lists all the way up.*

We shall argue that, even where there is lexical stipulation, it often involves access to information which already exists somewhere in the network of morphological knowledge. This idea is particularly important in our discussion of virtual paradigms in Chapter 6.

In our analyses we represent morphological knowledge in terms of *nodes* and *inheritance* between nodes. Nodes in Network Morphology can be conceived as containers for lists of rules. Sometimes one node can be the location for a large number of rules defining the paradigm of, say, a verb, as is true for our analysis of the the Gunwinyguan language Dalabon in Chapter 4. Alternatively, the rules yielding the forms associated with a lexeme's paradigm may be distributed around several nodes, as we illustrate in Section 2.2.5.

In order to grasp some of the key terminology, let us consider representations of the Russian noun lexeme *stol* 'table' as it would appear in the output of the full morphological model for Russian nouns (i.e. as the output of a morphological analysis of Russian nouns).[2] (The lexeme *stol* belongs to the same class as *zakon* 'law', namely Declension I, but has a different stress pattern.) In Figure 2.1 we represent the Russian noun lexeme *stol* 'table' as a container in which different types of information are combined, including information about its syntax (`syn`), semantics (`sem`), stem (`stem`) and inflectional morphology (`mor`). For example, the gender of *stol* is syntactically relevant, so we require information about `syn gender`. For *stol* this is `masculine`. For Russian, animacy is also important, as it plays a role in determining both the form of the accusative and associated agreements in syntax. In the plural, the accusative of animates is the same as their genitive, whatever that may be. In the singular, the rule is essentially restricted to Declension I, associated with masculine gender; even for Declension II nouns which are animate and masculine, such as *deduška* 'grandfather', the accusative is the exponent for that declension. This demonstrates the morphological nature of the rule. So we require information about `syn animacy`. For *stol* the value is `inanimate`. We also see an example of the semantic information associated with the noun, namely that it is semantically inanimate (`sem animacy = inanimate`). If we were looking at the analysis from which this morphological model would be generated, we would expect to equate syntactic animacy by default with semantic animacy, of course.

The syntactic category of *stol* is noun, and its syntactic gender (i.e. for agreement) is masculine. The container presented could provide more information about the lexeme's semantics, such as whether the noun is count or mass, and so on. We limit ourselves here to the simplification of the English gloss 'table', as our focus is on the morphology. The lexeme's stem is *stol*, and its inflectional morphology consists of a paradigm of twelve case and number combinations with associated inflections and stress. The information in Figure 2.1 represents the kind of information we would expect to find in the full morphological model. And, of course, the full morphological model will repeat lots of information redundantly. A good morphological analysis will, of course, show how the different forms of the lexeme are inherited, just as they are for thousands of other nouns.

```
Stol
```

syn	
cat = noun	
gender = masculine	
animacy = inanimate	
sem	
animacy = inanimate	
gloss = table	
stem = *stol*	
mor	
sg nom = *stol*	pl nom = *stol-í*
sg acc = *stol*	pl acc = *stol-í*
sg gen = *stol-á*	pl gen = *stol-óv*
sg dat = *stol-ú*	pl dat = *stol-ám*
sg inst = *stol-óm*	pl inst = *stol-ám'i*
sg prep = *stol-é*	pl prep = *stol-áx*

Figure 2.1 *The lexeme* Stol *'table' (with forms in transcription)*
Note: subsets of nouns also have additional second locative and second genitive forms. We discuss the second locative in Section 2.2.3.

The information in Figure 2.1 can be represented in DATR syntax as in (5). Each statement about the lexeme *stol* in (5) is expressed in the form of an *equation*. For example, the first equation states that the lexeme's syntactic category is noun. In DATR the single = is used for equations which represent the theorems belonging to the full morphological model (i.e. the outcomes of a morphological analysis), whereas if (5) were part of a morphological analysis, this would be represented in DATR by the use of == in the equation.

(5)

```
Stol:
  <syn cat> = noun
  <syn gender> = masculine
  <syn animacy> = inanimate
  <sem animacy> = inanimate
  <gloss> = table
  <stem> = stol
  <mor sg nom> = stol
  <mor sg acc> = stol
  <mor sg gen> = stol-á
  <mor sg dat> = stol-ú
  <mor sg inst> = stol-óm
  <mor sg loc> = stol-é
  <mor pl nom> = stol-í
  <mor pl acc> = stol-í
  <mor pl gen> = stol-óv
  <mor pl dat> = stol-ám
  <mor pl inst> = stol-ám'i
  <mor pl loc> = stol-áx
```

The information in (5) represents what we would expect our analysis to generate, but it also groups the information in a particular way so as to indicate that it is related. The different case and number forms are related, as they are treated as belonging to the same lexeme. The label `Stol` stands for the lexeme in (5). The label is given before the colon, but the choice of label is formally irrelevant. Any label would do. (Of course, the label chosen is helpful for a human looking at the representation.)

We talk of the *equations*, such as in (5), as being *facts* which consist of a left-hand side (LHS) and right-hand side (RHS). There are sixteen facts in (5). Each LHS contains a *path* notated with angle brackets, and each *path* contains a set of ordered *attributes*. Consider the fact in (6).

(6)

```
<mor sg dat> = stol-ú
```

The LHS in (6) consists of a path which contains three attributes, `mor`, `sg` and `dat`. In Chapter 1 we represented combinations of morphosyntactic features using the curly bracket notation. The LHS in (6) contains information that we referred to in Chapter 1, Section 1.1 as {NUM:SG, CASE:DAT}, for example. There the features were typed so that we could see that the value SG belongs to the feature NUM, and the value DAT belongs to the feature CASE. The path in (6) is ordered, and we can readily interpret that order as expressing an implicit typing. Network Morphology imposes an additional layer of interpretation onto the DATR attributes in terms of the linguistic notion of *feature* (and *feature value*). Features are sets of properties which belong together (e.g. 'case' is a feature). Feature values are the individual properties which belong to the set (e.g. 'dative' is a feature value belonging to the feature case). The attributes in (6) can be interpreted as in (7).

(7) {MODULE:MOR, NUM:SG, CASE:DAT} = *stol-ú*

In (7) `module:mor` is a special instance of typing, where the feature `module` has the feature value `mor` (for morphology, as opposed to `syn` for syntax, for example). Some Network Morphology constraints appeal to such implicit treatment in terms of features, and they do so by interpreting the ordering of attributes. As the additional information in (7) is implicit in the attributes we use, we do not employ the notation in (7), but we do appeal to the concepts 'feature' and 'feature value'. A particular appeal of the ordering approach to attributes is that it suggests a structure to the paradigm, and we shall discuss this further in Section 2.2.3.

It is also possible that linguistic features (as opposed to feature values) can appear as attributes. This can be seen in the equation which expresses information about *stol*'s gender, repeated in (8).

(8) `<syn gender> = masculine`

The purpose of (8) is to state that the syntax module must have the lexeme *stol*'s value for gender available to it.

Returning to (6) we note that the RHS just consists of the value *stol-ú*. In the full morphological model, the RHS can only contain values like these, specifying either morphological forms or feature values relevant for syntax. But in a morphological analysis, it is possible for an RHS to contain paths or combinations of paths and atoms. Indeed, equations which contain a path on the RHS involve inheritance of some kind, and so are important for making generalizations.

As we are interested in morphological analysis, much of what is listed in (5) should, in fact, be inferred from sources distributed across the network of morphological information, because the purpose of morphological analysis is to provide the rules and generalizations from which the surface facts in (5) can be inferred. In the next section, when we consider information distributed across the network, we also encounter attributes of intermediate status which are not required in the full morphological model, but which are internal to the morphological analysis. These are pure morphological features, as discussed in Chapter 1, Section 1.2.1.

2.2 Lexemes as part of a network

In a morpheme-based theory, the affixes which realize the different number and case combinations would have a similar status in the lexicon to roots and stems, such as *stol*, being treated as minimal signs which concatenate onto the stem. In contrast to this, as was explained in Chapter 1, Section 1.5, in an inferential–realizational theory the affixes and other exponents of grammatical features are associated with rules. Network Morphology is a default inheritance-based version of inferential–realizational morphology, and the rules of exponence are located within the network of information from which lexemes inherit.

In Chapter 1, Section 1.1 we discussed the lexeme as an item with multiple layers of information brought together. Matthews (1972: 160) describes the lexeme as the 'lexical element' to which the forms of a paradigm belong. As Stump (1998: 13) puts it, 'A *lexeme* is a unit of linguistic analysis which belongs to a particular syntactic category, has a particular meaning or grammatical function, and ordinarily enters into syntactic combinations as a single word…' Under a lexeme-based theory, a root or stem has associated meanings and part of speech, and rules apply to determine the correct inflectional forms. Hence, a lexeme can be associated with multiple inflected forms (the lexeme GIVE can be associated with *give*, *gives*, *gave*, *given*, for example).

So far we have presented lexemes as locations which combine various levels of information. But much of this information is predictable. For example, the fact that the lexeme *stol* is assigned to the masculine gender is not an accidental and unpredictable property of that item. As Corbett (1982; 1991) and Fraser and Corbett (1995) demonstrate, gender in Russian is usually predictable from either semantics (i.e. biological sex of higher-order animates) or declensional class. In the case of *stol*, the noun is assigned masculine gender because this is associated with the set of inflections it has – its declension. The individual exponents of noun case and number themselves are not directly associated with gender for a number of reasons. As we saw in Chapter 1, Section 1.0.1 in our discussion of paradigmatic relations, some inflections can be used across different declensional classes, and these declensional classes may assign different genders. For instance, the prepositional singular inflection *-e* is used in Declensions I, II and IV, and these declensions are associated with three different genders. Sometimes there is a mismatch between the declensional class and gender, as we saw in Chapter 1, Section 1.2 where the noun *d'ad'a* 'uncle' is masculine gender but belongs to Declension II, a class normally associated with the feminine gender. Another example of this type is the noun *deduška* 'grandfather'. We see this in (9), where the agreement on the adjective is masculine.

(9) star-yj deduška-a
old-SG.NOM.M grandfather-SG.NOM
'old grandfather'

For the noun *deduška* in (9), and others, there is a conflict between gender assignment on the basis of semantics and gender assignment by declensional class. In such circumstances we expect the semantics to take precedence (Corbett 1991: 37–8, 68–9). The forms of the noun *deduška* are entirely predictable, once we accept that the oddity arises from its membership in the wrong declension. Membership in declensional class also has a default semantic basis, as the analysis in Fraser and Corbett (1995) shows, but this is a separate matter from gender assignment. Nouns denoting males are assigned to Declension I by default. Hence, *deduška* is odd because it is assigned to the wrong declension, whereas it is perfectly normal in its gender assignment. For other nouns (those which denote inanimates and non-sex-differentiable animates), declensional class is stipulated in the lexical entry. In Network Morphology, a declensional class will be a node containing information about nouns' inflections. The noun *stol*, along with thousands of other nouns, belongs to a specific declensional class, and its inflections are therefore predictable once it is stipulated in its lexical entry to which declensional class it belongs, as part of its morphological level of description. In Chapter 3 we also show how there is inheritance structure within inflectional classes.

We have talked of lexemes as containers for information. In fact, we can treat morphological knowledge as a *network* of nodes at which information is located. These nodes are locations for equations about morphology. The flow of information between nodes is *inheritance*, and the links between nodes are *inheritance relations*. For the noun in (5), it turns out that much of this information is shared across most nouns of the Declension I. We can therefore distribute this information among nodes in order to capture the sharing of facts among lexical items.

2.2.1 Inheritance relations

Information is distributed across the network so that shared traits need only be stated once. Ultimately, the information in (5) can be reduced to a lexical entry in (10), with what is predictable provided by inheritance. Lexical entries in Network Morphology are *lexemic nodes* because the entry generalizes over all forms of the item and associated syntactic information. They are nodes, of course, because they are locations in a network. A typical lexemic node will have inheritance relations with other nodes but need not itself be the inheritance source for another node. Syntax can query a lexemic node registering the appropriate morphosyntactic features so that it will provide a fully inflected form for the corresponding syntactic position. (Recall that Network Morphology adopts a featural, rather than a formative, communication between syntax and morphology.)

(10)
```
Stol:
  <> = NOUN
  <declensional_class> == N_I:<mor>
  <gloss> == table
  <root> == stol
  <stress_index> == 2.
```

Let us consider the information in (10). Note that there is no gender information provided in the lexical entry in (10). This is because the gender can be determined by either the semantics of the noun or its declensional class membership, as we have just argued. Our complete network of morphological knowledge provides this. Ultimately, the dissociation of gender information from individual inflections, more easily expressed in an inferential–realizational framework, provides for a lexicon with greater efficiency, as nouns such as *deduška* 'grandfather' still inherit from Declension II, which normally assigns feminine gender, without acquiring the gender information. (The gender information is inherited from a rule of semantic assignment.) Because Network Morphology is based on default inheritance, in particular on the default inheritance of the kinds of paradigmatic information we argued to be important for morphology in Chapter 1, Section 1.0.1, it provides a straightforward way of doing this.

In (10) there is one LHS paired with a non-atomic RHS, namely the one in which it is stated that the declensional class of the noun is I (`<declensional_class> == N_I:<mor>`). This is morphology-internal information. The attribute `declensional_class` plays a role in the morphological analysis by specifying a source for information about the noun's paradigm. The RHS contains a node and path specification which, when paired with the LHS in question, states that declensional class information can be obtained by looking at extensions of paths beginning with the `mor` attribute at the node `N_I`. This is where the realizations for case and number features are specified. The information paired with `root` is specific to the lexical item, rather than being inherited from a more general class. In contrast, the LHS with attribute `stress_index` and value `2`, as explained in Brown, Corbett, Fraser, Hippisley and Timberlake (1996),[3] is used to evaluate the inheritance of stress for the noun in question. In effect, the index states that this noun takes the second choice stress pattern for a noun of its declensional class. Again, indices of this kind, are specific to morphology. They are suggestive of a distinct morphological component, as we argued in Chapter 1, Section 1.2.1. Furthermore, they provide access to different morphological rules, highlighting our earlier point in (3) that there are many ways for a lexeme to access the same morphological rule. As we see in Section 2.2.6, for Russian the specification of stress pattern choice is only interpretable relative to the declension of which the lexeme is a member, and so while it is possible to alter the information about the pattern, this is constrained by the declensional class membership.

In terms of inheritance we can distinguish between a main source of inheritance, with the source representing the core information with which the lexeme is associated, and orthogonal sources, where additional information is located. Information from the main source is inherited by *hierarchy relations*, and the main inheritance relations from higher nodes to lexical entries constitute a lexemic hierarchy. Information from the orthogonal sources is inherited by *network relations*. We discuss attribute ordering and network relations in Sections 2.2.3 and 2.2.5. We now go on to discuss hierarchy relations, which provide inheritance from the main source of information.

2.2.2 *Hierarchy relations*

If we consider the noun in (10), given again as (11), we can note that it inherits information from a node labelled here NOUN. As it inherits via the empty path <>, this is the maximally underspecified source of inheritance, and so in principle it can inherit anything from NOUN, unless otherwise specified.

(11)
```
Stol:
  <> = NOUN
  <declensional_class> == N_I:<mor>
  <gloss> == table
  <root> == stol
  <stress_index> == 2.
```

The node NOUN is the main inheritance source for the lexeme *stol*, so it is in a hierarchy relation with that node. Similarly, verbs inherit directly from a node VERB. What kind of information is stored at these nodes? The purpose of nodes such as NOUN and VERB and those for other parts of speech is that they are sources for the major generalizations about the lexemes which belong to them. This is why items such as (11) are part of the core hierarchy within the network, which we refer to as the *lexemic hierarchy*. And this is why Network Morphology can be seen as an inheritance-based version of inferential–realizational morphology. Generalizations at nodes in the lexemic hierarchy can take the form of rules which are either direct statements or declarations of where in the network to obtain specific types of information. For example, the syntactic category associated with nouns is stated at `NOUN` directly. As all nouns inherit from the node `NOUN`, this therefore generalizes over all nouns in the lexicon. The node `NOUN` can also specify where to obtain information about the semantics associated with nouns, such as the statement that by default a noun will denote a non-dynamic (i.e. non-processual) thing, for instance the noun *stol* 'table'.[4] Of course, there are also semantic properties which noun and verb lexemes may share. For example, nouns or verbs can denote situations and will need to inherit the semantics associated with these. In addition to default facts about the semantics of particular parts of speech, the lexemic hierarchy will also contain facts of a more axiomatic flavour, for example that each word belonging to a syntactic category will function as the head of its respective phrase. Information on the semantics shared across parts of speech and default statements about syntactic properties are located at a `WORD` node. A simple lexemic hierarchy for Russian is represented in Figure 2.2. (We have concentrated here on the nominal part of the hierarchy.)

In Figure 2 the lexical item *stol* 'table' has the `NOUN` node as its main source of inheritance. Information flows from the higher nodes to the lower nodes in the inheritance hierarchy, as indicated by the arrows. As this is a default inheritance hierarchy, information may be overridden at particular points, as outlined in Chapter 1, Section 1.3. For example, in the case of the noun *stol* the value for the `stress_index` path, which determines the stress properties of the lexical item, overrides the default for nominals. (Where there is an overt inflection for the noun *stol*, this will be stressed, the pattern associated with the value `2` for `stress_index`. In contrast, more generally for nouns or adjectives, the stress will be fixed on the stem throughout the singular and plural, the pattern associated with the value `1` for `stress_index`.)

We expect every natural language to have a core lexemic hierarchy, even if the information stored there is minimal. In contrast, inheritance from additional orthogonal sources may be less important in languages where either morphology plays a minimal role or its structure lines up with what is expected from the syntax. As we discuss later in Section 2.2.5 we use orthogonal inheritance, introduced in Chapter 1, Section 1.3.2, in the form of *network relations* to treat the morphology associated with inflectional classes as autonomous. Although there is still room for a great deal of variation cross-linguistically, we expect semantic, syntactic and even phonological knowledge to be less subject to language-specific variation than morphology. This is one of the reasons why morphology represents such a challenge. This is partly due to the intuition that

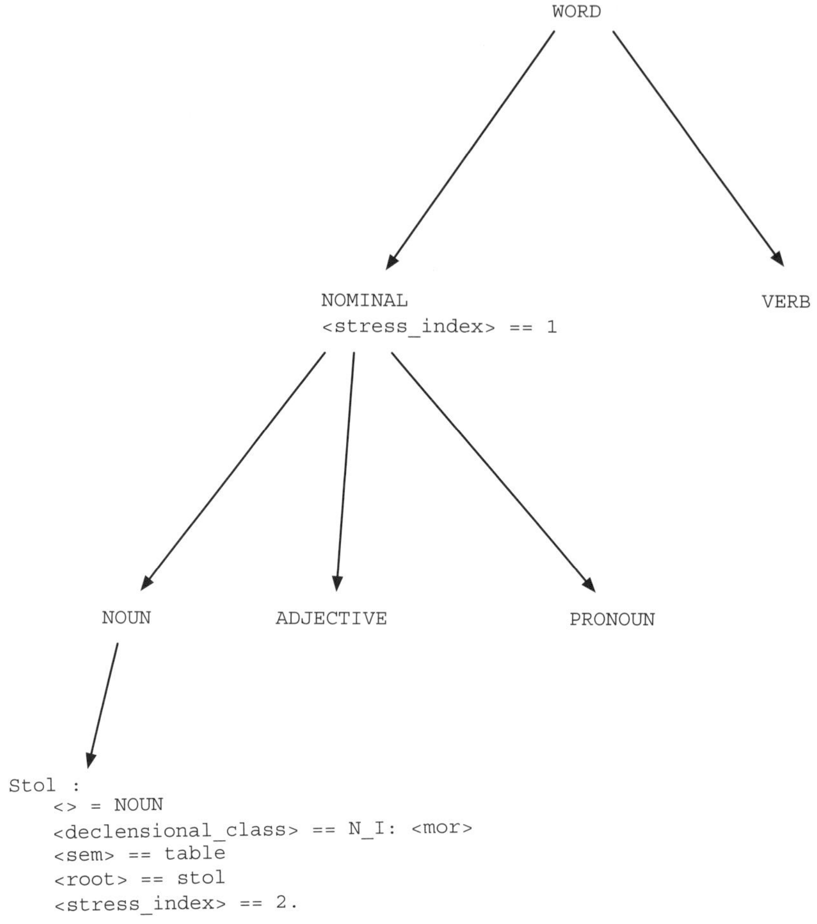

Figure 2.2 *The lexemic hierarchy with example lexical entry for the noun* stol *'table'*

semantic category comes as given and that syntax reflects this to some extent. Phonological knowledge is partly constrained by the inventory of phonological features made available cross-linguistically. Pure morphological knowledge, on the other hand, appears to be subject to more language-specific factors. Within the typology which emerges from our Network Morphology analyses, we can distinguish at least three types of relationship between syntax and morphology, which we summarize later in Section 2.4: (a) where, because the relationship with syntax is a direct one, the morphological information can be specified directly as part of the lexemic hierarchy; (b) where there is slippage between syntax and morphology in the use of morphosyntactic features; and (c) where there is a separate morphological hierarchy. Russian, it is claimed, is a language which displays morphological behaviour of type (c), as well as type (b), and this can be seen in (11) in that there is a path which refers to declensional class. This information is used to access a morphological hierarchy, an orthogonal source of information, which is separate from the lexemic hierarchy. In order to understand how this works, we need to consider attribute ordering.

2.2.3 *Attribute ordering*

As we have noted, attributes are ordered. This property of the Network Morphology framework imposes constraints on possible representations and leads to predictions in relation to a wide variety of morphological phenomena. For every Network Morphology representation of morphological phenomena, a decision has to be made about the order of attributes, and this has far-reaching effects. At one level Network Morphology can be interpreted as a framework which is based on the notion paradigm. The use of paths and attribute ordering actually means that it defines the shape of paradigms, while at the same time treating them in terms of partial functions (similarly to Stump 2001: 31–4). The pervasive nature of the attribute-ordering issue means that it leads to predictions ranging from the nature of the relationship between syntax and morphology through a variety of morphological phenomena, including neutralization, syncretism (discussed in Chapter 4) and deponency (discussed in Chapters 5 and 6), as well as claims about the most likely types of default information to be shared across parts of speech (see Section 2.3.1). We saw in (6) that Network Morphology equations consist of an LHS path which contains attributes. Let us consider the path from (6), with associated subpaths, in (12).

(12)
a. `<mor sg dat>`
b. `<mor sg>`
c. `<mor>`
d. `<>`

The path (12a) is an *extension* of the path in (12b), and the path in (12b) is an extension of the path in (12c). Finally, (12c) is an extension of the empty path. The attributes in these paths are ordered. The ordering of attributes is a property of the DATR language, but the actual choice as to how they should be ordered is a theoretical matter. Network Morphology treats attribute ordering as a way of expressing structural relationships between features in a paradigm, which is why we pointed out that the ordering of attributes is akin to an implicit typing of the feature values, as illustrated in our discussion of examples (6) and (7). Not only is a path which contains number and case information more specific than one which contains just number information, it also rules out the opposite possibility, namely that case is ordered before number. In Network Morphology, because it is an inferential–realizational framework, the notion of extension and attribute ordering, as illustrated in (12), does not necessarily entail a particular ordering of affixes (as argued by Brown 1998a). Attribute ordering allows us to make statements about words as signs, so it makes predictions about the distinctions made by particular word-forms within the paradigm of a lexeme. And as paths allow us to treat the paradigm as partial functions, attribute ordering allows us to talk about the design of the paradigm in terms of the distinctions which can be made. This ordering of attributes reflects an overall cross-linguistic tendency which can be violated by particular language-specific properties. Crucially, key rule types of the framework may be required simultaneously with the attribute ordering constraints, thereby suggesting interesting interactions of the language-specific and the general. We illustrate this in Chapter 4, Sections 4.4.3 and 4.5 when we discuss referrals, indexing and underspecification in the treatment of syncretism.

What evidence is there for ordering case attributes after number, as in (12)? One argument is that where case and number occur together, typically the number *feature* may determine the number of case distinctions, but not the other way around. In Russian, for example, in addition to the cases given in (5) there are second locative and second genitive cases in a small subset of nouns in the singular. These do not, however, occur in the plural. The prepositional (or first locative) case, as given for the noun in (5), would be used with the prepositions *o* 'about', *pri* 'at', *v* 'in' and *na* 'on'. For a small number of nouns, however, there is a separate form used with *v* and *na*. This is illustrated in (13), which is taken from a 1996 novel *Narkota* by V. P. Dorenko, cited in Brown (2007: 63–4).

(13)	*prosteršis´*	*na xolodn-om*	*tsementn-om*	*pol-ú* (transliteration)
	prostrated	on cold-SG.PREP.M	cement-SG.PREP.M	floor(M)-SG.LOC2
	'prostrated on the cold cement floor'			

In (13) we can see that the noun *pol* 'floor' occurs with a stressed *-ú* affix after the preposition *na* 'on'. This noun belongs to the same declensional class as *stol* in (5), but the two contrast in that *pol* belongs to a set of nouns which have a second locative form in stressed *-ú* after the prepositions *v* and *na*. In contrast, they still take the standard prepositional case inflection *-e* when used with *o* and *pri*. Hence, the formal distinction is associated with a different syntactic distribution, so this is a new case value.

Russian exponence of case and number values is cumulative. Each affix realizes both simultaneously. The evidence from texts indicates that the second locative developed sometime in the middle of the seventeenth century (Unbegaun 1935: 105; Černyx 1953: 262; Stang 1952: 15; Kiparsky 1967: 36; Thorndahl 1974: 918–19; Brown 2007: 63). The innovation of the second locative arose from the restructuring of Russian declensional classes. In (14) we see the singular paradigms for the *o*-stem and *u*-stem nouns in Old Russian. The forms of the locative case in (14) (the ancestor of the prepositional case) were all used with the same syntactic distribution (i.e. with the prepositions *v* 'in', *na* 'on', *pri* 'at' and *o* 'about'). This means that there was no second locative in Old Russian and that the form in *-u* was an inflectional allomorph of one case.

(14) *Singular of* o-*stems and* u-*stems in Old Russian* (Matthews 1960: 104, 106)

SG	*stolъ* 'chair' (*o*-stem, masculine)	*lĕt-o* 'summer' (*o*-stem, neuter)	synъ 'son' (*u*-stem, masculine)
NOMINATIVE/ACCUSATIVE	*stolъ*	*lĕt-o*	*synъ*
GENITIVE	*stol-a*	*lĕt-a*	*syn-u*
DATIVE	*stol-u*	*lĕt-u*	*syn-ovi*
INSTRUMENTAL	*stol-omь*	*lĕt-omь*	*syn-ъmъ*
LOCATIVE (>PREPOSITIONAL)	*stol-ĕ*	*lĕt- ĕ*	*syn-u*

Over time *u*-stem nouns migrated into the *o*-stem class, gaining its genitive, dative, instrumental and prepositional inflections. However, for a small group of nouns the original *u*-stem locative inflection was specialized to be used with the prepositions *v* 'in' and *na* 'on', as depicted in (15).

(15) *Distribution of the second locative in Contemporary Standard Russian*

	Most nouns	A few nouns
pri, o	Prepositional	Prepositional
v, na	Prepositional	Locative 2

This is not a process in which a new morphological distinction is created as the result of a formerly independent word becoming a new affix. Instead, the paradigm undergoes a restructuring to create a new distinction within one number. As this brings about a new syntactic distribution in the singular (i.e. restricting the form's use to particular prepositional phrases), it could also be considered a marginal instance of yesterday's morphology creating today's syntax. Most importantly, in relation to our understanding of attribute ordering, it demonstrates that this primarily reflects the structure of the paradigm. This structure need not be derived from an assumed deep set of morphemes as signs. Exponence in the Russian nominal system was cumulative throughout the period of this restructuring, thus there is no evidence to support the view that this new distinction was the product of a historical process creating a new distinction from smaller elements.

As would be expected from an inferential-realizational theory with attribute ordering, such as Network Morphology, the attribute order does not entail the need for separate case and number affixes in a particular linear order, and indeed the evidence from languages such as Russian suggests that this is not what is important. Of course, it is possible for separate affixes to reflect this distinction, but it is not necessary. Furthermore, as the constraint on attribute ordering is placed on number and case, rather than particular values of these, it is also possible for there to be asymmetry whereby a distinction is formally realized in the plural and not the singular. For example, in German nouns it is possible for the dative case to be overtly realized with the *-n* formative in the plural, when that case may not be formally distinguished from the other cases for the same noun in the singular.[5]

The attribute ordering in (12) also suggests that the paradigm can be affected in different ways along particular dimensions. The existence of *singularia* or *pluralia tantum* nouns is one example. This ordering is an expression of Universal 115 in the Konstanz universals archive. It is associated with Greenberg (1963: 103) and Uspensky (1965: 210). In Chapter 4, Section 4.2 we note that there are potential counterexamples to the attribute ordering of case and number. The Chukotko-Kamchatkan language Koryak in (16) is an example.

(16) *Koryak noun declensions* (Žukova 1972; Baerman, Brown and Corbett 2005: 115)

	Declension I 'father'			Declension II 'papa'		
	SG	DU	PL	SG	DU	PL
ABS	en'pič	en'piči-t	en'piči-w	appa	appa-nte	appa-w
ERG-INS	en'piči-k	en'piči-k		appa-na-k	appa-jək	
LOC	en'piči-te	en'piči-te		appa-na-k	appa-jək	
ABL	an'peče-ŋqo	an'peče-ŋqo		appa-na-ŋqo	appa-jəka-ŋqo	
TRANS	an'peče-jpəŋ	an'peče-jpəŋ		appa-na-jpəŋ	appa-jəka-jpəŋ	
DAT	an'peče-ŋ	an'peče-ŋ		appa-na-ŋ	appa-jək-əŋ	
ADIT	an'peče-jtəŋ	an'peče-jtəŋ		appa-na-jtəŋ	appa-jəka-jtəŋ	

DES	en'piči-nu	en'piči-nu	appa-na-no	appa-jəčge-no
NARR-CAUS	en'piči-kjit	en'piči-kjit	appa-na-kjet	appa-jə-kjet
CONT	en'piči-jite	en'piči-jite	appa-jeta	appa-jəka-jeta

In (16) we see that in Koryak Declension I loses all number distinctions outside the absolutive case. In Declension II dual and plural are syncretic outside the absolutive case, but the singular is still distinguished from them. Declension II also exhibits syncretism between the locative and ergative-instrumental cases. So, case syncretism is also found, suggesting that there are two different types of regularity operating simultaneously in the language. In this example, we argue that underspecification associated with attribute ordering is simultaneously accompanied by rules of referral which involve a degree of underspecification. In Chapter 4, Section 4.4 we will apply a similar argument for the pronominal paradigm of Dalabon.

With languages such as Russian it is possible to analyse the whole of the nominal system (adjectives, nouns, pronouns) as linked by various default relationships. Certain aspects of these relationships are also predicted by attribute ordering. In particular, when we come to adjectives and third-person pronouns – targets for agreement – the feature of gender has to be introduced. (Note the different representation of gender for nouns in (5) where gender is associated with the whole lexeme, as it is inherent, but is not a feature of the noun's inflectional paradigm.) Gender will extend paths containing number or case information. However, it should be noted that, given the empirical orientation of Network Morphology, these features are only considered to exist in a given language if there is overt formal evidence for them, as emphasized in Chapter 4, Section 4.1. So, the attribute-ordering constraints are not claims about the requirement for one feature in the presence of another. Instead, they are statements about what happens if a language has both features. As these are typological claims about strong cross-linguistic tendencies, they are constraints on the full morphological model and consequently on the associated morphological analyses. Ordering constraints can be summarized as follows:

(17) *Number and case (a constraint on the full morphological model)*
In paths containing case and number attributes, case attributes will extend number attributes. (e.g. `<mor sg nom>`)

(18) *Number and gender (a constraint on the full morphological model)*
In paths containing gender and number attributes, gender attributes will extend number attributes. (e.g. `<mor sg masc>`)

(19) *Case and gender (a constraint on the full morphological model)*
In paths containing gender and case attributes, gender attributes will extend case attributes. (e.g. `<mor nom masc>`)

There is no requirement that paths should contain the attributes mentioned in (17)–(19), but when they do we should expect to find reflexes of this manifested in the morphology. Example (17) has been discussed, and (18) represents a more liberal version of Greenberg's (1963: 112) Universal 37. This states that there never will be more genders in non-singular numbers than in the singular. The effect of (18) is that it predicts that there will be differences between numbers in terms of gender, but does not require them to take the specific manifestation of Greenberg's Universal 37, namely that there are never more genders in the non-singular than in the singular because there are counterexamples to this.[6] For instance, Biak, a member of the South Halmahera – West New Guinea subgroup of Austronesian, is known to have an animate–inanimate gender distinction in the plural but not the singular (Steinhauer 1985; Plank and Schellinger 1997; van den Heuvel 2006: 66; Mofu 2008: 26–38, 102–6).

(20) *Gender distinctions in third-person plural in Biak* (based on Mofu 2008: 27 and Steinhauer 1985: 471)

Free pronoun					Pronominal prefixes (type 1 agreement pattern)				
SG	DU	PAUC	PL AN	PL INAN	SG	DU	PAUC	PL AN	PL INAN
i	*su*	*sko*	*si*	*na*	*i-*	*su-*	*sko-*	*si-/s-*	*na/n-*

As Steinhauer (1985) and Plank and Schellinger (1997) indicate, this violates the claim that there are never more genders in the plural than the singular, as here there are none in the singular. Jakobi (1990: 102–3) describes another instance of this for the Nilo-Saharan language Fur, which has a human/non-human distinction in the plural but not the singular. From the point of view of Network Morphology, these examples still obey the generalization that gender has a special affinity for syncretism across number, whichever value may be involved (see Baerman, Brown and Corbett 2005: 82 and Corbett 1991: 155–6).

The constraints on the paradigm in (17)–(19) naturally treat contextual inflection in the sense of Booij (1996) as defining the paradigmatic structure which extends the larger subparadigms of number. That is, case and gender are contextual features which are imposed by government or agreement. However, we do not assume that this need be reflected in affix order. The claim is that these are best viewed as constraints on rules of exponence or referral in a realizational framework. Furthermore, as syntax and morphology are different things, these constraints are different from the syntactic mechanisms which yield the 'reduced' or 'partial' agreement phenomena that have been interpreted as potential challenges to the principle of syntax-free morphology, discussed in Chapter 1, Section 1.2.1. In such cases the use of a reduced feature set is associated with particular syntactic configurations. For instance, in Modern Standard Arabic, when VSO order is used and the subject is plural and denotes humans, the verb will be in the singular but will agree in gender (Corbett 2006: 154). As the interface between syntax and morphology is feature-based, syntax determines the feature values required in such a configuration, but the morphology does not need to know the syntactic configuration as such.[7]

A further issue for constraints such as those in (17)–(19) is Corbett's (forthcoming) criterion of 'exhaustiveness' in his canonical typology of morphosyntactic features. We give this in (21).

(21) *Exhaustiveness*
Every lexical item of every part of speech has available all values of all features. (Alternatively: every feature value applies to all lexical items.) (Corbett forthcoming)

For example, in Russian, number is a fairly exhaustive feature because it is realized on verbs and nominals (nouns, adjectives and pronouns). It is not totally exhaustive, as it is unavailable to prepositions, for instance. Furthermore, its near exhaustiveness cannot be explained on the basis of semantics, as Corbett argues, because number on the Russian verb expresses information about the nominal arguments, not the event itself. In contrast, gender is not as exhaustive in Russian, because it is not realized inflectionally on nouns (where it is an inherent feature). Case, on the other hand, fails to be exhaustive because it is not a feature of the lexical items which assign it (i.e. verbs and adpositions), but only of the items to which it is assigned. The exhaustiveness criterion is relevant for attribute ordering because it suggests that an exhaustive feature could serve as a shared 'spine' running throughout the inflectional morphology of a language. That is, we might expect number to appear left-most in the path for all lexical items, as it has a tendency to be shared by most of them. Of course, Bybee's (1985) notion of relevance is important here. We expect features which are highly relevant to a particular part of speech to define the first level of paradigmatic division for that part of speech. For example, aspect, tense and mood define a level of the paradigm for verbs which can be further specialized by person and number agreement, which are less relevant. According to Bybee (1985), the opposing factors that determine which featural distinctions are most likely to be realized are generality, on the one hand, and relevance on the other. Any distinction which is either too specific (and therefore potentially restricted to one subset of a part of speech) or too general (and therefore lacking in relevance for any part of speech) is less likely to be realized. It is the middle between these extremes which is preferred (Bybee 1985: 23).

As noted, the attribute orders in (17)–(19) appear to follow from the fact that case and gender are contextual inflection, that number is both relevant to nouns and often expressed across several parts of speech. For number agreement, it is probably the general requirement of quantification which supports it in its role for first-order paradigmatic organization. As they involve case, the constraints (17) and (19) will typically be limited to the nominal domain (although they will be relevant for participles, for example). The constraint (18) will apply to verbs which agree in gender and number. These constraints impose structure in terms of the features in question (i.e. number, case, gender) rather than creating structure which is internal to the features' values (e.g. singular, plural; nominative, accusative; masculine, feminine, neuter etc.). They reflect cross-linguistic tendencies, but they also interact with other morphological mechanisms, as we argue in relation to syncretism in Chapter 4, for example.

2.2.4 Flexible paradigm signatures

For those languages which have the relevant features, the constraints in (17)–(19) will apply. However, in Network Morphology it is not assumed that an ordering will always be available for all features relevant to inflectional morphology, such that the ordering will apply consistently across all languages. There is clearly a great deal of cross-linguistic variation in morphology. While we might expect tense, aspect or mood to be ordered before person or number, for instance, there is still a whole variety of possible orderings which are not ruled out. It is also possible that the same part of speech may split its paradigms in such a way that different features are involved. The shape of paradigms defined by the attribute structure must be sufficiently *flexible* so as to accommodate this.

The past and non-past forms of a Russian verb, such as *delat'* 'to do' in (22), split the paradigm in terms of the features involved. This is true for all verbs in Russian, irrespective of the conjugational class to which they belong or the behaviour of their stems.

(22) *Russian verb* delat' *'to do' (transliteration)*

Attributes	Form
NON-PAST 1ST SG	*delaju*
NON-PAST 2ND SG	*delaeš'*
NON-PAST 3RD SG	*delaet*
NON-PAST 1ST PL	*delaem*
NON-PAST 2ND PL	*delaete*
NON-PAST 3RD PL	*delajut*
PAST SG MASC	*delal*
PAST SG FEM	*delala*
PAST SG NEUT	*delalo*
PAST PL	*delali*

This split is a property of the morphology itself because, as Baerman *et al.* (2005: 32) argue, the person and gender features are still relevant to syntax, irrespective of the tense distinction. They attribute the split in the morphology to uninflectedness, where morphology is insensitive to all morphosyntactic feature values of a given feature in the presence of another feature value. In the non-past, the morphology of the Russian verb is insensitive to the gender distinction, and in the past it is insensitive to the person distinction. Evidence that the gender feature is syntactically relevant in the non-past is provided by (23), taken from Baerman *et al.* (2005: 32).

(23) Esli vopros okazyva-et-sja glup-ym…
if question turn.out-PRS.3SG-REFL stupid-M.SG.INS
'If the question turns out to be stupid…'

Although the verb in (23) does not realize gender, the predicate adjective does, indicating that gender is relevant for the whole syntactic structure. We can contrast this with the past tense equivalent in (24).

(24) Esli vopros okazyva-l-sja glup-ym…
if question turn.out-PST.SG.M-REFL stupid-M.SG.INS
'If the question turned out to be stupid…'

The difference between the verb in (23) and in (24) is a matter of the agreement morphology. In (23) the verb agrees in person and number, whereas in (24) it agrees in gender and number. It appears that the underlying structure of the clause is the same for both (23) and (24). Gender is still syntactically relevant in (24), as indicated by the predicate adjective which agrees with the subject in gender.

An analysis of Russian verb morphology need not, however, make mention of person in the past tense or gender in the non-past. If the paradigm of the Russian verb were treated as a sorted structure in which both person and gender were required to be present in the morphology, irrespective of tense, then the issue of where to place gender or person relative to each other would be problematic. As the features are relevant in both contexts syntactically, the issue is a morphological one. So a way is required for determining how best to represent splits of this kind. In fact, we argue that the constraint required for this provides a means for checking attribute orders. We might expect splits of this kind to fit with other morphological phenomena in terms of feature structure. The notion that the split is associated with tense is in accord with this because it suggests that tense is a high-level paradigmatic distinction which leads to the split. The appropriate formulation of the constraint is to treat it as local to the relevant part of speech. This means that it will be a constraint on the shape of the paradigm determined for the morphology of that part of speech.

(25) *Paradigm signature constraint* (constraint on the morphological analysis)
For two paths A and B in the morphological analysis, if feature value V_a in path A and feature value V_b in path B belong to different features, F_1 and F_2, then paths A and B cannot be extensions of the same subpath. (Based on Brown 2007: 73)

We refer to the implicit shape of the paradigm represented by attribute ordering as its *paradigm signature*. The constraint in (25) treats paradigm signatures as having a certain degree of flexibility but constrained in relation to the notion *subpath*, and also the notion *feature*. Recall that paths in (12) illustrate the notion *extension*. If a path A extends path B, then path B can be considered a subpath of A. For example, (12b) is a subpath of (12a). As we saw in our discussion of (7), attribute ordering represents an implicit constraint involving the notion *feature*. Because subpath refers to ordered attributes, in linguistic terms this entails that the same feature values must be involved. For example, in (26) the feature values `fem` and `masc` share the same subpath, namely `<mor sg nom>` and as they are different values of the same feature set, gender, this subpath sharing is not in violation of (25).

(26) *Same subpaths*

```
<mor sg nom fem>
<mor sg nom masc>
```

In (27), on the other hand, `fem` and `masc` extend different subpaths, namely `<mor sg inst>` and `<mor sg nom>`, respectively. (The attributes `ins` and `nom` belong to the same feature, of course, but that is not relevant for the definition of subpath.)

(27) *Different subpaths*
<**mor sg ins** fem>
<**mor sg nom** masc>

The paradigm signature constraint in (25) is therefore a constraint which requires knowledge of features to which the extension belongs, while treating subpath identity in terms of attributes. As (25) is a constraint on sets of LHS paths defined at a node, it means that we can only talk of illicit combinations of LHS paths. This is another contrast with the feature-ordering constraints we presented in (17)–(19).

The constraint imposed by (25) is sufficient to rule out certain combinations without being overly inflexible. The upshot is that the combinations of LHS paths in (28a) and (28b) are acceptable, whereas those in (28d) are not. (As noted, (25) only rules out incompatible combinations of LHS paths.)

(28)
a. <mor non-past sg first>
<mor past sg masc>
b. <mor non-past first sg>
<mor past sg masc>
c. <mor sg non-past first>
<mor sg past masc>
d. *<mor sg first non-past>
*<mor sg masc past>

In (28a) the attributes first and masc represent feature values which belong to different features, but these extend different subpaths, namely <mor non-past sg> and <mor past sg>. The paradigms described by (28b) and (28c) are potentially well-formed according to the paradigm signature constraint because the feature values which split the paradigm, namely those for tense, still occur before the gender and person features. In contrast, the subpath in (28d), namely <mor sg>, is extended by attributes representing values belonging to two different features, one a person value (first), and one a gender value (masc).

The principle presented in (25) provides an independent check on constraints related to feature ordering, such as those in (17)–(19). For instance, we expect tense, aspect or mood features to occur before agreement features such as number, gender or person. If we had to violate (25) in order to satisfy an ordering constraint, similar to those in (17)–(19), this would indicate that the ordering constraint is wrong. The orderings in (28a) and (28b) are consistent with the treatment of tense as the basic paradigm distinction for Russian verbs, and therefore ordered to the left of paths in the full morphological model.[8] It should be possible to allow for varying degrees of underspecification. Were it not for (25), it would be possible to find underspecified paths which lead to indeterminacy in realizing morphology. For example, in a situation where tense was underspecified, the paths <mor sg third> and <mor sg masc> would be equally valid possibilities for realizing the form of the third-person singular masculine. This situation does not arise, of course, but the ordering also suggests that splits of the type exhibited in (22) should affect whole slabs of the paradigm or, alternatively, lead to highly specialized morphology. This occurs because the constraint can be satisfied in two ways: (i) by specifying early in the path the different values of the same feature which license the split (as in (28a) where non-past and past contrast), thus leading to the definition of a paradigm which is split into identifiable slabs; (ii) by ensuring that the distinction is so specialized that the paradigmatic opposition with a value belonging to a different feature is hardly likely to occur, or occurs rarely.

The paradigm signature constraint in (25) rules out paradigms which would be viable under the attribute-ordering constraints in (17)–(19). Constraints on the relationship between gender and number have nothing to say about (28d), for example. Conversely, it would be possible to order gender before tense and number in order to satisfy the paradigm signature constraint, but this would fall foul of the ordering of gender after number in (18).

One of the interesting facets of (25) is that it accounts for two apparently different effects. We see in the Russian verb that it accounts for the split in the paradigm into two recognizable slabs, the past and non-past. But, as Brown (2007) argues, it is also partly responsible for the marginal status of the second locative case in Russian. If the second locative is treated as a subcase <mor sg prep loc> which extends the prepositional case <mor sg prep>, then the subcase value loc conflicts with the paradigm signature of adjectival paradigms, where, for example, <mor sg prep fem> is the specification for the feminine prepositional singular. Such a combination of paths for adjectives is ruled out by (25), as fem and loc belong to different features (gender and subcase, respectively). So there is no realization unique to the second locative on Russian adjectives, while there may be for nouns, because they do not realize gender inflectionally.

We have seen that there are constraints on the ordering of attributes in Network Morphology which are only partial. In addition, as there is some flexibility in the shape of the paradigm, it is perfectly possible for there to be splits in the paradigm. The shape of paths naturally allows us to pick out subparts of the network of linguistic knowledge, and it is to these which we now turn.

2.2.5 Network relations

The paths given in the previous section begin with a mor attribute. This is because they involve statements about morphology, an expression in the framework of morphology's autonomous status. Equally, paths which are about syntax, semantics or phonology would start with syn, sem or phon attributes. Different linguistic levels or components are represented by these attributes, and because they occur first in their paths, linguistic rules are able to define default relationships between whole linguistic components, a notion introduced in Chapter 1, Section 1.3.2. We return to this topic in Section 2.4 in our discussions of different degrees of autonomy. The ordering of attributes in this way also allows for a particular kind of multiple inheritance, called orthogonal multiple inheritance (an option outlined in Chapter 1, Section 1.3.2), which Network Morphology adopts. It is therefore possible for a node in the network to inherit from more than one source. The orthogonal property means that the nature of the inheritance is specified.

Returning to (11), we note the equation <declensional_class> == N_I:<mor>. This involves a *network relation*, as the LHS path is more specific than the empty path which specifies the main inheritance source (the NOUN node). The network relation points the lexical entry in (11) to a node N_I to inherit its inflectional morphology. The existence of a separate node N_I is justified for Russian because of the existence of separate declensional classes which cross-cut syntax. This is additional structure above and beyond what is in the lexemic hierarchy. For Russian we require four such declensional class nodes, but in Figure 2.3 only the network relation between the lexeme *stol* and the node N_I is illustrated.

As with all nodes, the name of the node N_I is purely mnemonic. In principle, it could be anything, such as the number 42. Nodes are locations for information. Most importantly, we see that the lexical item *stol* inherits parallel information from at least two local sources, illustrating the property of lexemes in Network Morphology as signs built from distributed information. Of course, *stol* belongs to one of four major declensional classes in Russian, so the node N_I is itself connected to other nodes containing information about inflection. These nodes constitute an orthogonal morphological hierarchy. We show in the next chapter, Chapter 3, Section 3.2, that such a hierarchy is licensed if its inheritance structure is not isomorphic with that of the lexemic hierarchy. Whether a separate morphological hierarchy is required to represent the morphology of a language is a matter of typological variation.

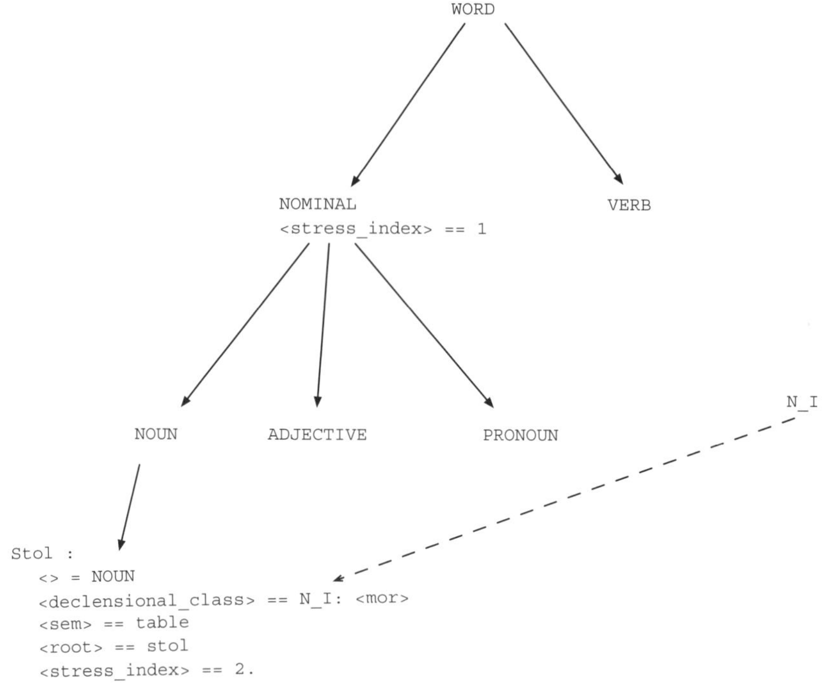

Figure 2.3 *The lexical entry for the noun* stol *'table' inherits inflectional information from an orthogonal source*

2.2.6 *Morphology as a network*

Morphology as conceived in the framework we are presenting here is distributed across a network. In a language where the relationship between the morphological elements and the syntactic properties is a very direct one, there may be no need for a separate set of nodes relating specifically to morphology. In other words, there is no separate morphological hierarchy. The morphology can be predicted from other properties of the lexeme (syntactic, semantic, phonological), as the inheritance structures for both will be isomorphic. However, in some languages, such as Russian, where inflectional classes and other autonomous structures (such as stem classes) are found, an orthogonal inheritance hierarchy for morphology may be required, where the independent regularities specific to that system are stated. The combined morphological and lexemic hierarchies for any language taken together form a complete, single network. As the lexemic hierarchy is the core of this network, it plays the key role of addressing the distributed inheritance sources for morphological and other information. Lexical items such as *stol* are part of the lexemic network. Information is either stipulated locally about these items or inherited.

The nominal stress system of Russian provides a good illustration of the way in which morphological information can be distributed around the network. It is paradigmatic (sensitive to morphosyntactic features), not susceptible to direct metrical assignment, and it can be viewed as an additional paradigmatic layer on top of the affixal morphology. We see in (29) the paradigms for the four declensions of Russian, which we introduced in Chapter 1. Here we include information about stress.

(29)

	I	II	III	IV
Singular				
NOMINATIVE	zakón	kárt-a	rúkop´is´	bolót-o
ACCUSATIVE	zakón	kárt-u	rúkop´is´	bolót-o
GENITIVE	zakón-a	kárt-i	rúkop´is´-i	bolót-a
DATIVE	zakón-u	kárt-e	rúkop´is´-i	bolót-u
INSTRUMENTAL	zakón-om	kárt-oj	rúkop´is´-ju	bolót-om
PREPOSITIONAL	zakón-e	kárt-e	rúkop´is´-i	bolót-e
Plural				
NOMINATIVE	zakón-i	kárt-i	rúkop´is´-i	bolót-a
ACCUSATIVE	zakón-i	kárt-i	rúkop´is´-i	bolót-a
GENITIVE	zakón-ov	kart	rúkop´is´-ej	bolót
DATIVE	zakón-am	kárt-am	rúkop´is´-am	bolót-am
INSTRUMENTAL	zakón-am´i	kárt-am´i	rúkop´is´-am´i	bolót-am´i
PREPOSITIONAL	zakón-ax	kárt-ax	rúkop´is´-ax	bolót-ax

In (29) the stress of the nouns is fixed on the stem and remains so throughout the paradigm.[9] This is the most common pattern. However, in addition to this fixed stress paradigm (pattern A), there are a further three basic patterns, giving a total of four basic patterns defined according to whether stress is on the stem or ending in each of the two numbers (Redkin 1971; Fedjanina 1976; Zaliznjak 1977). Pattern B, the next most common, has fixed stress, but this occurs on the ending in both the singular and the plural. This is illustrated in (30), where the forms of the nominative singular, dative singular and dative plural are given to illustrate the situation throughout the cases in the singular and plural.

(30) *Pattern B stress (on the ending in both singular and plural)*

	I *stol* 'table'	II *čert-*á 'characteristic'	III *voš* 'louse'	IV *veščestvó* 'substance'
Singular				
NOMINATIVE	stól	čert-á	vóš	veščestv-ó
DATIVE	stol-ú	čert-é	vš-í	veščestv-ú
Plural				
DATIVE	stol-ám	čert-ám	vš-ám	veščestv-ám

As can be seen, the overt inflection bears the stress. Where there is no ending, the stress will normally fall on the last syllable of the stem (Zaliznjak 1967: 152). While this is not visible in the monosyllabic stems *stol* or *voš*, it can be seen in nouns with polysyllabic stems belonging to pattern B, such as the noun *bogáč* 'rich man'.

Pattern A and pattern B stress patterns are found in all declensions, although pattern B is marginal in Declension III. (It should also be noted that the Declension III instrumental singular inflection *-ju* never bears stress and therefore contrasts with all the other case and number inflections in Russian, as these can occur with or without stress.) Stress pattern C, illustrated in (31), is restricted to Declensions I and IV.

(31) *Pattern C stress (on the stem in the singular and ending in the plural)*

	I *plug* 'plough'	II	III	IV *télo* 'body'
Singular				
NOMINATIVE	plúg	–	–	tél-o
DATIVE	plúg-u	–	–	tél-u
Plural				
DATIVE	plug-ám	–	–	tel-ám

Because nouns of Declensions II and III can have patterns A or B, and therefore the associated individual endings can occur either stressed or unstressed, a constraint which prevents the generation of stress pattern C for nouns belonging to these declensions cannot involve stipulations at the level of the individual endings. On the other hand, stipulation of the facts with the individual lexical items would go only part way to addressing this issue, as the patterns are shared by many nouns. Instead, just as nouns can be grouped into declensional classes, so nouns in Russian can be grouped according to stress patterns. Within Network Morphology this can be achieved by network relations where inheritance is determined by a stress index, as illustrated for *stol* in (11). Like declensional class this is a morphological feature. In the case of pattern C and Declensions II and III, network relations are defined in such a way that there is no inheritance route from pattern C to Declensions II and III, so these combinations do not occur.

Stress pattern D, where the stress is on the ending in the singular and the stem in the plural, is given in (32).

(32) *Pattern D stress (on the ending in the singular and stem in the plural)*

	I *rožók* 'little (animal) horn'	II *dirá* 'hole'	III	IV *s´ol-ó* 'village'
Singular				
NOMINATIVE	rožók	dir-á	–	s´ol-ó
DATIVE	rožk-ú	dir-é	–	s´ol-ú
Plural				
DATIVE	róžk-am	dír-am	–	s´ól-am

Pattern D is found with Declensions I, II and IV. So, in contrast with pattern C, there must be an inheritance route from pattern D to Declension II.

There are a further four subpatterns which involve deviation from the main patterns. The possible deviations are limited. Deviation from a pattern only occurs when the ending would otherwise be stressed. This means that only patterns B, C and D may have deviations. For the plural, deviation from the relevant major patterns where there is ending stress in this number – patterns B and C – is restricted to the nominative plural and therefore also the accusative plural if the noun is inanimate. In the singular, deviation from the relevant major patterns – patterns B and D – is restricted to the accusative singular when the realization of this is determined by a rule of exponence rather than referral, because in the latter case the form of the accusative singular is identical with the form of the nominative singular or genitive singular (if the noun is masculine and animate). Consequently, accusative singular deviation is possible only for nouns of Declension II. There is a further constraint in that if deviation is theoretically possible in the accusative singular, then this may happen only if the nominative plural is stem stressed. This, therefore, means that there are four subpatterns: two subtypes of pattern B (ending stress in singular and plural), one subtype of pattern C (ending stress in plural), and one subtype of pattern D (ending stress in singular, stem stress in plural), as in Halle (1970: 172–3).

Indicative frequencies for the stress patterns and declensions are given in (33), together with information about the particular preference of each declension for each pattern. For example, pattern C is the third most frequent choice for Declension I. We also give the subpatterns of B, C and D in (33), labelled as Bi, Bii, Ci and Di respectively.

(33) *Stress patterns and Russian noun declensions*[10]

Pattern	Description sg/pl	Decl I	Decl II	Decl III	Decl IV	Total (pattern)
A	stem/stem	18122 (choice 1)	12884 (choice 1)	3811 (choice 1)	5486 (choice 1)	40303
B	ending/ending	2104 (choice 2)	420 (choice 2)	5 (choice 3)	148 (choice 2)	2677
(Bi)	B, nom pl has stem stress	5 (choice 6)	39 (choice 4)	0	4 (choice 5)	48
(Bii)	Bi, acc sg has stem stress	0	21 (choice 5)	0	0	21
C	stem/ending	394 (choice 3)	0	0	43 (choice 4)	437
(Ci)	C, nom pl has stem stress	50 (choice 4)	3 (choice 7)	113 (choice 2)	2 (choice 6)	168
D	ending/stem	15 (choice 5)	229 (choice 3)	0	83 (choice 3)	327
(Di)	D, acc sg has stem stress	0	15 (choice 6)	0	0	15
Total (per declension)		20,690	13,611	3,929	5,766	43,996

As we have argued, stress patterns A and B can occur with any declension, so in principle any ending can be either stressed or unstressed. At the same time membership of a declension constrains a noun to a particular ranking of choices of stress pattern. Consequently, the required lexical constraint is associated with the declension, rather than the level of the individual ending. We shall argue that the stress patterns themselves form a mini hierarchy, and the nodes in this hierarchy are attached via network relations to the nodes representing declensional classes, such as the node `N_I`. (The Network Morphology treatment of this also relies on *evaluable paths* which we explain in Section 2.2.8, but we shall finesse this in our explanation in this section.) We first outline what the basic hierarchy for stress looks like, leaving out the minor patterns dealt with in Brown *et al.* (1996) for the sake of exposition.

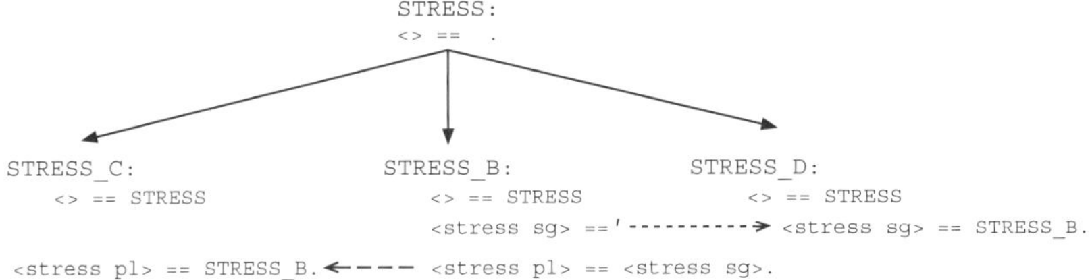

Figure 2.4 *A partial stress hierarchy for Russian*

Figure 2.4 is a partial hierarchy which defines inflectional stress for Russian nominals. (It is partial because we have not represented the minor stress patterns here, although they are included in the full theory.)

The default is for ending stress to be undefined, which is why the top node, STRESS, in this small hierarchy associates the empty path with no stress. This will account for fixed pattern A stress. The nodes which define the three other major stress patterns inherit from STRESS by hierarchy relations. The node STRESS_B provides a value for stress in the singular (as represented by ') and also states that the plural is the same as the singular. So this node defines pattern B stress, where the ending is stressed throughout the singular and plural. Through its hierarchy relation, STRESS_C inherits from STRESS the lack of ending stress in the singular (as this is an extension of the empty path at STRESS). STRESS_C also has a network relation for plural stress with the node STRESS_B. As STRESS_B has ending stress for the plural, so will STRESS_C.[11] So STRESS_C will therefore have stem stress in the singular and ending stress in the plural. In the case of the node STRESS_D, the singular is inherited from STRESS_B, and the plural is inherited via a hierarchy relation from STRESS.

The hierarchy in Figure 2.4 is, of course, part of a larger network of information. Our example noun *stol* inherits its inflections from Declension I, as we have illustrated in Figure 2.3. But it has a less common stress pattern. As can be seen from *stol*'s complete paradigm in (5) and its lexical entry in (11), *stol* has the second choice stress pattern for its declensional class. This is stated by the use of the equation <stress_index> == 2. In the lexical entry for *stol* in (11), the inheritance source for this noun is specified as the node N_I (representing Declension I). The second choice stress pattern for Declension I (as indeed for the other declensions except Declension III) is pattern B. We saw in Figure 2.2 that any NOMINAL lexeme would inherit the first choice stress pattern (i.e. pattern A) unless otherwise specified. Individual lexical items such as *stol* may override this. A value for stress will be provided only if the stress index stipulated by the lexical item is used within the morphological hierarchy. So far we have seen only the node N_I in the morphological hierarchy. But this node inherits from a node N_O (which generalizes over Declensions I and IV) and in turn from MOR_NOUN (for noun morphology) and MOR_NOMINAL (for nominal morphology). We justify the shape of this morphological hierarchy in greater detail in Chapter 3.

As an illustration of how the information is put together, let us consider the way in which the dative singular form of the lexeme *stol* is inferred, together with its stress. We, therefore, wish to infer the form associated with the path in (34).

(34)
```
<mor sg dat>
```

The most specific matching path for (34) at the node which defines the lexeme *stol* in (11) is the empty path which specifies the hierarchy relation with the lexemic node NOUN. As indicated in Figure 2.3, NOUN in turn inherits from the node NOMINAL. It is here that a path <mor> is specified. This requires the evaluation of the root's form in order to determine whether the nominal in question is inflectable, a matter which we will finesse here. The result of this evaluation is that for inflectable nouns such as *stol*, extensions of the path <mor> will be determined by their declensional class membership. That is, extensions of the path <mor> will be extensions of the path <declensional_class>. In (35) we see that declensional class membership may be dependent on the semantic sex of the referent.

(35)
```
NOUN:
  <> == NOMINAL
  <declensional_class> == DECLENSION:< "<sem sex>" >
  ...
```

However, the node Stol overrides this specification, because for inanimate nouns declensional class membership is more or less arbitrary. We repeat (11) as (36). In (36) we see that extensions of the path <declensional_class> at the node Stol can be found by looking at extensions of the path <mor> at the node N_I.

(36)
```
Stol:
  <> = NOUN
  <declensional_class> == N_I:<mor>
  <gloss> == table
  <root> == stol
  <stress_index> == 2.
```

Some of the relevant steps of inference can be seen as involving particular questions to be answered along the way. In (37a) we ask the question, 'What is the singular dative form of the lexeme defined by the node Stol?' By inheritance it can be inferred that it is a matter of what the singular dative of nominals is, as defined in (37b). After a number of evaluations, this will then depend on the specification of the singular dative at the declensional class associated with the noun *stol*, as given in (37c). In turn, because of the equation containing the LHS path <declensional_class> in (36), this will be the same as the value associated with singular dative at the node N_I, as shown in (37d).

```
(37)    a.  Stol:<mor sg dat>
        b.  NOMINAL:<mor sg dat>
        c.  Stol:<declensional_class sg dat>
        d.  N_I:<mor sg dat>
```

The node N_I inherits from the node N_O. This is because Russian Declensions I and IV share many of their inflections in the singular. Among other things the node N_O contains the information in (38).

```
(38)    N_O:
          <> == MOR_NOUN
          <mor sg dat> == "<stem sg>" ^ u "<stress sg>"
          ...
```

The singular dative is therefore the concatenation of the singular stem and the ending *-u*, together with the appropriate value for singular stress. The form of the stem ultimately depends on a default statement at the nominal level or higher that the stem is the same as the root. (As the attribute sg extends the path, we need say nothing about singular or plural stems unless there is a difference.) The default statement that a word's stem is the same as its root can, of course, be overridden in lexeme-formation, as we see in Chapter 7, and for some sets of Russian lexemes where there is an additional stem augment. For the noun *stol* the default applies, and this means that its root stol is used as the singular stem in (38). This is concatenated with the singular dative ending *-u* and the appropriate singular stress.

We turn now to the inference of the singular stress value for the singular dative form of the lexeme *stol*. The lexemic node in (36) overrides the default value for stress index. The node NOMINAL contains, among other things, the information in (39). In the chain of inheritance between the node representing the lexeme *stol* and the NOMINAL node, the path <stress> is the most specific path matching with <stress sg>.

(39)

```
NOMINAL:
  <stress> == <mor "<stress_index>">
  ...
```

The determination of *stol*'s singular stress can therefore be seen as a matter of answering the following questions:

(40)
a. Stol:<stress sg>
b. NOMINAL:<stress sg>
c. NOMINAL:<mor 2 sg>
d. Stol:<mor 2 sg>

As the LHS path <stress> in (39) is the most specific matching path for the query <stress sg>, the answer to the question of what the value is for singular stress of the noun *stol* involves answering the intermediate question, 'What is the value for singular stress of nominals?' This is indicated in (40b). Because of the RHS in (39), the answer is that the value for singular stress of nominals will depend on the stress index of the nominal. In the case of *stol* the index is 2. The overall effect is to evaluate the stress index for the lexeme and use this to extend the <mor> path. As the LHS in (39) is extended by the attribute sg so will the RHS be. This is why (40c) contains the attribute sg after the index 2. Therefore, the singular stress value for *stol* will be found by looking in the morphological hierarchy for the second stress pattern associated with *stol*'s declensional class and the value which that pattern associates with the singular, as indicated in (40d). The relevant equation at the MOR_NOMINAL node is given in (41).

(41)

```
MOR_NOMINAL:
  <mor 2> == STRESS_B:<stress>
  ...
```

In (42e) and (42f), we see the additional questions in the chain of inheritance which can be inferred from (41).

(42)
a. Stol:<stress sg>
b. NOMINAL:<stress sg>
c. NOMINAL:<mor 2 sg>
d. Stol:<mor 2 sg>
e. MOR_NOMINAL:<mor 2 sg>
f. STRESS_B:<stress sg>

As we see in the partial hierarchy in Figure 2.4, the value associated with <stress sg> is ending stress. This will, therefore, be the value for <stress sg> used in the RHS in (38).

In Figure 2.5 we have placed the stress hierarchy for Russian alongside the relevant part of the morphological hierarchy associated with nouns belonging

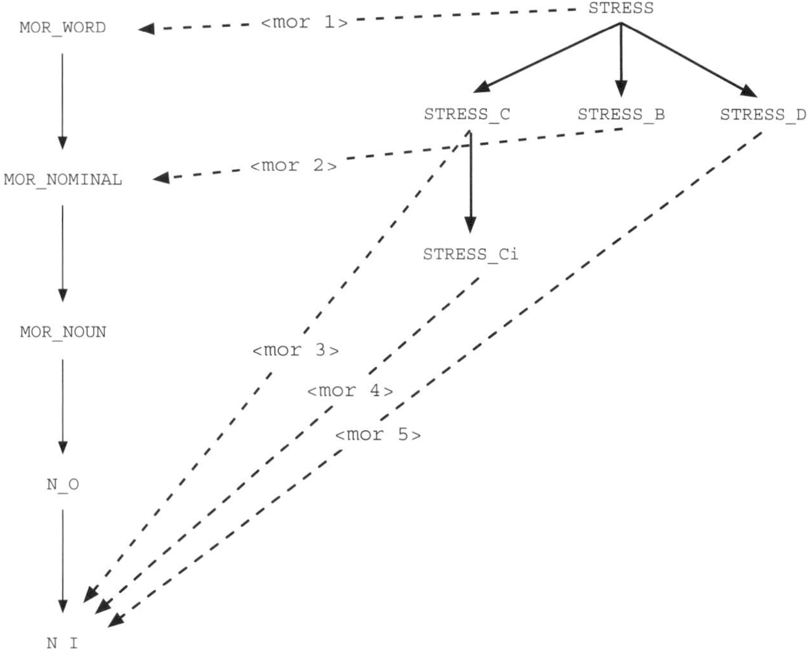

Figure 2.5 *The hierarchy and network relations associated with Russian Declension I morphology and stress*

to Declension I. In other words, this relates to those nouns which inherit their morphology from the node N_I. The morphological hierarchy, of which we introduced the noun portion in Chapter 1, Section 1.3, is represented here as a vertical structure with no branches, but this is because the other nodes for noun declensional classes, as well as those for adjectives, have been omitted. The hierarchy relations are represented as solid lines with the direction of inheritance represented by the arrows. The network relations are represented as dashed lines. The relevant path information is also given (e.g. <mor 1>, <mor 2> etc.), so that the default stress pattern (fixed on the stem) is the first choice for any word. The second choice for nominals (at MOR_NOMINAL) is inherited from the node STRESS_B. The third, fourth and fifth choices for nouns belonging to Declension I are associated directly with that class (as indicated by the network relations instantiated by <mor 3>, <mor 4> and <mor 5>).

Inspection of the data in (33) shows us that Declension I can be associated with most of the stress patterns, except the subpatterns Bii and Di (which are restricted to the singular accusative of Declension II). Declensions II and III, on the other hand, do not have any nouns which belong to pattern C. As the patterns are accessed by evaluating the stress index for the noun in question and using network relations between the stress hierarchy and the morphological hierarchy, the inheritance of the stress pattern is partly constrained by declensional class.

We have taken the nominal stress system to illustrate Network Morphology's status as a special kind of inferential–realizational framework. The different elements which contribute to the realization of a complete word-form can be treated as mini hierarchies located at particular positions in the network. For Russian, the stress hierarchy is accessible via the morphological hierarchy, with lexemes either inheriting or specifying indices which determine their inheritance of particular rules. This also highlights another big issue, namely that there is no hard-and-fast contrast between rules and lexical specification. Rather, we must make a distinction between the rule on the one hand and how the lexeme accesses that rule. Different lexemes may access the same rule in different ways. Furthermore, as our treatment of stress in Russian nominals shows, a rule itself may access other rules, some of which a lexeme may inherit via a general route, while others are more directly specified by the lexeme. Given the consideration of the inheritance route, we turn now to an important distinction between the local and the global context.

2.2.7 Local and global context

The lexical item *stol* in (11) inherits from the NOUN node via a hierarchy relation. We give three other equations from the NOUN node below in (43). The first of these states that the node NOUN inherits from NOMINAL, which is the formal representation of the inheritance relation shown in Figure 2.3. The next equation is a statement about the syntactic category, which involves an atomic RHS (namely `n`).

(43)
```
NOUN:
  <> == NOMINAL
  <syn cat> == n
  <syn animacy> == "<sem animacy>"
  ...
```

In the next equation, syntactic animacy is stated as being the same as semantic animacy. Animacy is known to play an important role cross-linguistically, of course, and in Russian it is involved in determining the form of the accusative case, as illustrated in (44). The animacy rule cross-cuts all declensional classes in the plural, whereas in the singular, its application is determined partly by declensional class. This claim is supported by the fact that Declension II (which usually contains feminine nouns) also contains some masculine animate nouns, but these still have the same accusative singular inflection as the examples given for Declension II in (44).

(44) *Accusative in Russian*

	Declension I		Declension II	
	zakon (animate) 'law'	student (animate) 'student'	Karta (inanimate) 'map'	žona (animate) 'wife'
SG NOM	zakon	student	kart-a	žon-a
SG ACC	zakon	student-a	kart-u	žon-u
SG GEN	zakon-a	student-a	kart-i	žon-i
PL NOM	zakon-i	student-i	kart-i	žon-i
PL ACC	zakon-i	student-ov	kart-i	žon
PL GEN	zakon-ov	student-ov	kart	žon

Syntactic animacy is equated with semantic animacy by default. For Russian, this generalization is quite robust, but in certain instances it does not hold. Pronouns are syntactically animate (i.e. have genitive/accusative syncretism) even if their referents are inanimate (Corbett 1980), and certain dances, such as *trepak* 'trepak', behave as animates in certain contexts (Zaliznjak 1977: 440, Klenin 1983: 9). In the West Slavonic language Polish, the generalization is subject to a greater number of overrides, with nouns such as *banan* 'banana' and *lód* 'ice-cream' behaving syntactically as animates.

In the equation in (43), the RHS path for semantic animacy is quoted. This is known as *global inheritance*.[12] The reason for this is that syntactic animacy will take the value for semantic animacy specified for the lexical item. Global inheritance requires the value to be inherited from the global context, rather than the local context (here, the local context is the node NOUN). In effect, this is a statement which says that the value for syntactic animacy for any noun, for example *stol*, is determined by the value for semantic animacy for that noun, whatever that may be. In essence, the ability to refer to the global context allows us to talk about properties which may be specific to lexical items without requiring us to state all the specific values in order to formulate the rule. Global inheritance is, therefore, also very important for allowing us to talk about things such as stems, roots and so on, where these differ from one lexeme to the next, but where generalizations can readily be made on the basis of these abstractions. We now move on to consider how information available to the lexical item can be used to evaluate and determine the inheritance source for other information and, therefore, turn to the issue of *evaluable paths.*

2.2.8 Evaluable paths

Returning to the node for Russian nouns in the lexemic hierarchy in (45) below, we have introduced two additional equations. The first of these tells us more about semantic animacy. As just discussed, syntactic animacy will depend on whatever the value for semantic animacy is for the noun in question. And the semantic animacy in turn depends on the value for semantic sex specified in the lexical entry.

(45)
```
NOUN:
  <> == NOMINAL
  <syn cat> == n
  <syn animacy> == "<sem animacy>"
  <sem animacy> == ANIMACY:< "<sem sex>" >
  <sem sex> == undifferentiated
  ...
```

In (45) semantic animacy (`<sem animacy>`) is determined by taking the value for semantic sex (here `<sem sex>`) and using this as an attribute in a path at a node `ANIMACY`. This is known as an evaluable path.[13] In the next equation in (45), a value `undifferentiated` is provided by default for the `<sem sex>` path at the node `NOUN`. The evaluable path `<sem sex>` used to determine the value of `<sem animacy>` is quoted, because the value will be whatever the lexical entry specifies or inherits. A lexical item could override the default value `undifferentiated` for `<sem sex>`. The value `undifferentiated` at the node `NOUN` is inherited by noun lexemes, if they do not specify `<sem sex>` directly. The node `ANIMACY` is given in (46).

(46)
```
ANIMACY:
  <> == animate
  <undifferentiated> == inanimate.
```

If an item inherits the default value for biological sex (i.e. `undifferentiated`), then this will be inserted in the evaluable path, and the value `inanimate` will be returned for semantic animacy. In contrast, other values for sex (i.e. `male` or `female`) will lead to the value `animate` being returned, as this is paired with the empty path and so will match with anything else.

Let us consider how this works with our example noun *stol*, repeated here as (47). (The information given in (47) is the full lexical entry associated with the morphological analysis and, together with the rules dispersed across the network, is sufficient to infer all of the information we saw in (5) and Figure 2.1.) As it does not specify a value for `<sem sex>` itself, the noun *stol* inherits the value `undifferentiated` for `<sem sex>` from NOUN. As it does not specify a value for `<sem animacy>` either, the noun *stol* also inherits the equation for `<sem animacy>` from NOUN. As we know from (45), this equation uses the value associated with `<sem sex>` in an evaluable path. This will, of course, mean that the noun *stol* inherits the value inanimate for animacy, as specified in (46), because it inherits the value `undifferentiated` for `<sem sex>` from NOUN; this will be inserted into the evaluable path so that it will match with the LHS in (46) associated with the value `inanimate`.

(47)

```
Stol:
  <> = NOUN
  <declensional_class> == N_I:<mor>
  <gloss> == table
  <root> == stol
  <stress_index> == 2.
```

The assignment of animacy here shows how it is possible to infer one piece of information about a lexical item on the basis of other information, as long as this is inherited at some point by the item in question. This also highlights an important point about Network Morphology, namely that it is not just a question of either information being listed or produced by rule. Instead, it is possible for lexical information to be partly specified lexically, while at the same time having rule-like properties, because as we noted earlier in (3), there is a variety of routes to the same rule. This notion of specification in entries, while at the same time involving some degree of regularity, will be important in our discussion of defaults in the next sections.

2.3 Defaults

The term *default* is associated with a variety of notions. Various criteria have been used to identify defaults, including the following: the notion of 'elsewhere', associated with underspecification and Pāṇinian Determinism (as discussed in Chapter 1, Section 1.3.1); what is productive; what is used in the normal case; what is used in the exceptional case. In Section 2.3.1 we discuss the Network Morphology approach to underspecification in relation to path extension, a topic we introduced in Section 2.2.3. In Section 2.3.2 we introduce the key Network Morphology constructs of *exceptional case default* and *normal case default*, and then go on to consider in Section 2.3.3 the relationship between defaults and productivity.

2.3.1 Path extension and underspecification

As Network Morphology is an inferential–realizational framework, it exploits default inference to model morphology. This means that, in the absence of any information to the contrary, it is possible to infer morphological forms by using the most specific subpaths, as discussed in Section 2.2.3. For example, in (48) the default morphological word in Russian can be treated as some combination of a stem with stress. The stem and stress information will either be inherited by lexemes or specified in the lexical entry. This is why the paths are quoted, as the information is taken from the global context.

(48)
```
MOR_WORD:
  <mor> == "<stem>" "<stress>"
  ...
```

As well as accounting for uninflected words such as adverbs, the specification in (48) allows us to infer the nominative singular for noun Declensions I and III because the declensional class nodes associated with these classes will ultimately inherit from `MOR_WORD`. As `<mor sg nom>` is an extension of `<mor>` and there is no more specific path intervening in the inheritance, these classes will determine their nominative singular forms in this way. An equation of this type fulfills the function of Stump's (2001: 53) Identity Function Default. This fits with the notion of underspecification as a kind of morphological default.

We can also associate the sharing of morphology between parts of speech with path extension. Consider the realization of the dative plural across the nominal parts of speech of Russian, as illustrated in (49).

(49) *The shared dative plural of Russian nominals*

	All nouns	First person	Second person	Third person	Adjective
Example	*zakon-a-m*	*n-a-m*	*v-a-m*	*j-i-m*	*nov-i-m*
Abstract pattern			*STEM-Theme Vowel-m*		

The realization of the dative plural in Russian can be characterized as a rule involving concatenation of the stem, a theme vowel associated with the part of speech and the exponent *-m*. The theme vowel is *-a-* for nouns and non-third-person pronouns, and *-i-* for third-person pronouns and adjectives. We can make a similar analysis for the instrumental plural in Russian.[14] This abstract analysis can also be tied in with the sharing of morphology across parts of speech, especially in the plural in Russian where the classes which realize gender agreement in their morphology lose gender distinctions in the plural.

As we move from left to right in (49), the parts of speech progress from those which are more noun-like (i.e. those for which gender is not an inflectional feature) to those which are more adjective-like (i.e. those for which gender is an inflectional feature). In Russian, this split occurs between the nouns and non-third pronouns on the one hand, and the third person pronouns and adjectives on the other. (Syntax still requires gender information about the former, of course, but the gender is not expressed directly in the inflectional forms.) Adjectives and third-person pronouns realize gender inflectionally. Because gender attributes extend paths containing case and number attributes in line with the constraints (17)–(19), gender can be neutralized in these contexts. In Russian, of course, gender is neutralized throughout the plural (Baerman *et al.* 2005: 28–30).

Network Morphology allows for generalizations about morphology which relate to superclasses of parts of speech. Shared morphology, such as that in (49), shows that there is a recognizable superclass of nominals in Russian. Some morphosyntactic features will be inflectional for some subclasses (e.g. gender is expressed inflectionally on adjectives and third-person pronouns), but not for others (e.g. gender is not expressed inflectionally on nouns and non-third-person pronouns). The shape of the inheritance structure for morphology of this type is partly determined by the following Network Morphology principle.

(50) *The Overextended Ancestor Prohibition* (constraint on the morphological analysis)

If a node A representing the morphology for a part of speech is in a *hierarchy relation* with a node B representing a superclass generalizing over the morphology of parts of speech, no LHS *path* at B may contain features which are irrelevant for the part of speech represented by node A.

In a situation such as the Russian one in (49), gender is neutralized throughout the plural and therefore does not appear in LHS paths. Consequently, the associated morphology can be readily shared by nouns, pronouns and adjectives. This principle, therefore, connects the neutralization of gender, through attribute ordering such as in (17)–(19), with morphological sharing. We discuss this further in Chapter 3.

The *Overextended Ancestor Prohibition* in (50) can be used with attribute ordering to determine if certain morphological classes are permissible.

For example, unless it plays a role in marking possession or some other construction where it may be imposed externally by syntax, gender is an inherent unchanging property of a noun lexeme and, therefore, not specified in a noun's inflectional paradigm. In contrast, for adjectives, because they are agreement targets, gender may appear in their paradigms in some languages. In Russian, for instance, this means that certain adjectival equations will contain paths that specify gender, whereas noun paths do not. Given the possibility that gender on agreement targets can be neutralized or syncretized in line with the constraints in (17)–(19), the *Overextended Ancestor Prohibition* in (50) suggests the possibility that such morphology may have default status beyond the part of speech where its featural information is reduced.

Returning to (49), we note that the Russian dative plural realization can be shared across nouns, pronouns and adjectives. In fact, this is also true for the instrumental plural. If we compare in (51) the realizations of the plural instrumental of the Russian adjective *novyj* 'new' and the Russian noun *gostinica* 'hotel', we see that their *paths* are equal in specificity. (The Russian example is given in transcription.)

(51)
```
<mor pl dat> = nov _i _m'i.
<mor pl dat> = gost'in'ic _a _m'i.
```

Furthermore, this morphology is also shared with the pronouns, the instrumental plural of the first-, second- and third-person pronouns being *n-a-m'i*, *v-a-m'i* and *n'-i-mi*, respectively. This suggests that there is a valid morphological class of nominals in Russian, which is a locus for default information of this kind. Note that this kind of default is constrained by attribute ordering. Here, morphology may be shared between classes for which gender is inflectional and those for which it is not, precisely in those parts of the paradigm where gender is neutralized in the presence of number and case. This notion of default is based on feature structure, where feature structure is reduced so that defaults can emerge in larger classes. It is associated with underspecification, which is relevant for our discussion of syncretism as default inference in Chapter 4, Section 4.2. We now turn to a different concept of default, namely the distinction between exceptional and normal case default.

2.3.2 *Exceptional and normal case defaults*

The distinction between the exceptional case default and the normal case default is key for our understanding of how inflectional morphology works, particularly in relation to differing degrees of regularity. In order to understand this distinction it is useful to take a non-linguistic example (from Evans, Brown and Corbett 2002: 119):

> Mary and John both work for a firm based in London. Mary is the personnel manager and works in the office in London. Occasionally, she goes to Paris on a training course. By default, then, Mary works in the office in London. John is a salesman. He normally spends Mondays in the south of England, Tuesdays in the west, and Wednesdays and Thursdays in the north. If, however, a client cancels an appointment, or he has a problem with his car, or there is a department meeting, he goes to the office in London. On Fridays he often plays golf, but if it rains he goes to the office. By default, then, John also works in the office in London. Intuitively the two cases are rather different. Mary is 'normally' at the office, John is not. And yet at a higher level of abstraction the office is the default workplace for both. It is these two types of default, both reasonable uses of the term, that have led to differences in usage in the literature, and to confusion. This is why we make the distinction: for Mary, working at the office in London is the normal case default, while for John, working in London is the exceptional case default.

Within Network Morphology the difference between the normal case and the exceptional case default is most readily observable in lexical entries. A lexeme which is highly regular will inherit the expected normal case defaults with little additional specification in its entry. As with Mary in the non-linguistic analogy, very little needs to be said about the default values to be inherited. With lexical items where the exceptional case default plays a role, there will be marking that something is odd, although the lexical item does not specify directly how this is resolved. We can compare this with the situation with John where there is a whole variety of events which may happen, but his exceptional case default location is predictable. The key point is that the exceptional case default differs radically from complete lexical specification where almost any exceptional morphological realization could be used. We argue that exceptionality based on the exceptional case default is to be expected over the less common full specification of irregular information. Furthermore, as we argue in Chapter 6, the exceptional case default provides an incremental mechanism for regularization over time, lexeme by lexeme, thereby obviating problems with rules which rely on an all-or-nothing switch for all lexemes.

We now turn to three examples which illustrate the interaction of exceptional and normal case defaults. The first shows their role in choosing an exponent of case and number, namely nominative plural, in Russian. The next looks at gender and morphological class assignment in Bininj Gun-wok, a language of the Gunwinyguan family spoken in central Arnhem Land in Australia's Northern Territory (Evans 2004). The third example illustrates the role of the normal and exceptional case default in assigning gender and animacy values in Polish. For all of these examples, we find that, given a particular domain of application, there is a normal expectation for a particular rule to apply. This is the normal case default in a sense similar to what happens with Mary or with John, if there are no cancellations or other problems.

2.3.2.1 Example 1: case and number morphology in Russian nouns

In (29) the Russian Declension I noun *zakon* illustrated the typical pattern of exponence associated with this declensional class. We also saw in Section 2.2.6 that there is a mini hierarchy of stress patterns within the morphological network for Russian. The stress patterns are defined in terms of morphosyntactic features (number, and also case for the minor patterns). They are overlaid onto the declensional classes. The noun *zakon* belongs to the default stress pattern, pattern A. Declensional classes are, of course, fuzzy things, and some lexemes are better members of their declensional classes than others. When a noun belongs to Declension I but has stress pattern C (ending stress throughout the plural and stem stress in the singular), its nominative plural is more likely to end in *-a*, than *-i*. Figures from Zaliznjak (1977) show that the inflection in *-a* predominates if a Declension I noun has stress pattern C. Overall, Zaliznjak (1977) lists about 390 Declension I nouns with this pattern. Of these, over two-thirds take the inflection in *-a*, while the inflection in *-i* (the expected inflection for Declension I) is found in the other third. The normal case default is what we expect to happen given a particular set of conditions. So, given pattern C stress and membership of Declension I, the normal case default exponent of nominative plural for this group is actually *-a*. Typically for Declension I nouns, and in fact for nouns in general, the normal case default would be *-i* for the nominative plural. Returning to our analogy, it is a similar situation to John's in that there are a number of places where he is normally expected to be under certain conditions. In contrast, the use of the *-i* exponent is the exceptional case default for these nouns, just as the office is the exceptional case default for John. (And, just as the office is the normal case default for Mary, so *-i* is the normal case default exponent for nominative plural for most Declension I nouns.) Some examples are given in (52).

(52) *Normal case and exceptional case defaults for Russian Declension I nouns with stress pattern C*

	Normal case default nominative plural	Exceptional case default nominative plural
tórmoz 'brakes'	*tormoz–á*	
ókorok 'ham'	*okorok–á*	
sneg 'snow'	*sneg-á*	
lesosád 'country park'		*lesosad-í*
dólg 'debt'		*dolg-í*
gról 'coffin'		*grob-í*

For Declension I nouns, the normal rule of nominative plural assignment takes the stress pattern into account. If the noun has pattern C, it will be inflected with *-a*. If it does not have pattern C, the noun will take *-i*, which is to be expected for Declension I. As pattern C is not the first-choice stress pattern for Declension I, or indeed any declension, most Declension I nouns will have the inflection in *-i* as their normal stress pattern. For Declension I other than the set with pattern C stress, the normal case default for nominative plural exponence is *-i*. For this group, however, *-i* is the exceptional case default and *-a* the normal case default. The noun *grob* 'coffin' is just such an example. We can compare the lexical entries for the noun *sneg* 'snow' in (53) and the noun *grob* 'coffin' in (54). They both belong to Declension I, and they both have the third choice of stress, pattern C as shown in (33). In (54), however, we see that the noun *grob* specifies the nominative plural by accessing directly the node which specifies high-level default information about noun morphology `MOR_NOUN`.

(53)

```
Sneg:
  <> == NOUN
  <declensional_class> == N_I:<mor>
  <gloss> == snow
  <root> == sneg
  <stress_index> == 3.
```

(54)

```
Grob:
  <> == NOUN
  <declensional_class> == N_I:<mor>
  <gloss> == coffin
  <root> == grob
  <mor pl nom> == MOR_NOUN
  <stress_index> == 3.
```

The noun in (54) is, therefore, in a certain respect odder than the noun in (53), even though it has the exponent which is normally expected for nouns in its declensional class, and nouns overall in fact. When we talk of an exceptional case default, we mean that the lexeme resorts to a default which is unexpected *relative* to the other information associated with it. Furthermore, this illustrates directly the important theoretical point which was made in (3). There are indeed many ways to access a rule. On the one hand, in (54) there is a specification that *grob* overrides its expected nominative plural, but on the other, the source of the realization rule which it uses for the nominative plural is located somewhere else in the network.

We have seen with this first example how the normal case default for a subgroup of lexemes can be overridden by an exceptional case default which itself involves a switch back to a pattern which is in fact the normal case for the majority of items. Indeed, we argue that this is a recurring kind of exceptionality, and it still involves accessing a rule, but via a different route than for the nouns for which that rule is the normal case.

For the next example, we illustrate with gender and morphological class assignment in Bininj Gun-wok. Here the interaction is quite complex, but the underlying analysis is that the morphological class assignment system is based on animacy. There are normal case default assignments to morphological class for animates (to have no prefix) and inanimates (to have a morphological class prefix assigned on the basis of the noun's gender). The exceptional case default for each of these groups (animate and inanimate) is to switch to what would be the normal case for the other group. The gender assignment principles are sensitive to a number of semantic categories and subcategories. For each category there is a normal case default, with masculine also serving as an exceptional case default. We illustrate this with an analysis of nouns for birds and provide figures for how well this analysis fares.

2.3.2.2 Example 2: morphological class and gender assignment in Bininj Gun-wok

For the purposes of our discussion, we will focus on the Kunwinjku dialect of Bininj Gun-wok, where nouns are assigned to one of four genders (masculine, feminine, vegetable or neuter). These genders are marked by a prefix. Nouns are also assigned to one of five morphological classes, four of which are marked by a prefix, with the fifth being the class where there is no prefix. (Morphological classes are similar to inflectional classes. The key point is that the morphology of the noun is what is involved. We have not used the term inflectional class here, as it might suggest that case is involved.) While there may be formal identity between a noun's morphological class prefix and the prefix marking its gender on agreement targets, there are many examples of mismatches between the two systems. The set of prefixes and associated morphological class and gender information is given in (55).

(55) *Morphological class and gender in Bininj Gun-wok*

Prefix	Morphological class	Gender
na-	Class I	masculine
ngal-	Class II	feminine
man-	Class III	vegetable
kun-	Class IV	neuter
(no prefix)	Class V	–

In (56) we give the possible combinations of gender and morphological class. Where the prefix on the noun (its morphological class) is identical with the gender agreement it takes, we have referred to this situation as 'congruent'.

(56) *Gender and morphological class combinations*

	Class I *na-*	Class II *ngal-*	Class III *man-*	Class IV *kun-*	Class V (no prefix)
masculine *na-*	congruent				
feminine *ngal-*		congruent		*kundung 'sun' only*	
vegetable *man-*			congruent		
neuter *kun-*				congruent	

The information in (56) is a simplification of that available in Evans *et al.* (2002). The shaded areas are combinations of morphological class and gender which are impossible in Bininj Gun-wok. Nouns can belong to Class V (i.e. have no prefix) and be assigned to any of the four genders. It is also possible for a masculine gender noun to belong to any one of the five morphological classes. Nouns can belong to Class IV and belong either to the congruent gender (i.e. neuter) or any of the non-congruent genders, although the noun *kundung* 'sun' is the only one which can be both Class IV and feminine gender (Evans *et al.* 2002: 126). Evans *et al.* (2002) show that the principles of assignment for the two systems differ, although both gender and morphological class assignment can be described by reference to a system of normal case and exceptional case defaults.

In essence, the main distinction for morphological class assignment is animacy. In the normal case, there are a number of default rules which assign nouns to genders on the basis of their semantics. For gender there are more specific rules, but as the rules for morphological class involve congruence, this means that the semantic assignment of gender will overlap with the morphological class rules. For our purposes it is not necessary to specify all of the rules here. (The reader is referred to Evans *et al*. 2002 and Evans 2004 for details.) The key rules for our purposes are as follows:

(57) *Morphological class*
Normal case default for animates: Class V
Normal case default for inanimates: class congruent with gender
Exceptional case default for animates: class congruent with gender
Exceptional case default for inanimates: Class V

Some of the gender assignment rules
Normal case default for higher animates: gender based on biological sex
Normal case default for animates: masculine
Normal case default for birds: feminine
Normal case default for inanimates, such as plants: vegetable
Normal case default for landscape: neuter
Exceptional case default: masculine

We have not specified all of the rules here. The motivation for the normal case default for a given domain is frequency based in that the majority of nouns having the semantics in question will follow the pattern. For instance, the majority of animates would be expected to have no morphological class prefix. The majority of birds would be expected to have feminine gender. The exceptional case default, on the other hand, will be less common for a given domain, but be a possibility across all of them. Given the rules in (57), the normal case default for a noun with higher animate denotation, such as a human being, would be to have no prefix and to have gender assigned according to its biological sex. The noun *daluk* 'woman' is an example, as it has no morphological class prefix but has feminine agreements in the singular. The normal case default for inanimates is to have a morphological class prefix which is congruent with the gender prefix, and this essentially means an overlap in the semantic categories which assign gender and morphological class. For example, the noun *kun-ngarlk* 'valley' is assigned to the neuter gender, because it denotes a landscape item, and the overt prefix on it shows that it follows the normal case default for inanimates, namely to have a morphological class congruent with its gender.

We now go on to show how the normal case and exceptional case defaults interact for the domain of birds. The default assignment rule for nouns that denote birds places them in the feminine gender. In addition to this, the normal case for animate nouns is to be assigned to the class with no prefix (Class V).[15] Seen from the perspective of our non-linguistic analogy, the noun *biwidj* 'little grebe' in (58) is similar to Mary in that we can readily predict its gender and morphological class without any further specification. In addition to information about its root and specific meaning, all that is specified about it in the lexical entry is that it inherits all other information from the NOUN lexeme node and its semantics from the node BIRD.

(58)
```
Biwidj:
  <> == NOUN
  <sem gloss> == little grebe
  <root> == biwidj
  <sem> == BIRD.
```

The relevant equations at the node NOUN are given in (59).

(59)
```
NOUN:
  <> == NOMINAL
  <mor prefix> == MOR_NOMINAL:
                  <mor "<morphological_class>" >
  <morphological_class> == MORPHOLOGICAL_CLASS:
                           < <eval_morphological_class> >
  <eval_morphological_class> == "<prag register>"
                                "<sem cat>"
  <congruence> == CLASS_FROM_GENDER:
                  < "<syn gender>" >
  ...
```

The equation with the LHS path <mor prefix> ultimately provides the correct form of the noun prefix by evaluating the noun's morphological class. The information required for evaluating the morphological class is associated with the LHS path <eval_morphological_class>. We need information about the register (<prag register>) and the semantics (<sem cat>). The register distinguishes between the ordinary language and the avoidance register – which is used in certain contexts to show respect. (For the purposes of exposition we do not discuss the avoidance register further.) This information is then used to determine the morphological class at the node MORPHOLOGICAL_CLASS. A further relevant equation is the one which states that congruence involves evaluation of gender in order to determine class at the node CLASS_FROM_GENDER. At the node MORPHOLOGICAL_CLASS in (60) the ordinary language (o_1) treats inanimate nouns as congruent and animate ones as belonging to Class V. This provides a complete partition of the lexicon, of course, as any noun will be animate or inanimate. However, there is also the maximally underspecified possibility which allows for a switch at the node EXCHANGE (not shown here) so that items normally assigned to Class V (i.e. animates) are congruent, and items which are normally assigned to the congruent class (i.e. inanimates) are assigned to Class V. This switch itself is the exceptional case default.

(60)
```
MORPHOLOGICAL_CLASS:
  <> == EXCHANGE:< "<eval_morphological_class>" >
  <o_l entity which_is inanimate> == "<congruence>"
  <o_l entity which_is animate> == v
  ...
```

The noun *biwidj* (which belongs to the ordinary language) denotes an animate entity and thus is assigned to Class V. Its gender is assigned by a rule which says that birds are assigned to the feminine gender. The output theorems are shown in (61). In (61) the forms have been generated as part of a syntactic phrase in which the noun is modified by the adjective *kimuk* 'big' to its right. The prefix *ngal-* appears on the adjective *kimuk* as an exponent of feminine gender. In contrast the head noun *biwidj* has no marker on it.

(61)
```
Biwidj:<syn / mod noun> = [ [ biwidj ] ngal _ kimuk ].
Biwidj:<syn gender> = feminine.
Biwidj:<morphological_class> = v.
```

In contrast to *biwidj*, the noun *ngalkordowh* 'brolga',[16] is assigned the normal case default for gender but takes the exceptional case default for morphological class (<ecd>).

(62)
```
Ngalkordowh:
  <> == NOUN
  <sem gloss> == brolga
  <root> == kordowh
  <morphological_class> == MORPHOLOGICAL_CLASS:<ecd>
  <sem> == BIRD.
```

The exceptional case default for animates is for them to have a morphological class which is congruent with their gender. A key point to note here is that an inferential–realizational theory based on inheritance marks the irregularity in terms of the inheritance of the appropriate rule and does not need to specify information on all possible instances of exceptionality in the actual exponent itself. In (62) the lexical entry for *ngalkordowh* 'brolga' contains an additional statement that its morphological class information is inherited from the MORPHOLOGICAL_CLASS node. It should be noted that the attribute ecd – which is a mnemonic for exceptional case default – is meaningless from the point of view of the morphological class assignment. Indeed, we could replace it with any arbitrary attribute, such as `foo` or `spanner`, or leave it out entirely. There is no rule at the MORPHOLOGICAL_CLASS node which uses this attribute. Instead, the attribute matches with the least specific path, and `<eval_morphological_class>` is treated as an evaluable path to determine the morphological class at the node EXCHANGE where, as we have explained, the morphology is switched to congruent if the normal case is Class V and to Class V if the normal case is congruent. As the normal case for animates is Class V, the noun *ngalkordowh* ends up with the exceptional case for morphological class, namely to have a congruent prefix. As it is assigned the normal case gender for birds, however, this congruent prefix is the Class II prefix. The results of this are shown in (63).

(63)
```
Ngalkordowh:<syn / mod noun> =
            [ [ ngal _ kordowh ] ngal _ kimuk ].
Ngalkordowh:<syn gender> = feminine.
Ngalkordowh:<morphological_class> = ii.
```

Another option is for the gender to be assigned as an exceptional case default. Nouns such as *benuk* 'scrub turkey' and *karnamarr* 'black cockatoo', while following the normal case default for morphological class, are assigned to the gender of last resort, the masculine. It is also possible to resort to the exceptional case defaults for both morphological class and gender, as is true for *namaddorl* 'wedge-tailed eagle'.

(64)
```
Namaddorl:
  <> == NOUN
  <sem gloss> == wedge-tailed eagle
  <root> == namaddorl
  <morphological_class> == MORPHOLOGICAL_CLASS:<ecd>
  <syn gender> == GENDER:<ecd>
  <sem> == BIRD.
```

The forms which can be inferred for *namaddorl* are given in (65).

(65)
```
Namaddorl:<syn / mod noun> =
          [ [ na _ namaddorl ] na _ kimuk ].
Namaddorl:<syn gender> = masculine.
Namaddorl:<morphological_class> = i.
```

We have used the portion of the Bininj Gun-wok lexicon associated with birds to illustrate the importance of the distinction between normal case and exceptional case defaults. But we can account for the whole lexicon on the basis of this distinction. For example, inanimates are assigned to the vegetable gender, or they may be assigned to the neuter, if they belong to specific categories such as those relating to the weather or body parts. There is, however, always the possibility that they can take the exceptional case default for gender, namely masculine. Words such as *bakki* 'tobacco', *bim* 'painting', *bokurlurl* 'full moon' and *djirla* 'salt' are assigned to the masculine gender as exceptional case defaults. These words also have the inanimates' exceptional case default for morphological class, as they have no prefix. (As noted, having a morphological class prefix is the normal case for inanimates but the exceptional case for animates.) We can see in (66) the figures for a lexicon of 258 Bininj Gun-wok nouns that a combination of the exceptional case and normal case defaults assigns gender correctly for 95 per cent of the lexicon and morphological class for 94 per cent of the lexicon.

(66) *The role of normal case and exceptional case defaults in gender and morphological class assignment in Bininj Gun-wok* (based on Evans *et al.* 2002: 152)

	No specification (fully regular)	Exceptional case default	Direct specification
Gender	212 (82%)	33 (13%)	13 (5%)
Morphological class	179 (70%)	63 (24%)	16 (6%)

Exceptional case and normal case defaults can account for a wide variety of phenomena in a wide variety of languages where morphology plays a role. As we have seen, it works well for the gender and morphological class assignment in a Gunwinyguan language. Fraser and Corbett (1997) originally used this distinction in Network Morphology to account for noun class and gender assignment in Arapesh, drawing on the work of Aronoff (1992a) and the data in Fortune (1942). Just as with the example of the nominative plural in Russian, we can see from the lexical entries for the nouns in our case study of birds that lexical specification of exceptional case default involves referring to another inheritance source in the network, as opposed to complete lexical exceptionality. It is this property of Network Morphology, where the rule and the route to that rule are distinguished, which allows us to express this distinction of normal case and exceptional case default.

We now move on to discuss the role of normal case and exceptional case defaults in the assignment of gender and subgender in Polish. Subgender is a term for agreement classes which 'control minimally different sets of agreements' (Corbett 1991: 163). Animacy in the Slavonic languages is a subgender because its effects are restricted to a small part of the paradigm, typically the form of the accusative case, although the effects vary across the different

Slavonic languages. What is of interest in Polish is that the animacy subgender has three values, `inanimate`, `animate` and `person`. The exceptional case default for subgender involves hitting the middle of these three values. That is, a semantically inanimate noun can take the animate value for subgender as its exceptional case default, and a noun which denotes a person could also take the animate value as its exceptional case default. We find both of these effects, so the exceptional case default is responsible for two apparently unrelated phenomena in Polish.

2.3.2.3 Example 3: Gender and subgender assignment in Polish

The number of genders in Polish is a matter for debate.[17] As we show in our analysis, certain differences in gender distinctions can be achieved by distinguishing between the main gender and the subgender and allowing for switches between the normal case and exceptional case for these. We treat Polish as having four genders (masculine, masculine personal, feminine and neuter), and an animacy subgender with three values: inanimate, animate and person. We consider subgender first and then conclude this example by looking at the main gender system.

In (67a) the noun *pokój* is assigned to the masculine gender in virtue of its declensional class membership. Its accusative is the same as its nominative because it is an inanimate noun, and agreement targets accordingly have an accusative form which has the same form as the nominative (*nowy* 'new'), thereby expressing the inanimate value of subgender. In (67b) the noun *chłopiec* 'boy' has an accusative form the same as the genitive because it denotes a person. This is reflected in the form of the agreement target *nowego* 'new' which has the same form as the genitive singular, thereby expressing the `animate` or `person` value of the animacy subgender. As with *chłopiec*, the noun *pies* 'dog' has an accusative singular which is syncretic with genitive singular, and this is reflected on the agreement target, where the accusative–genitive syncretism again expresses the animate value for the animacy subgender. This is illustrated in (67c).

(67) a. Widz-ę now-y pokój
see-1SG new-SG.ACC.MASC.INAN=SG.NOM room.SG.ACC = SG.NOM
'I see the new room.'

b. Widz-ę t-ego chłopc-a
see-1SG this- SG.ACC.M.PERS = SG.GEN boy-SG.ACC = SG.GEN
'I see this boy.'

c. Widz-ę t-ego ps-a
see-1SG this- SG.ACC.M.AN = SG.GEN dog-SG.ACC = SG.GEN
'I see this dog.'

We can conclude from the examples in (67) that animacy determines the form of nouns in the accusative singular and the corresponding agreement forms. This animate/person distinction is a subgender distinction, because, unlike the main gender distinctions (which appear throughout the adjectival paradigm for example), the agreement pattern is restricted to the accusative singular. This subgender distinction is only relevant for nouns of masculine gender in the singular. In the plural, however, and in contrast to nouns which are masculine and denote persons, animate nouns of masculine gender behave similarly to inanimate nouns. That is, animate nouns have nominative–accusative syncretism in the plural, just as the inanimate ones. In (68a) the accusative plural form of *pokój* has the same form as would be used in nominative plural contexts. While the exponent differs in (68c) from that in (68a), the accusative plural of *pies* 'dog' (i.e. *psy*) is also the same form as used in nominative plural contexts for that noun. Furthermore, both *pokój* and *pies* take the same agreements in the accusative plural, where a form which is syncretic with the nominative plural is used. (We have used an adjective and a demonstrative, respectively, in (68a) and (68c), but these require the same inflection with *pokój* and *pies* in the accusative plural and could be used with either, of course.) So nouns which are masculine and animate (but not personal) behave in the plural as nouns which are masculine and inanimate. In contrast, the nouns which are masculine and denote humans have genitive–accusative syncretism and take agreement which has genitive–accusative syncretism.

(68) a. Widz-ę now-e pokoj-e
see-1SG new-PL.ACC.M.INAN = PL.NOM room-PL.ACC = PL.NOM
'I see the new rooms.'

b. Widz-ę t-ych chłopc-ów
see-1SG this-PL.ACC.M.PERS = PL.GEN boy-PL.ACC = PL.GEN
'I see these boys.'

c. Widz-ę t-e ps-y
see-1SG this-PL.ACC.M.AN = PL.NOM dog-PL.ACC = PL.NOM
'I see these dogs.'

The nouns in (68a) and (68c) also take the same agreement pattern in the plural as nouns belonging to neuter and feminine genders. This is illustrated by *dziewczynka* 'girl' (69a) and *miasto* 'city' (69b). These would take feminine and neuter agreements, respectively, in the singular.

(69) a. Widz-ę t-e dziewczynk-i
see-1SG this-PL.ACC.F = PL.NOM girl-PL.ACC = PL.NOM
'I see these girls.'

b. Widz-ę now-e miast-a.
see- 1SG new-PL.ACC.N = PL.NOM town-PL.ACC = PL.NOM
'I see the new towns.'

So far we have seen the role of subgender in the accusative. In the nominative, subgender does not play a role. Instead, the following main gender values determine agreement.

(70) *Main genders in Polish*

`masc`	masculine
`masc person`	masculine personal
`fem`	feminine
`neuter`	neuter

The masculine personal gender is a 'structured gender' (Brown 1998a), and this means that the value assciated with it it is an ordered set (`masc person`). This structured value combines the value `masc` with the value `person` assigned for the subgender. As the subgender is not relevant outside the accusative, and there is no masculine personal agreement in the singular, a masculine personal noun will, therefore, have masculine agreements in the singular. In the nominative plural, on the other hand, the agreements differ. In (71) we see that the masculine personal contrasts with the other three main genders, which all have the same form. Furthermore, this distinction is also to be found in personal pronouns and in verbs, thereby confirming the status of masculine personal as a main gender distinction.

(71) *Nominative plural agreements in Polish as shown by the adjective* nowy *'new'*

	MASCULINE PERSONAL	MASCULINE	FEMININE	NEUTER
PL NOM	*now-i*	*now-e*	*now-e*	*now-e*

In all of the instances we have seen so far, the nouns are assigned to genders and subgenders according to the normal case default assignments. The normal case assignment works as follows: biological males are assigned to the masculine gender; biological females to the feminine; human males to the masculine personal; where there is no semantic basis, gender is assigned according to declensional class. In addition to the main genders, Polish has the values for subgender in (72).

(72) *Subgenders in Polish*

`inanimate`	inanimate
`animate`	animate
`person`	person

Subgenders are assigned as follows: semantically inanimate nouns are assigned the `inanimate` value; semantically animate nouns the `animate` value; nouns which denote people to the `person` value.

We now turn to instances where the exceptional case plays a role in the assignment of subgender. This is illustrated by the semantically inanimate nouns *banan* 'banana' and *lód* 'ice-cream'.

(73) a.

Dzieck-o	je	smaczn-ego	lod-a
child-SG.NOM	eat.3SG	tasty-SG.ACC.M.AN	ice.cream-SG.ACC
		= SG.GEN.M	= SG.GEN

'The child eats a tasty ice-cream.'

b.

Dzieck-o	je	smaczn-ego	banan-a
child-SG.NOM	eat.3SG	tasty-SG.ACC.AN	banana-SG.ACC
		= SG.GEN.M	= SG.GEN

'The child eats a tasty banana.'

In (73a-b) we see that the nouns *banan* 'banana' and *lód* 'ice-cream' behave syntactically as animates. In (74) we also see that this distinction carries through to other agreement targets, including the relative pronoun *który*. In (74a) the noun *banan* requires animate agreements, whereas the noun *tort* 'cake' in (74b) requires the expected inanimate agreements.[18]

(74) a.

Dzieck-o	je	banan-a,	któr-ego
child-SG.NOM	eat.3SG	banana-SG.ACC	which-SG.ACC.AN
		= SG.GEN	= SG.GEN.M

dostał-o	od	mam-y
get.PST-SG.N	from	mum-SG.GEN

'The child eats a banana which it got from its mum.'

b.

Dzieck-o	je	tort,	któr-y
child-SG.NOM	eat.3SG	cake-SG.ACC.INAN	which-SG.ACC.INAN
		= SG.NOM	= SG.NOM

dostał-o	od	mam-y
get.PST-SG.N	from	mum-SG.GEN

'The child eats a cake which it got from its mum.'

The noun *tort* will be assigned its value as inanimate by the normal rules of animacy assignment so that its lexical entry appears as in (75). (The information about the final element of the root is also obtained by inheritance to capture consonantal alternations, but this is not relevant for our purposes.)

(75)

```
Tort:
  <> == NOUN
  <gloss> == cake
  <declensional_class> == N_I:<>
```

```
<root> == tor
<root final> == T.
```

The noun *banan* specifies that it inherits its value for animacy directly from the node ANIMACY, as it takes the exceptional case default. As we see in (78), the value animate will be supplied as the default option in this instance.

(76)
```
Banan:
  <> == NOUN
  <gloss> == banana
  <declensional_class> == N_I:<>
  <root> == bana
  <root final> == N
  <syn animacy> == ANIMACY.
```

Again, the contrast between the items has to do with how the rules are accessed, rather than with direct lexical specification of the value. Both items inherit from the node NOUN.

(77)
```
NOUN:
  <> == NOMINAL
  <sem sex> == undifferentiated
  <syn animacy> == "<sem animacy>"
  <sem animacy> == ANIMACY:< "<sem sex>" >
  ...
```

From (77) both nouns will inherit the value undifferentiated for their biological sex. By default, syntactic animacy is based on semantic animacy, and for Polish the semantic animacy is normally assigned using evaluable paths where the biological sex is evaluated.[19] The node ANIMACY is as in (78).

(78)
```
ANIMACY:
  <> == animate
  <male> == person
  <undifferentiated> == inanimate.
```

Both the noun *tort* and the noun *banan* are assigned semantic animacy in the same way. As semantic animacy involves an evaluable path, the undifferentiated value for <sem sex> is used in the LHS at ANIMACY so that both nouns receive the value inanimate. The difference between *tort* and *banan* is that the latter in its lexical entry in (76) overrides the equation of syntactic animacy with semantic animacy stated at the NOUN node.

When a lexeme inherits its value for <syn animacy> by the normal route, information about its biological sex (<sem sex>) is used. The noun *tort* inherits the undifferentiated value for <sem sex>, and this is used to evaluate its animacy. It therefore receives the value inanimate. The node *banan*, on the other hand, inherits directly from the node ANIMACY. As no path at ANIMACY is specified, the value animate associated with the completely underspecified LHS path (the empty path <>) is the one which is inherited. This is the highest level default for animacy. In the full morphological model, therefore, the information in (79) is associated with the lexemes *banan* and *tort*.

(79)
```
a. Tort:<syn animacy> = inanimate.
   Tort:<sem animacy> = inanimate.
b. Banan:<syn animacy> = animate.
   Banan:<sem animacy> = inanimate.
```

From this the agreement rules will provide the correct agreements on the basis of the syntactic animacy of the nouns.

The exceptional case and normal case default system provides us with an overarching account of different phenomena related to Polish gender and subgender. So far we have seen how semantically inanimate nouns can be treated as animate in terms of the exceptional case default. But it turns out that nouns which would be given the value person for syntactic animacy can also be animate as the exceptional case default. We saw in (68b) that in the plural masculine personal nouns have genitive–accusative syncretism, but animate nouns in the plural, as in (68c), do not. In (80) we would expect the masculine personal noun to have genitive–accusative syncretism. Genitive–accusative syncretism is, in fact, a possibility, but in (80) it is not used. The phrase has a pejorative function.

(80) Zna-m t-e pijan-e
know-1SG this-PL.ACC.AN = PL.NOM drunk-PL.ACC.AN = PL.NOM
chłop-y
guy-PL.ACC = PL.NOM
'I know these drunk guys.' (Huntley 1980: 193)

Informant judgments differ about which nouns this can happen with. Where this does occur, we argue, the noun has switched from taking the person value for the subgender to taking the animate value. It is animate rather than inanimate because in the singular the noun would still require accusative–genitive syncretism, a characteristic of nouns that are masculine and animate. Hence, this example involves the same exceptional case default for syntactic animacy as with (75) and (76), but this time the normal case default would involve the other end of the set of animacy values, namely person. Hence, the exceptional case default for subgender accounts for these two different phenomena: promotion of inanimate nouns to syntactically animate; demotion of person nouns to syntactically animate.[20] The noun in (80) is characterized as 'devirilized' or 'depreciative' (Wertz 1977; Saloni 1988). As it turns out, there are two types of devirilization: type 1, partly illustrated in (80), where the exceptional case default for subgender (`animate`) is inherited by the lexeme, and this has an effect on the structured main gender value; type 2, where the exceptional case default for the main gender (`masc`) is used instead of masculine personal (`masc person`). With type 1 devirilization, accusative syncretism with the nominative in the plural, as illustrated in (80), entails that the noun also loses masculine personal agreement in the nominative plural (Brown 1998a: 209).

We have seen what happens with type 1, and we now turn to type 2 and the role of normal case and exceptional case defaults in assignment of the main gender distinctions in Polish. Instances of type 1 devirilization where the accusative is affected, such as illustrated in (80), are rarer than instances of type 2 devirilization where the main gender switches from masculine personal to masculine, but the accusative is unaffected (i.e. the noun keeps genitive–accusative syncretism). The main gender distinctions are expressed on a number of different agreement targets: pronouns, adjectives, other nominal modifiers, and verbs. As we have said, there are four main genders in Polish: masculine, masculine personal (virile), feminine and neuter. Nouns are assigned to genders according to a mixed system of semantic and formal assignment. Higher-order animates are assigned according to biological sex and, in the case of males, according to whether they are humans: male humans are assigned to the masculine personal (virile) gender; other males are assigned to the masculine gender; females are assigned to the feminine gender; otherwise nouns are assigned to genders according to their declensional classes. In instances where both sets of principles come into play, we expect the semantic principles will win over the morphological.[21] We treat the masculine personal gender as a 'structured gender' (Brown 1998a). This essentially means that the value is taken as an ordered set `masc person`. This structured value combines the value `masc` with the value assigned for the subgender. In the singular the masculine personal is not a relevant gender distinction. Because `masc person` contains `masc`, a noun belonging to this gender will take masculine agreements in the singular. It will also take the genitive–accusative syncretism in (67b) with appropriate agreements, as it belongs to one of the higher animacy values (`animate` or `person`). The agreement patterns associated with a noun in the nominative plural will depend on whether it is masculine personal or not. In (81) we see a masculine personal noun with examples of agreement in nominal modifiers and a past-tense verb. In square brackets underneath, we give the forms which would be required if the noun belonged to the other genders (masculine, feminine or neuter).

(81) C-i mężn-i rycerz-e walczy-l-i
this-PL.M.PERS brave-PL.M.PERS knight-PL.NOM fight-PST-PL.M.PERS
[t-e] [-e] [-ł-y]
'Those brave knights fought.' (Based on Rappaport 2010: 171)

Because the main masculine personal gender combines the value `masc` with the `person` value assigned for the subgender, if a masculine personal noun has its subgender value switched to `animate` from `person`, as we saw for the accusative example in (80), it will also take non-masculine personal agreement when it is in the nominative plural. This prediction appears always to be borne out: any noun with male human denotation which may optionally show the nominative–accusative syncretism, must also be able to show non–masculine personal agreement when in the nominative plural (Brown 1998a: 209). However, the converse is not true. Optional devirilization in the nominative plural does not necessarily mean that a noun may have optional nominative–accusative syncretism. Consider the following sentences:

(82) a. C-i głupi łajdac-y
this-PL.NOM.M.PERS stupid.PL.NOM.M.PERS scoundre-PL.NOM
posz-l-i do prac-y
go-PST-PL.M.PERS to work-SG.GEN
'Those stupid scoundrels went to work.'

b. T-e głupi-e łajdak-i
this-PL.NOM.NMP stupid-PL.NOM.NMP scoundre-PL.NOM
posz-ł-y do prac-y
go-PST-PL.NMP to work-SG.GEN
'Those stupid scoundrels went to work.'

In (82a) the noun *łajdak* 'scoundrel' takes masculine personal agreements. In (82b) it takes non-masculine personal agreements.[22] Although judgments differ, speakers who find (82b) acceptable do not necessarily allow for the noun to be used with an accusative plural which is syncretic with the nominative plural, analogous to (80) (Brown 1998a: 208–9). They may still consider the genitive–accusative syncretism and associated agreement, exemplified in (68b), to be the only possibility. How can this difference be accounted for? The answer is straightforward. The devirilization in (82b), without accompanying loss of genitive–accusative syncretism, involves switching the normal case default gender for these nouns (`masc person`) to the exceptional case default (`masc`). Here the lexical item accesses the gender assignment rule directly but is still assigned the `person` value for subgender, which is why genitive–accusative syncretism and the associated agreements are required. This approach, therefore, distinguishes two types of devirilization: one where the subgender takes the exceptional case default (animate), with concomitant effect on the main gender, where both the agreement patterns for the nominative and accusative are affected; and the other where the main gender switches to the exceptional case default (masc), affecting the agreement pattern for the nominative, but leaving the accusative syncretic with the genitive.

We summarize the assignments of genders and subgenders according to their normal case and exceptional case defaults in (83).

(83) *Polish gender and subgender: normal case and exceptional case defaults (based on Brown 1998a)*

	Gender: normal case default	Gender: exceptional case default	Subgender: normal case default	Subgender: exceptional case default
Male humans	masc person	masc	person	animate
Female humans	fem	(any noun)	person[23]	(any noun)
Animates	masc		animate	
Inanimates	masc/fem/neut[24]		inanimate	

Summary for exceptional and normal case defaults

Given the requisite information for a particular set of items, the normal case default usually applies. However, within the system there is available an exceptional case default rule. As we saw with the Russian example in Section 2.3.2.1, it may well be that the exceptional case default for a group subject to a more specific normal case default (to realize nominative plural suffix *-a* if the noun is Declension I and belongs to stress pattern C) is to return to what applies to most nouns (suffix *-i*). In the Bininj Gun-wok example in Section 2.3.2.2, for morphological class assignment, the nominal lexicon is partitioned into animate and inanimate nouns. The normal case for animates is to have no prefix, and the normal case for inanimates is to have one congruent with gender. The exceptional case involves a switch to follow the behaviour of the opposite group (i.e. the exceptional case is for animates to receive a prefix and inanimates to be unprefixed). For gender assignment in Bininj Gun-wok, there are several semantic assignment rules, with masculine as an exceptional case default. We illustrated the interaction of morphological class and gender assignment rules with examples from the bird domain and gave figures to show that the normal case default and exceptional case default system works well in accounting for the vast majority of the Bininj Gun-wok lexicon. The interaction of exceptional case assignment with normal case assignment for gender and subgender in

Polish, as illustrated in Section 2.3.2.3, allowed us to account for a wide range of complex phenomena using very general mechanisms.

A number of important properties fall out from these general mechanisms. First, as we can see, it is possible for items which fit the requirements for a particular rule not to follow that rule. This is, of course, what happens in areas of knowledge which are default-based. The examples we have shown demonstrate that what is often observed is that the exceptional case default allows a lexeme to opt out of a specific rule and return to a more general default rule which also functions as the normal case default for other items. This is true for the Russian case and number examples we saw and the Polish gender-assignment system. It is also true for the gender assignment in Bininj Gun-wok. For the Bininj Gun-wok morphological class system, on the other hand, we observe a switch to follow the behaviour of the opposing class of noun. This fits again with our point that there are a variety of routes to the same rule. With the Russian nouns in *-á*, there is a generalization that belonging to pattern C and Declension I predicts that realization.[25] But, the lexical entry may stipulate that a noun opts out of the expected rule and takes a direct inheritance source to a default. Sometimes there may be reasons external to morphology underlying the switch. For instance, the 'devirilized' items we discussed for Polish tend to have a pejorative function. At other times, it is less clear that there is an external reason. The inanimate nouns taking the exceptional case default for animacy, such as *banan* 'banana' and *lód* 'ice-cream', have a semantic connection, but this is not sufficient, as the noun *tort* 'cake' demonstrates. Knowledge that the noun behaves in an odd way for the class to which it belongs is morphological knowledge, and the morphology typically has a rule available, even if the route to it for other items is a very different one.

2.3.3 *Defaults and productivity*

Given the contrast between rules and how they are accessed, we naturally turn to the question of productivity. This is discussed in greater detail in Chapter 7, Section 7.4. There we expand on the different notions of productivity. As we have seen in our discussion of the exceptional and normal case defaults, there is a distinction between the degrees of specificity for a particular rule, which may be taken as highly productive if it typically applies under the right conditions. On the other hand, a lexeme may access a rule which is considered to be highly productive, but the access comes through an exceptional case default. Furthermore, as Network Morphology specifies different linguistic levels, it is perfectly possible for a rule to apply to a lexeme while certain aspects of it (such as the semantics) are subject to slippage.

The issue of productivity also touches on the relationship between syntax and morphology. We expect this relationship itself to be a matter of defaults, so to this we now turn.

2.4 The default relationship between syntax and morphology

As Network Morphology is a framework based on defaults, it also provides a way for dealing with the default relationship between syntax and morphology. This can be represented straightforwardly as follows:

(84) `<syn> == "<mor>"`

Here the information associated with morphology is available to syntax in a direct way, by default. However, as statements about morphology require the use of a path beginning with the `mor` attribute, morphology is potentially autonomous, meaning it can be separated in the system of rules. But this potential need not be manifested, as we will see in the following chapters. In Chapter 1, Section 1.2.1 we pointed to different types of dissociation between syntax and morphology. We turn now to the most straightforward type of relation. A key task for morphological theory is to allow for this straightforward, least exciting type, as well as the ones where the role of morphology is more articulated.

2.4.1 Non-autonomy

This is where the morphology directly reflects what is required by the syntax. The grammar contains none of the dissociation between syntax and morphology discussed in Chapter 1, Section 1.2.1. While there is an attribute identifying the morphological level, there is no need for a separate inheritance structure for morphological knowledge. As we shall see in Chapter 3, Section 3.2, a starting point is the general principle that morphological classes reflect parts of speech and that nodes of the morphological hierarchy will correspond to the nodes of the lexemic hierarchy.

(85) *Principle of Morphological Projection*
Morphological classes reflect parts of speech: by default we expect parts of speech to have a corresponding morphological class.

Of course, true autonomous morphology fails to meet the ideal entailed in (85). If however, there is no additional morphology cross-cutting the classes required by syntax, then an additional morphological hierarchy is superfluous, as it will be isomorphic with the lexemic hierarchy. While a *broad* Network Morphology assumes that there will be a separate hierarchy, the *narrow* version allows it to be reduced in line with a general principle for reducing redundant nodes.

(86) *Node Elimination*

If a node N_1 inherits from another node N_2 (where $N_1 \neq N_2$) via a non-evaluable inheritance relation, and there is no other node which inherits from N_2, then N_2 is eliminable and the associated information can be stated at N_1.

Node Elimination may be considered a principle of housekeeping, but it performs an important role. It will stop us, for example, from creating a unique class for one lexeme. And it will ultimately mean that a morphological hierarchy which is projected directly from parts of speech will be unnecessary, as there will be no need to switch between the nodes using evaluable paths. Thus, the bottom nodes of that hierarchy will be eliminable and in turn so will those from which they inherit. We now turn to the relationships where there is morphological autonomy.

2.4.2 *Morphosyntactic feature slippages*

One reason why an assumption of identity between syntax and morphology may be assumed is because the morphosyntactic features are shared by both. But sometimes there can be slippage between the two levels when apparently the same feature is involved. We will discuss this for syncretism in Chapter 4. Here the slippage is that the morphology fails to make a distinction which is relevant for syntax, characterized as one form having more than one function in Chapter 1, Section 1.2.1. This can take on a variety of different manifestations and have a number of different causes. If the lack of a distinction can readily be described in terms of feature structures for which there is external syntactic evidence, then this is an example of autonomy, because a morphosyntactic feature required in syntax fails to have a match in morphology. Certain syncretisms can be accounted for by rules of referral (Zwicky 1985b; Stump 2001: 212–41), which we discuss further in Chapter 4. Here one cell of the paradigm refers to another for the associated realization. This means, of course, that there may be significant slippage between the morphosyntactic features as interpreted by syntax and as interpreted by morphology. We will present a generalized version of referrals where they can accommodate a significant degree of underspecification, so that sets of cells of paradigms can be referred to other sets of cells, providing significant work for referrals within the morphology of some languages. The generalized referral mechanisms allow us to move from syncretism to deponency. This is an extreme type of slippage, because the morphosyntactic feature expressed by the morphology is the opposite of the one required by syntax. We reserved the term *mismatch* for this specific kind of dissociation in Chapter 1, Section 1.2.1. The classic example comes from

Latin, and we illustrate it here in (87) with an example where a passive form has active meaning. We discuss deponency in detail in Chapter 5.

(87) Plautus, *Mercator*, Act IV; lines 695–7 (Nixon 1924)

sed	coqu-os,	quasi	in	mar-i	sol-et
but	cook-PL.ACC,	as	at	sea-SG.ABL	be.wont-ACT.PRS.3SG

hortator	remig-es	horta-rier	ita
encourager-SG.NOM	oarsman-PL.ACC	exhort-PASS.INF (=ACT)	so

horta-batur
exhort-PASS.IPFV.3SG (=ACT)

'But he exhorted the cooks, just as a coxswain is in the habit of exhorting oarsmen.'

While they are different phenomena, both syncretism and deponency entail that morphology treats morphosyntactic features in a way which would not be expected from the point of view of the requirements of syntax. This may either manifest itself in terms of morphology's inertness to distinctions which are made in the syntax, or in terms of it expressing such distinctions with values which would normally be syntactically relevant, but in entirely the opposite context. We now turn to the other type of syntax–morphology relationship mentioned in Chapter 1, Section 1.2.1, where the morphology makes distinctions to which syntax is insensitive.

2.4.3 Autonomous morphological features

We have already seen examples of this type of autonomy. The `declensional_class` attribute is one in that it is entirely unnecessary from the point of view of syntax and is purely morphological. As we argue in Chapter 3, there is a need to set up nodes which generalize over inflectional classes for Russian, and this justifies the existence of a separate morphological hierarchy. In order for the rules of Russian morphology to determine the inheritance source for a lexeme, attributes of this kind are needed to address the appropriate node in the inheritance hierarchy for morphology. We see in Chapter 4, Section 4.5 that indices can also play a role in a particular type of syncretism where the syncretized values do not form a natural class from the perspective of syntax.

It is worthy of note that languages, even closely related ones, may differ in terms of the number and types of indices they require. In Polish, for example, nouns require declensional class information, but the stress assignment system is phonologically determined, with stress falling on the penult. Similar to Polish, Russian also requires declensional class information, but in addition to that it requires a stress index to determine which stress pattern a lexeme will inherit, as explained in Section 2.2.6. This is because the stress patterns in

Russian are a kind of morphological class and are not entirely predictable on phonological grounds.

2.5 Conclusion

Network Morphology is a framework that makes use of different types of default. It specifies principles of paradigmatic structure, such as those for attribute ordering and flexible signatures which determine the possibilities for the featural distinctions that morphology can make. These types of feature-related constructs can readily be related to morphological phenomena which involve some degree of inertness to syntactic distinctions when these can be expressed in terms of reduced combinations of features. We discuss this further in Chapter 4. We also saw how the differences between an actual rule and the way that rule is accessed could be accounted for using the notions of exceptional case and normal case default. This distinction will play a prominent role in our discussion of deponency in Chapters 5 and 6. In Chapter 7 we illustrate how Network Morphology can provide an account which integrates word-formation with inflectional morphology. In the next chapter, we return to the issue of morphological autonomy. As we argue, the default situation assumes that morphological categorization follows that of syntax. This means that nodes for morphological rules will be projected from the corresponding lexemic nodes. In and of itself, this principle will lead to an isomorphic hierarchy which can be eliminated. Only when there are discrete inflectional classes, or some other structure which cross-cuts the parts of speech required by syntax, can there be an autonomous hierarchy for morphology.

3 *Inflectional classes*

3.0 Introduction

In Chapter 1, Section 1.3.2 and Chapter 2, Section 2.2.6, we saw that morphology can be treated as a network of information, with rules located in a number of hierarchies distributed across the network. So lexemes can inherit from multiple sources. This was illustrated in Chapter 2, Section 2.2.5 with the Russian lexeme *stol* 'table', inheriting from the NOUN node in the lexemic hierarchy and from the node N_I for its morphology. We now turn to look at the hierarchy of which N_I is a part. In languages such as Russian, nodes such as N_I, which are locations for generalizations about inflectional morphology, are themselves part of an orthogonal morphological hierarchy. In particular, there are nodes which generalize over the individual inflectional classes. We also show that this separate morphological hierarchy is justified, only if the generalizations cannot be described using the same inheritance structure as for the lexemic hierarchy. Inflectional classes have to be addressed by the use of morphological indices or features, as discussed in Chapter 2, Section 2.4.3.

The redundant realization of the same inflectional information means that inflectional classes pose a learnability problem (see, for example, Goldsmith and O'Brien 2006). This is one of the reasons why researchers have tried to posit possible constraints on the potential complexity of inflectional classes. Carstairs' (1983) influential article on paradigm economy argued that languages tend to limit the number of possible inflectional classes based on the inventory of affixes. Carstairs gave examples from a number of languages to support this claim. Given, for example, the six cases and two numbers in Latin, the maximum possible number of inflectional classes available can be calculated from the number of affixes used for each combination. For Latin the total number could be 20,736 (Carstairs 1983: 118). The minimum number of possible inflectional classes could, of course, be the same as the number for the combination which has the most affixes. In Latin, under one treatment of theme vowels, this is three. Carstairs claimed that there is a general tendency for the number of inflectional classes, in languages which have them, to be as close as possible to this lower limit determined by the number of affixes used for a given feature combination. Carstairs-McCarthy's (1994) No Blur Principle imposed limits on the sharing of inflectional exponents across classes. The basic idea with No Blur is that an affix either identifies its class, or it is the default. Therefore, this rules out a pattern in which, for example, there is more than one affix which occurs in multiple inflectional classes. These principles are restricted to affixal morphology, excluding many potential counterexamples. There are several analytical issues related to this. A key one is the extent to which one can identify different inflections across classes, and the other is that we have to consider whether inflectional classes should be counted if they have a small number of members. Counterexamples have been suggested. For instance, Finkel and Stump (2007) demonstrate that both No Blur and Paradigm Economy are violated by the affixal morphology of the Nilo-Saharan language Fur.

Ackerman, Blevins and Malouf (2009) argue that inflectional classes are constrained to reduce entropy (i.e. unpredictability) in order to guarantee reliable inferences about a lexeme's inflectional variants. This tendency to reduce entropy entails that not all instances of particular inflectional exponents are equally probable. Parallel to this is the work on the more traditional notion of principal parts, or reference forms (Wurzel 1984). These are the cells of a lexeme's paradigm from which all other cells can be inferred. While the notion of entropy reduction may impose some upper limit on the potential complexity that inflectional classes create, there are still substantial differences between languages in terms of potential principal parts analyses. As Finkel and Stump (2007) point out, paradigmatic transparency (i.e. the extent of predictability between a lexeme's cells) is a matter of typological variation.

Defaults should typically reduce the degree of uncertainty associated with exponence. Underspecification-based defaults (in our framework those based on attribute ordering) may reduce the set of possible exponents as a natural consequence of reducing the set of features to be realized by the morphology. For example, Russian neutralizes gender distinctions in the plural, so the possible space of allomorphy is reduced to the case and number distinctions. And reduction in the set of features also brings with it the possibility that the morphology can be shared across parts of speech. As we showed in Chapter 2, Section 2.3.1 in line with the Overextended Ancestor Prohibition, rules for oblique morphology in Russian (i.e. dative, instrumental, and prepositional plural) are shared by nouns, pronouns and adjectives, facilitated by the fact that gender distinctions are neutralized in the plural. Other types of default will have differing effects in relation to their position on the hierarchy. As discussed in Chapter 2, Section 2.3.2, the morphological system makes available an exceptional case default. Often exceptional items opt out of subregularity and revert to a more general rule. While a lexeme may be irregular in making use of an exceptional case default, the use of the exceptional case default itself keeps the uncertainty as to its exponence within manageable bounds. Having access to recognizable classes and the exceptional case default requires that the lexeme be part of the network of information we described in Chapter 2, Section 2.2. Because of this we argue here that the traditional notion of inflectional classes as monolithic entities is misleading. Instead, they should be perceived as partial entities which can be modelled in terms of a specific hierarchy for inflectional morphology. But we also show that, in the absence of recognizable inflectional classes, this hierarchy can be reduced to the lexemic hierarchy under the principle of Node Elimination introduced in Chapter 2, Section 2.4.1. This, therefore, provides a point of typological contrast between languages: those for which a valid morphological hierarchy can be constructed, and those for which it cannot. In the next section we move on to consider inflectional classes within their wider typological space.

3.1 Inflectional classes within the wider typological space

We typically conceive of inflectional classes as discrete entities associated with one particular part of speech. But this may mean that the problem has been limited by drawing a boundary where none should exist. For instance, counting the number of realizations relative to the noun part of speech in Russian ignores related adjectival and pronominal classes which share nominal morphology with nouns.

In this section we look at inflectional classes from the perspective of canonical inflection. This allows us to consider possibilities which may be nonexistent or rare. In our case study of Russian nominals in Section 3.1.2, we consider the relationship between the lexemic hierarchy and the morphological hierarchy and show that the morphological hierarchy could be collapsed onto the lexemic hierarchy if there were no inflectional classes.

Our starting point for understanding the place of inflectional classes is the notion of canonical inflection, and we use this to define the Network Morphology relationship between the lexemic hierarchy and the morphological hierarchy. According to Corbett (2009), a canonical inflectional class would exhibit a number of characteristics which contrast with canonical inflection. The following is a crucial difference between inflection classes and canonical inflection:

(1) In canonical inflection each part of speech has only one realization per feature value.

We will finesse the issue of how many canonical parts of speech there are. This basically means that for any item which belongs to a particular part of speech, such as noun, we will know immediately what the possible realization of a morphosyntactic feature is, as there can only be one. It is important to note that (1) does not rule out parts of speech sharing inflectional features and morphology. Once we know the feature and part of speech required, however, nothing more need be said. In terms of Network Morphology, this means that the lexemic node for the part of speech in question could specify the morphology for the feature values, and there would be no need to have any additional subclasses inheriting from this node which specify alternative realizations. Network Morphology has built into the framework the possibility of morphological autonomy. Under the principle of morphological projection discussed in Chapter 2, Section 2.4.1 we could set up a morphological node, a container for information about the morphology of the part of speech, which would have the properties expressed in (2).

(2) For a lexemic node N_L there is a non-evaluable inheritance relation with a corresponding node N_M (the morphological node) via a `<mor>` path and its extensions.

We were introduced to the notion of evaluable paths in Chapter 2, Section 2.2.8. The reason why the inheritance relation in (2) does not require an evaluable path – and is therefore a non-evaluable relation – is that there are no alternatives to switch between. The morphology specified by the morphological node is inherited directly by the lexemic node. As with any other node in the network, if there are no other reasons for the existence of the morphological node in (2), then it can be eliminated in line with the principle of Node Elimination introduced in Chapter 2, Section 2.4.1. As we will see in Section 3.1.1 and later in our discussion in Section 3.2, the morphological hierarchy will be lost if the language has no inflectional classes, because the corresponding lexemic node does not need to switch between alternatives, and the conditions of Node Elimination will be met.

Let us imagine that a simplified version of English could be captured in terms of (3). There is a lexemic VERB node and a corresponding MOR_VERB node:

(3)
```
VERB:
  <syn cat> == verb
  <mor word> == "<stem>" "<mor affix>"
  <mor affix> == MOR_VERB.
```

```
MOR_VERB:
  <mor affix present> == s
  <mor affix past> == ed.

Eat:
  <> == VERB
  <stem> == eat.
```

Not only would the verb *eat* in (3) form its present tense in *-s* and past tense in *-ed*, all verbs in English would do so. So there are no inflectional classes. Now let us consider the principle of Node Elimination from Chapter 2, Section 2.4.1, which we repeat here in (4).

(4) *Node Elimination*

If a node N_1 inherits from another node N_2 (where $N_1 \neq N_2$) via a non-evaluable inheritance relation, and there is no other node which inherits from N_2, then N_2 is eliminable and the associated information can be stated at N_1.

The general principle in (4) can be used to optimize Network Morphology networks so that the number of nodes is reduced. If we try to apply (4) to (3), we get an interesting result. First, the node MOR_VERB is clearly eliminable, because the node VERB inherits from it via a non-evaluable inheritance relation (i.e. there are no evaluable paths in the RHS of <mor> == MOR_VERB). Consequently, (3) can be optimized to (5).

(5)

```
VERB:
  <syn cat> == verb
  <mor word> == "<stem>" "<mor affix>"
  <mor affix present> == s
  <mor affix past> == ed.

Eat:
  <> == VERB
  <stem> == eat.
```

If the lexical entry for *eat* in (5) were the only one in the theory, then we could apply (4) again and reduce the whole to a theory consisting of one node only. Of course, there will be many more lexical items in the language with thousands of nodes inheriting from VERB, so this step would not apply. The upshot of (5) is that we are left with a lexemic node which combines syntactic and morphological information. This represents an ideal where the realization of syntactic information by morphology is so direct that we do not need a special structure in the inheritance graph to represent inflectional morphology.

So far we have seen that the default principle of Morphological Projection allows us to assume the existence of autonomous morphological classes. But the principle of Node Elimination will do away with autonomous morphological nodes if morphology fails to show a different inheritance structure of its own. We saw in Chapter 2, Section 2.2.2 a possible structure of the lexemic hierarchy for Russian. In a language unlike Russian where the morphology maps straightforwardly onto the corresponding part of speech, we can locate information about morphotactics at the lexemic node corresponding to the relevant part of speech, as we see with our imaginary example in (5). Even under the situation where a part of speech uses inflection which is unique to it, this could be inherited straightforwardly without a separate morphological hierarchy, if the inheritance structure fits with the properties of the morphology. The top of the lexemic hierarchy which specified properties of lexemes could also make default statements about the morphotactics. For example, it could supply information that, by default, all words are suffixing. As long as the overrides associated with morphotactics lined up with part of speech, there would be no need to introduce a separate morphological structure. If, however, the ordering of affixes differed within a part of speech, there might be grounds for keeping an autonomous structure. This situation, where the different linguistic levels brought together in the lexeme behave in the same way in terms of the classes to which lexemes belong, is quite rare. On the one hand, in many languages parts of speech might be defined on the basis of semantics or syntactic distribution, while the morphology is uninformative or differentiates very little between these classes. On the other hand, even when there is a lot of morphology, this does not fit neatly with the parts of speech defined on distributional grounds. For example, nouns, pronouns and adjectives in Slavonic languages may partially share morphology amongst themselves but differ in terms of their distributional properties.

If there are inflectional classes in a language, then these can in principle use a variety of operations to realize morphosyntactic features – suffixing, prefixing, ablaut, metathesis, reduplication, and so on. Indeed, these operations are available even in the absence of inflectional classes. As we will see in Section 3.2, once we have separate nodes for the relevant inflectional classes, the nodes assumed by morphological projection – those corresponding to parts of speech – are then justified to store the default information about these classes. The default inheritance structure of the parallel morphological hierarchy under such circumstances will have some degree of correspondence to the lexemic hierarchy in terms of the higher default classes (such as for nouns, verbs and words) but, as the hierarchy is autonomous, will not be isomorphic with it.

Inflectional classes can be placed at one end of the dimension highlighted in (1) because the number of realizations associated with a morphosyntactic combination is greater than the number of parts of speech which may realize them. The canonical point for the dimension in (1) is the middle. At the other end of this dimension, we can place clitics, or at least some subset of what are termed clitics. Anderson (2005: 31–6) treats the combination of clitics and their hosts as a post-lexical matter. In line with Anderson, we also argue that there is reason to treat some clitics as part of the morphology, although as Network Morphology is a declarative framework, the combinatory properties are not treated as post-lexical. In Network Morphology clitics can be treated as a default realization for a particular feature value which generalizes across parts of speech. The relationship between the number of possible realizations of feature values (e.g. first person) and the number of relevant parts of speech is one dimension along which the distinction between affixes and clitics can be understood. We represent this in (6).

(6) *Inflectional classes at one end of the realizations-per-feature-value dimension*

the number of realizations (per feature value) is fewer than the number of relevant parts of speech	the number of realizations (per feature value) is the same as the number of relevant parts of speech	the number of realizations (per feature value) is greater than the number of relevant parts of speech
'clitics'	canonical mapping	inflectional classes

This suggests that, for this dimension, the canonical ideal of inflection lies between inflectional classes and word-level defaults. In an inferential–realizational theory, the interface between syntax and morphology is feature-based (i.e. based on morphosyntactic features) and not form-based, as discussed in Chapter 1, Section 1.2.1. Syntax can place a particular type of feature at the edge of the phrase or on the head of the phrase (or operate with both placement strategies depending on other factors), but this is an additional dimension to that given in (6). Anderson (2005) argues that the notion of an edge feature is problematic, although there are clear examples where edge features are required (Anderson, Brown, Gaby and Lecarme 2006). The syntax naturally requires the ability to make reference to the edge of the phrase, and this can be achieved through the use of an edge feature (see Klavans 1985; Miller 1992; Tseng 2003; Samvelian 2007). Network Morphology treats morphology as syntax-free, as we explained in Chapter 1, Section 1.2.1. The notion of morphology expressing information about syntactic constituency per se would, therefore, be problematic. We show that the morphology does not need to know that a feature is at the edge of the phrase. It just needs to realize the value, if required to do so by syntax. As with Luís and Spencer's (2005) treatment of clitics in European Portuguese, we do not need to assume in this treatment that the clitic-like elements are syntactic terminals. They are instead affixed in the morphology.

We present an example of the left-most type from (6) in the next section and then move on to the other end of this dimension, namely inflectional classes. While the purpose of our study of clitic-like elements here is to show how they fit at one extreme of a dimension where inflectional classes are at the other end, we can provide a formal implemented account of these phenomena, which relies on the syntax being able to refer to the edge of a phrase in order to place the morphosyntactic features to be realized, but where the morphology does not have knowledge of the feature which expresses the information about the edge. As we will see, in the absence of any distinctions which cross-cut those made in syntax, there is no need for a morphological hierarchy.

3.1.1 Example 1: No morphological hierarchy required

We take as our example Kokota, a language of the Santa Isabel subgroup of Northwest Solomonic (Palmer 2009). In Kokota there is a set of demonstrative markers which may occur at the right edge of a left-headed noun phrase. The marker may attach to one of a very small, closed class of adjectives, as in (7a), a verb (7b), or a noun (7c). In sum, the realization of the specific feature value is not dependent on the part of speech, which naturally means that the number of realizations for that feature value is fewer than the number of parts of speech. (In Kokota there is a wide range of demonstratives conveying deictic information (Palmer 2009), but these are different feature values.)

(7) a. (ira) mane tove=ro
ART.PL man old=DEM
'those old men'
b. (ira) mane dou=ro
ART.PL man be.big=DEM
'those big men'
c. (ira) mane vave=ro
ART.PL man in.law=DEM
'those men [who are] in-laws'
(Examples from Palmer and Brown 2007: 201)

Parallel to this, we find in the language, as argued by Palmer and Brown (2007), that possession marking attaches to the head of the noun phrase. The placement of the person and number markers used for indexing the possessor is dependent on how the syntax distributes the features onto heads of phrases. In (8) we see a directly possessed noun (more or less equivalent to inalienable possession) where the person marking attaches to the head of the phrase.

(8) (ia) nene-gu (ara)
ART.SG leg-1SG.POSS I
'my leg' (Palmer and Brown 2007: 202)

Alienable possession is typically marked using either a general host *no-*, for non-consumable possession, or a consumable host *ɣe-*. To this attaches the person and number marking which indexes the possessor. Palmer and Brown (2007) argue that this marking attaches to the head of the noun phrase, and that the hosts are a kind of noun. This can be seen in (9) with the general possession host and in (10) with the consumable possession host.

(9) (ia) no-gu suga (ara)
ART.SG GENPOSS-1SG.POSS house 1SG
'my house' (Palmer and Brown 2007: 202)

(10) (ia) ɣe-gu kaku (ara)
ART.SG CONSPOSS-1SG.POSS banana 1SG
'my banana (which I intend to eat)' (Palmer and Brown 2007: 202)

We have seen the person and number indexing of possessors on the heads of the noun phrases, but it should be noted that this marking can also attach to verbs (Palmer 2009: 274; Palmer personal communication). So within Kokota we can see two types of marking which are closer to the left-end of the idealized view in (6), in that they can be used across parts of speech. Their appearance is a matter of how the syntax distributes the feature value.

In Figure 3.1 demonstrative morphology and person–number morphology, specified at the node MOR_WORD, can be inherited by any part of speech. There is little morphological autonomy here, and the node MOR_WORD could be eliminated under Node Elimination in (4), with the necessary equations located at the WORD node. (For the purposes of our exposition we will keep the rules at the MOR_WORD node, but we should bear in mind that this node can be eliminated.) The syntax distributes the feature values, and this determines whether the morphology is actually required to realize them. In (11) the node WORD at the top of the lexemic hierarchy specifies that words are made up of stems and inflections (<mor>).

(11)
```
WORD:
  <mor> == MOR_WORD
  <word> == "<stem>" "<mor>"
  <stem> == "<root>".
```

In (12) the MOR_WORD node specifies the morphology and its linear order without making reference to edge features. (The syntax, which we have not given here, can make reference to the edges and heads of the phrases, of course.[1])

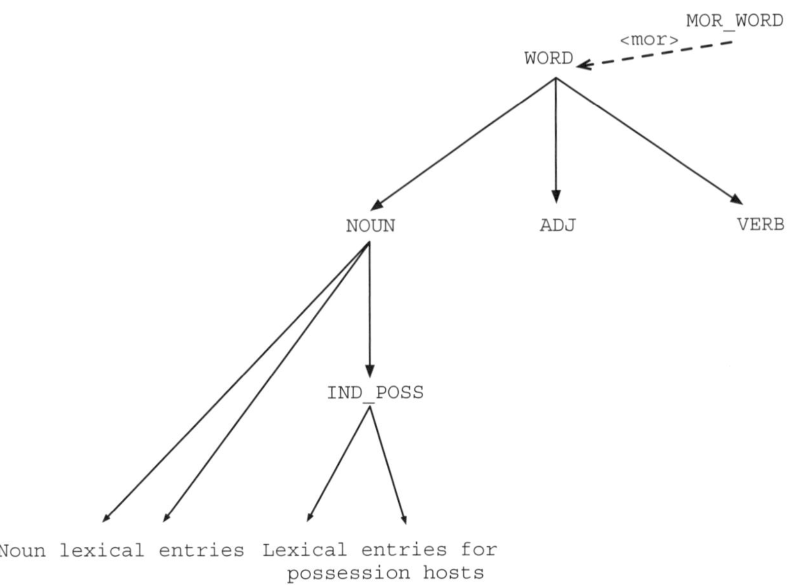

Figure 3.1 *A fragment of Kokota morphology*

(12)
```
MOR_WORD:
  <mor> ==
  <mor dem pl not_visible> == -ro
  <mor dem sg not_visible> == -no
  <mor dem sg within_reach> == -ine
  <mor poss first sg> == -gu "<mor>"
  <mor poss first pl> == -mai "<mor>".
```

The equations involving the possession marking allow for the possibility that further morphology may follow. (This further morphology may default to nothing, of course, if the syntax provides no features for it to spell out.) As an illustration of how this works, consider the associated lexical entries for *mane* 'man' and *tove* 'old' in (7a). These are given in (13) and (14).

(13)
```
Mane:
  <> == NOUN
  <root> == mane
  <gloss> == man.
```

(14)
```
Tove:
  <> == ADJ
  <root> == tove
  <gloss> == old.
```

The noun *mane* is the head of the phrase into which the separate words *mane* 'man' and *tove* 'old' are inserted. The noun *mane* inherits from the NOUN node in the lexemic hierarchy, and in turn therefore from the WORD node. The adjective *tove* inherits from the ADJ node and in turn from WORD. As a consequence they both inherit the generalizations in (12). For the example in (7a), the syntax uses an edge feature to place the `plural`, `demonstrative` and `not_visible` features at the edge of the phrase, and as *tove* is at the right edge, it will form a word consisting of a stem (which is the same as its root) and the morphology associated with the features in question, as demonstrated by the output theorems in (15). (The output `<syn form>` refers to the form of the phrase after lexical insertion. The other outputs provide information about the features associated with that phrase.)

(15) EXAMPLE15:<syn form> = mane tove -ro.
EXAMPLE15:<syn poss> = undefined.
EXAMPLE15:<syn dem> = dem pl not_visible.

In (16) the noun *kame* 'hand' is both the head of the phrase meaning 'my hand within reach' and at the right edge. The morphology is required to provide the (inalienable) first-person singular marking *-gu* on the head of the phrase with the demonstrative *-ine*. As we can see in (12), the morphology specifies only that the possession marking may have further morphology outside it but does not make reference to the syntactic notions of head or edge.

(16) EXAMPLE16:<syn form> = kame -gu -ine.
EXAMPLE16:<syn poss> = poss first sg.
EXAMPLE16:<syn dem> = dem sg within_reach.

In (17) the consumable possession host *γe-* is the head of the phrase with first-person possession marking, while the noun *nene* 'leg' has the edge-marking demonstrative attached to it. This example output, which is a prediction of the fragment rather than an attested phrase, demonstrates that the head and edge marking are distributed correctly by the theory, which also rules out the unexpected possibilities. We have marked the head and the edge words of the phrase in bold.

(17) EXAMPLE17:<syn form> = **γe** -gu **nene** -ro.
EXAMPLE17:<syn poss> = poss first sg.
EXAMPLE17:<syn dem> = dem pl not_visible.

Returning to (12) we pick out one particular equation from it and place it in (18). The combination `γe -gu` in (17) is not followed immediately by `-ro` because syntax does not place the features `dem pl not_visible` on the head, as this does not coincide with the right edge of the phrase in this instance. In this case the path `"<mor>"` in the RHS in (18) defaults to nothing. This is, of course, the identity function default we discussed in Chapter 2, Section 2.3.1.

(18) `<mor poss first sg> == -gu "<mor>"`

Our purpose in looking at the placement of clitics and head marking in Kokota is to demonstrate that the theoretical means available to us to deal with inflectional classes, a very different type of morphology, are sufficient to account for head inflection and clitic morphology, given the ability of syntax to refer to the head and the edge of phrases. We have also demonstrated that this does not require the morphology to make reference to syntax-specific notions, such as head or edge, which would be a violation of syntax-free morphology, a principle we argued for in Chapter 1, Section 1.2.1. This situation is the mirror image of the problem we face with inflectional classes, where the syntax should not make reference to morphology-internal properties. As we specified earlier, Figure 3.1 indicates that we can optimize the network further in line with Node Elimination in (4). This would eliminate the `MOR_WORD` node and mean that there is no specific inheritance structure for morphology, as the lexemic hierarchy would be sufficient for this. The morphological inheritance structure can be accounted for using the lexemic inheritance structure for Kokota. The degree of morphological autonomy is reduced to the limiting case, namely that morphology is syntax-free, thereby ruling out the possibility that morphology's realization rules or rules of exponence should make reference to `head` or `edge`, for example.

3.1.2 Example 2: Morphological hierarchy required

So far we have looked at a kind of morphology which appears to be more tightly related to syntax, and now we move on to the other extreme, where the inheritance structure associated with inflectional classes does not pattern with part of speech. Given that the issue of natural classes in morphology is often dealt with by looking at it from *within* a given part of speech, this is an important issue. On the one hand, the sharing of morphology across lexemes in general could be a problem if it turned out not to pattern with the sharing of structure across parts of speech, as defined in the lexemic hierarchy. In the limiting case from the previous example, morphology is shared across lexemes. This is because the morphology is a default which can apply to any word. We can envisage a range of dissociations between morphology and the parts of speech defined by syntax. For Indo-European languages, we can typically posit lexemic hierarchies which contain, among others, the following nodes:

(19) a. `NOMINAL`
b. `ADJ`

c. NOUN
d. PRONOUN

The node NOMINAL defines a class of syntactic objects, nominals, which share specific syntactic properties. Nouns and pronouns, together with adjectives in NPs lacking a head noun, can appear in subject position and control agreement on verbs, for example. This node is the inheritance source for syntactic and semantic properties which are shared across adjectives, nouns and pronouns. This will include shared information, such as their distribution in NPs. The nodes ADJ, NOUN and PRONOUN inherit from NOMINAL and can override some of the default properties stated there. The extent to which there is a correspondence between morphological expression and the distribution patterns and semantics defined at these nodes is a matter of variation. In Russian, we argue, there is a need for the morphological nodes in (20) that correspond to nodes in the lexemic hierarchy. (We have omitted inflectional class nodes.)

(20) *Nodes for Russian nominal morphology*
a. MOR_NOMINAL
b. MOR_ADJ
c. MOR_NOUN

The reason why we do not require a node for pronoun morphology is that the third-person pronouns have adjective-like morphology, and the non-third-person pronouns have noun-like morphology. We illustrate this in (21) using the dative singular.

(21)

	Adjectives *novij* 'new'	Third-person pronouns	Non-third pronouns	Nouns
SG DAT	*nov-omu* (M/N)	*j-omu* (M/N)	*mn'-e* ('me')	*zavod-e* 'factory' (Decl I)
	nov-oj (F)	*j-(e)j* (F)	*teb'-e* ('you')	*komnat-e* 'room' (Decl II)
				tel-e 'body' (Decl IV)

In (21) we can see that masculine and neuter singular dative forms of the adjective *novij* 'new' are similar to that of the 'he/it' form of the third-person pronoun, while the feminine singular dative form is similar to the 'she' form. The first- and second-person pronouns, on the other hand, have dative singular forms which share the exponent with nouns from three of the four declensional classes.[2] We have also seen in Chapter 2, Section 2.3.1 that there is a recognizable morphological class of nominals where rules of exponence for the plural oblique forms are located, among other things. This is why there is a node MOR_NOMINAL.

We can contrast the Russian situation with Latin, for example, where it is difficult to identify specifically adjectival inflection, so that adjectival inflection is essentially taken from noun declensions. We require a node NOMINAL in the lexemic hierarchy for Latin, along with the others specified in (19), in order to describe the shared syntactic and semantic properties of the nominal parts of speech. But there is no need for a MOR_ADJ node, because the node ADJ can inherit via network relations from the inflectional class nodes defining noun morphology and add information about gender accordingly. As there is no MOR_ADJ for Latin, there is no need for a MOR_NOMINAL node to generalize over the morphology of nouns and adjectives. Latin has inflectional classes, of course, and will therefore have a morphological hierarchy, but its shape differs from that of Russian.

The reason for positing a separate morphological hierarchy is because there is autonomous structure which cross-cuts the distinctions necessary for syntax. Just accepting that there are inflectional classes, however, is not enough. Figure 3.2, where the noun lexical entries inherit from the respective inflectional class nodes, is a possibility for representing Russian nominal morphology, but it does not address the fact that morphology may be shared across inflectional classes, and it does not tell us anything about morphology shared across parts of speech.

In this simplified version, there is no node MOR_NOUN corresponding to the class of noun lexemes. Instead, there are just nodes N_I, N_II, N_III and N_IV. There is little *morphological systematicity*, because the inflectional classes appear to share nothing with each other. There is, on the other hand, a significant degree of *morphological autonomy*, because the multiple inflectional classes correspond to one part of speech and are, therefore, redundant from the perspective of syntax. Of course, theorists, such as Carstairs-McCarthy (1994), have posited constraints on the extent of autonomy, by limiting the degree to which inflectional classes can differ from each other. We argue that inflectional classes can diverge quite significantly in practice, and that the constraining factor in morphology is actually that it must be *default-based* at some point. The Principle of Morphological Projection, however, means that we assume that there is some limit to autonomy. The morphological hierarchy will account for the sharing of morphology between the different declensional classes and allow for morphological classes which generalize beyond an individual part of speech, an issue which goes largely unaddressed when considering the role of defaults in morphology.

Our starting point is the Principle of Morphological Projection which we introduced in Chapter 2, Section 2.4.1.

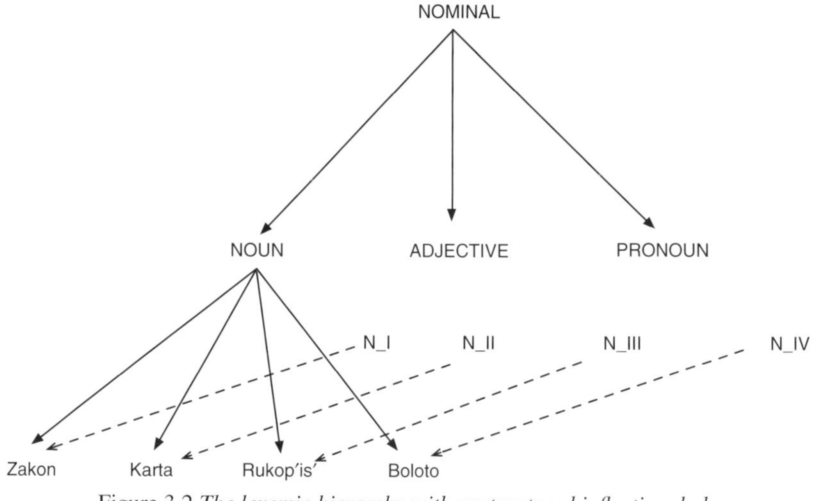

Figure 3.2 *The lexemic hierarchy with unstructured inflectional classes*

(22) *Principle of Morphological Projection*
Morphological classes reflect parts of speech: by default we expect parts of speech to have a corresponding morphological class.

This means that nodes in the lexemic hierarchy should have corresponding nodes in a morphological hierarchy. We can recognize at least three classes of nominal within Russian: adjectives, nouns and pronouns. These classes are related syntactically in that they occur in NPs and may be subject to the same related syntactic operations. We have already explained that there is no need for a separate node for pronoun morphology. There are three recognizable adjective declensions and four declensions for nouns. This provides us with the initial morphological hierarchy in Figure 3.3. As we saw in Chapter 2, Section 2.2, nodes serve as containers of partial information about lexemes, and the nodes in the morphological hierarchy are containers specifically for information about lexemes' inflections.

The next step is to populate these nodes with rules of exponence or rules of referral. In order to do this, we adopt a majority default heuristic, as stated in (23).

(23) *Heuristic: Majority default*
The rule of exponence or rule of referral which is shared by most inflectional classes is treated as the default.

This heuristic allows for the location of default information at nodes which may already be established, because of (22). Given the heuristic in (23) it is

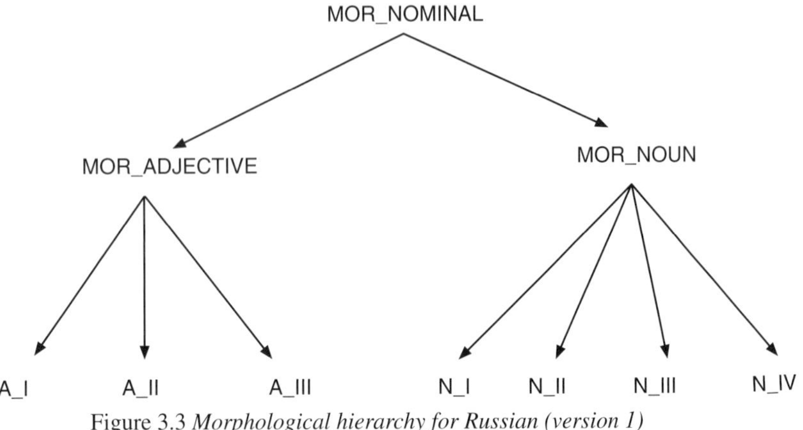

Figure 3.3 *Morphological hierarchy for Russian (version 1)*

always possible that there can be a tie between rules. In the absence of other evidence, there may well be no way of resolving a tie between rules of exponence. However, given the inferential–realizational nature of the framework, (23) also applies to referrals. Where a rule of referral and a rule of exponence are in competition on the basis of (23), the heuristic in (24) applies.

(24) *Heuristic: Rules of referral beat rules of exponence*
Where there may be competing candidates, which cannot be determined by *Majority Default*, rules of referral take precedence over rules of exponence.

We set out the noun inflections in (25).

(25)

	I	II	III	IV
Singular				
NOMINATIVE	zakón	kárt-a	rúkop´is´	bolót-o
ACCUSATIVE	zakón	kárt-u	rúkop´is´	bolót-o
GENITIVE	zakón-a	kárt-i	rúkop´is´-i	bolót-a
DATIVE	zakón-u	kárt-e	rúkop´is´-i	bolót-u
INSTRUMENTAL	zakón-om	kárt-oj	rúkop´is´-ju	bolót-om
PREPOSITIONAL	zakón-e	kárt-e	rúkop´is´-i	bolót-e
Plural				
NOMINATIVE	zakón-i	kárt-i	rúkop´is´-i	bolót-a
ACCUSATIVE	zakón-i	kárt-i	rúkop´is´-i	bolót-a
GENITIVE	zakón-ov	kárt	rúkop´is´-ej	bolót
DATIVE	zakón-am	kárt-am	rúkop´is´-am	bolót-am
INSTRUMENTAL	zakón-am´i	kárt-am´i	rúkop´is´-am´i	bolót-am´i
PREPOSITIONAL	zakón-ax	kárt-ax	rúkop´is´-ax	bolót-ax

We can compare them with the main declensional class for Russian adjectives in (26).

(26) *Declension I Russian adjectives (`A_I`), as shown by* novij *'new'*

	Masculine	Neuter	Feminine
Singular			
NOM	nov-ij	nov-oje	nov-aj-a
ACC	INAN = SG NOM	nov-oje	nov-uj-u
	an = sg gen		
GEN	nov-ovo		nov-oj
DAT	nov-omu		nov-oj
INS	nov-im		nov-oj(u)
PREP	nov-om		nov-oj
Plural			
NOM	nov-i-je		
ACC	INAN = PL NOM		
	AN = PL GEN		
GEN	nov-i-x		
DAT	nov-i-m		
INS	nov-i-m´i		
PREP	nov-i-x		

The next type is rarer. It contains possessive adjectives such as *mam´in* 'mother's' as well as some related to animals. The third-person pronouns also basically follow a similar pattern, as indicated by (21). The crucial difference in comparison with the adjectives in (26) lies in the forms of the masculine nominative singular, the nominative and accusative singular of the neuter and feminine, and the nominative plural. The inflections in these cells are shared with nouns. The form of the masculine accusative singular is also determined by a rule of referral that is shared across nominals. The accusative singular will have the same form as the genitive singular, if the agreement controller is masculine and animate. The genitive singular form is itself an adjectival form.

(27) *Declension II Russian adjectives (`A_II`), as shown by mam´in 'mother's'*

	Masculine	Neuter	Feminine
Singular			
NOM	mam´in	mam´in-o	mam´in-a
ACC	INAN = SG NOM	mam´in-o	mam´in-u
	AN = SG GEN		

GEN	mam´in-ovo	mam´in-oj
DAT	mam´in-omu	mam´in-oj
INS	mam´in-im	mam´in-oj(u)
PREP	mam´in-om	mam´in-oj
Plural		
NOM	mam´in-i	
ACC	INAN = PL NOM	
	AN = PL GEN	
GEN	mam´in-i-x	
DAT	mam´in-i-m	
INS	mam´in-i-m´i	
PREP	mam´in-i-x	

The third class of adjectives (A_III) which appears in Figure 3.3 is extremely rare and is restricted to a small number of adjectives such as *otcov* 'father's'. This class is essentially the same as A_II, except that in the singular genitive and singular dative the masculine and neuter forms are the same as for the genitive and dative singular of Declensions I and IV nouns, namely *-a* and *-u*, respectively.

As we showed in Chapter 2, Section 2.3.1, in line with the Overextended Ancestor Prohibition, neutralization of gender contrasts will make morphology more likely to be shared across nominals, as gender is not an inflectional feature for nouns. Essentially, it is not an inflectional feature when it fails to be a target feature. We summarize the differences amongst nouns, adjectives and pronouns in (28) in relation to the Network Morphology notions of <syn gender> – the inherent gender of a controller – and the specification of gender in the morphological path (namely extensions of <mor>). For nouns, gender is not part of the inflectional paradigm, as it is an inherent feature of the noun. The gender assignment system will provide a value for <syn gender> of nouns, and this will typically be an invariant property of the noun.

(28) *Gender properties of Russian nouns, adjectives and pronouns*

Nominal type	Gender specified in <mor> path	Value defined for <syn gender>	Value for <syn gender> invariant	Controller or Target?
Nouns	No	Yes	Yes	Controller
First-person pronoun	No	Yes	No	Controller

Second-person pronoun	No	Yes	No	Controller
Third-person pronoun	Yes	Yes	No	Both
Adjectives	Yes	No	n/a	Target

Typical adjectives are the opposite of nouns in all these regards. They realize gender in their paradigms but are not assigned an inherent value for gender.[3] First- and second-person pronouns do not realize gender but require it to be defined so that agreement targets may agree with them for gender. However, the gender feature for second- and first-person pronouns is not invariant, as it will depend on the referent. Third-person pronouns are both targets for agreement, in virtue of anaphoric reference, and also controllers of agreement. Hence, they realize gender in their inflectional paradigms, as well as imposing it on other constituents syntactically. While they differ in terms of the status of gender, all the nominal classes in (28) realize number and case in their inflectional paradigms.

As they share morphology, any analysis which seeks to consider the status of defaults here must take account of classes beyond those associated with the specific parts of speech (adjectives, nouns and pronouns). Given our arguments about attribute ordering in Chapter 2, Section 2.2.3, gender will occur last in the path for nominal morphology. Russian has three genders (masculine, neuter and feminine). In the adjectives there is gender syncretism between masculine and neuter in all case and number combinations except the nominative and accusative singular. As the syncretism entails underspecification for gender, it naturally means that the morphology could potentially be shared with all nominal classes, including those which do not inflect for gender (i.e. nouns and non-third-person pronouns). In addition to this, as was explained in Chapter 2, Section 2.3.1, morphology will default to the bare stem at the MOR_WORD level (from which MOR_NOMINAL inherits). This default will account for singular nominative of Declension I nouns in (29) and the singular nominative masculine for adjectives such as *mam´in* 'mother's' in (27). Here the morphology is shared, because neither N_I nor A_II specifies a rule for the singular nominative or singular nominative masculine. The most specific matching path is the one at MOR_WORD which specifies the identity function.

Those parts of the adjectival morphology which are underspecified for gender (i.e. the masculine and neuter forms outside the nominative and accusative) are, therefore, potential candidates for default status at the MOR_NOMINAL level. We give the rules in (29). (We have used the affixes as proxies for the rules of exponence and used the term 'referral' where a rule of referral is required.)

(29) *Nominal morphology in Russian*

	A_I *nov-ij* 'new'	A_II *mam'in* 'mother's'	A_III *otcov* 'father's'	N_I *zakon* 'law'	N_II *karta* 'map'	N_III *rukop'is'* 'manuscript'	N_IV *boloto* 'marsh'
SG NOM	**n/a**	-Ø	-Ø	-Ø	-a	-Ø	-o
SG ACC	referral	referral	referral	referral	-u	referral	referral
SG GEN	-ovo	-ovo	-a	-a	-i	-i	-a
SG DAT	-omu	-omu	-u	-u	referral	referral	-u
SG INS	-im	-im	-im	-om	-oj(u)	-ju	-om
SG PREP	-om	-om	-om	-e	-e	referral	-e
PL NOM	-ije	-i	-i	-i	-i	-i	-a
PL ACC	referral	referral	referral	referral	referral	referral	referral
PL GEN	referral	referral	referral	-ov/-ej	-Ø/-ej	-ej	-Ø/-ej
PL DAT	-i-m	-i-m	-i-m	-a-m	-a-m	-a-m	-a-m
PL INS	-i-m'i	-i-m'i	-i-m'i	-a-m'i	-a-m'i	-a-m'i	-a-m'i
PL PREP	-i-x	-i-x	-i-x	-a-x	-a-x	-a-x	-a-x

The justification for assuming that there is a rule of referral associated with a particular cell is the asymmetric nature of the identity, typically coupled with systematicity across the classes. (This is discussed in Baerman, Brown and Corbett 2005.) For instance, the accusative referrals involve use of the genitive, if the noun is animate, or the nominative if the noun is inanimate. But the actual form of the genitive or nominative will differ across the classes. Similarly, if one looks in (29) at the dative singular, its form differs in Declensions II and III, but in both cases it is identical with the prepositional singular. The *-e* realization of the prepositional singular is shared across three classes, while the *-e* form of the dative singular is restricted to Declension II, as can be seen in (29). This suggests that the dative singular refers to the prepositional singular. This also fits with what we know about the frequency distribution of these cases, where typically the referred-to cell is less frequent (Brown, Tiberius and Corbett 2004; 2007). The rule for the genitive plural restricted to the adjectival classes refers to the prepositional plural form. This is justified by the fact that the prepositional plural realization is *-V-x* across all the adjective and noun declensional classes and is, therefore, the basic exponent of that feature combination.

We have only given the affixal realizations for each class in (29), but it should also be noted that the realizations for, say, genitive singular and nominative plural in Declensions II and III cannot be taken as syncretic, because the stress may differ between these in subsets of nouns belonging to these classes. In contrast, the identity of accusative plural with either nominative or genitive plural is absolute, as the stress pattern is always the same for both. Brown *et al.* (1996: 80) pointed to this as one justification for a referral-based approach to accusative-related syncretism in Russian. (The main justification for referrals is, of course, the asymmetry in exponence.)

Given our heuristics we can place the rules at different positions in the morphological hierarchy. Furthermore, as Network Morphology is based on defaults, we can allow for some degree of overriding between classes. Indeed inflectional classes are not an all-or-nothing category. They are a fuzzy notion which allows for items to be members with some degree of aberrant behaviour. We, therefore, introduce two principles which are relevant for inflectional classes. These are the principle of *Generalization Violation*, which determines the extent to which classes are allowed to override information from the superclasses of which they are members, and the principle of *Inflectional Proximity*, which determines the extent to which we can consider two inflectional classes to be members of a larger superclass. We turn to Generalization Violation. This constraint influences where we can place the rules of exponence and rules of referral.

(30) *Generalization Violation*

(i) Where a node A inherits from a node B by a hierarchy relation, the number of matches between LHS at A and LHS at B should be no greater than one, with the exclusion of the hierarchy relation itself.
(ii) A match is where the LHS paths are identical.

Given the Majority Default heuristic in (23) and the data in (29), the rules for the singular accusative, plural nominative, plural accusative, and the oblique cases in the plural can be placed at the MOR_NOMINAL node. The identity function default is stated at the MOR_WORD level above MOR_NOMINAL for all words, so this will account for the singular nominative realization by the bare stem. The referral of the plural genitive to the plural prepositional is not the majority rule for nominal declensions, but we have placed it at MOR_NOMINAL, because it is also true of pronouns. (As we have argued, pronouns do not have a node of their own in the morphological class.) This yields the defaults in (31) at the MOR_NOMINAL node, represented in DATR as in (32).

(31) *Defaults at the* `MOR_NOMINAL` *node*

SG ACC	referral
PL NOM	*-i*
PL ACC	referral
PL GEN	referral
PL DAT	*-V-m*
PL INS	*-V-m'i*
PL PREP	*-V-x*

(32)

```
MOR_NOMINAL:
  <> == MOR_WORD
  <mor sg acc> == ACCUSATIVE:< sg "<syn gender>"
                    "<syn animacy>" >
  <mor pl nom> == "<stem pl nom>" ^ i "<stress pl nom>"
  <mor pl acc> == ACCUSATIVE:< pl "<syn animacy>" >
  <mor pl gen> == "<mor pl prep>"
  <mor pl dat> == "<stem pl>" "<mor theme_vowel>"
                    "<stress pl>" ^ m
  <mor pl inst> == "<stem pl>" "<mor theme_vowel>"
                    "<stress pl>" ^ m'i
  <mor pl prep> == "<stem pl>" "<mor theme_vowel>"
                    "<stress pl>" ^ x
  ...
```

We can see in (32) straightforward rules of exponence, such as that for the plural dative, which states that this is realized by the plural stem, a theme vowel, the value for plural stress and the formative `m`. We have already discussed how the stress is inherited in Chapter 2, Section 2.2.6. It should be noted that the accusative plural forms for all classes will depend on the evaluation of animacy: animate nouns will have a form the same as the genitive plural (whatever that may be), and inanimate nouns will have a form the same as the nominative plural (whatever that may be). The accusative singular also requires evaluation of the gender of the noun, as the animacy rule in the accusative singular only applies to masculine nouns and their agreement targets. The node `MOR_ADJ` will receive the following adjective-level defaults, as these are the realizations favoured by the majority of adjective declensions.

(33) *Defaults at the* `MOR_ADJ` *node*

SG GEN	*-ovo*
SG DAT	*-omu*
SG INS	*-im*
SG PREP	*-om*

At the MOR_ADJ level, most of the defaults are singular, because the rules for the plural are already available at MOR_NOMINAL.

Before moving on to consider what is located at MOR_NOUN, let us look at the exponents of dative and genitive singular in classes N_I and N_IV and the rare adjectival type A_III. These are *-u* and *-a*, respectively. Although they are not used in the majority of the classes throughout the nominals, they occur in the greatest number of classes. And because they may occur in one of the adjectival declensions, we might consider making them nominal defaults. However, this will be ruled out by Generalization Violation, because it would lead to more than one match between MOR_NOMINAL and MOR_ADJ for the LHS paths of the rules for dative and genitive singular, as the gender information is underspecified. The node A_III will have to inherit these exponents from the noun portion of the hierarchy via orthogonal network relations, but this is readily justifiable, because there are only a handful of adjectives which inflect like this, and they occur rarely.

For the nouns the genitive plural forms in (29) are determined by evaluation of the properties of the stem. Whether the stem is functionally soft (i.e. palatalized or palatoalveolar) is an important factor for all classes, but in Declensions II and IV stress information also plays a role (Brown and Hippisley 1994). All nouns in Declension III have functionally soft stems, so they will receive the inflection *-ej*. We have referred to this as EVAL in (34), as it involves evaluable paths, as we can see from the rule for the genitive plural in (35). In fact, the animacy rules for the accusative in (32) also involve evaluable paths, but they are referrals in the sense that the evaluation determines which cell of the paradigm is referred to (nominative or genitive). In the case of the evaluation for genitive plural, the rule uses information about stem properties without referring to another paradigm cell.

(34) *Defaults at the MOR_NOUN node*

SG DAT	referral
PL PREP	-e
PL GEN	EVAL

(35)
```
MOR_NOUN:
  <> == MOR_NOMINAL
  <mor sg dat> == "<mor sg prep>"
  <mor sg prep> == "<stem sg>" ^ e "<stress sg>"
  <mor pl gen> == MGP:<"<mor stem hardness>" pl gen>
  ...
```

Given the default status of the rule of referral for the dative singular in (35), the question naturally arises: how is it possible to express the sharing of the dative singular between Declensions I and IV? In fact, we allow for intermediate inflectional classes to generalize over other classes if there is a significant degree of inflectional proximity between them. We define inflectional proximity as follows:

(36) Two classes are inflectionally proximate if they share a greater proportion of the inflectional rule system (significantly more than half).

We can count the overlap for each class in terms of shared realizations or rules (rules of exponence or rules of referral).[4] We illustrate this in (37) for the nouns where it is immediately apparent that the inflectional proximity of classes `N_I` and `N_IV` is very great. In essence, they share three-quarters of their inflectional rules, including rules of referral. (They share seven rules of exponence, the rule of referral which determines the form of the accusative in the plural, and the referral for the singular accusative.)

(37) *Inflectional proximity of noun declensions*

	N_I	**N_IV**	**N_II**	**N_III**
N_I	12	9	6	7
N_IV	9	12	6	5
N_II	6	6	12	7
N_III	7	5	7	12

It could be argued that, in virtue of the shared genitive and dative singular exponents, the rare `A_III` type adjective in (29) has inflectional proximity with `N_I` and `N_IV`. However, (29) only represents the parts of the adjectival paradigm which are underspecified for gender (i.e. where masculine and neuter are syncretic). Once the rules associated with feminine gender are included, the overlap does not account for more than half from the perspective of adjectival morphology.

Example (37) shows that there is significant inflectional proximity between `N_IV` and `N_I`. The two classes are sufficiently alike that we can treat them as belonging to a superclass of their own. This provides justification for the existence of a superclass `N_O` as first argued for by Corbett and Fraser (1993). The other declensions in (37) do not come close to this situation. For any of the others, the overlap may be marginally over half the paradigm, and that includes rules of referral.

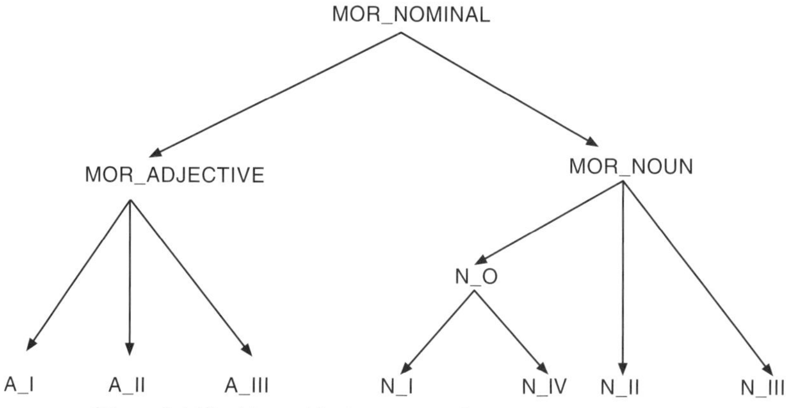

Figure 3.4 *The hierarchical structure of Russian declensional classes*

(38) *Inflectional proximity of noun declensions*

	N_O	**N_II**	**N_III**
N_O	9	5	5
N_II	5	12	7
N_III	5	7	12

In (38) we have contrasted the superclass N_O with classes N_II and N_III. Class N_O is defined for only nine paradigm cells (the ones which overlap between classes N_I and N_IV). It should be noted that N_II and N_III both have the same inflectional proximity with N_O (5/9), and this is quite similar to their inflectional proximity with each other (7/12). In both cases it is just over half the potential overlap. The use of the notion of *inflectional proximity* allows us to define the set of classes in our hierarchy for noun morphology. For nouns the relevant nodes are: MOR_NOUN (on the basis of (22)), N_I, N_II, N_III, N_IV and N_O (the latter established on the basis of inflectional proximity).

Given (22) and the justification of N_O on the basis of inflectional proximity, we have the inheritance hierarchy for Russian nouns first argued for by Corbett and Fraser (1993). This is shown in Figure 3.4, together with the inheritance structure for adjectival morphology, with the node MOR_ADJ again established on the basis of (22). The node MOR_NOMINAL corresponds to NOMINAL in the lexemic hierarchy. This is also justified on the basis of (22).

Guided by the heuristics in (23) and (24), and obeying Generalization Violation, the rules of exponence and rules of referral relevant for nouns are distributed in the hierarchy, as indicated in (39).

(39) *Russian noun inflections and the position of the rules in the hierarchy*

Morphosyntax	Realization	Shared by	Number of noun declensions sharing	Locations
PL ACC	*REFERRAL*	N_I, N_II, N_III, N_IV	4	MOR_NOMINAL
PL DAT	-*V-m*	N_I, N_II, N_III, N_IV	4	MOR_NOMINAL
PL INS	-*V-mi*	N_I, N_II, N_III, N_IV	4	MOR_NOMINAL
PL PREP	-*V-x*	N_I, N_II, N_III, N_IV	4	MOR_NOMINAL
SG ACC	*REFERRAL*	N_I, N_III, N_IV	3	MOR_NOMINAL
PL NOM	-*i*	N_I, N_II, N_III	3	MOR_NOMINAL
SG PREP	-*e*	N_I, N_II, N_IV	3	MOR_NOUN
SG NOM	-*Ø*	N_I, N_III	2	MOR_WORD[5]
SG DAT	*REFERRAL*	N_II, N_III	2	MOR_NOUN
PL GEN	EVAL (hard/soft)	N_I, N_III	2	MOR_NOUN
SG GEN	-*a*	N_I, N_IV	2	N_O
SG GEN	-*i*	N_II, N_III	2	N_II, N_III[6]
SG INS	-*om*	N_I, N_IV	2	N_O
SG DAT	-*u*	N_I, N_IV	2	N_O
PL NOM	-*a*	N_IV	2	N_IV
SG NOM	-*a*	N_II	1	N_II
SG ACC	-*u*	N_II	1	N_II
SG NOM	-*o*	N_IV	1	N_IV
PL GEN (HARD)	-*ov*	N_I	1	N_I
PL GEN	EVAL	N_IV	1	N_IV
PL GEN	EVAL	N_II	1	N_II
SG INS	-*oj(u)*	N_II	1	N_II
SG INS	-*ju*	N_III	1	N_III
SG PREP	*REFERRAL*	N_III	1	N_III

We have seen the rules for the nominals in (32) and for nouns in (33). The information in (39) shows where in the hierarchy the different rules for inflection are inherited by Russian nouns. The 'number sharing' column shows how many declensional classes for nouns are subject to the rule. (This means, for instance, that the number of classes sharing the plural dative is given as four, while in fact it is seven, if adjectival classes are included.) The rules have been sorted in descending order according to position in the hierarchy. The genitive plural rule is worthy of comment, as it involves a number of evaluations. It is sensitive to whether the stem of the noun is hard or soft, as we can see in the equation in (35) with the use of the evaluable path. In (40) we see that the Declension I nouns *stol* 'table' and *žitel´* 'inhabitant' differ in terms of their genitive plural inflections. This is because the stem of the noun *žitel´* ends in a palatalized consonant and is, therefore, soft. The evaluation in (35) involves determining what the final element of the stem is so that the correct inflection is chosen.

(40) *Declension I hard and soft genitive plural*

Nominative singular *stol* table[NOM.SG] 'table'	Nominative singular *žitel´* inhabitant[NOM.SG] 'inhabitant'
Genitive plural *stol-ov* table-GEN.PL 'of (the) tables'	Genitive plural *žitel-ej* inhabitant-GEN.PL 'of (the) inhabitants'

Declension III contains only nouns which have soft, or functionally soft stems,[7] and so it will inherit the exponent *-ej*, as we can see for the noun *rúkop´is´* 'manuscript' in (29). For Declensions II and IV, there is an additional layer of evaluation. Declension II nouns, which are soft, can potentially have no overt exponent in the genitive plural or use the exponent *-ej*. Brown and Hippisley (1994) showed how the stress information available elsewhere in the network, which we saw in Chapter 2, Section 2.2.6, could be used to determine how the genitive plural is realized for Declension II nouns with soft stems. Basically, if the genitive plural of a soft Declension II noun requires ending stress, according to the pattern of which it is a member, then it will most likely be realized by *-ej*. Declension IV also has stem evaluation which follows a set of criteria similar to that followed by Declension II.

In Russian there is a recognizable morphological class of defaults associated with the syntactic class of nominals: the instrumental plural and the dative plural are shared by adjectives, pronouns and nouns, and the prepositional plural is shared by adjectives, third-person pronouns and nouns. Equally, the prepositional singular is naturally associated with the morphological class MOR_NOUN. Given the lack of inflectional proximity between Declensions II and III, the referral of dative singular to prepositional singular is also naturally housed at MOR_NOUN, in line with the heuristic that rules of referral are more likely defaults than rules of exponence. Recall that the class N_O accounts for the forms shared by N_I and N_IV alone. One way in which Network Morphology differs from other default-inheritance-based approaches is that it is assumed that classes such as N_O, as well as the more abstract classes MOR_NOM, MOR_NOUN and MOR_ADJ, are different in nature from the inflectional class nodes, because defaults at this level describe lexemes only partially.

The morphological hierarchy in Figure 3.4 provides a solution to a long-standing issue within Russian linguistics, where the tradition has generally been to group Declensions I and IV together as one class. Corbett (1982; 1991) argues that gender need not be specified in lexical entries, because it can be predicted either from the inflectional class or from the semantics of the noun, which must be specified anyway. It can only be predicted, however, if one adopts the four-class approach.[8] Viewing the noun portion of the hierarchy from the top down, we see that there are three declensional classes at one level (N_O, N_II and N_III). In contrast, looking from the bottom up, there are four (N_I, N_IV, N_II and N_III). Not only does the hierarchy capture the shared morphology, it also allows for the gender assignment system to work on the basis of the four bottom nodes in the morphological hierarchy.

We have outlined how the morphological hierarchy is set up. In contrast with the Kokota example in Section 3.1.1, a morphological hierarchy is required because of the cross-cutting morphology. In Section 3.2 we will show that the existence of MOR_ADJ, MOR_NOUN, and consequently MOR_NOMINAL, is actually dependent on the existence of the inflectional classes N_O, N_I, N_II, N_III and N_IV. If the latter were not present, then the former would be eliminable with application of principle (4). However, there is one situation which is not necessarily ruled out. Inflectional classes could be monolithic entities without any shared defaults. These would be similar to the canonical inflectional classes we shall discuss in Section 3.2. As we argue, even with the examples which appear to be like this, defaults are required to capture shared patterns of syncretism. Our next task is to explain the relationship between the lexemic hierarchy and the morphological hierarchy and account for the gender and animacy rules.

3.1.3 Inheritance between the lexemic and morphological hierarchies

The lexemic hierarchy and the morphological hierarchy are related by *interdependency nodes*. These nodes make use of information specified in the lexical entry, or inherited by it, to determine which node in the morphological hierarchy a lexeme may inherit from. They make use of evaluable paths, a concept we explained in Chapter 2, Section 2.2.8. In order to determine a noun's inflection, it must be assigned a declensional class. Russian noun roots (and therefore stems) end in a consonant. If the noun is a loanword that ends in a vowel which cannot readily be reanalysed as an inflection, then the noun will be indeclinable (Fraser and Corbett 1995: 132; Worth 1966). This can also hold for other nominals. At the node `NOMINAL` in the lexemic hierarchy, some of which is given in (41), it is stated that a nominal's inflectional morphology – defined by the `<mor>` path – is determined by evaluating the final element of the root and using this information at the interdependency node `PARADIGM`. The node `NOMINAL` also contains a default statement that the final element of the root is a consonant.

(41)
```
NOMINAL:
  <mor> == PARADIGM:<"<root final>">
  <root final> == consonant
  ...
```

At the node `PARADIGM` in (42), the animacy of the lexeme will be evaluated, if the root ends in a vowel. This is relevant for a rule of gender assignment located at the node `ADJ_OR_NOUN` but is not relevant for declensional class assignment. Ultimately, the items whose stem ends in a vowel will inherit their form from the node `MOR_WORD`, and this will be the identity function we introduced in Chapter 2, Section 2.3.1.[9] As we see in (42), where the lexeme's root ends in a consonant, as is true for the vast majority, the morphology will be inherited from the declensional class. The RHS path `"<declensional_class>"` is quoted, because the value will be the one taken from the global context (i.e. whatever the lexeme is), rather than the local context (which would be the node where the rule is stated, namely `PARADIGM`).[10]

(42)
```
PARADIGM:
  <vowel> == ADJ_OR_NOUN:<"<sem animacy>">
  <consonant> == "<declensional_class>".
```

The declensional class of a lexeme is largely predictable, if the noun denotes a sex-differentiable higher-order animate. If it denotes a male, then the noun will belong to Declension I, and if it denotes a female, then the noun will belong to Declension II (Fraser and Corbett 1995: 132). It is worth reiterating at this point that declensional class and gender are two separate things, so that it is possible for the semantic assignment rules to be overridden for declensional class, while being obeyed for gender, as explained in Chapter 2, Section 2.2 for the noun *deduška* 'grandfather'. The node NOUN in (43) specifies that declensional class involves evaluation of the semantics of biological sex associated with the lexeme. This information is used at an interdependency node to determine the declension from which to inherit the morphology.

(43)
```
NOUN:
  <> == NOMINAL
  <declensional_class> == DECLENSION:< "<sem sex>" >
  ...
```

In (44) we see that lexemes which denote males will inherit their morphology from Declension I (represented by the node N_I), and nouns which denote females will inherit their morphology from Declension II (represented by the node N_II).

(44)
```
DECLENSION:
  <male> == N_I:<mor>
  <female> == N_II:<mor>.
```

Where a noun does not denote a higher-order sex-differentiable animate, then it will stipulate its declensional class in its lexical entry. We saw this with the lexeme *stol* in Chapter 2, and we give its lexical entry here again in (45).

(45)
```
Stol:
  <> = NOUN
  <declensional_class> == N_I:<mor>
  <gloss> == table
  <root> == stol
  <stress_index> == 2.
```

The noun *ženšč'ina* 'woman', on the other hand, does not need to specify its declensional class, as this is ultimately determined at (44), where it is stated that if a noun denotes a female, then it will inherit from Declension II. We give the lexical entry for *ženšč'ina* in (46).

(46)
```
Ženšč'ina:
  <> == NOUN
  <gloss> == woman
  <root all> == ženšč'in
  <sem sex> == female.
```

The noun *bik* 'bull' does not need to specify its declensional class, as this is also determined at (44). We give the lexical entry for *bik* in (47).

(47)
```
Bik:
  <> == NOUN
  <gloss> == bull
```

```
<root all> == bik
<sem sex> == male
<stress_index> == 2.
```

We noted in Chapter 2, Section 2.2 that nouns such as *deduška* 'grandfather' are masculine in gender but are assigned to the wrong declensional class. The noun *mužč'ina* 'man', for which we give the lexical entry in (48), is another example.

(48)
```
Mužč'ina:
  <> == NOUN
  <gloss> == man
  <declensional_class> == N_II:<mor>
  <root all> == mužč'ín
  <sem sex> == male.
```

The lexical entry in (48) has to specify the declensional class, but once this is done, everything else follows. All of the morphology of the noun will be inherited from Declension II. Before we move on to the system of gender assignment, it is worth reflecting on the advantages of this approach. Nouns such as *deduška* 'grandfather' and *mužč'ina* 'man' are odd, because they belong to the wrong declensional class. However, once they belong to this class, they obtain the inflections that most other members of the class inherit. Consider the relevant outputs for the full morphological model for the noun *mužč'ina* in (49). The accusative singular is the same as for all other members of the declensional class.

(49)
```
Mužč'ina:<gloss> = man.
Mužč'ina:<mor sg nom> = mužč'ín ^ a.
Mužč'ina:<mor sg acc> = mužč'ín ^ u.
Mužč'ina:<mor sg gen> = mužč'ín ^ i.
Mužč'ina:<mor sg dat> = mužč'ín ^ e.
Mužč'ina:<mor sg inst> = mužč'ín ^ o ^ j ( u ).
Mužč'ina:<mor sg prep> = mužč'ín ^ e.
Mužč'ina:<mor sg prep loc> = mužč'ín ^ e.
Mužč'ina:<mor pl nom> = mužč'ín ^ i.
Mužč'ina:<mor pl acc> = mužč'ín.
Mužč'ina:<mor pl gen> = mužč'ín.
Mužč'ina:<mor pl dat> = mužč'ín ^ a ^ m.
Mužč'ina:<mor pl inst> = mužč'ín ^ a ^ m'i.
Mužč'ina:<mor pl prep> = mužč'ín ^ a ^ x.
Mužč'ina:<syn gender> = masc.
Mužč'ina:<syn animacy> = animate.
```

If we wished to associate gender directly with the inflections of Declension II nouns (which are typically feminine), then we would need to find some way of guaranteeing that nouns such as *mužč'ina* would inherit all of the associated inflections of that class (given that, under such a view of the matter, it would have the wrong gender for these inflections). In other words, we would need to make sure that once it has a Declension II inflection in one cell of the paradigm, then it will in the others as well. But the oddity of nouns such as this is their declensional class membership, while their syntactic behaviour and gender are as expected and in line with the notion that syntax is morphology-free. So in (50) the agreement target is masculine, and it is subject to the animacy rule which says that singular accusative masculine animate is the same as the singular genitive. However, the noun *mužč'ina* controlling the agreement in (50) is not subject to the animacy rule in the singular, because it is a well-behaved member of its declensional class. It is its membership *in* the declensional class, rather than its behaviour *as* a member of that class, which is unexpected, given its semantics.

(50) et-ovo mužč'in-u
this-SG.ACC.AN = SG.GEN man-SG.ACC

Now that we have explained how declensional class is assigned, we move on to look at the assignment of gender, which for Russian and similar languages is a mixed semantic-formal system (Corbett 1991). This means that gender can be predicted from semantics or declensional class. We provide further information about the NOUN in (51).

(51)
```
NOUN:
  <> == NOMINAL
  <syn cat> == n
  <declensional_class> == DECLENSION:< "<sem sex>" >
  <syn gender> == GENDER:< "<sem sex>" >
  <syn animacy> == "<sem animacy>"
  <sem animacy> == ANIMACY:< "<sem sex>" >
  <sem sex> == undifferentiated
  ...
```

The crucial equation for gender assignment is the one which contains the `<syn gender>` LHS path. In the RHS an evaluable path is used to evaluate (biological) sex and determine the gender at the node GENDER. Note that the default value for `<sem sex>` is `undifferentiated`. This will be subject to further refinement in our treatment of derivation in Chapter 7 Section 7.1. The contents of the node GENDER appear in (52).

(52)
```
GENDER:
  <male> == masc
  <female> == fem
  <undifferentiated> == "<mor formal gender>".
```

Nouns which denote males are assigned to the masculine gender. Nouns which denote females are assigned to the feminine gender. If a noun denotes entities which are undifferentiated for biological sex, then its gender will be the same as its formal gender (the gender associated with its declensional class). A noun such as *mužč'ina* in (48) inherits the gender assignment rule from `NOUN` and, as it denotes a male, will be assigned the value `masc` for its gender according to (52). This can be seen for `<syn gender>` in the outputs of the analysis in (49). Only if the semantics cannot provide an answer will the declensional classes play a role. The noun *stol* in (45) will inherit the value `undifferentiated` for biological sex and have its gender assigned as the value for formal gender. As this is a path which begins with the `mor` attribute, it will be inherited via the equation at the `NOMINAL` node in (41). For any noun which inflects – that is, whose stem ends in a consonant, as stated at (42) – the declensional class will provide the formal gender value. For Declension I the value is masculine. For Declension II it is feminine. For Declension III it is also feminine. For Declension IV it is neuter. In Chapter 7, Section 7.3.2 we will see that this formal feature has a role in the derivation of diminutives in Russian.

We saw in Chapter 2, Section 2.2.7 that the syntactic animacy of Russian nouns is based on their semantic animacy and that semantic animacy can be determined by default for sex-differentiable nouns. We also saw in Chapter 2, Section 2.3.2.3 examples from Polish where animacy is further differentiated in that we have inanimate, animate and person. Additionally, we saw in our discussion of exceptional case and normal case defaults in Polish that the semantic–syntactic animacy distinction is important, as some nouns can exhibit dissociations between the two. And we have just seen that the animacy rule is itself not a purely syntactic one, as its application is blocked by declensional classes where the noun in question otherwise has the relevant syntactic features. This is the situation in (49) and (50), for example, where the accusative form of the noun is determined by its declensional class membership, rather than its syntactic properties. In contrast, the form of the adjective agreeing with the noun, as shown in (50), is determined by the noun's syntactic properties. In (53) we repeat the relevant defaults we placed at the `MOR_NOMINAL` node for Russian.

(53)
```
MOR_NOMINAL:
  <> == MOR_WORD
  <mor sg acc> ==
  ACCUSATIVE:< sg "<syn gender>" "<syn animacy>" >
  <mor pl acc> == ACCUSATIVE:< pl "<syn animacy>" >
  ...
```

The evaluable path in the first rule for the singular accusative places gender and animacy values after the number attribute. In the plural, only animacy is used in the evaluable path, as gender is not relevant there. The `ACCUSATIVE` node referred to is given in (54).

(54)
```
ACCUSATIVE:
  <sg> == "<mor sg "<mor case>" >"
  <pl> == "<mor pl "<mor case>" >".
```

Given the evaluable paths in (53), the path for the singular at (54) will be extended with gender and animacy, and the path for the plural will be extended with animacy only. If a noun is masculine and animate, for example, the effect is that we can infer the following in (55).

(55)
```
ACCUSATIVE:
  <sg masc animate> == "<mor sg
                          "<mor case masc animate>" >"
  <pl animate> == "<mor pl "<mor case animate>" >".
```

The values associated with these evaluable paths can then be used. For example, additional equations at MOR_NOMINAL, given in (56), specify that <mor case masc animate> is the same as <mor case animate masc> and, as it is an extension of <mor case animate>, it is associated with genitive (gen).

(56)
```
MOR_NOMINAL:
  <> == MOR_WORD
  <mor case masc animate> == "<mor case animate masc>"
  <mor case> == nom
  <mor case animate> == gen
  ...
```

This means that we can further infer from (55) the following in (57).

(57)
```
ACCUSATIVE:
  <sg masc animate> == "<mor sg gen>"
  <pl animate> == "<mor pl gen>".
```

And as the RHS paths are quoted, the forms to be inherited will depend on the lexeme in question, of course. Because these rules are specified at MOR_NOMINAL, they are relevant for adjectives as well.

We have seen how nouns can be assigned to declensional classes which are represented as nodes in the morphological hierarchy. Syntactic animacy is generally determined by semantic animacy. Gender, on the other hand, is determined either by semantic values or inheriting the information about formal gender from the declensional classes. These relationships between the lexemic and morphological hierarchies are captured by interdependency nodes. They are, however, only required if there is a dissociation between the lexemic and morphological hierarchies. We now move on to show that a morphological hierarchy can be eliminated if it is isomorphic with the lexemic hierarchy.

3.2 Justifying morphological hierarchies

As we saw in Chapter 2, Section 2.4.1 and again in (22), our starting point is the principle that morphological classes should reflect parts of speech to some degree. For example, we expect a syntactic class of verbs to be associated with an identifiable morphology for verbs, or a syntactic class of nouns to be associated with identifiable morphology for nouns, and so on. In Section 3.1 we saw that the structure created by this principle could be reduced by Node Elimination in (4). As we shall see, reduction by Node Elimination is not possible once we have inflectional class nodes, because the corresponding node for the morphological class (e.g. a MOR_NOUN node for nouns) is required in order to make generalizations over the inflectional classes. The MOR_NOUN node is therefore the inheritance source for multiple (inflectional class) nodes, which means it cannot be subject to Node Elimination.

The existence of arbitrary inflectional classes requires a location for default statements about the morphology of a particular part of speech. So for languages with inflectional classes, or similar structures, knowledge of a language's morphology is made manageable by the existence of partial morphological classes associated with that part of speech. (The classes are partial because they share information with other classes, or because the default knowledge may have gaps in it.) This knowledge may consist of default rules of referral, rules of exponence, or network-directed links to parallel structures for stress or other information.

In order to see how the principle in (22) works with Node Elimination in (4) consider the two parallel hierarchies in Figure 3.5.

In Figure 3.5 the lexemic hierarchy and the morphological hierarchy are isomorphic, with a network relation from each node in the morphological hierarchy to its corresponding node in the lexemic hierarchy. For example, WORD inherits from MOR_WORD, NOMINAL inherits from MOR_NOMINAL, and ADJ inherits from MOR_ADJ. This network is both interesting and problematic. It clearly is in accordance with the Morphological Projection in (22), because there is a corresponding morphological class for each part of speech as represented by a node in the lexemic hierarchy. However, the morphological hierarchy is basically unnecessary, because the generalizations in it can be reproduced by the inheritance structure of the lexemic hierarchy. In this situation the inheritance structure in the lexemic hierarchy would be sufficient to capture generalizations about the morphology.

The situation in (22) can be accounted for in terms of Node Elimination. This is because the nodes MOR_NOUN, MOR_ADJ, MOR_PRONOUN and MOR_VERB are

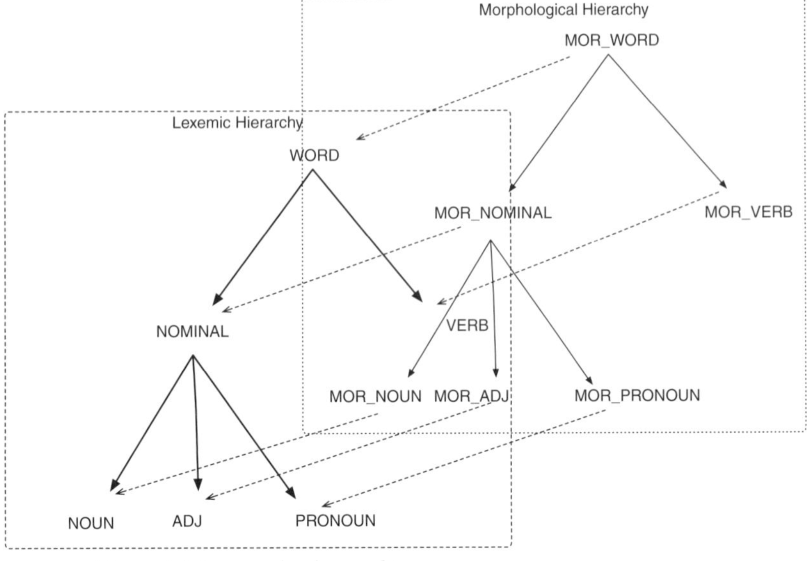

Figure 3.5 *Isomorphic hierarchies*

eliminable under the definitions in (4), as nothing else inherits from them. And if MOR_NOUN, MOR_ADJ and MOR_PRONOUN are eliminated, then MOR_NOMINAL can be eliminated, leaving only MOR_WORD to be eliminated in turn under (4). It is worth dwelling on the consequences of this and comparing it to the situation in Figure 3.2 before we move on. In Figure 3.2 the inflectional class nodes appear to represent discrete entities, but if the separate nouns in Figure 3.2 inherited from MOR_NOUN, then this would stop Node Elimination from applying, because now MOR_NOUN would have the inflectional class nodes inheriting from it. Once inflectional classes exist, they create the possibility of additional morphological structure *above* them, which may also involve the potential for dissociation.

The upshot of our discussion of (22) is that something like inflectional classes *must* exist for there to be morphological systematicity which is independent of the classes established by syntax. The question of whether just anything can happen with inflectional classes, which we raised at the beginning of this chapter, can be tentatively answered in relation to the generally assumed principle in (22): inflectional classes create autonomous morphology, but some classes within the morphological structure will reflect parts of speech in accord with principle (22). However, these classes which reflect parts of speech (classes such as MOR_NOUN in Figure 3.2) have a justified independent existence, because they are required to make generalizations about inflectional classes, and these cannot be achieved readily by using the inheritance structure for lexemes alone. We, therefore, expect there to be morphological defaults which reflect parts of speech established on other grounds.

According to Corbett (2009: 8) Burmeso, a language of the Mamberamo River area of Western New Guinea (Donohue 2001; Ross 2005), comes close to having canonical inflectional classes, where a large number of distinctions are made with a small inventory, and the phonological realizations are completely different across the classes. This idea of canonicity may appear to go against the claim that we expect there to be defaults associated with inflectional classes and that these should mirror (i.e. correspond to) parts of speech. As Corbett (2009: 8) points out, the two classes in (58) share the same syncretisms. Some of these syncretisms may arise from underspecification or partial underspecification, similar to the superclassing effects noted for genders by Evans (1997), but other elements may be the result of referrals of one number and gender combination to another.

(58) *Verbal inflectional classes in Burmeso* (Corbett 2009; Donohue 2001: 100, 102)

		Inflectional class 1		Inflectional class 2	
		e.g. *-ihi-* 'see'		e.g. *-akwa-* 'bite'	
	Assignment	SG	PL	SG	PL
I	Male	*j-*	*s-*	*b-*	*t-*
II	female, animate	*g-*	*s-*	*n-*	*t-*
III	miscellaneous	*g-*	*j-*	*n-*	*b-*
IV	mass nouns	*j-*	*j-*	*b-*	*b-*
V	banana, sago tree	*j-*	*g-*	*b-*	*n-*
VI	arrows, coconuts	*g-*	*g-*	*n-*	*n-*

If it is true that referrals are required, then they must be stated somewhere, and the most plausible place is a node which abstracts over verb morphology (i.e. MOR_VERB). This fits the intuition that the morphology of different classes determines the more abstract shape of the paradigm for the particular part of speech, an intuition which is covered by our heuristic in (24), which entails that referrals are more likely to be defaults than rules of exponence. The intuition behind this is that rules of referral determine the particular shape of paradigms. Indeed, Stump (2005a) makes a contrast between rules of abstraction and rules which deal with rule-block interaction. He classifies referrals as falling under this abstraction type. The notion that the shape of the paradigms is more fundamental fits under Corbett's (2009: 4) criterion, which states that canonical inflectional classes realize the same distinctions. Also, it means that even when we find canonical inflectional classes we expect them to make use of the same default paradigm signatures.

The Burmeso inflectional classes in (58) are highly predictable and, as any given cell of the paradigm can be used to predict the rest of the paradigm, any element can serve as a principal part. The one thing they have in common is the patterning of syncretisms in the paradigm, something which could be expressed by rules of referral. So Burmeso comes close to a patterning where the only defaults are referral-like and the rules of exponence are specific to the inflectional classes. This fits with the intuition about the role of referrals in defining the shape of paradigms and, therefore, being more likely to be defaults. However, we might imagine a situation where the inflectional material is shared by all classes (i.e. it is default material), and the only thing which differs from one class to the next would be the pattern of referral used. In (59) we give a small subset of inflectional classes for nouns in Nuer, a Nilo-Saharan language spoken in Sudan. The patterns in (59) could be interpreted as resulting from such a rule system. That is, the various formal patterns of stem alternation and affixal marking can be used to express different case and number combinations but with no particular formal realization restricted to one case and number combination. It could be argued, therefore, that Nuer comes close to a situation in which the only defining characteristic of an inflectional class is its pattern of (potentially referral-based) syncretism.

(59) Nuer inflectional classes *(Frank 1999: 84–6; Baerman* et al. *2005)*

	'dog'	'egret'	'girl'	'bug'
NOM SG	jiök	bööŋ	nyal	baan
GEN SG	jiö̃k	bööŋkä̃	nyal	baankä
LOC SG	jiö̃ö̃k	bööŋkä̃	nyaal	baan

Nilo-Saharan languages are known for the complexity of their nominal morphology. Ladd, Remijsen and Manyang (2009) report on the nominal system of Dinka, a language related to Nuer. They showed that there is a great deal of variation in the use of different combinations of means for expressing the singular–plural distinction. The number distinction is expressed by a variety of combinations of tone, vowel length, vowel height, vowel breaking, voice quality and consonantal alternation (Ladd *et al.* 2009: 664). In the study by Ladd *et al.*, the ten most frequent combinations among monosyllabic nouns account for 57 per cent of this group, and the ten most frequent combinations among polysyllabic nouns account for 59 per cent of that group. One of the arguments adduced for monotonic inheritance systems – that is, those where inheritance is mandatory (discussed in Chapter 1, Section 1.3.1) – is that, as one progresses from the most frequent items to those which occur rarely, knowledge of the set of classes is complete, and so, given this complete knowledge, there is no need for an override and default mechanism. But a default-based system, such as Network Morphology, is more robust in the face of partial knowledge. Given a new item which looks in some respects like what has gone before but different in other respects, we can allow it to be a fuzzy member of an already established class and override the information to which it does not conform. The system of defaults we propose does not rely on the notion that paradigm cells necessarily predict other cells. Instead, it is the default values, used either as normal cases or exceptional cases, which are reliable.

We considered in Chapter 2, Section 2.3.2.1 Russian Declension I nouns which have their plural nominative in *-a*, such as *tórmoz/tormoz-á* 'brakes'. The *-a* inflection is typically associated with Declension IV. Given this fact, the predictability and predictiveness associated with plural nominative *-a* is less than if we consider the major inflectional patterns for Russian in (25). Plural nominative *-a* would predict a singular nominative in *-o* and a zero realization for the genitive plural, and in turn these would predict plural nominative *-a* (i.e. what one would expect for Declension IV). But this cannot be maintained given the existence of nouns such as *tórmoz/tormoz-á* 'brakes'. And, of course, there are examples where Declension IV nouns have plural nominative inflection in *-i* (*jabloko* 'apple') and genitive plural in *-ov* (*oblako* 'cloud'). Under the approach we take, items such as these are taken as fuzzy or aberrant members of the larger inflectional class. This itself is a point of contrast with other approaches which also treat inflectional classes in terms of hierarchies, but where microclasses have to be established for the smallest subset of lexemes (such as in the Natural Morphology treatment of inflectional classes in Dressler, Kilani-Schoch, Gagarina, Pestal and Pöchtrager 2006). Some items are allowed to be poorly behaved members of their inflectional class. While new lexemes items may come along and be slightly different, potentially overriding information, defaults constitute reliability in the system.

3.3 Conclusion

We started out this chapter by considering the redundancy in inflectional classes and the limits on variation. In contrast, many systems have little autonomous morphological structure. We have shown how we can progress from phenomena such as clitics (as default affixes) to inflectional classes which represent the opposite end of the scale in terms of morphological autonomy. Where there are inflectional classes, we argue that trying to constrain the possibilities in terms of natural classes for morphosyntax will not succeed. Instead, we should consider degrees of autonomy and degrees of default-hood. Inflectional classes represent structure which is redundant from the perspective of syntax. In the extreme, morphology could create word-forms which cross-cut standard morphosyntax entirely. However, even where there is autonomy we can predict the following: (i) that there will be defaults for inflectional classes (generalizations which hold across classes); (ii) that partial generalizations which constitute defaults for inflectional classes will correspond to distributionally recognizable parts of speech.

4 *Syncretism*

4.0 Introduction

In the previous chapter we have shown how, in some languages, morphology may provide an autonomous structure due to the existence of inflectional classes, where the correspondence with parts of speech is many-to-one, thereby making more distinctions than are required by the syntax. In this chapter we consider a different kind of motivation for autonomy, where some parts of the morphology fail to make a distinction required by syntax. This failure to make a syntactically relevant distinction is syncretism, where a single form has more than one grammatical function (Spencer 1991: 45; Trask 1997: 215). Baerman *et al.* (2005: 2) provide the following key properties:

(1)
- a. a morphological distinction which is syntactically relevant (i.e. it is an inflectional distinction)
- b. a failure to make this distinction under particular (morphological) conditions
- c. a resulting dissociation between syntax and morphology[1]

In the previous chapter, we saw how the sharing of exponents across inflectional classes could be treated as a default inheritance hierarchy. Inflectional class nodes are locations for sets of realization rules which capture the horizontal paradigm relations, described in Chapter 1, Section 1.0.1, within such an autonomous hierarchy. Syncretism, on the other hand, is different from this in that it involves a failure to distinguish morphosyntactic features (i.e. features which have syntactic relevance).[2] This means that it affects vertical paradigm relations, as explained in Chapter 1, Section 1.3. So the challenge here is to determine the degree to which autonomous morphology lines up with relevant distinctions.

Syncretism may be the result of a number of different diachronic processes. As such it can have radically different effects on the shape of morphological paradigms and may also obscure the underlying paradigmatic design. In this chapter we show in Section 4.2 that some syncretisms can be accounted for using default inference (based on underspecification), where the form of a particular morphosyntactic combination is provided by default using path extension, which was introduced in Chapter 2, Section 2.3.1. We also show that there are examples of syncretism where default inference alone is not sufficient to account for the data (Section 4.3) and argue that referrals are required (Zwicky 1985b; Stump 2001: 212–41), where one part of the paradigm refers to another for the appropriate form or forms. We then demonstrate that both default inference using path extension and referrals are required to account for other instances of syncretism, such as the avoidance morphology of the Dalabon verbal paradigm, thereby confirming the need for both representational means (Section 4.4). We also show that the shape of the paths assumed for default inference provides the underlying basic structure of paradigms which are cross-linguistically more prevalent, while referrals allow us to state more language-specific properties, without obscuring the more general tendencies. Similarly, a combination of both stem indices and default inference is required for the Dhaasanac verb paradigms presented in Section 4.5.

4.1 Definitions

Syncretism is defined language-internally in terms of a subset of lexemes belonging to a particular part of speech having a form corresponding to more than one morphosyntactic feature value. An effective and rigorous way of defining the values of a feature is to follow the method of the Set Theoretic School (described in van Helden 1993 and Meyer 1994). Zaliznjak (1973, 2002) provides a rigorous definition of case within this tradition. Comrie (1991) employs a similar method in defining distributional case that can be generalized to other features.

> For each nominal in the language, establish the distinct forms that this nominal can show [i.e. its array of formal cases]. Now compare the distributions of all nominals. If some distribution is of a distinct form for all nominals, then this is a [distributional] case. If the distribution (a) of some form of some nominal is a proper subset of the distribution (a+b) of some form of any nominal, then the distribution or subdistribution defined by a and b are distinct [distributional] cases for all nominals. If the distribution (c+d) of some form of some nominal mutually and nonexhaustively overlaps the distribution of (d+e) of some form of any other nominal, then each of c,d, and e is a distinct [distributional] case for all nominals.
> (Comrie 1991: 46)

The notion of distributional case allows us to determine the set of values required for the case feature in a given language. (We can develop similar distributional versions for the other features.) Formal cases are the actual forms for a particular set of lexemes, and these may be fewer than the number of distributional values determined for the language. Returning to the Russian nominal paradigm in (2), which we have seen in Chapter 1, Section 1.0.1, Chapter 2, Section 2.2.6 and Chapter 3, Section 3.1.2, we illustrate the distinction between formal and distributional case.

(2) *Distributional and formal cases in Russian*

	I	II	III	IV
Singular				
NOMINATIVE	zakon	kart-a	rukop´is´	bolot-o
ACCUSATIVE	zakon	kart-u	rukop´is´	bolot-o
GENITIVE	zakon-a	kart-i	rukop´is´-i	bolot-a
DATIVE	zakon-u	kart-e	rukop´is´-i	bolot-u
INSTRUMENTAL	zakon-om	kart-oj	rukop´is´-ju	bolot-om
PREPOSITIONAL	zakon-e	kart-e	rukop´is´-i	bolot-e
Plural				
NOMINATIVE	zakon-i	kart-i	rukop´is´-i	bolot-a
ACCUSATIVE	zakon-i	kart-i	rukop´is´-i	bolot-a
GENITIVE	zakon-ov	kart	rukop´is´-ej	bolot
DATIVE	zakon-am	kart-am	rukop´is´-am	bolot-am
INSTRUMENTAL	zakon-am´i	kart-am´i	rukop´is´-am´i	bolot-am´i
PREPOSITIONAL	zakon-ax	kart-ax	rukop´is´-ax	bolot-ax

To illustrate, let us consider the prepositional case (also known as the locative).[3] The syntactic distribution (prepositional singular) of the forms *zakone* and *bolote*, belonging to the nouns *zakon* 'law' and *boloto* 'marsh' respectively, is a proper subset of the syntactic distribution (prepositional singular and dative singular) of the form *karte* of the nominal *karta* 'map'. In other words, if we take the syntactic constructions in which *zakone* and *bolote* can be used, we will find that these are a proper subset of the constructions in which *karte* can be used. Hence, there are distinct distributional cases prepositional and dative in the singular for Russian.

As has been discussed, syncretism involves a dissociation between syntactic distribution and form, where a particular form corresponds to the sum of distributions of other forms. In (2), for example, there is prepositional singular and dative singular syncretism in Declension II, and syncretism of prepositional, dative and genitive in the singular of Declension III.[4] Because the singular dative and singular prepositional syncretism occurs in two different classes with two different realizations we can also conclude that it is systematic.

Looking at (2) we might be led to the conclusion that there is no separate distributional case nominative or accusative in the plural, because there appears to be no separate nominal with a form whose distribution is a proper subset of the distribution of any of the other nominals. In the singular, of course, there is a distinct form for nouns of the *karta* type, which is sufficient to establish the accusative as a distributional case. In the plural the accusative case can be established on the basis of overlap in forms, as demonstrated in (3). Although there is no unique form, the genitive–accusative form of animates overlaps with the nominative–accusative form of inanimates, as illustrated in (3). (It is also worth noting the clear role of morphology in the animacy-based syncretism in (3), as only the singular forms in Declension I are subject to the animacy rule, which one would expect to apply across all classes, if it were purely semantic.)

(3) *Accusative in Russian (animate nouns)*

	Declension I	Declension II	Declension III	Declension IV
	student 'student'	žona 'wife'	miš 'mouse'	čudov'išč-o 'monster'
Singular				
NOM	student	žon-a	miš	čudov'išč-o
ACC	student-a	žon-u	miš	čudov'išč-o
GEN	student-a	žon -i	miš-i	čudov'išč-a
Plural				
NOM	student-i	žon-i	miš-i	čudov'išč-a
ACC	student-ov	žon	miš-ej	čudov'išč
GEN	student-ov	žon	miš-ej	čudov'išč

This method can be used to identify values for other morphosyntactic features, such as those for person, number, gender, tense and so on, and consequently also dissociations between their formal realization and syntactic distribution. We find, for instance, that the form *bid* of the English verb *to bid* can be used for past or present, whereas most other verbs have different forms for past and present. Therefore, other verbs can be found which have forms which are a proper subset of the distribution of the form *bid*. We can thus talk of distributional tense as opposed to formal tense, for example.

As Baerman *et al.* (2005: 27–36) explain, there are a number of related phenomena which come within the purview of syncretism: uninflectedness, neutralization and canonical syncretism. As we shall see in Section 4.2, neutralization gives us an insight into how to treat syncretism in a formal model.

It is the limiting case of syncretism and can be treated straightforwardly using default inference. We now use this to distinguish between neutralization, uninflectedness and syncretism. Where we talk of loss of values of a particular feature, or lack of distinctions, in (4i), (5i) and (6i), the values referred to have been established on distributional grounds in a way similar to the method used for case by Comrie (1991), and in line with the set-theoretic tradition.

(4) *Neutralization*

i. In the presence of a particular combination of values of one or more other features (the context), there is a general loss of all values of a particular feature F found elsewhere in the language.

ii. No syntactic objects distinguish any values of feature F in the given context, and feature F is therefore syntactically irrelevant in that context.

(Baerman *et al.* 2005: 30)

An example of neutralization, as defined in (4), is gender agreement in the plural in Russian. While there are three main gender contrasts in the singular, no agreement target in Russian distinguishes gender in the plural. In other words, all gender distinctions are eliminated in the plural. As the definition indicates, the lack of any distinction is merely a reflex of the feature's syntactic irrelevance in that context. Neutralization is a morphological phenomenon which closely reflects syntactic requirements and, therefore, does not necessarily involve a high degree of morphological autonomy. It does, however, suggest how to deal with straightforward syncretism in terms of default inference. A related phenomenon, which can also suggest a straightforward way of dealing with syncretism, is uninflectedness.

(5) *Uninflectedness*

i. There is, in certain lexemes only, a loss of all values of a particular feature F found elsewhere in the language. This loss may depend on the presence of a particular combination of values of one or more other features (the context).

ii. Other syntactic objects distinguish values of feature F, either generally or in the given context, and feature F is therefore syntactically relevant.

(Baerman *et al.* 2005: 33)

Uninflectedness, as defined in (5), can also be treated in terms of feature structure and default inference but represents a greater degree of morphological autonomy, as the morphology is inert in the presence of feature values which are relevant for syntax. We discuss neutralization and uninflectedness in relation to syncretism in the next section. We now turn to canonical syncretism in (6), which is more challenging to deal with, because certain parts of the morphology are still sensitive to the syntactic distinctions, while others are not.

(6) *Canonical syncretism*

i. There is, in certain contexts, a loss of distinctions between some but not all values of a particular feature F. This loss may depend on the presence of a particular combination of values of one or more other features (the context).
ii. Other syntactic objects distinguish those values of feature F, and they are therefore syntactically relevant.

(Baerman *et al.* 2005: 34)

In (2) we can see, for example, that for Declensions II and III there is syncretism between the dative and prepositional cases. This is not neutralization, because there is not a total loss of the distinction of cases in the presence of the feature value singular. Because they align naturally with the structure of morphosyntactic features, neutralization and uninflectedness suggest a treatment for straightforward instances of syncretism in terms of default inference, as discussed in Chapter 2, Section 2.3.1, and we now turn to this.

4.2 Syncretism by default inference

We saw the main Russian adjectival declension in Chapter 3, Section 3.1.2, as represented by the paradigm of *novij* 'new', repeated in (7).

(7) *Paradigm of the Russian long-form adjective*

	Masculine	Neuter	Feminine
Singular			
NOM	nov-ij	nov-oje	nov-aj-a
ACC	INAN = SG NOM	nov-oje	nov-uj-u
	AN = SG GEN		
GEN	nov-ovo		nov-oj
DAT	nov-omu		nov-oj
INS	nov-im		nov-oj(u)
PREP	nov-om		nov-oj
Plural			
NOM	nov-i-je		
ACC	AN = PL GEN/INAN = PL NOM		
GEN	nov-i-x		
DAT	nov-i-m		
INS	nov-i-m´i		
PREP	nov-i-x		

In the plural there are no gender distinctions. And, as this is generally true of targets for gender agreement in Russian, this is therefore an example of neutralization, as defined in (4). We also see that there is no differentiation of neuter and masculine genders in the genitive, dative, prepositional and instrumental cases in the singular. However, this is an instance of syncretism, as defined in (6), because there is still a contrast with the feminine gender, and so gender distinctions have not been lost completely.

In Chapter 2, Section 2.3.1 we explained default inference and path extension, where the most specific path wins when realizing morphosyntactic features. The fact that gender is neutralized in the plural and that it is syncretized in particular cases in the singular speaks for an analysis of gender syncretism in Russian in terms of path extension, because the syncretism can be treated in terms of gender underspecification. In other words, we specify the number and case attributes in the path but do not specify the gender, in accord with the attribute ordering of gender after case and number from Chapter 2, Section 2.2.3. The paths which contain only the number and case attributes in the analysis will be the most specific matching subpaths from which the forms in the full morphological model are inferred. The default singular adjectival paradigm in (8) is located at the node `MOR_ADJ` which we saw in the morphological hierarchy in Chapter 3, Figure 3.4. The adjective declensional classes inherit from this.[5]

(8)
```
MOR_ADJ:
  <> == MOR_NOMINAL
  <mor sg gen> == "<stem>" "<mor vowel sg>"
                  "<stress sg>" ^ vo "<stress pronoun>"
  <mor sg gen fem> == "<mor sg prep fem>"
  <mor sg dat> == "<stem>" "<mor vowel sg>"
                  "<stress sg>" ^ mu "<stress pronoun>"
  <mor sg dat fem> == MOR_NOUN
  <mor sg inst> == "<stem>" ^ i "<stress sg>" ^ m
  <mor sg inst fem> == N_II
  <mor sg prep> == "<stem>" "<mor vowel sg prep>"
                   "<stress sg>" ^ m
  <mor sg prep fem> == "<stem>" "<mor vowel sg>"
                       "<stress sg>" ^ j
  ...
```

As we saw in Chapter 3, Section 3.1.2, the adjectival node `MOR_ADJ` in (8) inherits from the more general node `MOR_NOMINAL` information about plural forms of adjectives. The adjective *novij* 'new' is specified as belonging to class `A_I` (not given here). This class specifies the singular nominative forms and associated stress. It inherits from the `MOR_ADJ` node in (8). In order to determine the form of the singular genitive neuter of the adjective *novij* 'new' we look for the appropriate path at the node `A_I`. The most specific matching path there is the hierarchy relation (i.e. empty path) with the node `MOR_ADJ`. At `MOR_ADJ` there is no exact match for `<mor sg gen neut>`, but the most specific matching path will win. This is `<mor sg gen>`, the second equation given in (8), so the form of the singular genitive neuter of *novij* is the concatenation of the stem *nov* with the vowel *o* and the formative *-vo*. (The vowel may also be associated with a value for singular stress, but this is undefined for *novij*, as it is stem-stressed.) The forms of the singular dative, instrumental and prepositional neuter will be generated in similar fashion. Because `<mor sg gen masc>` is also an extension of `<mor sg gen>`, the masculine form is also determined in the same way, and is therefore syncretic with the neuter. The masculine forms for the singular dative, instrumental and prepositional are treated similarly.

The beauty of this approach is that we treat the syncretism as reflecting the design of the paradigm, whereby gender is always an extension of paths beginning with number and case attributes. We also have reasons for ordering the case attribute after the number attribute. As we saw with the second locative in Chapter 2, Section 2.2.3, Russian nouns actually make a greater number of case distinctions in the singular than in the plural. This is summarized in (9) where with the prepositions *v* 'in' and *na* 'on' a small number of nouns take a second locative form in the singular, even though all nouns are alike in taking the prepositional case in the plural.

(9) *Distribution of the second locative in Contemporary Standard Russian*

	Singular most nouns	 a few nouns	Plural all nouns
pri, o	Prepositional	Prepositional	Prepositional
v, na	Prepositional	Locative 2	Prepositional

This is an example of overdifferentiation, as a small number of lexemes use a new form associated with a specific syntactic distribution, and they therefore distinguish a morphosyntactic value which is not expressed by the majority of items. The verb *be* in English is another example, as it is the only verb to have a distinct form for the first-person singular. As overdifferentiation is associated with a new syntactic distribution, it naturally follows that it should be most readily treatable in terms of morphosyntactic feature structure, as the distinction is relevant to syntax. It is linked to uninflectedness, as defined in (5), but in contrast with many instances of uninflectedness, which we might expect to affect a minority of lexemes, the majority of lexemes are inert in the presence of the second locative distinction.

The second locative is not the only case distinction which is limited to one number. In addition to the second locative, there is also a second genitive for a small number of nouns in the singular, as in (10). This has a partitive function (Švedova *et al.* 1980: Section 1179).

(10) ja xoč-u čaj-u
I want-1.SG tea-SG.GEN2
'I want some tea.'

Overdifferentiation in the singular follows from treating case as extending paths containing number.[6]

We observe in the adjectival paradigm in (8) that the (target) gender distinction between masculine and neuter is lost in the oblique cases. This suggests that gender attributes extend paths consisting of number and case attributes, and that case attributes extend paths consisting of number attributes, as we have argued in Chapter 2, Section 2.2.3. This also lines up with the existence of overdifferentiation splits across number values, as illustrated by the additional case distinctions. Gender neutralization in the plural, as illustrated in (7), is similar in that this is limited to one number value.

This chapter is about syncretism, but the treatment of the paradigm in terms of path extension is justified for other reasons as well, as this is manifested in a variety of different ways, including neutralization, uninflectedness and syncretism. It naturally extends to deponency, as we show in Chapter 5. Linguists have discussed different kinds of relationships between features. Noyer (1997) treats gender as a feature which is lower than number in terms of a universal hierarchy. Hjelmslev (1943: 79; 1961: 88–9), for example, uses the term 'dominance' and illustrates with an example from Latin, claiming that the neuter 'dominates' the 'overlapping', or syncretism, of the nominative and accusative. Nouns which are neuter in gender have nominative–accusative syncretism where nouns belonging to the same declension, but a different gender, may not. In (11) the Declension II noun *servus*, which is masculine, differs from *bellum*, which is neuter.

(11) *Latin Declension II*

	bellum 'war' (neuter)	*servus* 'slave' (masc.)
NOM SG	bell-um	serv-us
ACC SG	bell-um	serv-um
GEN SG	bell-ī	serv-ī
DAT SG	bell-ō	serv-ō
ABL SG	bell-ō	serv-ō

The generalization underlying the pattern in (11) is that neuter nouns will have nominative–accusative syncretism (and potentially other differences in exponence) no matter which declension they belong to. Elsewhere, of course, we find gender syncretism in Latin. These apparent counterexamples are to be accounted for as referrals and involve an asymmetry so that, for example, the exponent *-um* is associated primarily with the accusative singular (Baerman *et al.* 2005: 140).

The idea of feature dependencies can be found in Carstairs (1984) who talks of 'triggering feature' and changes this to 'contextual property' in later work (Carstairs-McCarthy 1992). Aikhenvald and Dixon (1998) also use examples of syncretism as illustrations of dependencies between grammatical features. As we have argued, the ordering of features is not about the order of affixes per se. In principle, it would be possible for a case affix to occur inside a number affix, even if this is less common (Greenberg 1963: 95, Universal 39). Within an inferential–realizational approach, the important question is where in the paradigm morphology realizes particular distinctions and where these distinctions are lost. Given the separation between morphosyntactic features and form in Network Morphology, in virtue of its being an inferential–realizational framework, the order of attributes is about the contrasts made by paradigms, which is itself an orthogonal issue to the order of affixes. There is, therefore, a substantive difference from approaches to morphology which propose hierarchies of functional categories (see, for example, Wunderlich and Fabri 1995: 246–7), where claims about the order of exponents are made. Because of its separation of morphosyntax from exponence, Network Morphology avoids the problems associated with the assumptions of a one-to-one relationship between morphological and syntactic representation, which we discussed in Chapter 1, Sections 1.2.2 and 1.2.3.

Neutralization can also be relevant for the sharing of morphology at a level of generalization above the recognizable morphological classes associated with parts of speech, but this will depend on whether the language makes a morphological distinction between those parts of speech in the first place. As we saw in Chapter 3, Section 3.2, the existence of inflectional classes in Russian facilitates the maintenance of higher default nodes in the morphological hierarchy as locations for default generalizations. However, languages with autonomous morphology will differ in terms of the higher-level nodes they require to store default information in the morphological hierarchy. For instance, in many languages, even those with autonomous morphology, it may be difficult to isolate a morphologically separate class of adjectives. In Latin, for example, the adjectives can be analysed as reusing the noun inflections. In contrast, Russian has a clearly identifiable morphology for adjectives, which we saw in Chapter 3, Section 3.1.2 and in (7). While Russian has some morphology that is unique to adjectives, it also has a recognizable nominal morphology in that certain realizations are shared by nouns, adjectives and pronouns. Neutralization may play a role in determining which parts of the morphology are likely to be shared. In a language such as Russian, where adjectives and pronouns are targets for gender agreement, systematic sharing of morphology with nouns (which are not targets for gender agreement) is most likely to occur when gender is neutralized. Russian gender is neutralized throughout the plural in adjectives and the third-person pronouns. So, for example, the oblique case endings of nominals *-i*, *-m*, *-m´i*, *-x* do not distinguish gender. Given the ordering of attributes in paths within the morphological component and the Overextended Ancestor Prohibition discussed in Chapter 2, Section 2.3.1, it follows that, for languages like Russian, loss of gender distinction in the plural brings with it a greater likelihood for sharing plural morphology between nouns and adjectives (Brown 1998b: 196).

We have discussed phenomena that can be accounted for in terms of path extension in order to demonstrate that this does not just provide a neat account for the straightforward types of syncretism. Another important indication of the ordering relation between number and case in Russian can be found in *singularia tantum* and *pluralia tantum* nouns. We can typically talk of *singularia tantum* and *pluralia tantum* nouns, for example, where the split reflects the structure of the paradigm imposed by the shape of the path for morphology. In languages such as Russian, there are examples in which a particular case may be problematic, but this is limited to a certain number. For example, the Russian noun lexeme *mečta* 'dream' has a defective genitive plural according to Zaliznjak (1977: 213), and the sixteenth edition of Ožegov's dictionary (Švedova 1984) states that *mečtan´ij* is used in its place for this part of the paradigm. Baerman and Corbett (2010: 1) provide corpus figures which reflect these claims. The point to note is that the singular genitive, along with the other parts of the paradigm, presents no problem. There is evidence that defectiveness can follow morphomic patterns, where the gaps are not distributed in accord with a morphosyntactic natural class. The verbal systems of Romance languages contain examples of this phenomenon, as discussed in Maiden and O'Neill (2010) and Boyé and Cabredo Hofherr (2010). In other instances the defective gaps can be defined in terms of the feature structure. So where a language has case and number morphology on its nouns, we expect the gaps to occur either in one case and number cell or throughout a particular number.[7]

So far we have seen examples of a number of phenomena which can be explained in terms of path extension, including neutralization. Unlike defectiveness, as discussed above, neutralization reflects syntactic requirements quite directly. Another phenomenon that can be accounted for in terms of the treatment of feature structure as path extension is uninflectedness, which we defined in (5). This is where the morphology is inert in the presence of syntactically relevant distinctions. An example is the Russian noun *pal′to* 'coat', which does not inflect at all, but which can in principle be used in any syntactic context. A more complex example of the same phenomenon comes from the related West Slavonic language Polish, where certain nouns inflect in the plural, but not the singular, such as *muzeum* 'museum' (Kotyczka 1980: 95, 105–6; Tokarski 1993: 257). The noun *muzeum* can be used in the singular in all cases, but its form does not change. In contrast, its form changes in the plural according to case. These nouns are in a sense partially inflectable, but they also show that there is a stage between total uninflectedness and being fully inflecting. And this stage is defined in terms of number first (rather than case), in line with the attribute ordering for which we have argued.

The phenomena we have considered are logically independent of syncretism, yet path extension links syncretism of the type we have seen in Russian adjectives in (7) with facts about *pluralia tantum* nouns, additional case distinctions, full and partial uninflectedness and neutralization. Hence, it appears to reflect some underlying design feature of languages like Russian. However, the fact that a paradigm may contain within it evidence both for and against a particular feature ordering clearly indicates that an approach based on feature ordering alone, or feature geometry, will be insufficient to account for all patterns of syncretism.

As Network Morphology associates the attributes in a path with particular features (case, number, etc.), rather than feature values (nominative, accusative, or singular, plural, etc.), the ordering of features differs from feature geometries, where the values are broken down further. This affects the nature of the claims arising from feature ordering because no expectation of a particular feature value being adopted in the presence of another one is imposed. For instance, the claim that gender syncretism occurs within a certain number does not entail that a particular value of that number is involved. Nor does it stipulate which values of gender should be syncretized. The ordering constraints represent tendencies associated with the particular features, and they can be obscured or overridden by language-specific systematicities.

Some counterexamples to feature ordering may have straightforward explanations, however. Consider the relation between gender and number in the Dravidian languages Kannada (Sridhar 1990: 244) and Tamil (Asher 1985:

144, 173). In the future tense of Tamil verbs, no distinction is made between singular and plural non-rational (Asher 1985: 173–4), thereby indicating that a number distinction may be lost in a particular gender. (Note that there is the feature of tense to be taken into account here as well.) In certain varieties of Tamil, singular and plural may not be distinguished in the third-person neuter of the pronoun (Asher 1985: 144). In Kannada, verbs are less likely to mark the plural of third-person neuter subjects (Sridhar 1990: 244), and in the varieties of Tamil which have no number distinction for the third-person neuter pronoun there will be no number distinction for third-person neuter on the verb (Asher 1985: 173). Both Kannada and Tamil have a strictly semantic gender assignment system (Asher 1985: 136–7; Sridhar 1990: 198; Corbett 1991: 8–11), and because of this, grammatical gender and the semantics of the noun (in this case animacy) line up very closely. However, the optionality of number marking for the nouns in question is a function of their position below the rationals on the animacy hierarchy (Smith-Stark 1974), rather than this being attributable to the relation between gender and number in morphosyntax.

If we consider the paradigms in (12) for the Indo-European language Kashmiri, we see that there are examples where the absolutive singular and absolutive plural of the noun *beni* 'sister' have the same form. Hence, this is an example where number syncretism occurs within absolutive case. This is not an instance of neutralization under the definition we have given in (4), because, although the failure to distinguish singular and plural involves total loss of number distinction, the loss of number distinction does not always occur in the presence of the absolutive case. This is demonstrated by the forms of the noun *gur* 'mare', where the absolutive singular is distinct from the absolutive plural.

(12) *Syncretism in Kashmiri Declension III* (Baerman 2002)

	Default type 'mare'		Stems in *-i* 'sister'	
	SG	PL	SG	PL
ABS	gur	guri	beni	
DAT	= pl abs	gur'an		ben'an
ABL		gur'av		ben'av
ERG				

The Kashmiri example of absolutive singular and absolutive plural syncretism, therefore, runs against our ordering of case after number in the paradigm. We could represent the syncretism of *beni* 'sister' as in (13).

(13)
```
BENI_TYPE:
  <mor abs> == "<stem>" _i
```

However, this would fail to capture the identity throughout the singular and violates the feature ordering we have suggested. Of course, problems of this type are legion. Closer examination of our earlier Russian adjective example in (7) – where neuter and masculine are syncretized in the oblique cases in the singular, but case syncretism occurs in the feminine gender – and the Kashmiri example in (12) reveals what we can term a feature interaction paradox:

(14) *Feature Interaction Paradox*
Feature values of feature A may be syncretized in the presence of a feature value of feature B in one part of the same paradigm, and feature values of feature B may be syncretized in the presence of a feature value of feature A in another part of that paradigm.

So in (7) we see that masculine and neuter (feature A) are syncretized in the presence of the oblique cases (feature B), whereas the genitive, dative and prepositional cases (feature B) are syncretized in the presence of the feminine gender (feature A). In the Kashmiri example in (12), the dative, ablative and ergative (feature A) are syncretized in the presence of singular number (feature B), whereas number (feature B) is syncretized in the presence of the absolutive case (feature A) in the set of nouns like *beni* 'sister'. Corbett (2000: 271–80) gives examples of reciprocal relationships of this kind in his discussion of the interaction of other features with number.

The existence of such reciprocal interaction between features might falsely lead one to believe that we should not try to establish any cross-linguistically valid claims in relation to the structure of morphological syncretism. A number of things speak against this. As we have seen with Russian, the masculine and neuter syncretism fits with the paradigmatic design we would expect from consideration of gender neutralization (where number, namely plural, conditions total loss of gender). If one moves to look at a wider picture, an interesting pattern emerges. Work using a detailed relational database (Baerman, Brown and Corbett 2002) to capture all instances of syncretism in thirty diverse languages (see Brown (2001) or Brown, Tiberius, Chumakina, Corbett and Krasovitsky (2009) for a description of the database) allows us to examine the relationship between features by counting the instances where number was a context for syncretism, for example, or where case was. For the Kashmiri example in (12), we can say that for the noun *beni* 'sister' a value of case (absolutive) serves as a context for number syncretism, and this could be summarized as in (15).

(15) *Feature interaction (number and case)*

Number	*Case*
Syncretic	Context

In contrast, feature ordering would lead us to expect the relationship in (16).

(16) *Feature interaction (number and case)*

Number	*Case*
Context	Syncretic

The Arabic sound plural (17), where genitive and accusative plural are syncretized, fits this pattern.

(17) *Arabic sound plural* (Fischer 1997: 194–6;[8] Baerman 2002)

	'animal' DEF	INDF
PL NOM	hayawa:n-at-u	hayawa:n-a:t-u-n
PL GEN PL ACC	hayawa:n-at-i	hayawa:n-a:t-i-n

We can visualize the syncretisms as a web of lines expressing the binary pairs such as in (15) and (16). We count the number of times each of these pairs occurs in the database and rate this using a threshold. A link is strong if it occurs more than thirty-five times, medium if it occurs fifteen times, and weak if it occurs fewer than fifteen times. (Even though there are only thirty languages in the database, it is possible for a pair such as (16) to occur more than thirty-five times, because it can occur in different domains within the same language.) The links between the context and syncretized values of nominals (noun, pronoun, adjective) are given in Figure 4.1. The three strengths of link in Figure 4.1 are as follows: strong (thick line), medium (thinner line) and weak (dotted line). There may also be multiple connections where context is involved more than once, or where syncretic values are connected more than once. For example, dative plural of gender III has the same form as the dative singular of gender III in the Nakh-Daghestanian language Tsakhur, so both gender and case will be counted as a pair of contexts (where number happens to be syncretized). This is why there are connections between context gender and context case, for example.

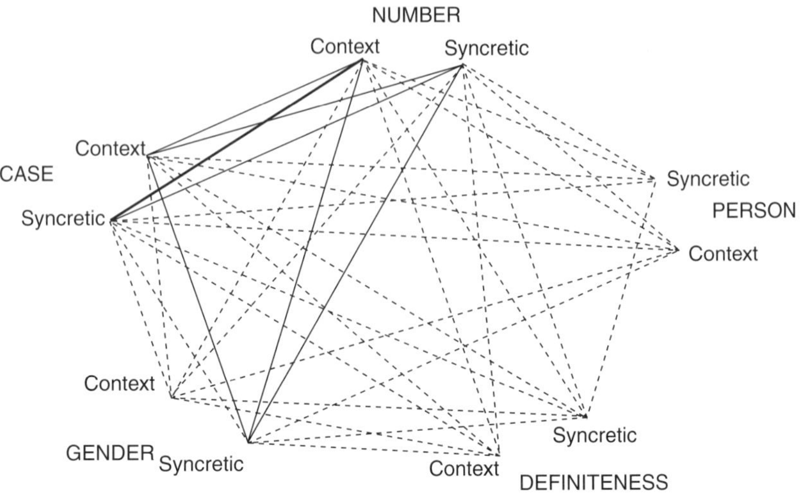

Figure 4.1 *Web of nominal categories and syncretism from a thirty-language sample*

There is only one strong link, and that is between number as a context for syncretism and case as the feature which is syncretized. The opposite does occur with reasonable frequency, with case as the context for number syncretism, but this is only a medium-strength link. Gender is an inflectional feature for adjectives and some pronouns (and may also be for nouns when possession is marked) and typically occurs less often than case and number. For this reason gender does not have any strong links. But its strongest links (the medium ones) always involve it as the syncretized feature.

In sum, the web of nominal categories shows that: (a) number occurs as a context for syncretism more than a syncretized feature; (b) case occurs as a syncretized feature more often that it does as a context for syncretism; (c) but when case co-occurs with gender, case is more likely to be a context, and gender syncretized; (d) gender is typically syncretized. So while the paradox in (14) is a very real one, there is some evidence that the structuring we assume from the attribute-ordering constraints in Chapter 2, Section 2.2.3 appears to reflect a more general tendency. Furthermore, there are two more generalizations about case and gender from the thirty-language study which give additional support to this structuring: if case is a context for some other syncretism in Language A, then case must be syncretized somewhere in Language A; if gender is a context for some other syncretism in Language A, then gender must be syncretized somewhere in Language A. Both of these generalizations are true of all languages in the database which have case (eighteen) or gender (twelve for nominals, thirteen including verbs). This suggests that the best approach to the paradox in (14) is to maintain the underlying paradigm design suggested by the structuring in Chapter 2, Section 2.2.3 and to use an additional representational mechanism for the less common syncretisms which go against the tendency suggested by Figure 4.1. Further justification for this comes from the fact that we actually require the additional mechanisms *simultaneously* with the other representational means (referrals or stem indexing). This indicates that these additional mechanisms are a necessity in some languages.

We have already demonstrated that we require some way of accounting for two apparently different types of syncretism: one which reflects a general tendency across languages in terms of feature structure (*syncretism by default inference*), and another which is able to analyse properties which are specific to a particular language or language group (*syncretism by autonomy*). Syncretism by autonomy can further be divided into *syncretism by referral* and *syncretism by indexing*. In the next section (Section 4.3), we introduce referrals and present language-specific analytical justifications for doing so, which adds further weight to the general evidence we have given here. In Section 4.4 we demonstrate that introducing referrals is justified by showing that we may require referrals and default inference *simultaneously* to model syncretism in one language. We present a similar justification for syncretism by indexing.

4.3 Syncretism by referral

Referrals are rules which refer one set of cells of the paradigm to another set of cells of that paradigm in order to obtain the correct forms. This means that a particular syncretic form can be interpreted as having a primary morphosyntactic meaning associated with it (the primary meaning being the cell referred to). In this section we show that referrals are appropriate to capture certain syncretisms which cannot be treated by path extension as described in Chapter 2, Section 2.2.3.

Corbett and Fraser (1997) discuss how different kinds of syncretism are best represented. On the basis of data from Slovene, they argue that the asymmetrical relation that referrals represent is indeed to be found in linguistic systems. In (18) we see that the dual genitive is the same as the plural genitive, as is generally the case with Slovene nouns.[9]

(18) *Paradigm of the Slovene noun* člověk *'person'* (based on Priestly 1993: 401)

	Singular	Dual	Plural
NOM	človek	človeka	ljudje
ACC	človeka	človeka	ljudi
GEN	človeka	**ljudi**	**ljudi**
DAT	človeku	človekoma	ljudem
INST	človekom	človekoma	ljudmi
LOC	človeku	**ljudeh**	**ljudeh**

As Corbett and Fraser (1997: 136–7) point out, this shows that syncretism can be asymmetric, as the suppletive plural stem is taken up by the dual paradigm. We cannot argue that the syncretism is the product of underspecifying the number and case affix alone, as we still need to ensure that it attaches to the correct stem. Grouping the plural and dual together as taking a plural stem is insufficient, as the other forms in the dual paradigm use the stem which appears in the singular. Hence, the most natural way to account for the syncretisms in the genitive and locative dual is to treat them as whole-word referrals, whereby the genitive dual refers to the genitive plural, and the locative dual refers to the locative plural.

We can refine our analysis further. If we combine the orderings of case after number from Chapter 2, Section 2.2.3 with a referral analysis, a requirement of our theory, then we can reduce the formal representation of the syncretism to one simple referral, which is *simultaneously combined* with default extension (underspecification). This will be as in (19).

(19)
```
<mor du> == "<mor pl>"
```

The beauty of (19) is that it is a succinct statement that dual morphology will default to plural in the absence of any specific statements about case. Any extension of the plural will be an extension of the dual, unless the realization of a particular case in the dual is explicitly stated. We must explicitly state the realizations of the dual nominative, dual accusative, dual dative and dual instrumental.[10] However, the forms of the genitive and locative need not be explicitly stated, as these will be taken over from the plural paradigm. Note that this would not be possible, if we assumed the opposite ordering of case and number.

The Slovene example shows us that syncretism can involve subtle interaction of both referrals and underspecification. We may also consider this in relation to Noyer's (1998) notion of *impoverishment* within Distributed

Morphology, where a feature is deleted in a particular context. A rule of referral in Network Morphology relies on interaction with default inference, so that in (19) we do not need to specify genitive or locative, as these will be inferred as extensions of both dual and plural in the absence of any information to the contrary. In an impoverishment-based analysis, on the other hand, the feature value dual would be deleted and replaced with the feature value plural in the context of genitive or locative, which must be specified. (We can also contrast this property of Network Morphology with the typological exposition above where, in contrast, reference is also made to context.) One of the predictions of impoverishment is that the deleted feature will be replaced by an 'unmarked' feature. In the case of Slovene, a persistent redundancy rule [-sg] → [+pl] is required in addition (Bobaljik 2002: 81–2 fn14), so that the singular is not used, as that is the least 'marked' feature. As Network Morphology is a declarative framework, the relationship in (19) is all that needs to be stated to capture the relevant syncretisms. As we shall see in our treatment of Dalabon in the next section, the combination with default inference without having to specify a context is a desirable property of Network Morphology referrals in that it allows us to pick out whole subparadigms (something which we also require in our treatment of deponency in Chapter 5). This interaction of feature order and referral is also a point of contrast with Paradigm Function Morphology, as noted by Stump (2001: 275).

But this is not the end of the story. The Slovene adjectival paradigm (Priestly 1993: 412), as well as the paradigm of the demonstrative pronoun (Priestly 1993: 410), involves the same syncretism between plural and dual for all genders. Hence, (19) is a highly predictive default for nominals and can be placed very high in the nominal class hierarchy. As the referral simultaneously involves implicit quantification over all path extensions, we need make no further statements about gender, and the ordering established in Chapter 2, Section 2.2.3 is observed because any gender will be an extension of `<mor du loc>` or `<mor du gen>` and therefore of `<mor pl loc>` and `<mor pl gen>`. Hence, referrals in the Network Morphology sense do much more than 'state the observed facts directly' (Bobaljik 2002: 80 fn12). They predict whole sets of cells in paradigms (a point we shall discuss in depth in Section 4.4). They are also constrained by the feature ordering discussed in Chapter 2, Section 2.2.3. Consequently, an advantage of Network Morphology-style referrals is that, while constrained by the feature ordering, they readily combine with default inference, an advantage over similar representational mechanisms such as impoverishment.

4.4 Case study for generalized referrals: Dalabon verbal morphology

In the previous section we have already pointed out that referrals may be combined with default inference (underspecification), thereby demonstrating the need for both means of representation, or something similar to them. Basing our exposition on the analysis of Evans, Brown and Corbett (2001), we now proceed to show how the combination of referrals with underspecification, which we term *Generalized Referral* (Baerman *et al.* 2005: 186–204), can account for the large verbal paradigm of the Australian language Dalabon, which belongs to the Gunwinyguan family. In Dalabon the intransitive paradigm is realized by bound prefixes, and the transitive paradigm is realized by a combination of a bound pronominal prefix and, for non-singular objects, by an object clitic pronoun.[11] While there are object clitics, the prefixes in the transitive paradigm still realize information about the object. For example, the prefix *dah-* is used to realize combinations involving a second-person singular subject acting on third-person objects, and it therefore provides information about the person of the object. Other prefixes, such as *yilah-*, provide person and number information about the subject and, as they are a form which is specifically transitive, indicate that there is an object. Second-person singular objects are realized by portmanteau prefixes. For example, *djilah-* is used for third-person plural subjects acting on second singular objects.

In Table 4.1 we see the forms of the intransitive paradigm given between square brackets in the top row under the appropriate person and number combinations. (Where there is an additional form marked by A, this is the form of the transitive subject.) There is clearly no syncretism in the intransitive paradigm, as there is no form which corresponds to more than one intransitive subject. In contrast to this, the transitive paradigm has a significant number of syncretisms where there is failure to distinguish the subject. In particular, there is syncretism of second- with third-person transitive subjects and also of first- with third-person transitive subjects. In fact, Evans *et al.* (2001: 207) summarize the subject syncretisms in the following way, using variables.[12]

(20) a. 2[n = α]> 1[n = β] uses the form for 3[n = α]> 1[n = β] where n is number
b. 1[n = α]> 2SG uses the form for 3[n = α]> 2SG where n is number

In our generalized referral approach, we do not use the variables in (20), as this information is underspecified. The paradigm cells referred to are the *source*, and those doing the referring are the *goal* (Corbett 2007: 33–5).

Table 4.1. *Paradigm of Dalabon subject/object combinations, including object clitics; unmarked realis series (Evans, Brown and Corbett 2001: 209).*

A first inclusive distinction is also expressed in the pronominal marking in Dalabon, but this has been omitted here (see Evans *et al.* 2001: 209).

Subject [intr. /tr. form] Object [free pronoun]	1sg [*ngah-*]	2sg [*djah-*] [A *dah-*]	3sg [*kah-*]	1dis [*ngeh-*]	2dis [*deh-*]	3dis [*keh-*]	1du [*yarrah-*] [A *yirrah-*]	2du [*narrah-*] [A *nurrah-*]	3du [*barrah-*] [A *burrah-*]	1pl [*yalah-*] [A *yilah-*]	2pl [*nalah-*] [*nulah-*]	3pl [*balah-*] [A *bulah-*]
1sg [ngey]		***kah-*** **[20a]**	*kah-*		***keh-*** **[20a]**	*keh-*		***burrah-*** **[20a]**	*burrah-*		***bulah-*** **[20a]**	bulah-
2sg [njing]	***djah-*** **[20b]**		*djah-*	***djirrah-*** **[20b]**		*djirrah-*	***djirrah-*** **[20b]**		*djirrah-*	***djilah-*** **[20b]**		*djilah-*
3sg [---]	*ngah-*	*dah-*	*kah- / bvkah-*	*ngeh-*	*deh-*	*keh-*	*yirrah-*	*nurrah-*	*burrah-*	*yilah-*	*nulah-*	*bulah-*
1du [njerr]		***njerr kah-*** **[20a]**	*njerr kah-*		***njerr keh-*** **[20a]**	*njerr keh-*		***njerr burrah-*** **[20a]**	*njerr burrah-*		***njerr bulah-*** **[20a]**	*njerr bulah-*
2du [norr]	*norr ngah-*		*norr kah-*	*norr ngeh-*		*norr keh-*	*norr yirrah-*		*norr burrah-*	*norr yilah-*		*norr bulah-*
3du [bu(l)nu]	*bunu ngah-*	*bunu dah-*	*bunu kah-*	*bunu ngeh-*	*bunu deh-*	*bunu keh-*	*bunu yirrah-*	*bunu nurrah-*	*bunu burrah-*	*bunu yilah-*	*bunu nulah-*	*bunu bulah-*
1incl du [njeh]			*njeh kah-*			*njeh keh-*			*njeh burrah-*			*njeh bulah-*
1pl [njel]		***njel kah-*** **[20a]**	*njel kah-*		***njel keh-*** **[20a]**	*njel keh-*		***njel burrah-*** **[20a]**	*njel burrah-*		***njel bulah-*** **[20a]**	*njel bulah-*
2pl [nol]	*nol ngah-*		*nol kah-*	*nol ngeh-*		*nol keh-*	*nol yirrah-*		*nol burrah-*	*nol yilah-*		*nol bulah-*
3pl [bulu]	*bulu ngah-*	*bulu dah-*	*bulu kah-*	*bulu ngeh-*	*bulu deh-*	*bulu keh-*	*bulu yirrah-*	*bulu nurrah-*	*bulu burrah-*	*bulu yilah-*	*bulu nulah-*	*bulu bulah-*
1incl pl [ngorr]			*ngorr kah-*			*ngorr keh-*			*ngorr burrah-*			*ngorr bulah-*

(21) *Generalized referral*

a. One feature specification (the goal) may refer to another feature specification (the source) for its realization.
b. As with other realization rules, referrals may be underspecified.
c. Extensions of the goal will be realized by extensions of the source.

A generalized referral as defined in (21) can be exemplified by (19), where dual is the goal and plural is the source. The statement in (19) is sufficient for us to know the genitive or locative dual, because, by default, extensions of the plural will be extensions of the dual.

Returning to (20a), we note that the realizations of paradigm cells involving a second-person subject acting on a first-person object will be syncretic with the realizations of paradigm cells involving a third-person subject acting on first-person object. (The relevant goal cells in Table 4.1 have been annotated **[20a]** to indicate which ones (20a) accounts for.) This means that 2 > 1 shares the same number forms as 3 > 1, so the generalization is valid for multiple cells of the paradigm.

In (20b) cells realizing a first-person subject acting on a second-person singular object are syncretic with cells realizing a third-person subject acting on a second-person singular object. (The relevant goal cells in Table 4.1 have been annotated **[20b]** to indicate which ones (20b) accounts for.) The fact that the subject number has to be treated as a variable in (20b) means that this syncretism also involves multiple cells of the paradigm. We shall treat this syncretism as a referral, but we do not need to make use of variables as such, because of the role of path extension in generalized referrals, as defined in (21c).

For both types of syncretism in (20), it is stated that the relevant cells containing either a second- or first-person transitive subject take their form from the corresponding third-person transitive subject cells. The third person is, therefore, taken to be the basic meaning associated with the forms in question. The reason for this is that the transitive paradigm for third-person subjects is clearly based on the third-person intransitive paradigm, and in the intransitive paradigm third-person subjects are differentiated from first- and second-person subjects. (The intransitive forms are given in square brackets at the top of each column.) For example, the third-person singular intransitive subject *kah-* differs from both the second-person singular intransitive subject *djah-* and the first-person singular intransitive subject *ngah-*. This indicates that the third-person subject forms have a unique third-person interpretation in certain contexts.

Further evidence that third person is the basic meaning associated with the forms can be found in the disyllabic prefixes found in the dual and plural. The forms of any dual or plural transitive subject prefix (when the object is third person) are transparently based on the corresponding intransitive ones, by altering the first vowel of the prefix to *-i-*, if the first element of the prefix is *y-* (CaLah → CiLah, where C is a laminal and L is a liquid), or by altering the first vowel of the prefix to *-u-* otherwise (CaLah → CuLah, where C is a laminal and L is a liquid) (Evans *et al.* 2001: 202). Again, the intransitive prefix forms are given at the top of each column in Table 4.1 in square brackets. Immediately below them, preceded by the letter A, are the corresponding transitive forms. For example, the form *yirrah-* is used in paradigm cells where the first-person dual is the transitive subject, and this form is based on that of the prefix for the first-person dual intransitive subject, namely *yarrah-*.

We argue that underspecification is insufficient to account for the patterns indicated by (20). Or to be more precise, it is most certainly insufficient, if we establish the set of feature values using the distributional method in a similar way to that illustrated earlier in this chapter in Section 4.1. It is the case that one can account for phenomena of this type, if a sufficiently abstract feature system is adopted (see Müller 2008: 216, 218). The empirical justification for the Set Theoretic method is that it establishes the maximum number of distinctions that can be justified as syntactically relevant. But as the abstract features involved are required for the purposes of selecting the correct form, their role is morphology-internal and not related to syntactic distribution. Later, in Section 4.5, we consider abstract morphological features in relation to the distribution of stems in Dhaasanac.

Returning to Dalabon, we note a number of intractable challenges for an underspecification-based analysis. For instance, the second-person plural subject form *nulah-* (based on intransitive *nalah-*) would be more specific than the form *bulah-* (based on intransitive *bulah-*), if this latter were treated as a marker of plural subject only (i.e. underspecified for person). This would mean, however, that we would expect *nulah-* to be the prefix in both the 2PL > 1 and 2PL > 3 cells, because it would be more specific than *bulah-*. But this is not what happens. Instead, we get *bulah-* in 2PL > 1 and *nulah-* in 2PL > 3. We would expect the second-person dual subject form *nurrah-* (based on intransitive *narrah-*) to be the prefix in both 2DU > 1 and 2DU > 3. However, *nurrah-* is not used in the 2DU > 1 paradigm.[13] Instead *burrah-* is used, and this is based on the unambiguously third-person dual intransitive subject form *barrah-*. Furthermore, in the intransitive disharmonic[14] paradigm we see that *deh-* is unambiguously the marker of the second-person disharmonic subject, and this would lead us to expect that *deh-* should fill the transitive 2DIS > 1 cells. Instead these cells are filled by the prefix which is the unambiguous realization of third singular subject in the intransitive paradigm, namely *keh-*. Underspecification of *keh-* for person will not work here, as it would be less specific than *deh-* and therefore fail to fill the 2DIS > 1 cells as subject. This indicates the inadequacy of underspecification. Certain forms could be treated in terms of underspecification, of course, such as the 2SG > 3 form *dah-* in the singular paradigm. This could be analysed as marking a third-person object, being underspecified for subject person and number. We will show that these facts can be accounted for by combining underspecification based on attribute ordering with referrals.

The paradigm of the second singular object has a special portmanteau prefix. Here there is a slightly different issue. For example, the prefix *djah-* is 1SG > 2SG (the same form as the second singular intransitive subject, an absolutive patterning). On a purely underspecification-based analysis, this prefix must be associated with second-person singular, with information about the subject person omitted, because *djah-* can realize the first-person and third-person subject in combination with the second-person singular object. In contrast, the prefix *ngah-* must be associated with first-person singular subject, as it is used to express only combinations containing a first-person subject. In underspecification terms there would, therefore, be two prefixes with information content which is compatible to realize the 1SG > 2SG cell in the transitive paradigm: *djah-* (specified for second singular objects) and *ngah-* (specified for first singular subjects). On what basis does the second singular object marking win over the marking of first singular subject? This can be accounted for by the combination of attribute ordering and referrals.

According to Evans *et al.* (2001: 208), the principle governing the choice of transitive prefix is based on 'avoidance', a phenomenon observed by Heath for both Australian languages (1991) and languages of the Americas (1998). When forms expressing speech-act participants are combined, the speaker–addressee relation is played down, as the combination is pragmatically sensitive. Dalabon has gone one step further by grammaticalizing the relations in (20). In particular, the form of one person (namely the third person) is substituted for another (namely the first or second). This grammaticalization is most naturally expressed by the use of rules of referral.

Another set of patterns which become observable from the implemented Network Morphology analysis is the following:

(22) Where first- or second-person subjects are involved, each associated object cell is always differentiated (i.e. 2 > 1 always differs from 2 > 3, 1 > 2 always differs from 1 > 3, and 1 > 3 cells always differ from 2 > 3 cells).

If we look down the first-person subject and second-person subject columns in Table 4.1, we see that where there is a combination of bound pronominal prefix and object clitic pronoun in one row there will be non-identity with another row in the same column. For example, the 1SG > 2DU cell is not identical to the 1SG > 3DU cell. For non-singular objects this is due to periphrasis in that the clitic marker will distinguish the object. For the non-periphrastic forms in 1 > 2SG and 1 > 3SG cells, however, it is the referral (20b) which guarantees non-identity between these sets of cells. It does this at the expense of making 1 > 2SG cells syncretic with 3 > 2SG cells, of course. Furthermore, while the referrals may create identity between certain third-person subject cells and certain first- or second-person subject cells, the 1 > 3 cells always differ from 2 > 3. The pattern in (22) follows as an additional consequence of combining the referrals-based approach with the ordering of attributes we argue for in this section. If there were no avoidance-based referrals, the pattern in (22) would not hold with the relevant singular objects. It is clearly also a pattern based on the top two elements of a person hierarchy, as it is not true of the third-person subject forms, where first-person singular and third-person singular objects fail to be differentiated in the presence of third-person subjects.[15]

4.4.1 The Dalabon paradigm without referrals

We will now proceed to consider what we term the shape of the verbal paradigm. In other words, we impose an ordering on the attributes used to represent the Dalabon syncretisms.

The idea that certain features may dominate others was noted in Chapter 2, Section 2.2.3. Dominance is often associated with ordering of marking. For example, Bybee (1985) and Bybee, Perkins and Pagliuca (1994) have analysed the relationship between verbal categories and the proximity of marking to the verbal root, and both Wunderlich and Fabri (1995) and Noyer (1997) also use hierarchies to make predictions about the order of affixes. However, as we have argued, there is an important difference between the linear order of affixes and the distinctions made in a paradigm. Dalabon has a first-person inclusive (not given in Table 4.1), and this is incompatible with singular, because the lowest cardinality associated with first inclusive is two. Morphologically, the first inclusive dual and the first inclusive plural look like the singular and dual forms, respectively, of the other persons. As person determines which numbers are available, we order the person attributes before the number attributes for a given argument (intransitive subject, transitive subject and object). Again, the attribute ordering reflects a more general cross-linguistically observable tendency.[16]

(23) For a given argument of the verb, person attributes are ordered before number attributes.

```
<mor infl s 2nd sg>
<mor infl a 2nd sg o 1st_exclusive sg>
```

We now address how object marking and subject marking should be represented. In Table 4.1 the non-singular object clitics appear before the bound prefixes. This might lead us to claim that object attributes (followed by their person and number attributes) should occur first in the path. We argue, in fact, that this is the case for third- and second-person objects, because only when the object is third- or second-person may there be clear marking of the person of that object on the *bound* pronominal prefixes, again reinforcing the point that affix ordering and distinctions in the paradigm are logically independent. So, the second-person singular object is clearly marked on the portmanteau bound pronominal prefix. Furthermore, second-person singular object conditions syncretism of the disharmonic transitive subject with the dual transitive subject. We can also claim that there is one example of a bound pronominal prefix clearly marking third person: the third-person singular higher animacy object (Table 4.1). The form *bvkah-* is used only when the object is a higher animacy third-person singular, not when it is first-person exclusive, as indicated by the contrast in this regard between the 3 > 1SG and 3 > 3SG paradigms, which are otherwise the same. Hence, this form definitely identifies a third-person object. In contrast to this, there is no *bound* pronominal prefix where an object is clearly marked as first person. We therefore order attribute combinations of object with second and third person before any attribute combinations of transitive subject (and any associated person and number marking). Here we see that, in contrast to (22), it is the bottom two elements of a person hierarchy, namely second and third person (singular), which pattern together in terms of bound pronominal forms marking objecthood.

There is no unambiguous bound prefixal marking of the first-person exclusive object. For the bound pronominal paradigm, third-person transitive subjects condition loss of distinction between first-person singular and third-person singular objects. These two facts lead us to claim that, in contrast with the other persons, the object attributes for first-person exclusive occur last in the path. So, we treat the generalizations about the availability, or lack, of bound forms which mark an object as related to the order of attributes. We give the generalizations in (24) and (25) together with example paths to illustrate. The paths are those we require for the full morphological model. The paths in the analysis may well be underspecified relative to these.

(24) Second- and third-person object attributes are ordered before transitive subject attributes (i.e. second- and third-person object paradigms have extensions).
Examples:

```
<mor infl o 3rd sg a 2nd sg>
<mor infl o 3rd du a 2nd sg>
<mor infl o 2nd pl a 1st_exclusive sg>
```

(25) First-person object attributes are ordered after transitive subject attributes (i.e. first-person object paradigms extend subject paradigms and, therefore, have no extensions themselves).
Examples:

```
<mor infl a 2nd sg o 1st_exclusive sg>
<mor infl a 3rd sg o 1st_exclusive du>
<mor infl a 2nd du o 1st_exclusive pl>
```

In (24) and (25), we have examples of the shape of the paradigm for which we would expect the theory to yield the appropriate forms. The actual analysis may contain less specific, and therefore more general, facts than those given in (24) and (25). From these the fully specified forms can be inferred.

4.4.2 *Relating prefixes and clitics*

For the purpose of our exposition, we need to recognize at least three types of morphological entity in the Dalabon paradigm: bound prefixes (represented as `<mor prefix>`; clitics (represented as `<mor cl>`); inflected forms (whole words which contain bound prefixes and/or clitics, represented as `<mor infl>`). In a Network Morphology representation of the Dalabon verbal system, there is a node `MOR_VERB`, referred to by the lexemic node for verbs in general, which represents default facts about the verbal morphology. Here it is stated, among other things, that the realization for any morphology which is not specified will default to nothing (the Identity Function Default as discussed in Chapter 2, Section 2.3.1 and Chapter 3, Section 3.1.1). Furthermore, it is stated that a verb will consist of a root with some morphological complex (clitic or otherwise) before it. These two generalizations are given in (26).

(26)

```
MOR_VERB:
  <mor> ==
  <mor infl> == <mor cl> "<root>"
  ...
```

If no clitic is available to realize the particular attribute combination in question, then the morphology will delve into the bound pronominal forms proper (27).

(27)
```
<mor cl> == <mor prefix>
```

In (27) we see the generalization that the morphological cluster will default to bound prefixal marking if there are no available clitic pronouns. The prefixes referred to in (27) are the bound markers in Table 4.1. When clitics appear, they are typically specified as in (28).

(28)
```
<mor cl o 3rd du> == bunu+ <mor prefix>
<mor cl o 3rd pl> == bulu+ <mor prefix>
```

In (28) the clitic realizations are attached to the prefixal realizations, which will extend the object person and number combinations with information about the transitive subjects. The object clitics for other combinations are similarly specified.

4.4.3 *Adding referrals*

The rules in (26), (27) and (28), together with the appropriate information about bound prefixes and clitics, will output some of the Dalabon verbal paradigm. In particular, any 1 > 3 combination and any 2 > 3 combination will be correctly predicted, and because of generalization (25), the 3 > 1 paradigm is treated as a default extension of the third-person subject paradigm. However, the 1 > 2 paradigm would incorrectly be predicted to differ from the 1 > 3 paradigm. We also require that the 1 > 2SG paradigm takes on the special forms of the 3 > 2SG paradigm, namely *djirrah* 3DU > 2SG and *djilah* 3PL > 2SG.

For the 1 > 2SG paradigm, we introduce a referral which captures generalization (20b). The referral of the 1 > 2SG to the 3 > 2SG combinations illustrates that generalized referrals, that is a referral with a degree of underspecification, are required. The underspecified element is the number of the transitive subject, and given that subject information is ordered after information about the second-person objects, as we generalized in (24), this means that we infer the correct number form by default. We state the referral in (29).

(29)
```
<mor infl o 2nd sg a 1st_exclusive> ==
  <mor infl o 2nd sg a 3rd>
```

In (29) all extensions of paths for 1 > 2SG can be obtained by referring to the extensions of 3 > 2SG. These extensions will, of course, be those for number of the transitive subject, as this is what is not specified in the referral in (29). Hence, we predict multiple cells in a paradigm by combining referrals with default extension as generalized referrals.

Recall that we claimed in (25) that the first exclusive object attributes should be specified as occurring last in any path. We argued that this had to do with the fact that there is no person-specific bound pronominal marking for the first exclusive object, in contrast to the second and third person at least, where the second singular object is clearly marked, and there is marking of the higher-animacy third singular object. As this means that first exclusive object marking is an extension of the third-person paradigm, the referral of 2 > 1 to 3 > 1 takes the form in (30).

(30) <mor infl a 2nd> == <mor infl a 3rd>

This states that the second-person transitive subject finds its extensions from the third-person transitive subject. Here, the ordering of attributes in (25) plays a role, because from (25) it follows that only first exclusive object attributes can extend a path which starts with transitive subject attributes, such as in (30). Note the high degree of underspecification involved. The referring paradigm of second-person transitive subject obtains its transitive subject number, together with the first exclusive object person and number information, from the third-person paradigm.

We have argued that the use of underspecification alone is insufficient to predict the correct forms of the Dalabon verbal paradigm. In particular, certain underspecified forms would lose out to more specific ones on Pāṇinian grounds. However, adding referrals with a certain degree of underspecification, in the form of generalized referrals, allows us to capture generalizations about 'avoidance' and, therefore, predict multiple paradigm cells. It should also be noted that the need for additional representational means or constraints is recognized for Dalabon by other theoretical approaches. For example, Wunderlich (2001) introduces 'taboos' as a constraint in his correspondence-theoretic account of Dalabon. As the mechanisms involved in this account basically take fully specified input and delete certain features, they behave in a similar way to referrals. An advantage claimed for impoverishment rules (Halle and Marantz 1993: 124, 172 fn12) and the constraints Wunderlich introduced is that they predict that a 'marked' feature value will always be replaced by an 'unmarked' one. Hence, for Dalabon the third person is used in the place of the first. As we saw, this claim does not quite work for the Slovene in Section 4.4, where the form which substitutes for the 'marked' dual is not the 'unmarked' singular but the plural. Bobaljik (2002: 81–2 fn14) argues that this can be accounted for by combining a persistent redundancy rule with impoverishment. The use of an additional rule type suggests that this is not as unmarked as expected. Furthermore, Spencer (2000a) highlights Koryak and Chukchi transitive agreement paradigms for first-person object which involve syncretism with the antipassive. This is another instance involving takeover of a 'marked' feature value by an 'unmarked' one. In any event, this indicates that there is clearly a general consensus in morphological theory that underspecification is insufficient to deal with syncretism of the type found in Dalabon and elsewhere. The fundamental issue is how to interpret these additional mechanisms. If one understands them as representing tendencies specific to a particular language or language grouping, then it may not be so surprising that the 'resort to the unmarked' does not always work. It is probably better if one interprets them as a cross-linguistically general mechanism with language-specific manifestations (i.e. independent of feature structure) and typically, therefore, with some diachronic dimension. For example, the referral-based approach readily fits with historical analyses based on analogical extension, as argued by Hansson (2007) for North Saami. And the referral-based approach also allows us to capture a more general intuition behind the Dalabon syncretisms, while at the same time allowing us to see its language-specific consequences. That is, the syncretisms are motivated by the potential inappropriate combination of first and second person. It is transitivity which conditions the loss of person distinction.

4.4.4 Summary

Clearly, the referrals of Dalabon are particular to that language. If we tried to make the syncretisms which arise from them appear to result from underspecification alone, we would not be in a position to distinguish Dalabon's more general cross-linguistic properties from what makes it special. In fact, we can find hierarchical properties within Dalabon person marking, such as the generalization in (22). But, we will not be able to see these more general properties if we obscure them by trying to treat language-specific systematicities as anything other than that. While certain syncretisms may reflect the typical underlying paradigmatic design of particular language types, which we would expect to occur much more frequently cross-linguistically, others will be of a more parochial nature. The challenge is fitting the two together.

4.5 Combining stem indexing and default inference

In the previous section, we saw how referrals are used simultaneously with default inference to capture syncretism in Dalabon. Here, we consider the Dhaasanac verbal paradigm (Tosco 2001). This is an example of morphological systematicity where the syncretized values do not form a natural class. Verbs have A and B forms. The A and B forms are realized as stem alternations, sometimes involving the stem-initial consonant (e.g. *yes* ~ *ces*), sometimes the stem-final consonant (e.g. *kufi* ~ *kuyyi*) and sometimes vowel alternations (e.g. *seð* ~ *sieti*). This is illustrated in (31).

(31) *Dhaasanac stem forms* (Tosco 2001: 123–206; Baerman *et al.* 2005: 106)

Form A	Form B	
a. leeði	leeti	'fall down.PRF'
b. kufi	kuyyi	'die. PRF'
c. guurma	guuranna	'migrate. IPFV'
d. ʔuufumi	ʔuufeeni	'cough. PRF'
e. seð	sieti	'walk. PRF'
f. yes	ces	'kill. PRF'

The A and B forms are used to mark subject person in the perfect and imperfect positive paradigm, as well as the dependent positive and short past (Tosco 2001: 123–206). The distribution of the A and B forms is given in (32). This is a very good example of 'morphology by itself' (Aronoff 1994), where the features involved do not constitute a natural class, as discussed in Chapter 1, Section 1.2.1.

(32) *Dhaasanac syncretisms* (Baerman *et al.* 2005: 106)

	SG	PL
1INCL	– – –	A
1	A	B
2	B	B
3 F	B	A
3 M	A	A

In the case study, we show how we can capture this autonomous morphological systematicity and still associate it with the relevant morphosyntax using default inference. While the person and number patterns are incompatible, as we have noted, the patterning itself generalizes across the positive paradigms in Dhaasanac.

The other important aspect of the Dhaasanac data is that they are an instance of mediated polarity (see Baerman *et al.* 2005). Importantly, the B form is always used for the second person, both singular and plural. This is, therefore, an example of underspecification of number in the presence of second person, but this still needs to be combined with indexing of the forms. The paradigms in the full morphological model which we assume for Dhaasanac are as in (33). Here `pos` stands for positive, `pf` for perfect, `1st sg` for first-person singular, and so on.

(33)
```
<mor pos pf 1st sg>
<mor pos pf 2nd sg>
<mor pos pf 3rd sg fem>
<mor pos pf 3rd sg masc>
<mor pos pf 1st_excl pl>
<mor pos pf 1st_incl pl>
<mor pos pf 2nd pl>
<mor pos pf 3rd pl>
```

The ordering of attributes in (33) reflects the fact that it is negation (or its absence) and TAM which determine whether there are A and B forms, because the negated paradigms and the imperative do not distinguish A and B forms. It is the role of our formal analysis to infer the correct forms for the positive paradigms.

In (34) we give the lexical entry for the verb *fúr* 'to open', which belongs to the class of verbs whose stem ends in a coronal consonant.

(34)
```
Fúr:
  <> == VERB
  <form> == CORONALS
  <gloss> == 'open'
  <stem type> == one_vowel
  <stem cons_1> == f
  <stem vowel_1> == _u
  <stem final> == _r.
```

The node Fúr inherits from the node VERB, which includes the information in (35). (We have omitted some of the information given at VERB.)

(35)
```
VERB:
  <> ==
  <syn> == verb
  <index> == _A
  <index 2nd> == _B
  <index 3rd sg fem> == _B
  <index 1st_excl pl> == _B
  <mor pos impf> == "<form impf <index> >"
  <mor pos pf> == "<form pf <index> >"
  ...
```

Extensions of the path `<mor pos pf>`, for example, will involve attributes for person and number (in that order), and for the third-person singular, also gender. Hence, in the absence of any more specific information, the form of the perfect paradigm will be determined by looking at the equation associated at VERB with `<mor pos pf>`, namely `<mor pos pf> == "<form pf <index> >"`. The right-hand side of the equation `"<form pf <index> >"` involves an evaluable path (the <index> part). This equation basically means that the morphology of the positive perfect is determined by looking for the form of the perfect and inserting the appropriate index for that form. Let us consider the morphology for the path <mor pos pf 2nd sg>. In (36) we have an example of an evaluable path which takes a value from the local context at VERB and uses this to infer the correct forms of the paradigm. This evaluable path also works on the basis of underspecification. The rules of inference mean that, among other things, we can infer (37) from (36). That is, if we are looking for extensions of the positive perfect paradigm (and these will be in terms of person and number of the subject), then the index will be the appropriate one associated with that extension. Let us take the second-person singular form as our example.

(36) From:

```
<mor_pos_pf> == "<form_pf_<index>_>"
```

(37) We can infer that:

```
<mor pos pf 2nd sg> == "<form pf <index 2nd sg> >"
```

Note that (37) is not stated explicitly but can be inferred from the theory. In (35) it is also stated that the index B is associated with the second person (among others). We repeat this here as (38).

(38)

```
<index 2nd> == _B
```

Because <index 2nd> is the most specific path matching with the evaluable path <index 2nd sg> in (37), the index value _B is placed into the path, thereby leading to the inference in (39).

(39) We can infer that:

```
<mor pos pf 2nd sg> == "<form pf _B>"
```

We should note from (34) that the lexical item *fúr* inherits information about its associated forms from the node CORONALS. Even though *fúr*'s A and B forms may differ from those of other verbs, the equations at VERB can generalize across all verbs, irrespective of the specific realization of the A and B forms. In the case of *fúr*, we can obtain the forms in (40) for the perfect paradigm.

(40)

```
Fúr:<mor pos pf 1st sg> = f _u _r -i.
Fúr:<mor pos pf 2nd sg> = f _u _ɗɗ -i.
Fúr:<mor pos pf 3rd sg fem> = f _u _ɗɗ -i.
Fúr:<mor pos pf 3rd sg masc> = f _u _r -i.
Fúr:<mor pos pf 1st_excl pl> = f _u _ɗɗ -i.
Fúr:<mor pos pf 1st_incl pl> = f _u _r -i.
Fúr:<mor pos pf 2nd pl> = f _u _ɗɗ -i.
Fúr:<mor pos pf 3rd pl> = f _u _r -i.
```

The other TAM, person and number combinations work in the same way. This is a realizational approach to morphology because it separates the morphosyntactic specification from the actual form with which it may be associated. Thus, by treating the inventory of forms available as separate from the associated morphosyntax, it is possible to capture the morphological systematicity of the Dhasaanac verb. At the same time, the morphology is still constrained, because these indexed items have to match up with well-formed feature specifications. Again, the language-specific systematicity is contained within more general structures.

4.6 Conclusion

Inflectional syncretism within a language is the product of a number of different factors. There are examples where syncretism is a parochial property of a language or language family, the result of particular historical changes. There are also more widely occurring patterns, such as gender syncretism conditioned by number or case, which we have illustrated with examples from Slavonic. Gender syncretism across number is known to be highly prevalent (see Baerman *et al.* 2005: 82). We have argued that formal models need to use different representational means for these different types of syncretism. For the more general cross-linguistic patterns, we can represent certain syncretisms as resulting from the ordering of grammatical attributes, as we argued in Section 4.2. As we noted for Slovene, it is possible that referrals and attribute ordering can be combined, so that the language-specific statement that the dual may use forms from the plural relies on the more general tendency that case extends number. This need for referrals and underspecification based on path ordering, suggested by our examination of Slavonic, finds additional justification when we look further afield at the avoidance morphology of Dalabon. When referrals and underspecification based on path ordering come together, we have a combination of language-particular properties reacting with more general tendencies. And, as we have seen with stem indexing in Dhaasanac, a similar combination of the language-specific and the general is required.

In the next chapter, we look at deponency. We have demonstrated here that a range of phenomena which fall under the rubric of syncretism can be accounted for by use of underspecification, referrals and morphomic indexing, and with many examples a combination of these, which demonstrates the requirement for all of them. The account of deponency we present needs little more than the principles we have outlined in Chapter 2, in particular the notion of exceptional case default, combined with the mechanisms available here. Indeed, looking at the referrals of Dalabon, it is worth noting that in some respects the phenomenon is more like deponency than syncretism. As Corbett (2007: 35) notes, canonical deponency affects a small number of lexemes but covers a large slab of the paradigm. For Dalabon a large slab of the paradigm is affected, but so are all verbs. This demonstrates that a whole range of phenomena can be accounted for by the theoretical constructs presented here; but the behaviour is intricate, and in the presence of such intricate behaviour we need implemented, computationally tested models.

5 *Morphological mismatch and extended deponency*

5.0 Introduction

We have seen that with syncretism there can be a dissociation between syntactic function and morphological form, specifically where separate syntactic words of a given lexeme converge on a single morphological form. In this chapter we discuss a different kind of dissociation which can be characterized as *mismatch* of function and form, namely deponency. This kind of dissociation therefore constitutes further evidence for an autonomous component of morphology whose interface with syntax is not always direct.

In Latin there is a class of irregular verbs that can be defined as displaying passive morphological form in active contexts. A member of this class is *hortor* meaning 'encourage' whose root is seen in the English verb 'exhort'. The following line appears in Plautus' comedy *Mercator* (The Merchant), written in the second century BC (briefly discussed in Chapter 1, Section 1.2.1 and Chapter 2, Section 2.4.2.).

(1) Plautus, *Mercator*, Act IV, lines 695–7 (Nixon 1924)

sed	coqu-os,	quasi	in	mar-i	sol-et
but	cook-PL.ACC,	as	at	sea-SG.ABL	be.wont-ACT.PRS.3SG

hortator	remig-es	horta-rier	ita
encourager-SG.NOM	oarsman-PL.ACC	exhort-PASS.INF (=ACT)	so

horta-batur
exhort-PASS.IMPF.3SG
(=ACT)

'but he exhorted the cooks, just as a coxswain is in the habit of exhorting oarsmen.'

The verb *hortor* is used twice, and both times it takes a direct object argument. In the first instance it occurs as an infinitive whose internal argument is the noun *remiges* 'oarsmen' appearing in the accusative, the case for canonical objects in Latin. In its second use its object is accusative-marked *coquos* 'cooks'. Despite its *active* distribution, its morphology is *passive* as seen in the gloss. This class of verbs is the deponents, and they involve a mismatch which we can schematize as follows.

(2)	Lexeme 1		Lexeme n		*Hortor*	
	ACT	PASS	ACT	PASS	ACT	PASS
	X-α	X-β	Y-α	Y-β	Z-β	–

Most lexemes have a pattern of exponence such that -α is used for ACTIVE syntax and -β for PASSIVE syntax. But, the lexeme HORTOR upsets the general system by using a different pattern of exponence for ACTIVE syntax. At the same time, this is the exact pattern used for PASSIVE syntax for other verbs, namely -β.

The evidence for autonomous morphology that we have collected, first discussed in Chapter 1, Section 1.2.1, is the existence of purely morphological properties such as theme vowels, dissociations such as inflectional classes and syncretism, and now mismatch phenomena – deponency. As we argued in Chapter 1, Section 1.2.1, the product of morphology is an encapsulated object, in which syntactic rules are blind to the process of its creation in a separate component. If a passive rule has been used and its output value is active, the syntax reads that value. In this way 'morphology may operate at cross-purposes with morphosyntax without apparently hindering the function of the system of correspondences' (Baerman 2007b: 18). Morphology is being kept out of syntax, the principle of morphology-free syntax. As we have shown, modularity of the grammar is expressed in Network Morphology by separate but orthogonally connected hierarchies. In this chapter we account for dissociation as mismatch through overriding the default link between the lexemic hierarchy, where morphosyntactic properties of a word are referenced, and the inflectional hierarchy, where morphological forms of a word are created. As discussed in Chapter 2, Section 2.4, the default link is expressed as `<syn> == "<mor>"`. In Corbett's terms, this is the canonical match of morphosyntactic features (function) and morphology (form). Deponency is not restricted to Latin verbs; it is a notion that can be extended beyond Latin, beyond voice features and beyond verbs (Corbett 2007: 29). In this chapter we account for 'extended' deponency as instances where a high-level normal case default is being overridden, and once overridden other lower generalizations can be made. Languages that override at the highest level may override at lower levels too, and these lower-level overrides can be used to express the full range of extended deponency. What marks out deponency from other irregularity phenomena in Latin is that once the normal case default is overridden, subsequent lower-level overrides result in the exceptional case default (Section 2.3.2). In other words, the exception is restoring 'mismatch' to 'match'. Related to this, deponency is also shown to be good motivation for the attribute order conventions discussed in Chapter 2, Section 2.2.3 since the 'source' feature combination employed matches the 'goal' feature combination in all but the leading feature value attribute. Although there is a mismatch, it is highly constrained in retaining the normal match amongst a significant subset of the features in the string of features involved.

In Section 5.1 we demonstrate how the properties associated with 'classical' deponency can be expressed as defaults at different hierarchical levels. This allows us to define extended deponency examples in relation to Latin through differences in the way defaults are overridden. In Section 5.2 we present the Network Morphology account of Latin verbs. We include some irregular verbs to contrast them with the special kind of irregularity that deponents represent. This sets the scene for our account of classical deponency as overriding defaults set at different levels, thereby inheriting the exceptional case default (Section 5.3). Then in Section 5.4 we offer an NM account of extended deponency, illustrating with the noun system of Archi, a Nakh-Daghestanian, Lezgian language. Finally, in Section 5.5 we consider whether Latin deponents really are mismatches, questioning the voice features that characterize the mismatch and bearing in mind the passive morphology's origin as middle voice marking.

5.1 Extended deponency as defaults-based rule interaction

Baerman (2007b) defines deponency with reference to Latin but in such a way that modifying parts of the definition allows non-Latin instances into the deponency realm. In this way deponency can be extended to other mismatch phenomena that are similar in kind to Latin deponents. The chapters in Baerman, Corbett, Brown and Hippisley (2007) provide extensive coverage of extended deponency cases. Baerman's definition can be divided into six characteristics which we list in (3). Only some of these are relevant to our discussion.

(3)

Characteristic number	*Definition*
1.	There is a mismatch between form and function.
2.	The resulting opposition is a formal morphological one.
3.	The opposition involves the active and passive features values.
4.	This mismatch assumes the context of a normal function:form mapping.

5. The mismatch irregularity is located at the level of the lexeme.
6. A consequence of the mismatch is that the normal function becomes unavailable. (Based on Baerman 2007b: 2)

The first characteristic directly expresses what we discussed, that deponency is a type of mismatch. The purpose of the second is to leave room for an instance of extended deponency where the realization of the function in question is not morphological but a syntactic construction. The speculative example Baerman gives is expletives (2007b: 4), a syntactic mapping with semantics which breaks down since no theta role is assigned to a constituent argument despite its getting a grammatical relation label. We restrict our discussion to instances where characteristic 2 is unaltered. Characteristic 3 captures the Latin situation but what features are involved can be altered for extended deponency examples. In Archi, the opposition involves a noun feature, specifically number, as we shall see. In both the Latin and Archi cases, mismatch implies a majority method of matching form and function, so there is a 'normal' context – characteristic 4. But a mismatch need not be exceptional. An example Baerman gives is valence-changing morphology in Ngiyambaa, where transitives productively derive intransitives by switching from one conjugation to another. Some transitive verbs belong to the target (intransitive) conjugation; however, these represent nearly half the free-root transitive verbs in the language (2007: 6). Altering characteristic 5 allows instances of extended deponency where the mismatch is not located in one lexeme, or set of lexemes, like the deponent verbs in Latin. Rather the mismatch is situated at a higher level of generalization – in how the realization rules for a subset of the paradigm of regular verbs can be characterized. Chukchi is an example of extending deponency in this direction where the transitive paradigm antipassive morphology markings are used in a subset of the cells (Baerman 2006a, based on Spencer 2000a: 206–7, Skorik 1977: 61–2, 73). This again is not relevant for present purposes, as our extended deponency example involves a subset of lexical items. Finally, the last characteristic of Latin deponents is that they are defective (characteristic 6). Transitive verbs like *hortor* cannot be used in passive constructions. This is indicated by the blank in (2), where there is neither an exponent nor a stem. This is relevant for our discussion, as it is one of the ways we distinguish the classical deponency instance (Latin) from an extended deponency instance (Archi).

5.1.1 The hierarchical characterization of deponency

The first characteristic in (3) is central to the definition of deponency. We could think of it in hierarchical terms as an override of the highest-level default: a given combination of *morphosyntactic* features in the lexemic hierarchy has an exact correspondent in the same combination of *morphological* features in the inflectional hierarchy. This is illustrated in (4) for the combination 'active imperfective present indicative singular second'.

(4)
```
VERB:
  <syn active impf pres ind sg 2> ==
    "<mor active impf pres ind sg 2>"
  ...
```

Paths expressing this particular feature combination and any other involving active voice are really extensions of <syn active> and <mor active>, by the principles explained in Chapter 2 and illustrated for inflectional classes and syncretism in Chapters 3 and 5. We can therefore express deponency quite succinctly as the specific override of the equation in (5).

(5)
```
VERB:
  <syn active> == "<mor active>"
  ...
```

In (5) the value of a morphosyntactic path held at a lexemic hierarchy node (VERB) is a morphological path, and this path's value is inherited from somewhere in the orthogonal morphological hierarchy. So, (5) is the Network Morphology expression of active morphosyntax and active morphology sharing the same realization *by default*.

Once this default is overridden, we enter the domain of Latin deponents. This domain carries its own set of expectations: if active morphosyntax is to match passive morphology, then all active feature combinations should be involved in the mismatch. We could think of this as a default of 'full participation'. This default is clearly situated at a lower level in the hierarchy, a generalization about the behaviour of a class of non-regular items. The lower-level default is expressed in (6). The second equation is both an override of the matching default at VERB as well the default of full participation for deponent verbs: values for active morphosyntax are shared with those of passive morphology. And the scope of this unusual situation extends to all combinations involving active voice, by default. Note that the mismatch is represented by a node in the lexemic hierarchy inheriting from VERB to express that the mismatch between syn and mor holds for a *subset* of lexemes.

(6)
```
DEPONENT:
  <> == VERB
  <syn active> == "<mor passive>"
  ...
```

It turns out that this lower-level default, namely that all feature combinations involving the active are included, is itself subject to overriding. Latin deponents do not fully participate in the mismatch: while the overwhelming majority of cells in a deponent paradigm are morphologically passive with active function, a few remain outside the deponent domain, as it were. For example, the future infinitive is active in form as well as function. One way of capturing this fact about Latin deponents is to say that we are dealing with an exception within an exception. In Network Morphology terms, the lower-level default of full participation stated in (6) is being overridden. But because this override characterizes Latin deponents, the profile of the lack of full participation – which feature combinations 'escape' the mismatch – can itself be stated as a default, albeit of an even lower order. This is partially expressed in (7), equation 3. (The full representation of this third order default capturing all the Latin details is presented in Section 5.4.)

(7)
```
DEPONENT:
  <> == VERB
  <syn active> == "<mor passive>"
  <syn active imperfective future infinitive> == VERB
  ...
```

The equation in question overrides the second order default (equation 2) by extending the `<syn active>` path and providing it with an alternative value. By Pāṇini's principle, the narrower statement overrides the more general statement, expressed as the longer path overriding the shorter path of which it is an extension (as discussed and illustrated in previous chapters).

What is the alternative value responsible for the full participation override? It is a value found at the node VERB, namely what we discussed from the start: the first-order default that active morphosyntax lines up with active morphology, as represented in (5). In other words, we have yet another instance of the exceptional case default, where overriding at a lower level results in inheriting the highest-level generalization (see Chapter 2, Section 2.3.2 for a definition and examples in Polish, Russian and Bininj Gun-wok). There is a subclass of deponents known as 'semi-deponents' since their paradigm is split by deponent behaviour, specifically they are deponent for the perfect subparadigm. We could think of this subclass as representing an override of the third-order default since the numeration of the cells that do not participate in the mismatch goes beyond the normal case. The consequence of overriding the third-order default is therefore institution of a fourth-order default, the default for semi-deponents. And again, overriding the normal case default is inheritance of the exceptional case default, the non-perfect slab of the paradigm that escapes the mismatch.

The profile of deponency in (3) begins with the characteristic that there is a mismatch between form and function. Thus far we have discussed the *functional* side of the mismatch. But once the highest-level default has been overridden, we can think of a default about the *form* of deponents, and this default sits in parallel with the second-order default about the function. The default is that the form used in a deponent is identical to the 'source' form. In other words, the passive form used to realize active morphosyntax is the very form used to realize passive morphosyntax for regular verbs. Conceivably it could be different; part of the form could include a 'signal' that this is really deponency and not a passive. Where it is different, we have an override of a form default. We will see that this override is in fact invoked in the extended deponency example we present, number in Archi nouns. Baerman's sixth characteristic in (3), that the normal function becomes unavailable for deponent items, is entailed by the form default. To avoid homonymy, a deponent lexical item dispenses with the source form's original passive function, resulting in a kind of systematic (because entailed) defectiveness. Conversely, we would expect the original function to be available in cases where the form default is overridden since there is no homonymy. And this is indeed what we see happening in another example, Archi case and number.

The way the defaults are spread over different levels of a hierarchy is summarized in Table 5.1.

The first column specifies the nature of the default and the level at which it is pitched and includes the three levels of default we have discussed. The second column specifies the override to which a default is subject. Overriding the first-order default leads to the second-order default, and overriding at this level leads to a third-order default. This cascading of defaults is indicated by the arrows. The specifics of the features involved in the override are given in the third column. Based on the information in these columns, we can draw a comparison between classical deponency (Latin) and our example of extended deponency, Archi (columns 3 and 4). The distinction between instances of deponency therefore amounts to what happens at a given default level: is the default inherited or overridden? And if overridden, in what way? We have not indicated the values of these features here. But as we discussed, overrides of second- and third-level defaults inherit the exceptional case default ('no mismatch'), so we could imagine arrows emanating from the 'Deponency type classical' column and returning to the first-order default: function lines up with form – morphosyntactic active and morphological active share the same form.

The possibilities at each level are viewed as one of five different kinds of property associated with deponency, Properties 1–5. Property 1 is about the

Table 5.1. *Deponency viewed as levels of default*

Default level and nature		Override	Deponency type: classical	Deponency type: extended	Property
1st order	function=form	–	*no override*	*no override*	n.a.
		mismatch	verb: voice	noun: number	1
2nd order	all cells participate	cells not participating	future infinitive and others	*no override*	2
3rd order	non-participation profile	cells outside profile	semi-deponent: non-perfect	n.a.	3
		Formal			
2nd order	deponent form = source form	deponent form different	*no override*	heteroclisis	4
	defectiveness (entailed by Property 4)	complete paradigm	*no override*	specific dep. form	5

nature of the mismatch – voice features in the classical scenario but other possibilities in extended deponency cases such as Archi. This property corresponds directly to characteristic 1 in (3), based on Baerman's definition. Property 2 deals with the set of cells involved in the mismatch, where the default that all are involved is inherited by Archi. Ancient Greek would also inherit at this level, directly corresponding to the canonical situation in Corbett's discussion of extended deponency (2007: 34). Property 3 applies only to the instance where not all cells participate in the mismatch, as it is a property entailed by overriding the second-order default. This is where semi-deponents fit into the picture. Whereas Properties 2 and 3 are about the functional side of the mismatch, Properties 4 and 5 are about form. In the classical scenario, the deponent form is identical to what would be used in the normal situation; this is the default. Archi overrides this default since heteroclisis interacts with deponency yielding non-identity between deponent form and source form. Property 5 is entailed by the specification of Property 4. Defectiveness falls out from form identity, where avoiding homonymy is the motivation. Corbett includes defectiveness in the canonical deponency profile, with the implication that deponent form and source identity are also canonical.

In the next sections, we show how these property types are expressed in Network Morphology through overriding defaults at different levels. We begin with the classical situation by presenting a Network Morphology account of Latin verbs.

5.2 The Network Morphology account of Latin verb inflection

In this section we construct a network that holds predictable facts about Latin verbal inflection. Our account includes both regular and non-regular verbs. The non-regulars fall into the 'lexically listed' category of non-regularity since both the override and the value that the overriding path inherits are listed. This distinguishes them from the deponent verbs which are 'network-directed' non-regulars. Their overrides are listed, but unlike the lexically directed, the values are inherited from somewhere else in the network (specifically at the PASSIVE node series, as we shall see in Section 5.4).

Latin regular verbs inflect according to four patterns of exponence, the four verb conjugations shown in Table 5.2; the table gives the indicative present paradigm of the verbs *amō* 'like, love', *moneō* 'advise', *regō* 'rule' and *audiō* 'hear'. The table also includes non-finite forms.

The full paradigm includes tense and aspect combinations involving present, future, past and imperfect and perfect, as well as subjunctive and imperative mood forms. The full paradigm of forms of all four verbs can be found in Kennedy (1962: 64–81), the source used for our account.

Table 5.2. *Latin present indicative of verbs of the four conjugations*

	Conjugation 1		Conjugation 2		Conjugation 3		Conjugation 4	
	ACTIVE	PASSIVE	ACTIVE	PASSIVE	ACTIVE	PASSIVE	ACTIVE	PASSIVE
Singular								
1	amō	amor	moneō	moneor	regō	regor	audiō	audior
2	amās	amāris	monēs	monēris	regis	regeris	audīs	audīris
3	amat	amātur	monet	monētur	regit	regitur	audit	audītur
Plural								
1	amāmus	amāmur	monēmus	monēmur	regimus	regimur	audīmus	audīmur
2	amātis	amāmini	monētis	monēminī	regitis	regiminī	audītis	audīmini
3	amant	amantur	monent	monentur	regunt	reguntur	audiunt	audiuntur
Inifinitive								
	amāre	amārī	monēre	monērī	regere	regī	audīre	audīrī
Participle								
	amāns	—	monēns	—	regēns	—	audiēns	—

The lexical entry for the first-conjugation verb *amō* 'like, love' is given in (8). The relevant parts of our Latin theory can be discussed with reference to the equations in (8).

(8)
```
Amō:
  <> == VERB
  <gloss> == love
  <root> == am
  <stem> == CONJ_1.
```

The first equation shows lexical entries like Amō inheriting from the node VERB in the lexemic hierarchy as its primary source. The secondary source of inheritance is a node holding generalizations about inflectional class, a conjugational class node from the inflectional hierarchy (equation 4). The VERB node contains the first-order default that morphosyntactic voice features correspond to morphological voice features, as discussed with reference to (5) in Section 5.1.1.

(9)
```
VERB:
  <syn active> == "<mor active>"
  <syn passive> == "<mor passive>"
  <mor active> == ACT_FORMS:<>
  <mor passive> == PASS_FORMS:<>.
```

The first two equations in (9) can be collapsed into `<syn> == "<mor>"` as the LHS and RHS are their respective leading subpaths. The next two equations point to nodes in the inflectional hierarchy where the realizations of active and passive feature combinations are to be gathered as values that are inherited by active and passive paths. Before we discuss the address nodes ACT_FORMS and PASS_FORMS, we should make it clear that our theory assumes a specific ordering of features, expressed as the sequence of attributes in an LHS path (see Chapter 2, Section 2.2.3, where we provided arguments for particular orderings of case, number and gender). The orderings we propose are given in (10).

(10) *Assumed feature ordering*
VOICE→ASPECT→TENSE→MOOD→NUMBER→PERSON

The consequence of this ordering is that the paradigm is first divided according to voice and subsequently according to aspect. As we shall show in the next section, motivation for this ordering comes from deponents and semi-deponents, for their behaviour hinges on voice and aspect distinctions. The ordering means that the first nodes to be visited in the inflectional hierarchy are nodes about voice realization, as shown in (11).

(11)
```
ACT_FORMS:
  <imperfective> == ACT_IMPF:<>
  <perfect> == ACT_PERF:<>.

PASS_FORMS:
  <imperfective> == PASS_IMPF:<>
  <perfect> == PASS_PERF:<>.
```

These nodes serve to redirect the query to aspect nodes, in accordance with (10). It may be helpful at this point to consider a query for the present second-person singular of the lexical entry for *amō*. Given Table 5.2, we see that the theory should deliver *amās*. The path to be evaluated is given in (12).

(12) *Query for present second-person singular of the lexical entry for* amō
```
Amō:<mor active imperfective present indicative sg 2>
```

In (13) the subpath `<mor active imperfective>` has been consumed, and its extension `<present indicative sg 2>` is passed on to the area in the subnetwork that handles tense feature values, including present. This is expressed by the nodes addressed in (13).

(13)
```
ACT_IMPF:
  <present> == ACT_IMPF_PRES:<>
  <past> == ACT_IMPF_PAST:<>
  <future> == ACT_IMPF_FUT:<>.
```

Here paths of the three tenses are redirected to appropriate nodes. At this point the original query path is consumed as far as the mood attribute, so that what is redirected is `<indicative sg 2>`. The final stage of the evaluation is provided at tense nodes, including the one in (14) for the present tense. Here we see the second- and third-person singular, as well as two non-finite form realizations.

(14)
```
ACT_IMPF_PRES:
  <indicative sg 2> == "<stem 1>" s
  <indicative sg 3> == "<stem 1>" t
  <infinitive> == "<stem 1>" re
  <participle> == "<stem 1 ext>" ns
  ...
```

The node in (14) provides the exponent of a particular combination of features (compare the endings in the respective cells of *amō*'s paradigm in Table 5.2). But part of the realization involves the selection of the right stem, here the lexical entry's first stem. Our theory incorporates the association of stem type with a set of feature combinations, i.e. the morphomic level of description (see discussion in Chapter 1, Section 1.2.1). The shape of the different stem types obviously varies with the lexical entries. But this variation is in part regulated by conjugation membership.[1] Each conjugational class is identified with a particular theme vowel, and the theme is used to build stems. For Conjugation 1 it is *-ā-*, for 2 it is *-ē-*; for 3 it is *-e-* and for 4 *-ī-*. The theme vowels can be discerned from Table 5.2. So, we can compare present infinitive *am-ā-re* (Conj 1) with *mon-ē-re* (Conj 2), *reg-e-re* (Conj 3) and *aud-ī-re* (Conj 4). The regulation of stem formation by conjugational class is expressed in the fourth equation of the lexical entry in (8), where a stem path inherits from the appropriate class. Stem formation itself involves the theme vowel, as shown in (15), the node for Conjugation 1.

(15)
```
CONJ_1:
  <stem theme> == ā
  <stem 1> == "<root>" "<stem theme>"
  <stem 2> == <stem 1> v
  <stem 3> == <stem 1> t.
```

From (15) we see that, in addition to a root form, a first-conjugation verb has three stems. For *amō* the forms are: *am-* (root), specified at the lexical entry; *amā-* (stem 1) built by concatenating the theme vowel of the first conjugation to the root; *amāv-* (stem 2) built on stem 1 with the addition of /v/; *amāt-* also built on stem 1 but with the addition of /t/ instead. We have already seen that stem 1 is associated with the present tense (expressed in (14)) as well as the future and past imperfective. Stem 2 is associated with the perfect and stem 3 with the passive, amongst other features. Some of these associations are shown in (16).

(16)
```
ACT_IMPF_PAST:
  <indicative sg 1> == "<stem 1>" bam
  <indicative sg 2> == "<stem 1>" bās
  <indicative sg 3> == "<stem 1>" bat
  …

ACT_PRES_PERFECT:
  <indicative sg 1> == "<stem 2>" ī
  <indicative sg 2> == "<stem 2>" istī
  <indicative sg 3> == "<stem 2>" it
  …

PASS_PRES_PERFECT:
  <indicative sg 2> == "<stem 3>" us es[2]
  <indicative sg 3> == "<stem 3>" us est
  <participle> == "<stem 3>" us
  …

ACT_IMPF_FUT:
  <participle> == "<stem 3>" ūrus
  …
```

From (16) we see that stem 1 is used for the imperfective past, stem 2 for the active present perfect and stem 3 for the passive present perfect. The third stem is truly morphomic since it is also used for active voice, imperfective aspect and future tense, as shown in the participle form in the last node. Theorems for the lexical entry `Amō` showing the three stems and evaluations of the paths in (16) are given in (17).

(17)
```
Amō:<gloss> = love.
Amō:<root> = am.
Amō:<stem 1> = am ā.
Amō:<stem 2> = am ā v.
Amō:<stem 3> = am ā t.
Amō:<syn active imperfective past indicative sg 1> =
    am ā bam.
Amō:<syn active imperfective past indicative sg 2> =
    am ā bās.
Amō:<syn active imperfective past indicative sg 3> =
    am ā bat.
Amō:<syn active imperfective future participle> =
    am ā t ūrus.
Amō:<syn active perfect present indicative sg 1> =
    am ā v ī.
Amō:<syn active perfect present indicative sg 2> =
    am ā v istī.
Amō:<syn active perfect present indicative sg 3> =
    am ā v it.
Amō:<syn passive perfect present indicative sg 2> =
    am ā t us es.
Amō:<syn passive perfect present indicative sg 3> =
    am ā t us est.
Amō:<syn passive perfect present participle> =
    am ā t us.
...
```

Theme vowels are used not only to guide the construction of a lexical entry's three stems but also the choice of exponent. In other words, they determine inflectional class-based allomorphy. For example, the active imperfective future first singular is realized by the exponent *-bō* for Conjugation 1 but *-am* for Conjugation 4. The way in which the correct exponent is negotiated by the lexical entry's theme vowel is partially shown by the nodes in (18).

(18)
```
ACT_IMPF_FUT:
  <indicative> == ACT_IMPF_FUT_INDIC:<"<stem theme>">
  <participle> == "<stem 3>" ūrus
  ...

ACT_IMPF_FUT_INDIC:
  <ā> == TYPE_1_ACT_FUT_INDIC:<>
  <ī> == TYPE_3_ACT_FUT_INDIC:<>
  ...
```

```
TYPE_1_ACT_FUT_INDIC:
  <sg 1> == "<stem 1>" bō
  ...

TYPE_3_ACT_FUT_INDIC:
  <sg 1> == "<stem 1>" am
  ...
```

The first node has an evaluable path that uses the theme vowel; evaluation takes place at the second node. When the theme is `ā` the path is directed to one type of future realization node, to another when it is `ī`.

We have presented the highlights of our Network Morphology theory of Latin verbs. The full theory appears in the accompanying website. Other aspects will emerge in our discussion of the non-regulars, including the deponents. For completeness, lexical entries for verbs of the other three conjugations in Table 5.2 are given in (19).

(19)
```
Moneō:
  <> == VERB
  <gloss> == advise
  <root> == mon
  <stem> == CONJ_2.

Regō:
  <> == VERB
  <gloss> == rule
  <root> == reg
  <stem> == CONJ_3.

Audiō:
  <> == VERB
  <gloss> == hear
  <root> == aud
  <stem> == CONJ_4.
```

5.2.1 Non-regulars excluding deponents

As discussed in previous chapters, Network Morphology captures degrees of non-regularity by expressing non-regular behaviour in the nature of a lexeme's relation to the network. Deponent verbs are *network-directed* non-regulars since the override that defines them as a group is the redirection of active paths to passive paths, whose values are available elsewhere in the network. Latin has other non-regular verbs, three of which we briefly discuss in this section: *ferō* 'I carry', *coepi* 'I have begun' and *aiō* 'I say yes'. Unlike the deponents, their non-regularity is more extreme since not only is the override lexically stipulated but so too is the alternative value. We begin with *ferō*, an example of a *lexically listed* non-regular. This lexeme's perfect active forms are based on the suppletive stem *tul-* and perfect passive *lat-*. Thus, 'I have carried' is *tulistī* and 'I was carried' *latus sum*. The distribution of suppletive stems corresponds to the distribution of stems 1, 2 and 3 for regulars like *amō*. Indexed stems and suppletive stems partitioning the paradigm in the same way were used as justification for a morphomic level of description in Chapter 1, Section 1.2.1. Given that our Latin theory integrates the morphomic level, i.e. the value of a realizational path includes an indexed stem, it is a straightforward matter to express the non-regularity of *ferō* by overrides involving its stems.

(20)
```
Ferō:
  <> == VERB
  <gloss> == carry
  <root> == fer
  <stem> == CONJ_3
  <stem 2> == tul
  <stem 3> == lat.
```

The overrides are restricted to stem specification. In other respects it is like other regular Latin verbs. And as such it belongs to a particular conjugational class: its pattern of exponence is like Conjugation 3 *regō*. At the same time, the overrides, which are Conjugation 3 stem-formation overrides, take their values from the lexical entry itself. The overrides thus locate precisely what constitutes the non-regular behaviour; but the class of this non-regular behaviour as lexically listed follows from where the overriding paths are directed.[3]

The verbs *coepi* 'I have begun' and *aiō* 'I say yes' are non-regular because their paradigms are incomplete. The paradigm of *coepi* lacks imperfective forms. Its non-regular behaviour is expressed in (21).

(21)
```
Coepi:
  <> == VERB
  <gloss> == have_begun
  <root> == coep
  <stem> == CONJ_3
  <stem 2> == "<root>"
  <syn active imperfective> == undefined
  <syn passive imperfective> == <syn active imperfective>.
```

The last two equations express its defectiveness[4] by overriding active imperfective paths with the value 'undefined', and referring the passive imperfective to the same evaluation. Again we are dealing with a lexically listed non-regular since the values for the overriding paths are found within the lexical entry. This verb's third stem is the root plus the formant /t/. Since this is how Conjugation 3 verbs form the third stem, we specify that it inherits stem formation from Conjugation 3. Stem 2 is not formed by adding /s/ directly to the root, the default method for Conjugation 3, so it must be overridden (equation 5).

Finally, the verb *aiō* 'say yes' is a 'worse' kind of defective as its defective cells include those that form a natural class and those that do not. The cells that are missing include the active perfect and active imperfective present first-person plural and second-person plural. The overrides are shown in (22).

(22)
```
Aio:
  <> == VERB
  <gloss> == say yes
  <root> == ai
  <stem> == CONJ_3
  <syn active perfect> == undefined
  <syn active imperfective present indicative pl 1> ==
    undefined
  <syn active imperfective present indicative pl 2> ==
    undefined
```

Path ordering allows us to reduce the number of equations expressing overrides since all active perfective feature combinations are implied by `<syn active perfect>`. This allows us to distinguish cases where the overrides hold for a class of feature combinations from those that do not. There are fewer overriding paths that inherit the value `undefined` in (21) than in (22). This does not take into account the 'extra' path needed in (21) due to *coepi* having a potential passive paradigm. We now turn to the very different kind of non-regularity displayed by deponents.

5.3 Classical deponency

Our Network Morphology theory captures the five properties listed in Table 5.1 that mark out classical deponency. First, deponents constitute a mismatch between morphosyntactic voice and its formal expression, specifically *active* morphosyntactic features are realized by *passive* morphology (Property 1). Second, a number of cells in the paradigm do not participate in deponency, as Table 5.2 demonstrates. These are the future infinitive (*amātūrus esse*), the present participle (*amans*) and the future participle (*amātūrus*). These facts combine to form Property 2. The third property (Property 3) is that amongst the deponents there is a group whose cells not participating in deponency fall outside what Property 2 describes. These are the semi-deponents whose perfect subparadigm is deponent but not their imperfective subparadigm. For all deponents the passive form used for the active corresponds exactly to the form that would have been used if the verb had been regular, where in theory it could have been different: this is Property 4. Finally, Property 5 is a kind of corollary of Property 4 as Latin deponents are defective for passive morphosyntax since those exact forms are in use doing 'active' duty. We base our account on Baerman's report of Latin deponency (Baerman 2006b), who in turn draws on Ernout and Thomas (1953), Flobert (1975) and Kühner (1955). The theorems are validated by checking against the Kennedy (1962) Latin primer.

5.3.1 Mismatch, Property 1: overriding the first-order default

Mismatch is expressed as overriding a first-order default, and we showed this with the DEPONENT node in (6). We repeat it here as (23).

(23)
```
DEPONENT:
  <> == VERB
  <syn active> == "<mor passive>"
  ...
```

The path that is being overridden is situated at the highest node in the hierarchy, the node VERB given in (9) and reproduced here in (24).

(24)
```
VERB:
  <syn active> == "<mor active>"
  <syn passive> == "<mor passive>"
  <mor active> == ACT_FORMS:<>
  <mor passive> == PASS_FORMS:<>.
```

The fourth equation in (24) expresses the fact that the default evaluation of <mor passive> is through the PASS_FORMS node in the morphological hierarchy. The force of the override in (23) is to redirect all <syn active> paths to the PASS_FORMS node by inheritance of the <mor passive> path and its default evaluation at VERB.

Lexical entries for deponent verbs such as our illustrative example (1) *hortor* 'encourage' inherit from DEPONENT, thereby inheriting the first-order override. For all other aspects about their morphology they inherit the default – for example, the associations between conjugational class and stem formation and pattern of exponence, which we discussed in (15) and (18). Example (25) gives lexical entries for Conjugation 1 *hortor* and Conjugation 3 *ūtor* 'use'.

(25)
```
Hortor:
  <> == DEPONENT
  <gloss> == encourage
  <root> == hort
  <stem> == CONJ_1.

Ūtor:
  <> == DEPONENT
  <gloss> == use
  <root> == ūt
  <stem> == CONJ_3.
```

If we compare these to regulars such as the lexical entry for *amō* given in (8), we see the only difference is the first equation, the inheritance of a lower-level node holding the first-order override. Because this lower-level node inherits from `VERB` we can pinpoint the difference between non-regulars and deponents, namely the second equation in (23). This equation itself is the redirection of a path to elsewhere in the network, expressing the fact that deponents constitute the special class of network-directed non-regulars. In scalar terms, they are 'low-level' non-regulars because the override inherits facts that are available and 'normal' under different circumstances, and the override itself is of the first-order.

5.3.2 *Lack of full participation, Property 2: overriding the second-order default*

Through DATR's mechanism of default inference, the overriding path `<syn active>` implies all its extensions. The override in this way is itself a default, albeit of a lower order: once a lexeme is determined to be deponent, it is expected to be deponent in all its manifestations. But we noted that for Latin deponents not all the cells are deponent, which is what distinguishes Latin deponents in relation to Property 2. In hierarchical terms, the Property 2 behaviour is viewed as overriding the second-order default that is expressed by the subpath equation `<syn active> == "<mor passive>"`. One of the feature combinations that does not participate is the future infinitive. Overriding for this feature combination was shown by the third equation in (7). We give this again as (26). The override is expressed as the extension of the `<syn active>` subpath and its inheriting an alternative value.

(26)
```
DEPONENT:
  <> == VERB
  <syn active> == "<mor passive>"
  <syn active impf future infinitive> == VERB
  ...
```

As we mentioned earlier, the alternative value comes from somewhere else in the network. Moreover, the value is the first-order default for verbs. The second level default is therefore being overridden by the first-order default, an example of inheritance of the exceptional case default.

At the beginning of Section 5.4 we noted that in addition to the future infinitive, two other feature combinations do not participate in deponency, namely the present participle and the future participle. We could include paths expressing these combinations alongside the future infinitive path in (26), but in doing so we would miss an important distinction between the future infinitive's lack of participation and the lack of participation by these others. For the active present and future participle forms, there is no counterpart in the passive paradigm. In this regard Latin displays a kind of systematic defectiveness: certain feature combinations that can occur in an active syntactic context cannot occur in a passive context. Thus, 'loving' in Latin is possible but not 'being loved'. We treat these cases as a different kind of override of the second-order default, one that directly falls out from defectiveness at the level of the inflectional system. The way we handle the present participle staying active, as it were, is shown in (27).

(27)
```
PASS_IMPF_PRES:
  <indicative sg 2> == "<stem 1>" ris
  <indicative sg 3> == "<stem 1>" tur
  <infinitive> == PASS_PRES_INF:<"<stem theme>">
  ...
  <> == ACT_IMPF_PRES.
```

The ellipsis denotes any other path expressing additional feature combinations, such as passive first-person plural, passive second-person plural, etc.; here as in other DATR representation examples, the ellipsis is not part of the theory. This means that the last equation is a catch-all: any other path not specified inherits from ACT_IMPF_PRES, the node for active present forms. In the case of deponent lexical entry Hortor the evaluation of the path <syn active imperfective present participle> is redirected to PASS_FORMS (26) equation 2, (24) equation 4 from where it is addressed to PASS_IMPF_PRES (27) for imperfective values. By this stage the path has been reduced to <participle>. This path is not listed in (27) but is covered by <> and addressed to ACT_IMPF_PRES. And consulting (14) above, we see that this is the concatenation of the formant /ns/ to the first stem. In the case of *hortor*, this will be *hortāns*. The future participle is dealt with in similar fashion.

The partial theorems of Hortor and Amō are given in (28). The active forms of Hortor coincide with the passive forms of Amō, excepting the future infinitive, the present participle and the future participle which are shown in bold type.

(28)
```
Hortor:<gloss> = encourage.
Hortor:<root> = hort.
Hortor:<stem 1> = hort ā.
Hortor:<stem 2> = hort ā v
Hortor:<stem 3> = hort ā t.
Hortor:<syn active imperfective present indicative sg 2>
       = hort ā ris.
Hortor:<syn active imperfective present indicative sg 3>
       = hort ā tur.
```

```
Hortor:<syn active imperfective present infinitive> =
      hort ā rī.
Hortor:<syn active imperfective present participle> =
      hort ā ns.
Hortor:<syn active imperfective future infinitive> =
      hort ā t ūrus esse.
Hortor:<syn active imperfective future participle> =
      hort ā t ūrus.
Hortor:<syn active perfect present indicative sg 2> =
      hort ā t us es.
Hortor:<syn active perfect present indicative sg 3> =
      hort ā t us est.
Hortor:<syn active perfect present participle> =
      hort ā t us.
...

Amo:<gloss> = love.
Amo:<root> = am.
Amo:<stem 1> = am ā.
Amo:<stem 2> = am ā v.
Amo:<stem 3> = am ā t.
Amo:<syn active imperfective present indicative sg 2> =
   am ā s.
Amo:<syn active imperfective present indicative sg 3> =
   am ā t.
Amo:<syn active imperfective present infinitive> =
   am ā re.
Amo:<syn active imperfective present participle> =
   am ā ns.
Amo:<syn active imperfective future infinitive> =
   am ā t ūrus esse.
Amo:<syn active imperfective future participle> =
   am ā t ūrus.
Amo:<syn active perfect present indicative sg 2> =
   am ā v istī.
Amo:<syn active perfect present indicative sg 3> =
   am ā v it.
...
```

5.3.3 *Semi-deponents, Property 3: overriding the second- and third-order defaults*

The second-conjugation verb *audeō* 'dare' is deponent but only in perfect contexts. Other perfect deponents include *gaudeō* 'rejoice', *fīdō* 'trust', *soleō* 'be wont' (see our Plautus extract in (1)). So, for example, while the active perfect infinitive displays passive morphology, *ausus esse*, the active imperfective infinitive is realized with active morphology, *audēre*. The converse situation is represented by *revertor* 'return', whose imperfective forms are deponent but whose perfect forms do not participate in the mismatch. Nodes for perfect deponents such as *audeō* and imperfect deponent *revertor* are given in (29).

(29)
```
PERFECT_DEPONENT:
  <> == DEPONENT
  <syn active imperfective> == VERB.

IMPF_DEPONENT:
  <> == DEPONENT
  <syn active perfect> == VERB.
```

Semi-deponent lexical entries inherit from one of the nodes in (29), depending on which features fail to participate in deponency. Both nodes are daughters of DEPONENT. This means that they inherit certain aspects of the broader class of deponents and override other aspects. For the IMPF_DEPONENT node, the mismatch of active imperfective features with passive counterparts is inherited information. The mismatch of perfect features is being overridden. As such the node holds the overriding of the second-order default. In this regard IMPF_DEPONENT itself represents a third-order default. Motivation for this hierarchical positioning of IMPF_DEPONENT under DEPONENT comes from the imperfective subparadigm of *revertor*. Although it is mainly deponent in this subparadigm, certain cells do not participate. These are the very cells that do not participate in the broader class of deponents: future infinitive and present and future participles. Rather than viewing this as a property peculiar to *revertor*, we see it as the broader property of deponents, and *revertor*, a semi-deponent, inherits it. This is expressed as inheritance by IMPF_DEPONENT of the third-order default held at DEPONENT, the lack of participation in the mismatch as discussed above. A subset of the theorems of the lexical entry for *revertor* is given in (30).

(30)
```
Revertor:<gloss> = return.
Revertor:<syn active imperfective present indicative sg 2>
        = revert e ris.
Revertor:<syn active imperfective present indicative sg 3>
        = revert i tur.
Revertor:<syn active imperfective present infinitive> =
        revert ī.
Revertor:<syn active imperfective present participle> =
        revert e ns.
Revertor:<syn active imperfective future infinitive> =
        revert s ūrus esse.
Revertor:<syn active imperfective future participle> =
        revert s ūrus.
Revertor:<syn active perfect present indicative sg 2> =
        revert istī.
Revertor:<syn active perfect present indicative sg 3> =
        revert it.
...
```

Turning to the PERFECT_DEPONENT node, the mismatch of perfect features is inherited from DEPONENT. And, *all* facts about imperfective features are overridden. These facts are of different kinds. The first kind is the second-order default that imperfectives are subject to mismatch, as expressed by the following equation: `<syn active> == "<mor passive>"` at DEPONENT since it implies `<syn active imperfective> == "<mor passive imperfective>"`, a path overridden at PERFECT_DEPONENT. There is also a second kind of fact that is being overridden, the third-order default about certain extensions of `<syn active imperfective>`, namely those paths that do not participate in the mismatch. So PERFECT_DEPONENT simultaneously overrides both the second- and third-order defaults at DEPONENT by holding the path `<syn active imperfective>` as an LHS of an equation. However, overriding the third-order default is vacuous since the alternative value is the exceptional case default: the inheritance of the path is from VERB. We give some of Audeō's theorems in (31).

(31)
```
Audeo:<gloss> = dare.
Audeo:<syn active imperfective present indicative sg 2> =
      aud ē s.
Audeo:<syn active imperfective present indicative sg 3> =
      aud ē t.
Audeo:<syn active imperfective present infinitive> =
      aud ē re.
Audeo:<syn active imperfective present participle> =
      aud ē ns.
Audeo:<syn active imperfective future infinitive> =
      aus ūrus esse.
Audeo:<syn active imperfective future participle> =
      aus ūrus.
Audeo:<syn active perfect present indicative sg 2> =
      aus us es.
Audeo:<syn active perfect present indicative sg 3> =
      aus us est.
Audeo:<syn active perfect present participle> = aus us.
...
```

The imperfective forms that do not participate in the mismatch coincide with those in Revertor's theorem. But, the two sets are arrived at differently. For Revertor it is through inheritance of the third-order default; for Audeō it is through overriding the third-order default and then using the exceptional case default as the alternative value. Vacuous overriding may raise questions about our Network Morphology analysis of the Latin facts, but it is the consequence of the correct location of the generalization. For perfect deponents, the generalization is that all imperfectives do not participate in the mismatch. The alternative to this single statement is two statements: (i) some imperfective cells do not participate in the mismatch because we are dealing with a special kind of deponent (semi-deponents); and (ii) some imperfective cells do not participate because we are dealing with a special kind of verb (deponents).

5.3.4 'Form' defaults and defectiveness, Properties 4 and 5

Up to this point we have focused the discussion on the functional side of the mismatch between function and form. Recall from Table 5.1 that deponents also hold the second-order default that the deponent form is identical to the source form. This *form* default for deponency is overridden in some instances of extended deponency, as we shall see in the next section. We argued that defectiveness in the subparadigm associated with the source forms ensues from this default because an item's paradigm would otherwise carry homonymous expressions. In the case of Latin deponents, the passive subparadigm is lacking. This is the last fact that is added to the DEPONENT node, shown in (32).[5]

(32)
```
DEPONENT:
  <> == VERB
  <syn active> == "<mor passive>"
  <syn active imperfective future infinitive> == VERB
  <syn passive> == undefined
  ...
```

Defectiveness plays another role in our analysis of Latin deponents. Recall that the exceptional case default for the future and present participles comes about because there are no passive counterparts for any Latin verbs. In other words, defectiveness in the inflectional system leads to the exceptional case default for deponents. A further systematic defectiveness is at play with the perfect participle. Regular verbs lack a perfect participle for active contexts. However, deponents recover this gap in the active subparadigm by supplying the passive perfect participle. In a somewhat perverse way, non-regular deponents are more canonical than regulars (since more complete) by virtue of what characterizes them as non-regular. When we compare the partial theorems of Hortor and Amō for non-finite paths, the regular lexical entry lacks the last listed theorem of the non-regular item.

(33)
```
Amo:<gloss> = love.
Amo:<syn active imperfective present infinitive> =
    am ā re.
Amo:<syn active imperfective present participle> =
    am ā ns.
Amo:<syn active imperfective future infinitive> =
    am ā t ūrus esse.
```

```
Amo:<syn active imperfective future participle> =
    am ā t ūrus.
Amo:<syn active perfect present infinitive> =
    am ā v isse.
…
Hortor:<gloss> = encourage.
Hortor:<syn active imperfective present infinitive> =
       hort ā rī.
Hortor:<syn active imperfective present participle> =
       hort ā ns.
Hortor:<syn active imperfective future infinitive> =
       hort ā t ūrus esse.
Hortor:<syn active imperfective future participle> =
       hort ā t ūrus.
Hortor:<syn active perfect present infinitive> =
       hort ā t us esse.
Hortor:<syn active perfect present participle> =
       hort ā t us.
…
```

5.4 Extended deponency and Archi nouns

Mismatch in Archi differs from Latin with respect to the feature involved: namely the noun feature NUMBER. Within a subclass of nouns, the form normally associated with one number value is exchanged for another number value. We briefly present our Network Morphology account of a fragment of Archi noun inflection and then show how deponent lexical entries containing these paths represent instances of extended deponency with reference to the five property types listed in Table 5.1.

5.4.1 The Network Morphology account of Archi nouns

The analysis of the Archi data that informs our account is taken from Baerman (2006c), which in turn draws on Kibrik (1977a, b). Archi nouns have distinct singular and plural stems to which suffix exponents of case are attached. Number distinction is expressed not by the case suffixes but the shape of the stem. While there is no allomorphy of the case exponents, there are three major patterns of stem formation. Lexical items representing the three stem-formation classes are given in (34) and (35), taken from Kibrik (1977a: vol. 3, 251, 254, 256).[6] The oblique case stem is equivalent to the ergative word-form, so genitive of *aˤrum* 'sickle' is the ergative *aˤrum-li* plus genitive suffix *-n*.

(34)

	'sickle'		'military division'	
	SG	PL	SG	PL
ABS	aˁrum	aˁrum-mul	aˁri	aˁri-tːu
ERG	aˁrum-li	aˁrum-mul-čaj	aˁri-li	aˁri-tːaj
GEN	aˁrum-li-n	aˁrum-mul-če-n	aˁri-li-n	aˁri-tːe-n
DAT	aˁrum-li-s	aˁrum-mul-če-s	aˁri-li-s	aˁri-tːe-s
COMIT	aˁrum-li-ɬːu	aˁrum-mul-če-ɬːu	aˁri-li-ɬːu	aˁri-tːe-ɬːu
COMP	aˁrum-li-χur	aˁrum-mul-če-χur	aˁri-li-χur	aˁri-tːe-χur
PERM	aˁrum-li-kɬ'əna	aˁrum-mul-če-kɬ'əna	aˁri-li-kɬ'əna	aˁri-tːe-kɬ'əna
PART	aˁrum-li-qˁiš	aˁrum-mul-če-qˁiš	aˁri-li-qˁiš	aˁri-tːe-qˁiš
SUPERLAT	aˁrum-li-tːik	aˁrum-mul-če-tːik	aˁri-li-tːik	aˁri-tːe-tːik
SUBLAT	aˁrum-li-kɬ'ak	aˁrum-mul-če-kɬ'ak	aˁri-li-kɬ'ak	aˁri-tːe-kɬ'ak

(35)

	'lover'	
	SG	PL
ABS	kɬ'annu	kɬ'annib
ERG	kɬ'annum-mu	kɬ'annim-maj
GEN	kɬ'annum-mu-n	kɬ'annim-me-n
DAT	kɬ'annum-mu-s	kɬ'annim-me-s
COMIT	kɬ'annum-mu-ɬːu	kɬ'annim-me-ɬːu
COMP	kɬ'annum-me-χur	kɬ'annum-me-χur
PERM	kɬ'annum-mu-kɬ'əna	kɬ'annim-me-kɬ'əna
PART	kɬ'annum-mu-qˁiš	kɬ'annim-me-qˁiš
SUPERLAT	kɬ'annum-mu-tːik	kɬ'annim-me-tːik
SUBLAT	kɬ'annum-mu-kɬ'ak	kɬ'annim-me-kɬ'ak

In the consonant-final base class represented by 'sickle', a *-li-* formative in the singular alternates with a complex *-mul-čaj-* formative in the plural. The same singular formative is used for 'military division' in the second class of vowel-final bases, but the plural is *-tːaj-*. Finally, in the third class of substantivized adjectives represented by 'lover', *-mu-* in the singular alternates with *-maj-* in the plural.

In our Network Morphology theory, we have a lexemic hierarchy containing the node NOUN. This node holds syntactic category information as well as default semantic features associated with the category. In Lieber's (2004) framework, this would be [- dynamic].

(36)
```
NOUN:
  <syn cat> == n
  <sem cat> == not_dynamic
  <syn> == "<mor>"
  <syn sg abs> == "<root sg abs>".
```

The lexemic hierarchy node also encodes the default alignment of morphosyntactic feature combinations, expressed as <syn> paths, with their corresponding morphological features, expressed as <mor> paths, as in the Latin theory for verbs (equation 3). The last equation captures the fact that realization of the singular absolutive may be based on a special version of the lexical item's root. For example, the word for 'cow' has the root *χˁon* for the singular absolutive and *χˁini* for the other case forms in the singular. We will take a closer look at the lexical entry for this item shortly. Many items do not have this special root. In these cases the path <root> at the lexical entry will imply <root sg abs>.

Lexical entries multiply inherit from the lexemic hierarchy via NOUN and a morphological hierarchy containing three class nodes that regulate stem formation and concatenate exponents of case to the stem. The lexical entry for *aˁrum* 'sickle' is given in (37).

(37)
```
Aˁrum:
  <> == NOUN
  <mor> == N_1:<>
  <gloss> == sickle
  <root> == aˁrum.
```

The path <mor> is the subpath of all number and case attribute combinations, for example <mor sg gen>. The values of these paths are inherited via stem-formation class nodes, such as N_1 (equation 2). Ultimately the values of <mor> paths are inherited by <syn> paths, a default stated at NOUN, as we just discussed. So, <syn pl gen> == <mor pl gen>. Example (38) shows how the <mor> value is retrieved from the network in the case of Aˁrum.

(38)
```
N_1:
  <> == N_0
  <pl> == "<root pl>" mul N_1_PL:<>.

N_1_PL:
  <> == čaj MOR_CASE:<>
  <abs> == .
```

```
MOR_CASE:
  <erg> ==
  <gen> == n
  <dat> == s
  <comit> == ɬɬu
  <comp> == χur
  <perm> == kɬ'əna
  <part> == qˁiš
  <superlat> == ttik
  <sublat> == kɬ'ak.
```

The subpath `<mor pl>` inherits the complex value consisting of the lexical entry's root `aˁrum` plus stem formative `mul`. Its extension `<gen>` is then pushed to the second node `N_1_PL` where a second formative `čaj` is picked up. This extra formative is not used for the realization of all cases. For absolutive, there is no `čaj` attachment (second equation). Moreover, the full realization of case exponents, including the genitive, is picked up at `MOR_CASE` except for absolutive. Therefore, the theory captures the fact that the absolutive word-form is distinct in two ways: (i) in the formation of its stem and (ii) in the lack of a case exponent. It also captures the effect of the obliques building on the ergative word-form. The final stage of the evaluation of `<mor pl gen>` is sent to `MOR_CASE:<gen>`, where the case exponent `n` is added. So, the complex value for `<mor pl gen>` ends up being `aˁrum mul čaj n`, and this is the value inherited by `<syn pl gen>` by the `<syn> == "<mor>"` default at `NOUN`.

For singular paths, e g. `<mor sg gen>`, evaluation begins at the node `N_0`, an abstraction over `N_1` and `N_2` since these two stem classes share stem-building mechanisms for singular word-forms. This sharing is expressed by the first equation at `N_1` in (38). The node `N_O` is given in (39) for completeness.

(39)
```
N_0:
  <sg> == "<root sg erg>" N_0_SG:<>.

N_0_SG:
  <> == li MOR_CASE:<>
  <abs> == .
```

The node captures the fact that the singular word-forms are based on the root. But through path extension, a special singular version of the root is used if there is one `<root sg>` or an even more special singular version of the root, the ergative singular root `<root sg erg>`. Since obliques are built on the ergative, the distinction will be seen throughout the oblique subparadigm. For example, the noun *χali* 'family' has the root *χali* and the truncated form *χal* for singular oblique word-forms. More dramatically *abbtu* 'father' has suppletive *um*. Further evaluation comes through the node `N_0_SG` where the stem formative `li` is added, and then the genitive case exponent is added at `MOR_CASE`, as discussed in (39). The absolutive is treated differently in the plural as in the singular, as discussed. Example (40) is a subset of the theorem of the lexical entry Aˤrum, showing the absolutive, ergative and genitive word-forms in singular and plural.

(40)
```
Aˤrum:<gloss> = sickle.
Aˤrum:<syn cat> = n.
Aˤrum:<root> = aˤrum.
Aˤrum:<syn sg abs> = aˤrum.
Aˤrum:<syn sg erg> = aˤrum li.
Aˤrum:<syn sg gen> = aˤrum li n.
Aˤrum:<syn pl abs> = aˤrum mul.
Aˤrum:<syn pl erg> = aˤrum mul čaj.
Aˤrum:<syn pl gen> = aˤrum mul čaj n.
...
```

5.4.2 *Integrating deponent lexical entries*[7]

The word for 'family' *χali* displays extended deponent behaviour in that its non-absolutive *singular* word-forms use formatives normally associated with *plural* word-forms. So, the ergative singular is *χalmaj* with the same formative used for class 3 plurals like *kɬ'annu* 'lover': *kɬ'annimmaj*. In relation to the deponent properties presented in Table 5.1, its Property 1 is the overriding of a first-order default associating distinct stem-formation processes with singular and plural word-forms. In this particular instance, the default is part of the description of class 2, the class to which *χali* belongs based on its plural forms. For example, the ergative plural of *χali* would be *χalittaj* (compare the paradigm of *aˤri* in (34)). Class 2 is represented by the node N_2 in our theory.

(41)
```
N_2:
  <> == N_0
  <pl> == "<root pl>" N_2_PL:<>.

N_2_PL:
  <> == ttaj MOR_CASE:<>
  <abs> == ttu.
```

Plural word-forms are built on a stem formed in ttaj (or ttu for the absolutive). The lexical entry for *χali* is given in (42), and it includes the override of this first-order default.

(42)
```
Xali:
  <> == NOUN
  <mor> == N_2:<>
  <mor sg> == <root sg erg> N_3_PL:<>
  <gloss> == family
  <root> == χali
  <root sg erg> == χal.
```

In (42) the second equation expresses the affiliation of this item with class 2. The third equation overrides the default evaluation of singular paths for this class, replacing them with an alternative evaluation that is normally used for plural word-forms, i.e. evaluation is at a plural node. This node is given in (43), showing the addition of the plural stem formative `maj` for non-absolutive word-forms.

(43)
```
N_3_PL:
  <> == maj MOR_CASE:<>
  <abs> == .
```

Turning to Property 2 and Property 3, properties concerning which cells participate in the mismatch, Archi deponents distinguish themselves from Latin in that all singular cells in a deponent's paradigm are involved in the mismatch. Some of the theorems of *χali* are given in (44), showing that all non-absolutive singular word-forms contain the plural stem formative.

(44)
```
Xali:<syn sg abs> = χali.
Xali:<syn sg erg> = χal maj.
Xali:<syn sg gen> = χal maj n.
Xali:<syn sg dat> = χal maj s.
Xali:<syn sg comit> = χal maj ɬɬu.
Xali:<syn sg comp> = χal maj χur.
Xali:<syn sg perm> = χal maj kɬ'əna.
Xali:<syn sg part> = χal maj qˤiš.
Xali:<syn sg superlat> = χal maj ttik.
Xali:<syn sg sublat> = χal maj kɬ'ak.
...
```

In our hierarchical organization of deponency, the second-order default specifying the mismatch is inherited for every cell that is subject to the mismatch. Recall that the absolutive is not subject to the mismatch since *-maj-* is not used for the absolutive plural (see (43)).

We now turn to Property 4 and Property 5, properties concerning the formal side of the function/form mismatch. We showed above how Latin deponency is characterized by formal equivalence of deponent form and source form: the passive used to realize active is, in all respects, the passive that we would have expected for passive realization. But in Archi this formal default is overridden since deponent form ≠ source form. The lack of equivalence comes about through heteroclisis. Looking at *χali*'s lexical entry in (42), we see that the default realization is through the `N_2` node, and this is overridden by going to a *different* stem-formation-class node for the singular, `N_3_PL`. If the deponent forms were picked up from `N_2`, then deponent and source forms would be equivalent. Entailed in overriding the formal default is the lack of homonymy amongst the deponent forms and the plural forms realizing plural function. This amounts to overriding the defective paradigms default in Archi where Latin inherits. We can now give those theorems of `Xali` corresponding to the plural subparadigm, where all cells are available and all are distinct from the deponent cells since they belong to a different class.

(45)
```
Xali:<syn pl abs> = χali ttu.
Xali:<syn pl erg> = χali ttaj.
Xali:<syn pl gen> = χali ttaj n.
  Xali:<syn pl dat> = χali ttaj s.
  Xali:<syn pl comit> = χali ttaj ɬɬu.
  Xali:<syn pl comp> = χali ttaj χur.
  Xali:<syn pl perm> = χali ttaj kɬ'əna.
  Xali:<syn pl part> = χali ttaj qˤiš.
  Xali:<syn pl superlat> = χali ttaj ttik.
  Xali:<syn pl sublat> = χali ttaj kɬ'ak.
  ...
```

In fact the formal default is overridden not only through a switch to another stem-formation class in the network but a more local switch in the lexical entry itself. In (42) singular word-forms are stated as being based on a singular version of the root, the ergative singular root form. When (44) and (45) are compared we see not only distinctions in the plural stem formative used but in the root itself: *χali* is used for the plural-functioning-as-plural forms and the truncated version *χal* for the deponent forms. In other words, there is a double distinction between deponent and source brought about by lexically specified differences in the root. This is even more dramatic in the case of deponent *c'aj* 'goat', where the singular and plural roots display stronger suppletion: *c'aj* for singular and *c'ohor* for plural. At the same time, the deponent stem formatives are from class 2 and the plurals from class 1. Some of the theorems of this item are shown in (46).

(46)
```
C'aj:<gloss> = goat.
C'aj:<syn cat> = n.
C'aj:<root> = c'aj.
C'aj:<syn sg abs> = c'aj.
C'aj:<syn sg erg> = c'aj ttaj.
C'aj:<syn sg gen> = c'aj ttaj n.
C'aj:<syn pl abs> = c'ohor.
C'aj:<syn pl erg> = c'ohor čaj.
C'aj:<syn pl gen> = c'ohor čaj n.
```

We end our discussion of extended deponency with a noun that displays full suppletion and is also deponent. Unlike *c'aj* and *χali*, the mismatch goes the other way: plural morphosyntax is matched with singular stem formatives. The item in question is the word for 'cow' which has three root forms: *χˤon* used for absolutive singular, *χˤini* for non-absolutive singular word-forms and *bucc'i* for the plural. The plural is formed according to the class 1 and class 2 *singular* pattern, expressed as N_O in the theory (39). The singular non-absolutive uses the *χˤini* root to which the case exponents are directly attached, and the plural uses the suppletive root. A subset of the item's theorems is given in (47).

(47)
```
Xˤon:<gloss> = cow.
Xˤon:<syn cat> = n.
Xˤon:<syn sg abs> = χˤon.
Xˤon:<syn sg erg> = χˤini.
Xˤon:<syn sg gen> = χˤini n.
Xˤon:<syn pl abs> = bucc'i.
Xˤon:<syn pl erg> = bucc'i li.
Xˤon:<syn pl gen> = bucc'i li n.
...
```

Overriding the formal default is manifested in using for the deponent forms the suppletive *bucc'i* to which is attached the singular stem formative li. The result is non-equivalence with the source singular forms in alternative root *χˤini*. A further distinction between deponent and source is the missing li in the singular paradigm. This occurs because, whereas the plurals inherit from N_O_SG, the singulars inherit from somewhere else; they avoid all stem-formation classes and inherit directly from the case exponents node MOR_CASE.

Archi is an example of extended deponency since it overrides the function/form default, the first-order default that characterizes all deponency, but does so with different features from Latin. At the same time, Archi sets itself apart from Latin in its inheritance/overriding behaviour for other deponency properties. For Property 2 it inherits rather than overrides the second-order default that all cells are included in the mismatch: there is no subset of singular cells which does not display deponency in *χali* or *c'aj*; nor is there a subset of plural cells in *χˤon*'s paradigm that lacks deponency. Property 3 does not apply: semi-deponency is predicated on overriding the full participation default. On the other hand, the formal default that deponent and source forms are identical is overridden in Archi through a combination of switching stem-formation class and switching root form for the deponent subparadigm. The consequence is complete paradigms, deponent cells together with cells carrying their original function. Finally, our example deponent nouns in Archi belong to the same non-regularity category as Latin deponents. They are network-directed non-regulars since the alternative value specified by the override is retrievable from nodes in the network supplying information for entirely regular nouns, the stem-formation nodes `N_0`, `N_1`, `N_2` and `N_3`.

Since these non-regular Archi examples involve the noun's number feature, the claim that there is a mismatch of syntactic function and morphological form is not a bold one. For the vast majority of count nouns in Archi there is a formal pattern associated with the singular function which is distinct from a pattern associated with the plural function. Deponents end up with the 'wrong' pattern for one of these functions. In the next section, we consider more carefully whether Latin deponents really do represent function/form mismatch. The feature involved is voice, but the history of the active/passive distinction, as well as its relevance to each and every lexical item, makes voice a less straightforward context for mismatch.

5.5 Is Latin deponency really morphological mismatch?

The *-r* morphology of passive voice in Latin originally served to encode middle voice, a reflex of the PIE two-voice system, active and middle (Baldi 1976).[8] A number of deponents reflect this middle-voice history, for example *morior* 'die' and *nascor* 'be born', so deponency could be a kind of *media tantum*, items with just middles (Kemmer 1993); in terms of 'subject affectedness', we would include reflexives and non-causatives. The association between non-causative semantics and deponents is especially strong amongst verbs derived from nouns and adjectives. Xu, Aronoff and Anshen (2007) carry out a thorough investigation into the correlation between verb semantics and Latin deponency, and they show that the vast majority of denominal deponent verbs are non-causative. Examples include *fatuor* 'play the fool' from *fatuus* 'silly', *copior* 'furnish oneself' from *copia* 'resources' and *ancillor* 'act like a handmaid' from *ancilla* 'handmaid'. This is corroboration of Flobert's earlier observation that derived deponents share a middle semantics (1975: 398). Peter Matthews in a recent paper argues that, given this history, it does not really make sense to view the *-r* morphology as an expression of voice opposition (Matthews 2007). And without opposition there is, of course, no mismatch. So, *morior* and *nascor* are functionally middles, hence they have the 'right' morphology. In other words, for these verbs at least, there is no mismatch between function and form. Conversely, *crescō* 'grow larger' has active morphology but is 'functionally' far from active, yet this verb is not viewed as mismatching function and form. Matthews argues that for non-causatives active and passive voice are simply irrelevant. Instead such items are unspecified for voice, or the voice feature is neutralized. What makes deponents anomalous is not the mismatch of function and form but neutralization co-occurring with what could be thought of as the more 'marked' morphology, i.e. *-r* morphology.

We could, of course, object that the deponent verb's patient argument might then be expected to take a non-nominative case. The fact that it does not actually makes them more anomalous: marked morphology *and* not making use of case forms associated with patients. There are in fact a number of arguments for viewing Latin deponency as morphological mismatch, despite the middle origins of *-r* morphology. Baerman (2006b) provides a good summary, drawing on the Latin deponent literature. The first argument is that not all deponents have middle semantics and not all are non-causative. Our running example has been the verb *hortor* 'encourage', surely occupying a high place on the Transitivity Hierarchy. Others include *fūror* 'steal', *potior* 'capture', *transgredior* 'omit' (for these and more, see Xu *et al.* 2007: 134–5). Flobert notes that it is difficult to put non-derived deponents into any semantic class, though this is the goal of the Xu *et al.* paper. After examining over five hundred deponent verbs, the very tentative conclusion they draw is that deponents tend not to be verbs that have a *physical* effect on an argument. Although this is in part what makes something canonically intransitive, it is a far cry from saying they have middle, or non-causative, semantics as the history would suggest. Even amongst the denominal deponents, where there is a strong non-causative correlation, transitives emerge: *architector* 'construct' derived from *architectus* 'master builder'. In these examples the *-r* morphology cannot be an expression of voice neutralization since voice opposition is relevant.

A second line of argument for mismatch is that voice opposition is actually manifested in a deponent's paradigm. The gerundive in Latin is a verbal adjective with passive function. For example, *amanda* is the gerundive form of *amō* which serves as the target of a female controller, meaning 'having to be loved'. In a deponent such as *sequor* 'follow', the gerundive *sequendus* with masculine controller 'maintains' the passive interpretation: 'having to be followed' (Ernout and Thomas 1953: 183). Of course, this intra-paradigmatic voice opposition is relevant only to transitive deponents. The third argument concerns so-called voice attraction. The verb *coepi* 'to have begun' was discussed as an example of a defective non-regular in Section 5.3.1. As an auxiliary it takes on the voice of its VP complement (at a particular stage of the language's history). Baerman cites Kühner (1955: 677) for this phenomenon. The example Baerman gives is displayed in (48), where the main verb appearing in the passive (*premi*) attracts passive voice on *coepi*, shown in bold.

(48) post a Pompei procurator-ibus sescent-is
after by Pompey.SG.GEN agent-PL.ABL 600-PL.ABL
prem-i **coeptus est**
press-PASS.PRS.INF began.PASS.PF.PRS.3SG
'afterwards he began to be pressed by scores (=600s) of Pompey's agents.'
(Cicero, *Ad Atticum*)

However, the attraction is strictly functional rather than formal. When the *-r* morphology on the main verb has an active function, in other words when there is mismatch, the auxiliary is 'not interested': in (49) the main verb is *insequor* 'pursue', and the auxiliary remains morphologically active.

(49) quem cum egredi-entem insequ-i
who.SG.ACC when go.out-PRS.PPLE.SG.ACC follow-PASS.PRS.INF
coep-issem
began-PST.PF.SBJV.1SG
'when I began to press upon him (=follow), as he was departing'[9]
(Cicero, *Oratio de Haruspicum Responso*)

Voice attraction sensitive to the functional passive only, intra-paradigmatic voice opposition in the gerundive and lack of a restriction on deponents to be middle or non-causative combine to suggest that Latin had active and passive voice opposition, and passive form was mismatched with active function in deponents. In the next chapter, we provide evidence for mismatch of a different kind, where deponents are diachronically 'realigned' so that active function is expressed by active morphology. One must suppose that realignment as a levelling pressure is based on perceived misalignment or mismatch.

5.6 Concluding remarks

Morphological mismatch entails a separate, autonomous morphological component whose interface with syntax is characterized as a relation between morphosyntactic features and the way they are systematically realized, but one that is by default and subject to overriding. Deponent lexical items represent a particular kind of non-regularity, where the override's alternative value is retrieved from a place in the network that holds generalizations for something different. In the case of Latin deponents, active paths override by inheriting generalizations about passive paths. Mismatch phenomena can vary within and across languages. This variation reflects the fact that deponency as non-regularity is a scalar notion. Through a hierarchical treatment of regularity, instances of deponency can be seen as occupying a particular hierarchical position. The lower positions represent a higher degree of non-regularity but with an interesting consequence: the alternative value ends up being the highest level default, what we have termed the exceptional case default in Chapter 2, Section 2.3.2. In this way the non-regularity is highly constrained: values are either those of the first (highest) override or those of the first (highest) default. Moreover, the override values themselves are constrained since they must be available from elsewhere in the network. Path-ordering principles enforce this constraint since values can only be inherited by the extension of the subpaths that are being overridden. For this reason the voice feature must be the first attribute, as that feature is the only one that is being overridden. Likewise, for semi-deponents, both voice and aspect are overridden so both must be expressed as attributes at the beginning of the attribute path in order for whole sets of cells to be affected.

In the next chapter, we look at morphological mismatch in a diachronic context and show that the restructuring of Latin deponent paradigms points to further evidence for autonomous morphology, as we propose that lexical entries hold two paradigms, one of which is purely a product of the morphological system with no syntactic consequence. The presence of morphological mismatch is felt, however, in the specific case of paradigmatic restructuring which we call paradigmatic realignment. We represent realignment as resetting the first-order default whose overriding is responsible for the mismatch.

6 *Defaults and paradigmatic restructuring: diachronic deponency*

6.0 Introduction

We showed in the previous chapter that deponency as morphological mismatch is further evidence for an autonomous level of morphology. In Chapter 1, Section 1.2.1 and Chapter 2, Section 2.4.2 we characterized it as a mismatch where the slippage between the two components is extreme. In this chapter we consider Latin deponency in a diachronic context. We find that deponent paradigms disappear by ceding their mismatch pattern of exponence to an aligned one. As we shall see, this move assumes the notion of 'virtual paradigm', the regular alternative paradigm that is called into the service of syntax at a later diachronic stage.

A number of centuries after Plautus penned the lines displayed in Chapter 5, a newer verb *hortor* is used, and patterns after any other regular first conjugation verb. Its virtual paradigm has been made real (1).

(1)	Horta-bat	ceter-os	Apostol-us:
	encourage-ACT.IPFV.PST.3sg	other-PL.ACC	Apostle-SG.NOM:
	recorda-mini	fratr-um	
	remember-PASS.IMP.2Pl	brother-PL.ACC	

'The Apostle exhorted the others: remember the brothers.'
(Luculentius, *Commentary on Romans XII 6*, first–second century AD)

We account for paradigm restructuring as the *realignment* of function with form by simply resetting the first-order default. The diachronic development of the verb *hortor* is sketched out in (2).

(2)			
	Stage N	`<syn active> == "<mor passive>"`	first-order default overridden
	Stage N + 1	`<syn active> == "<mor active>"`	first-order default restored

Realignment is lexical. In the Luculentius example, the word-form *recordamini* is passive in form but active in meaning. In other words, at the stage when *hortor* was no longer deponent, the verb *recordor* 'remember' still was. This means that (2) must be expressed within the lexical entry. We capture lexical change as the overriding of specific paths of a source/ancestral lexical entry. In the case of realignment, what is overridden is the `<syn active>` path. The alternative value is inherited from `VERB`. In other words, realignment is expressed as inheritance of the exceptional case default, a mechanism that allows for incremental change which is lexical, but formulated in terms of access to a rule.

(3)
```
Hortor_2:
  <> == Hortor
  <syn active> == VERB.
```

In this chapter we give a Network Morphology account of paradigmatic restructuring, specifically with reference to deponents. Virtual paradigms are central to our account, the product of morphology by itself and further evidence for autonomous morphology. In Section 6.1 we situate paradigmatic realignment in the context of paradigmatic restructuring, showing it to be the result of the same pressures found in cases of analogical levelling and extension. Section 6.2 is devoted to virtual paradigms, by-products of the morphological machinery that are never pressed into the service of syntax. In (3) `<syn active>` inherits from `VERB` and this means that it will inherit the equation which states that morphosyntactically active verbs are morphologically active, as we showed in the previous chapter. The double quotes in the RHS for stage N+1 indicate that the value is determined from the global context and so it will be available at the lexical entry. Despite being a deponent verb, ancestral *hortor* has available to it an active paradigm from the morphological system. This is of no use while the lexeme is deponent, but a descendent lexeme may make use of it. Section 6.3 is the Network Morphology account of deponency regularization as realignment due to default restoration and draws extensively on Flobert's (1975) survey of deponency. In Section 6.4 we consider some of the wider implications of an account that invokes virtual paradigms, and we discuss how our model might be extended to account for the emergence of deponents in the first place.

6.1 Diachronic deponency as paradigmatic restructuring

There are two ways of thinking about paradigmatic reorganization. First, it is the stems of a paradigm which become phonologically uniform where previously there was a distinction. This is analogical levelling. Alternatively in analogical extension, reorganization involves the exponents. In stem-based reorganization phonological changes can cause distinctions to arise in the stem of different word-forms in a lexeme's paradigm. To restore transparency between meaning and form – in this case stem – one of the stems is taken as the model for all the stems. An example is the reorganization of the Old English (OE) paradigm for the word 'choose', as discussed in Hock (1986: 168–9) and McMahon (1994: 73–4), given in (4):

(4)

	OE	Modern English	
present	cēo[z]-an	choose	[z]
past sg	cēa[s]	chose	[z]
past pl	cu[r]-on	chose	[z]
past participle	co[r]-en	chos-en	[z]

The OE stems are distinct because of different distributions of the vowel and stem-final consonant. There is a stem in [s], a stem in [z] and a stem in [r]. These distinctions are the outcome of phonological changes affecting the language as a whole.[1] By the time of Modern English, the disruption in the paradigm caused by these phonological changes is ironed out by analogy: the stem in [z] is used as the analogical model for the stem of all cells in the paradigm. In this way, levelling undoes phonological processes that have led to weak suppletion.

In cases of strong suppletion, the distinct stems in the paradigm come about for other reasons and are not the direct result of phonological rules. Nonetheless analogical pressure can still act to level the paradigm. An example of this is the Russian word for 'eye' whose chronology is given in (5) based on Chumakina, Hippisley and Corbett (2004).

(5)

Sg (nom)	Pl (nom)	Chronology
ok-o	oč′-i	10th–16th cent.
glaz-Ø	oč′-i	16th–19th cent.
glaz-Ø	glaz-a	19th cent. – present

The original paradigm had a uniform set of stems, albeit with a minor distinction in the stem-final consonant where /k/ alternated with the palatalized counterpart /č/ in the plural subparadigm. In the sixteenth century, we find a suppletive paradigm where the singular subparadigm is occupied by the completely phonologically distinct *glaz-*, the stem for a different lexeme meaning 'sphere', cognate with Polish *głaz* 'stone' (Vasmer 1986: 409). How did this come about? One account, from Unbegaun (1969), is seen in the context of local unmarkedness. The plural of this particular lexeme is the unmarked category, for obvious reasons. In marked contexts where speakers want to refer to the singular idea of 'eye', they are most likely referring to the eyeball, hence the association with sphere. Unbegaun's source is the *Kabal´nye knigi*, records of the pacts between Russian indebted peasants and their masters detailing their service obligations, the so-called 'kabala'. Physical descriptions of peasants were recorded, and many of these included a note on their eyes, identifying colour and any blemishes. One such example from the texts dated from the end of the sixteenth century to the beginning of the seventeenth is given in (6).

(6) oč´-i ser-i, na prav-om glaz-e bel´m-o
eye-NOM.PL grey-NOM.PL, on right-LOC.SG eye[ball]-LOC.SG blemish-NOM.SG
'the eyes are grey, on the right eye[ball] is a blemish'.

Over time the suppletive paradigm for 'eye' was reorganized in favour of the stem used in the singular paradigm. Though there are instances of *oč´i* in Pushkin (nineteenth century), these are stylistically marked.[2] In both examples it is the stem that is at fault, as it were, and paradigmatic reorganization involves innovation in the stem. Example (7) presents the Russian 'eye' example as stem-based reorganization.

(7)

Sg (nom)	Pl (nom)	Chronology
X-o	*X*-i	10th–16th cent.
Y-Ø	*X*-i	16th–19th cent.
Y-Ø	*Y*-a	19th cent.–present

Equally, we could have reorganization that involves the exponent. In Old English there were a number of rival affixes to mark plural, as shown in (8).[3] This system of plural exponence was reorganized in favour of one of the affixes used for masculine nouns. As with stem-based reorganization, the result of exponent-based reorganization is greater transparency in form and meaning correspondence. Where once there was a one-to-many mapping between the feature value PLURAL and its exponents, there is now (largely) a one-to-one mapping.

(8)

	Old English	Modern English
Masculine nouns:	stān-as	stone-s
	sun-a	son-s
	steorra-n	star-s
Neuter nouns:	word	word-s
	sper-u	spear-s
	ēag-an	eye-s
Feminine nouns:	car-a	care-s
	tung-an	tongue-s
	bēc	book-s

It is exponent-based reorganization that motivates the diachronic changes of Latin deponent paradigms. Morphological mismatch as represented by Latin deponents was schematized in Chapter 5, Section 5.0. Example (2) is given again here as (9).

(9)

LEXEME 1		LEXEME N		HORTOR	
ACT	PASS	ACT	PASS	ACT	PASS
X–α	X–β	Y–α	Y–β	Z–β	- - -

Given the range of *hortor*'s disorganization, mismatch coupled with defectiveness, (10) shows what it would mean for this verb to undergo reorganization. This is a *realignment* of function with the standard pattern of exponence and a kind of restoration of the defective pattern.

(10)

LEXEME 1		LEXEME N		HORTOR	
ACT	PASS	ACT	PASS	ACT	PASS
X–α	X–β	Y–α	Y–β	Z–α	Z–β

We see realignment as a two-step process: first passive realignment then active realignment. But whereas there are passive forms (the deponent forms) available to realign with, there are no active forms. Realignment presupposes something with which to realign. Our account relies on the presence of active forms in a deponent lexeme, which serve a virtual existence and are made 'real' only through realignment.[4] In (1) we had an example of active realignment. In (11) we give the same verb *hortor* after passive realignment: morphological passive corresponds to morphosyntactic passive.

(11) sic enim a Domin-o sub apostol-orum numer-o
thus for by Lord-ABL.SG under apostle-GEN.PL order-ABL.SG
hort-amur
encourage-1PL.PRS.PASS
(=PASS)
'for thus are we encouraged by the Lord under the order of the apostles'
(Jonas, *Vita Columbani* 2: 9; seventh–eighth century AD)

Our account provides for the fact that passive realignment and active realignment may happen at different diachronic stages.

Active realignment is in need of active forms, as we have said. An interesting fact about the behaviour of regularized *hortor* is that its active pattern of exponents follows the first conjugational class, the same class responsible for its passive forms. As we will see, in all instances of active realignment the forms that are used follow the pattern of the passive forms. In the next section, we show how virtual paradigms are the result of inheriting values from the morphological hierarchy that do not actually get used as realizations of morphosyntax due to the overriding of `<syn> == "<mor>"`.

6.2 Virtual paradigms and inheritance from the morphological hierarchy

As discussed in previous chapters, Network Morphology assumes autonomous morphology as represented by an inflectional hierarchy that lies orthogonal to a hierarchy of lexemes. A lexical entry inherits syntactic category information as well as default semantics from the lexemic hierarchy. From the lexemic hierarchy, it also inherits information about morphosyntactic realization through the path `<syn> == "<mor>"`, as we showed in the previous chapter. The effect of this equation is that two different sets of theorems can be inferred for a lexeme: a `<syn>` set of theorems generated by the equation and inherited from the lexemic hierarchy, and a `<mor>` set which has the same values as the `<syn>` set, but has independent status as something inherited from the inflectional hierarchy. A sample of both theorem sets of the lexical entry `Amō` is given in (12).

(12) a.
```
Amo:<gloss> = love.
Amo:<syn active imperfective present indicative sg 2>
    = am ā s.
Amo:<syn active imperfective past indicative sg 1>
    = am ā bam.
```

```
Amo:<syn active imperfective past indicative sg 2> =
    am ā bās.
Amo:<syn active imperfective past indicative sg 3> =
    am ā bat.
Amo:<syn passive imperfective present indicative sg 2> =
    am ā ris.
Amo:<syn passive imperfective past indicative sg 1> =
    am ā bār.
Amo:<syn passive imperfective past indicative sg 2> =
    am ā bāris.
Amo:<syn passive imperfective past indicative sg 3> =
    am ā bātur.
...
```

b.

```
Amo:<gloss> = love.
Amo:<mor active imperfective present indicative sg 2>
    = am ā s.
Amo:<mor active imperfective past indicative sg 1>
    = am ā bam.
Amo:<mor active imperfective past indicative sg 2>
    = am ā bās.
Amo:<mor active imperfective past indicative sg 3>
    = am ā bat.
Amo:<mor passive imperfective present indicative sg 2>
    = am ā ris.
Amo:<mor passive imperfective past indicative sg 1> =
    am ā bār.
Amo:<mor passive imperfective past indicative sg 2> =
    am ā bāris.
Amo:<mor passive imperfective past indicative sg 3> =
    am ā bātur.
...
```

When we check the paths and their values, we see that the <syn> paths in (12a) have the same values as the <mor> paths in (12b); this of course is the full list of inferences of <syn> == "<mor>" at VERB. Conversely, overriding the default has the effect of non-equivalence between the <syn> and <mor> paths, the morphological mismatch which Latin deponents like *hortor* represent. Example (13) are some <syn> and <mor> theorem sets for the lexeme *hortor*.

(13) a.

```
Hortor:<syn active imperfective present indicative sg 2>
       = hort ā ris.
Hortor:<syn active imperfective past indicative sg 1>
       = hort ā bār.
Hortor:<syn active imperfective past indicative sg 2>
       = hort ā bāris.
Hortor:<syn active imperfective past indicative sg 3>
       = hort ā bātur.
```

```
Hortor:<syn passive imperfective present indicative sg 2>
        = undefined.
Hortor:<syn passive imperfective past indicative sg 1>
        = undefined.
Hortor:<syn passive imperfective past indicative sg 2>
        = undefined.
Hortor:<syn passive imperfective past indicative sg 3>
        = undefined.
...
```

b.

```
Hortor:<mor active imperfective present indicative sg 2>
        = hort ā s.
Hortor:<mor active imperfective past indicative sg 1>
        = hort ā bam.
Hortor:<mor active imperfective past indicative sg 2>
        = hort ā bās.
Hortor:<mor active imperfective past indicative sg 3>
        = hort ā bat.
Hortor:<mor passive imperfective present indicative sg 2>
        = hort ā ris.
Hortor:<mor passive imperfective past indicative sg 2>
        = hort ā bār
Hortor:<mor passive imperfective past indicative sg 2>
        = hort ā bāris.
Hortor:<mor passive imperfective past indicative sg 3>
        = hort ā bātur.
...
```

A comparison of (13a) and (13b) reveals the nature of Hortor's non-regularity as a mismatch between the theorems inferable for syntax and those inferable for morphology. In principle the deponent lexeme has available to it the paradigm of other regular lexemes. In other words, mismatch and defectiveness are better viewed through an intra-lexeme rather than a cross-lexeme comparison. The mismatch is really the <mor> theorems having active forms as values of active attribute paths but the <syn> theorems having something different. And defectiveness in the <syn> theorems is implied by the presence of <mor passive> values in the <mor> theorems. In other words, the 'expected' word-forms that are traded for something else, making a deponent a deponent, lead a parallel existence in the deponent item's *morphological* paradigm.

The possibility of a lexeme having two paradigms is assumed in Paradigm Function Morphology (PFM) analyses of syncretism, heteroclisis and deponency. This is the purpose behind Paradigm Linkage theory, as proposed in a number of papers by Gregory Stump (Stump 2002; 2006; Stewart and Stump 2007). A lexeme's *syntactic* or *content* paradigm contains the set of forms that is licensed by particular syntactic configurations and that will be inserted into terminal nodes of phrase structure. The second paradigm, the *morphological* or *form* paradigm, is a repository of the output of standard realization rules operating over the lexeme's stem, or stems, in accordance with the inferential–realizational approach. Although a lexeme has two paradigms, the syntactic paradigm consults the morphological paradigm for all its values, rendering the two paradigms structurally indistinguishable *in most cases*. The reason why both paradigms are not indistinguishable in *all* cases is that the manner of consultation, i.e. the manner of 'paradigm linkage', may be altered for some subclass of lexemes, resulting in separate syntactic and morphological paradigms. Because the interface with syntax is featural rather than formative in paradigm-based approaches, as discussed in Chapter 1, Section 1.2.1, the syntax is sensitive to the morphosyntactic properties that a word-form carries but blind to its formal properties, such that cells in the syntactic paradigm can in principle be at odds with corresponding cells in the morphological paradigm. Since the link between the two paradigms is not direct for every lexeme, it is best viewed as a generalization or a default which can be overridden. The definition of paradigm linkage is given in (14).

(14) *Universal default rule of paradigm linkage* (Stump 2002; 2006)
Where *R* is *L*[exeme]'s root in language *l*
$\text{SPF}\ (<L, \sigma>) = \text{MPF}\ (<R, \sigma>)$

The definition is couched within the Paradigm Function Morphology framework and basically says that there is a cell in a lexeme's *syntactic* paradigm specified by a syntactic paradigm function (SPF) over the lexeme and a specific morphosyntactic feature set. There is also a cell in the same lexeme's *morphological* paradigm, i.e. a paradigm of cells specified by morphological paradigm functions (MPFs). This is a pairing of the same morphosyntactic property set with the lexeme's root (or stem). And, importantly, there is a direct link between the two cells belonging to the separate paradigms. It should be noted that in Paradigm Function Morphology the MPFs are realization rules, so that the cells in the morphological paradigm are outputs of realization rules. Finally, this linkage is described as a *default* rule, such that in theory one could have $\text{SPF}\ (<L, \sigma>) = \text{MPF}_2\ (<R, \sigma'>)$, where $\sigma \neq \sigma'$, an actual case of which is deponency (Stewart and Stump 2007: 393): active cells in the syntactic paradigm are not linked to active cells in the morphological paradigm but instead to passive cells. So for Latin deponents, the linkage is <*L*, {active…}> = <*R*, {passive…}>.

Lexeme 1,		*...,*	*Lexeme N,*	*...,*	*Lexeme D*
syn parad			syn parad		syn parad
ACT	PASS	ACT	PASS	ACT	PASS
L1-α	L1-β	L2-α	L2-β	LD-β	-------
⇑	⇑	⇑	⇑	⇑	
⇑	⇑	⇑	⇑	⇐	⇐
					⇑
mor parad			mor parad		mor parad
ACT	PASS	ACT	PASS	ACT	PASS
R1-α	R1-β	R2-α	R2-β	RD-α	RD-β
⇑	⇑	⇑	⇑	⇑	⇑
		Morphological realization rules			

Figure 6.1 *Paradigm linkage and Latin deponents*

It is important to note that (14) is *de facto* in operation in Network Morphology through the equation `<syn> == "<mor>"`. In Network Morphology separate paradigms naturally fall out from partitioning the network into lexemic and inflectional hierarchies, such that `<syn>` paths expressing the syntactic paradigm are inherited from the lexemic hierarchy and are themselves instantiated by `<mor>` paths expressing the morphological paradigms that are inherited from the morphological hierarchy. Paradigm linkage as a default that is overridden for Latin deponents is schematized in Figure 6.1.

Figure 6.1 shows that for most lexemes (Lexeme 1, Lexeme N) the syntactic paradigm containing the lexeme's morphosyntactic word-forms is informed by a separate morphological paradigm. Reading from the bottom of the figure, the output of morphological realization rules – in Network Morphology, evaluation in the morphological hierarchy – furnishes a lexeme's morphological paradigm – in Network Morphology, generates morphological theorems. In this example the active subparadigm is expressed by a pattern that modifies the root R with suffixation of -α and the passive subparadigm with suffixation of `-β`. The values of these cells are passed up to the syntactic paradigm, ready for lexical insertion, in Network Morphology `<syn> == "<mor>"`. Lexeme D represents a deponent lexeme. Looking from the bottom of the figure upwards, this lexeme is similar to other lexemes. Its active and passive morphological subparadigms hold the outputs of the same realization rules as for other lexemes; hence, it shares the same exponence. This is the deponent lexeme's morphological paradigm. What distinguishes Lexeme D from the other lexemes emerges when we move up the system, as it were, where we see the morphological paradigm passing information from its passive subparadigm to the 'wrong' place in the syntactic paradigm, i.e. to the active subparadigm. At the same time, nothing from its active subparadigm is passed. This will bring about defectiveness. This move renders the deponent lexeme's morphological paradigm *virtual*. From the point of view of the syntactic paradigm, we have passive morphology realizing active morphosyntax (deponency) – and passive morphosyntax with no formal content (defectiveness).

Through time the link between a deponent's virtual paradigm, i.e. its morphological paradigm, and its syntactic paradigm is readjusted. In our hierarchical account of deponency, this is a matter of recovering the first-order default `<syn> == "<mor>"`, the universal default of paradigm linkage, and making the virtual real. Paradigm restructuring in this special case is realignment of the morphological and syntactic paradigms. Diachronic deponency is outlined in the next section.

6.3 The Network Morphology account of diachronic deponency

Latin deponent verbs are non-regular but are by no means marginal. Flobert (1975) demonstrates that they have some currency in Classical Latin, using as evidence their occurrence in the colloquial-style comedies of Plautus (second century BC). Based on his sample of texts spanning various authors and diachronic stages, he gives 7 per cent as the mean deponent proportion of all verbs, with some texts over 10 per cent deponent (Flobert 1975: 512–13). Yet over time the subset of deponents that starts to follow the regular pattern increases in size, so that by Proto-Romance full regularization of deponents is complete (see Bonnet 1968: 402; Strecker 1929: 61 and Ernout 1945:182–8 amongst others).

To get a sense of deponency regularization, we can consider the fate of the deponent verb *lamentor* 'weep, wail'. An example of its classical usage is given in (15), from Plautus' comedy *Miles Gloriosus*, Act I, lines 5–6 (Lodge 1901–33: 879) from diachronic Stage I.

(15) nam ego hanc mechaer-am mihi
CONJ I.SG.NOM this.ACC.SG sword-ACC.SG me.DAT.SG
consol-ari[5] vol-o ne lament-etur
console-PRS.INF.PASS wish-1SG.PRS.ACT NEG wail-3SG.PRS.SBJV.PASS (=ACT)
'Verily I would comfort this blade of mine, lest he lament'[6]

Now compare (15) with (16–18), which are imperfective and perfect examples of the same lexeme appearing at different diachronic stages. They conform to the standard active pattern of exponence. All examples are taken from Flobert's survey[7]. For each we can supply the DATR path for which the word-form is the value. Examples (16–18) are from Flobert (1975: 313).

(16) *lamentat* `<syn active imperfective present indicative sg 3>`
sicut prophet-a lament-at clam-ans:
as prophet-NOM.SG wail-3SG.PRS.ACT proclaim-PRS.PPLE:
vir-i iniqu-i et dolos-[i]
man-NOM.PL unjust-NOM.PL and deceitful-NOM.PL
'as the prophet wails proclaiming: unjust and deceitful men'
(Petrus Chrysologus, *Sermons* 125: 98; Stage X)

(17) *lamentabit* `<syn active imperfective future indicative sg 3>`
qui hic pasc-itur, hic satur-atur… illic
who.NOM.SG here gratify-3SG.PRS.PASS here sate-3SG.PRS.PASS there
esuri-et, illic siti-et… illic
hunger-3SG.FUT.ACT there thirst-3SG.FUT.ACT There
lamenta-bit…
wail-3SG.FUT.ACT
'the man who here battens, here sates himself, here makes merry…shall hereafter hunger, thirst, mourn, wail…'[8]
(St Columba, *Instructiones* VII, 2; Stage X)

(18) *lamentavimus* `<syn active perfect present indicative pl 1>`
cantav-imus vo-bis et non salta-stis,
sing-1PL.PF.ACT you-DAT.PL and NEG dance-2PL.PF.ACT
lamentav-imus vo-bis et non plora-stis
wail-1PL.PF.ACT you-DAT.PL and NEG weep-2PL.PF.ACT
'we sang to you and you did not dance, we lamented to you and you did not weep'
(*Vetus Latina*: *Lucas Evangelium* 7, vol. 32; Stage VIII)

From (15) we see that *lamentor* is a Class 1 verb. In other words it follows the morphological patterning of *amō* 'love' in the passive. In (16–18) its active exponence also follows that of *amō*, a clear indication that the change is highly restricted: we start with a Class 1 verb and continue with a Class 1 verb. Instead of using passive morphology to realize active morphosyntax, the 'new' *lamentor* delivers an active paradigm, strictly in conformance with its inflectional class. Inflectional class stability is an important characteristic of the regularized deponents surveyed in Flobert, as we shall see. For each example we give its diachronic stage based on (19), which follows Flobert. A second point about these examples is that they all appear historically later than the original deponent lexeme.

(19)

Diachronic stage	Primary author(s)	Dates	Emperor(s)
Republic period			
I	Plautus	– 169 BC	n.a
II	Terence	169–80 BC	n.a
III	Cicero	80–43 BC	n.a
High Empire period			
IV	Virgil	43–14 BC	Augustus
V	Seneca	14 BC – 68 AD	Julio-Claudien dynasty
VI	Tacitus	AD 69–117	Flavius, Trajan
VII	Apuleius	AD 117–92	Hadrian, Antonine
Late period			
VIII	Tertullian	AD 193–337	Severius–Constantine
IX	(various)	AD 337–423	Constantine II
X	Gregory of Tours	mid 5th – end 6th cent.	n.a
XI	(various)	7th and 8th cent.	n.a

From (19) we see that deponent *lamentor* has currency in the Republic period, specifically at Stage I. Its non-deponent behaviour is subsequent: Stage VIII (18), Stage X (16, 17).

The examples we have seen so far show the regularization of a deponent lexeme as a matter of realigning active morphology with active syntax. Full regularization will be the reuse of the passive morphological paradigm for passive syntax. The verb *lamentor* may be either intransitive, as in examples (16)–(18), or transitive, as in (20).

(20) *lamenteris* `<syn active imperfective present subjunctive sg 2>`

Ego pol te faci-am, scel-us,
I.SG.NOM by.Pollux you.SG.ACC do-1SG.FUT.ACT scoundrel-VOC.SG

Te quoque… ips-um ut lament-eris
you.SG.ACC also… pro-ACC.SG COMP bewail-2SG.PRS.SBJV.PASS (=ACT)

'By the Lord, I'll make you, you villain, I'll make you mourn yourself as well.'[9]

(Plautus, *Persa*, Act IV, Line 743; Stage I)

This means that *lamentor* has the potential to be inserted into a passive configuration, as any other transitive verb. As part of its regularization, this potential is realized by matching its passive forms with passive syntax, as shown in (21), an example from the *Vulgate Bible* (Flobert 1975: 365).

(21) *lamentatae sunt* `<syn passive perfect present indicative pl 3>`

iuven-es	eorum	comed-it	ignis	et
youth-ACC.PL	them.GEN.PL	consume-3SG.PRF.ACT	fire-NOM.SG	and

virgin-es	eorum	non	sunt	lamentatae
virgin-NOM.PL	them.GEN.PL	NEG	AUX.3PL	lament.PASS.PPLE.3PL.F (=PASS)

'fire consumed their young men and their maidens were not lamented'
(*Vulgate: Psalms* 77: 63; Stage IX)

This means that regularization of a deponent has two parts: the 'innovation' of an active morphology for active syntax, and the reassignment of its passive morphology to passive syntax. The latter is relevant only to those lexemes with an internal argument that is expressed as a direct object in the accusative case. However, sometimes a deponent with a non-accusative internal argument is 'passivized' as part of the regularization process, as we will see in Section 6.4.2. With these three points in mind – morphological class stability, regularization as diachronically later, and the distinction between what Flobert calls the 'activation' of a deponent verb from its 'passivation' – we turn to our Network Morphology account of paradigmatic realignment.

6.3.1 *Activation of deponents*

Flobert is careful to separate activation of deponents from passivation, though as we shall see he argues that the two regularization processes are related. In this section we give our Network Morphology account of deponent *activation* as resetting the default that links the `<syn active>` paths of a deponent lexical entry to its `<mor active>` paths, as with the instance of a regular lexeme like `amō` (see (12)). In (22) we have an example of the verb *ūtor* 'use' from Plautus, showing its deponent behaviour in the Republic period.

(22)

At	enim	nimis	long-o	sermon-e	ut-imur
but	for	excessively	long-ABL.SG	talk-ABL.SG	use-1PL.PRS.PASS (=ACT)

'But see here, we're going in for [lit. using] too much talk.'[10]
(Plautus, *Trinummus*, Act III, 806; Stage I)

Lexical entries for *ūtor* and *hortor* are expressed as nodes inheriting the path description <syn active> == "<mor passive>" from the DEPONENT node, as discussed at length in Chapter 5. This is shown again in (23) and (24).

(23)
```
Ūtor:
  <> == DEPONENT
  <gloss> == use
  <root> == ūt
  <stem 3> == ūs
  <stem> == CONJ_3.
```

(24)
```
Hortor:
  <> == DEPONENT
  <gloss> == encourage
  <root> == hort
  <stem> == CONJ_1.
```

Note that regardless of their deponency the lexical entries need to be specified for conjugational class to inherit the correct passive morphology from the morphological hierarchy. This is achieved by the equation <stem> == CONJ_1 (see previous chapter for details).

Our hierarchical account of the activation of these items amounts to situating an alternative 'activated' lexical entry in the network such that it shares all facts with its deponent counterpart, except that the path equation <syn active> == "<mor passive>" inherited from DEPONENCY is overridden. This is shown in (25).

(25)
```
Hortor_ACT:
  <> == Hortor
  <syn active> == VERB.
```

The alternative value inherited by the override is the exceptional case default, the equation <syn active> == "<mor active>" available from VERB, a path that extends the first-order default <syn> == "<mor>".

Our model of paradigmatic restructuring as realignment is, thus, a hierarchical representation of diachronic stages of an item coupled with inheritance of the exceptional case default by the lexical entry at the later stage. For both lexical entries, the primary source of inheritance is the respective deponent counterpart. The historically earlier item dominates the innovative item. The nature of the innovation is expressed by the override.[11] This means that much of the old ūtor is preserved in the new ūtor: semantics, syntactic category, stem and, most crucially, inflectional class, in this case Conjugation 3. Deponent activation is expressed as inheritance by active <syn> paths of active <mor> paths. This represents the syntactic paradigm accessing a virtual morphological paradigm whose pattern of exponence follows the third conjugation. Example (26) contains some theorems for the morphosyntax of another Conjugation 3 verb, *rego* 'rule'.

(26)
```
Rego:<gloss> = rule.
Rego:<syn active imperfective present indicative sg 3> =
     reg i t.
Rego:<syn active imperfective present indicative sg 3> =
     reg i mus.
Rego:<syn active imperfective past indicative sg 3> =
     reg e bat.
Rego:<syn active imperfective past indicative pl 1> =
     reg e bamus.
Rego:<syn active imperfective past indicative pl 3> =
     reg e bant.
Rego:<syn passive imperfective present indicative sg 3> =
     reg i tur.
Rego:<syn passive imperfective present indicative pl 1> =
     reg i mur.
Rego:<syn passive imperfective past indicative sg 3> =
     reg e bātur.
Rego:<syn passive imperfective past indicative pl 1> =
     reg e bāmur.
Rego:<syn passive imperfective past indicative pl 3> =
     reg e bāntur.
...
```

In (22) we saw the deponent form *utimur* for first-person plural present. The same cell in *rego*'s paradigm is expressed as the eighth equation in the list in (26), and we see the same Conjugation 3 pattern of exponence, `regimur`. In (27–9) we give examples of activated *ūtor* taken from Flobert (1975: 310). They pattern in the same way as the active equations in `Rego`'s theorems.

(27) *utebat* `<syn active imperfective past indicative sg 3>`

absque	taedi-o	ute-bat	ips-o
without	disgust-ABL.SG	use-3SG.IPFV.PST.ACT	pro-ABL.SG

'[although she considered this vision to be meaningless] she made use of [it] without any actual distaste.'
(*Vita Landiberti* 20; Stage XI)

(28) *utebant* `<syn active imperfective past indicative pl 3>`

Arrian-orum	sect-a	ute-bant
Arrian-GEN.PL	mode-ABL.SG	use-3PL.IPFV.PST.ACT

'[Those who had settled in Cisalpine regions] practised the way of life of the Arrians.'
(Fredegarius, *Chronicles* III, 9; Stage XI)

(29) *utebamus* <syn active imperfective past indicative pl 1>

qu-am	aufer-entes	adiutori-o	ute-bamus
wh-ACC.SG	raise-PRS.PPLE.NOM.PL	support-ABL.SG	use-1PL.IPFV.PST.ACT

'which after we had raised we used supporting cable'
(*Vetus Latina: Actus apostolorum* 27: 17; Stage VIII)

At this point we need to ask: where do these active forms come from? Our answer is that they belong to the morphological paradigm of deponent *ūtor*, the output of productive morphological rules, in this case those rules available for regular Conjugation 3 verbs. Recall the `<mor>` theorems of a Conjugation 1 verb, `Hortor` (13b). Along with its other facts, the evaluation of these `<mor>` paths is inherited from ancestral `Ūtor` by activated `Ūtor`. And because of the 'new' path description `<syn active> == VERB` specified at activated `Ūtor`, they are given as the values of the `<syn active>` paths; in other words, for the first time they are instantiations of the syntactic paradigm and, hence, are objects for lexical insertion. Example (30) shows the theorems corresponding to the morphological imperfect past subparadigm of the lexical entry for `Ūtor`.

(30)
```
Ūtor:<mor active imperfective past indicative sg 1> =
     ūt e bam.
Ūtor:<mor active imperfective past indicative sg 2> =
     ūt e bās.
Ūtor:<mor active imperfective past indicative sg 3> =
     ūt e bat.
Ūtor:<mor active imperfective past indicative pl 1> =
     ūt e bamus.
Ūtor:<mor active imperfective past indicative pl 2> =
     ūt e batis.
Ūtor:<mor active imperfective past indicative pl 3> =
     ūt e bant.
```

In (31) we give the representation of the corresponding cells of the active *syntactic* paradigm of the innovative activated *ūtor*, and we see that the two sets of values are equivalent.

(31)
```
Ūtor_ACT:<syn active imperfective past indicative sg 1> =
         ūt e bam.
Ūtor_ACT:<syn active imperfective past indicative sg 2> =
         ūt e bās.
Ūtor_ACT:<syn active imperfective past indicative sg 3> =
         ūt e bat.
Ūtor_ACT:<syn active imperfective past indicative pl 1> =
         ūt e bamus.
```

```
Ūtor_ACT:<syn active imperfective past indicative pl 2> =
        ūt e batis.
Ūtor_ACT:<syn active imperfective past indicative pl 3> =
        ūt e bant.
```

We have a similar account for the activation of *hortor* (Flobert 1975: 327). For the regularized lexeme, the active forms that surface in syntax will be the forms that are inherited from the (historically prior) deponent lexeme's morphological paradigm. In other words, they are the output of active morphological operations for a regular Conjugation 1 verb, coerced into the syntactic paradigm for lexical insertion, and so pattern like `Amo` (see (12)). Activation for *hortor* was illustrated with the Luculentius excerpt in (1). Some other examples are given in (32) and (33).

(32) *hortabant* `<syn active imperfective past indicative pl 3>`
ut, si esset Domin-i voluntas,
COMP if be.3SG.PRS.SBJV Lord-GEN.SG desire.NOM.SG
face-ret quod horta-bant
do-3SG.IPFV.PST.SBJV.ACT wh.ACC.SG encourage-3PL.IPFV.PST.ACT
'[He promised to act in such a way] that, if it was the Lord's will, he would be doing what they exhorted him to do.'
(Jonas, *Vita Austrigislii Episcopi Biturigi*, 2; Stage XI)

(33) *hortaverunt* `<syn active perfect present indicative pl 3>`
atque hortav-erunt, ut… eum
and encourage-3PL.PF.ACT COMP him.ACC.SG
stude-rent manda-re sepulchr-o
take.pains-3PL.IPFV.PST.SBJV.ACT deliver-PRS.INF.ACT grave-DAT.SG
'and they encouraged (them) to take pains to deliver him to the grave'
(Jonas, *Passio Ragneberti* 6; Stage XI)

6.3.2 *Passivation of deponents*

One important property that deponents share is defectiveness: they have no formal means of realizing passive morphosyntax. Part of deponency regularization is to recover the passive paradigm, and this is what Flobert terms 'passivation'. But, we have to be careful about our meaning when we say that a deponent displays defectiveness. Consider how Corbett (2006) uses the term:

> Defectiveness depends on a notion of what can be reasonably expected… [it] implies the lack of specific forms, which the lexeme might reasonably be expected to have. (2006: 84)

The common Latin deponent verb *morior* 'die' lacks passive grammatical words, but are these 'specific forms, which the lexeme might reasonably be expected to have'? As this lexeme has only the non-agentive external argument, there is no internal argument to be promoted to subject, and no agent to be demoted. Therefore, it cannot be associated with a passive construction, and hence, there is no need for it to have passive grammatical words. On the other hand, the transitive *hortor* 'encourage' is defective in the real sense since it has an internal argument which is expressed as a direct object grammatical relation, marked with the accusative case. We return to our first deponent example from Chapter 5, given again here as (34).

(34) sed coqu-os, quasi in mar-i sol-et
but cook-ACC.PL, as at sea-ABL.SG be.wont-3SG.PRS.ACT
hortator remig-es horta-rier ita
encourager-NOM.SG oarsman-ACC.PL exhort-PASS.INF so
horta-batur
exhort-3SG.IPFV.PST.PASS
(=ACT)
'but he exhorted the cooks, just as a coxswain is in the habit of exhorting oarsmen'.
(Plautus, *Mercator*, Act IV, Line 695–7)

In (34) *coquos* 'cooks' is the direct object of *hortabatur* and *remiges* 'oarsmen' the direct object of *hortarier*. The personal noun *hortator* is derived from *hortor* and is the output of a rule of word-formation that productively takes transitive agentive verbs as its base (see Aronoff 1994: 37–9 for the *-or* agentive noun derivation built on the third stem). Because it has the right semanticosyntactic ingredients, 'what can be reasonably expected' is for the lexeme to combine with a passive construction. However, the lack of passive expression prevents it. This can be rectified by realigning its passive morphological paradigm with its passive syntactic paradigm. The result is passivation of the deponent, examples of which are given in (35)–(37), from Flobert (1975: 355).

(35) *hortamur* `<syn passive imperfective present indicative pl 1>`
sic enim a Domin-o sub apostol-orum
thus for by Lord-ABL.SG under apostle-GEN.PL
numer-o horta-mur
order-ABL.SG encourage-1PL.PRS.PASS
(=PASS)
'for thus are we encouraged by the Lord under the order of the apostles.'
(Jonas, *Vita Columbani* 2:9; seventh–eighth century AD; Stage XI)

(36) *hortaretur* `<syn passive imperfective past subjunctive sg 3>`
et ab ipso confessor-e beat-o
and by himself-ABL.SG confessor-ABL.SG blessed-ABL.SG

saepius oration-i insiste-ret
often.COMPAR prayer-DAT.SG pursue-3SG.IPFV.PST.SBJV.ACT
horta-retur
encourage-3SG.IPFV.PST.SBJV.PASS
'and so that he be encouraged by the blessed Confessor himself to stand fast in prayer more often'
(Gregory of Tours, *Vitae patrum* 7: 2; Stage X)

(37) *(ex)hortantur* `<syn passive imperfective present indicative pl 3>`
omn-es consola-ntur, aedifica-ntur,
all-NOM.PL console-3PL.PRS.PASS, edify-3PL.PRS.PASS,
(ex)horta-ntur, ut De-um rog-ent
exhort-3PL.PRS.PASS to God-ACC.SG ask-3PL.PRS.SBJV.ACT
(=PASS)
'All are consoled, edified and exhorted to ask God.'
(Augustine, *Epistulae* 228: 8; fourth–fifth century AD; Stage IX)

Note that in Latin the agent is demoted to a PP headed by *a(b)*, and the internal theme argument is promoted to subject, overtly shown in (37) *omnes* 'all people', which controls the plural agreement on the head verb.

We represent passivation in terms of realignment as in (38), where an override takes the exceptional case default since VERB contains the implied path `<syn passive> == "<mor passive>"`.

(38)
```
Hortor_PASS:
  <> == Hortor
  <syn passive> == VERB.
```

Theorems for the syntax of the regularized item are given in (39). What is immediately noticeable is that as a consequence of passivation there is homonymy in the active and passive subparadigms.

(39)
```
Hortor_PASS:<gloss> = encourage.
Hortor_PASS:<syn active imperfective present indicative
            sg 2> = hort ā ris.
Hortor_PASS:<syn active imperfective present indicative
            sg 3> = hort ā tur.
Hortor_PASS:<syn active imperfective present indicative
            pl 1> = hort ā mur
Hortor_PASS:<syn active imperfective present indicative
            pl 3> = hort ā ntur
Hortor_PASS:<syn active imperfective present subjunctive
            sg 3> = hort ētur.
Hortor_PASS:<syn passive imperfective present indicative
            sg 2> = hort ā ris.
```

```
Hortor_PASS:<syn passive imperfective present indicative
            sg 3> = hort ā tur.
Hortor_PASS:<syn passive imperfective present indicative
            pl 1> = hort ā mur
Hortor_PASS:<syn passive imperfective present indicative
            pl 3> = hort ā ntur
Hortor_PASS:<syn passive imperfective present subjunctive
            sg 3> = hort ētur.
...
```

In fact it is ambiguity in voice that Flobert argues leads to activation of the paradigm, as a means of disambiguation, and so passivation is 'anterior' to activation (Flobert 1975: 316, 343). For all regularized deponents, Flobert is careful to give the diachronic stage at which they are passivized and at which they are activated. In the overwhelming majority of cases, passivation occurs earlier. Thus, *hortor* has passive forms for passive syntax as early as Stage III, and activation does not occur until Stage X (Flobert 1975: 64).

We have argued that only truly defective deponents are subject to passivation. Their argument structure means that they are expected to appear in passive constructions, but their lack of a passive syntactic paradigm makes them passive deficient; they require and acquire a passive paradigm through realignment. Now recall the *lamentor* examples we gave at the beginning of this section. They were examples of activation except for (21), which showed the lexeme with passive morphology and a passive interpretation. But if *lamentor* is intransitive, then it is not defective, and so we would suppose not subject to passivation. Flobert suggests that valence change must be a contributing factor to passivation: 'la transitivation a dû contribuer…à l'activation' (Flobert 1975: 317). The lexeme must, therefore, develop a valence-based polysemy, and as a two-argument verb which is deponent, it is rendered defective. It is, therefore, in need of passivation. And indeed passivation is anterior: it is first attested at Stage VI, whereas activation is at Stage VIII (Flobert 1975: 79).

We end this section with a passivation puzzle. The examples of *ūtor* in (27)–(29) above show a verb with agent and theme semantic roles, but with an indirect object grammatical relation for the theme: the theme is an NP in the ablative case; in (22) this is *longo sermone*. Yet an historical development of this lexeme was passivation, as (40) shows (Flobert 1975: 360).

(40) *utitur* `<syn passive imperfective present indicative sg 3>`

quia	supellex	mult-a,	quae	non
because	chattels	much-NOM.SG.F	wh.NOM.SG.F	NEG

ut-itur,	em-itur	tamen
use-3SG.PRS.PASS (=PASS)	buy-3SG.PRS.PASS	nevertheless

'For a lot of furniture is bought even though it is not used'
(Novius, *Comedeia 13*, cited in Gellius *Noctes Atticae* XV, 13; Stage II)

How is this possible? Evidence that only transitive verbs can appear in the passive comes from the formation of the gerundive in the paradigm. Recall our discussion of gerundives in Chapter 5, Section 5.5, a verbal adjective with passive interpretation. But in fact, gerundives have a passive interpretation for only transitive verbs, e.g. *patria defendenda est* 'our country must be defended' (Schmitz 2004: 289), signifying 'something must be done'. The agent, if there is one, appears as an NP in the dative case, so *hoc mihi faciendum est* 'this must be done by me' (mihi = me.DAT). Formally they are like predicate adjectives, but only transitive gerundives are targets for agreement, with the theme argument as the controller: *defendend-a* expresses feminine singular agreement with *patri-a*. For intransitives they are formally and functionally different: they appear in the neuter singular only[12] and function as impersonal verbs of necessity: *mihi est eundum* 'I must go'. The gerundive of the intransitive lexeme *ūtor* falls into this class of expressions: *pane utendum est*: 'one must use bread'. However, because there is something prototypically agentive about this lexeme's semantics, there is pressure to use it in a passive context. In fact we could see it as having almost a suppletive passive supplied by the lexeme *usurpo* 'make use of'.

Flobert (1975: 343) lists a number of such deponents that employ the passive paradigm of a synonymous lexeme to supply their defective passive paradigm; and the pair *ūtor/usurpari* belong to that list. The gerundive is available to deponents, and for transitive deponents it is the one cell in a transitive deponent's paradigm that can express a passive function, as discussed in Chapter 5, Section 5.5, so shining a small light into the darkness of its passive defectiveness. Thus, even prior to passivation, *hortandus* means 'one who is to be encouraged' (Schmitz 2004: 289). For *ūtor* we see an early development of a transitive gerundive with passive meaning, also acting as an agreement target: *rei utendae causa* 'for the sake of the thing that must be used' (where *utend-ae* marks feminine agreement with *re-i*). Other intransitive, but agentive, deponent verbs that follow this course are: *fruor* 'enjoy', *fungor* 'administer' and *potior* 'acquire' (all taking an ablative object).

With the co-opting of a synonymous lexeme's passive paradigm, and the development of the transitive gerundive, there has to be a perception that *ūtor* is passive defective and so needs rescuing, revealing that it must be not only defectiveness but also perceived defectiveness that can act as the trigger for passivation. Alternatively passivation of *ūtor* is due to a prior reanalysis of the lexeme's argument structure. Evidence that this might be happening comes from classical examples where the argument *quod* 'which (acc.)' is in the accusative:

(41) *uti* `<syn active imperfective present infinitive>`

an bon-i quid usquamst quod quisquam
COMP good-GEN.SG wh. NOM.SG anywhere wh.ACC.SG anyone.NOM.SG
ut-i poss-et sine mal-o omn-i...
use-PRS.INF be.able-3SG.PRS without evil-ABL.SG every-ABL.SG

'[Tell me this] – is there such a thing as weal unmixed with woe anywhere, for anyone to enjoy [lit. 'which anyone is able to use']...?'[13]
(Plautus, *Mercator*, Act IV, Lines 145–6)

In either case, passivation is predicated on defectiveness, which with *ūtor* is either perceived or a by-product of a reanalysis of its argument structure.

6.4 Questions about virtual paradigms

The notion of a virtual paradigm falls out directly from paradigm linkage, since the link between the syntactic and morphological paradigm of a lexeme is specifically a *default* link, leaving open the possibility that certain cells in the morphological paradigm are never linked, hence rendered virtual objects only. Our account of deponent verbs presupposes the notion of virtual subparadigms: these are the `<mor active>` paths for a deponent lexeme that are never used in syntactic paradigms, i.e. are not shared with `<syn active>` paths. The actualization of the virtual subparadigm is what we have called paradigmatic realignment. In Stump's paradigm linkage terms, this restores 'the unmarked pattern of linkage':

> The morphological paradigm of a deponent lexeme's root has 'virtual' members which are morphologically active, and because these may be used as exploratory expressions[14] they afford the means of bringing a deponent lexeme's syntactic paradigm back into the unmarked pattern of linkage. (2002: 174)

While we have invoked virtual paradigms to account for the historical emergence of active forms of a deponent, Corbett (2007) uses the idea of virtual paradigm to account for its passive forms prior to regularization, i.e. while still a deponent. Intransitive lexemes cannot be passive, so the passive-looking values in its 'real' active paradigm must come from the passive values of virtual passive cells (Corbett 2007: 29, 33). It is the use of values of virtual cells for 'real' syntactic cells which makes deponency special and distinguishes it from canonical syncretism. In the next section, we look at some of the wider implications of analyses that rest on virtual paradigms.

6.4.1 Neo-deponents and virtual paradigms

We have shown historical change as a simple matter of resetting a default that at a prior stage was being overridden. Our defaults/overrides model will allow for the opposite situation as well, where a regular lexeme becomes deponent by overriding the default of a prior stage. In other words, our analysis predicts both regularization of deponents as well as 'irregularization' of lexemes *into deponents*. And such a class of objects does appear to exist as part of the colourful landscape of the diachronic Latin verb. These are the so-called neo-deponents (Flobert 1975: 410–19; Bonnet 1968: 411; Strecker 1929: 61). An example is the lexeme *continere* 'contain, retain' which appears as a regular lexeme in Plautus (Stage I), but which has been transformed into a deponent in the late period. Examples of both uses are given in (42)–(43).

(42) proin se domi contine-ant,
so pro.ACC at.home contain-3PL.PRS.SBJV.ACT,
vit-ent infortuni-o
avoid-3PL.PRS.SBJV.ACT misfortune-DAT.SG
'So let'em keep themselves at home and avoid danger.'[15]
(Plautus, *Curculio* Act II, Line 298; Stage I)

(43) capsul-a, qu-ae sanct-orum pignor-a
box-NOM.SG, wh-NOM.SG saint-GEN.PL pledge-ACC.PL
contene-batur[16]
contain-3SG.IPFV.PST.PASS
(=ACT)
'a (little) box which contained the pledges of the saints'
(Gregory of Tours, *In gloria martyrum* 75; fifth century AD;[17] Stage X)

The suggestion in Ernout and others that activated deponents were a feature of colloquial Latin tells only part of the story; 'deponentized' verbs were also coined in vulgar varieties, a point that Flobert is careful to make:

> On ne saurait accepter telle quelle l'explication trop souvent donnée: le déclin des déponents dans la langue parlée; c'est doublement faux: les vulgarismes ne sont pas à sens unique, car il y a des déponents vulgaires…[18]
> (Flobert 1975: 308)

Of course a development such as this would also entail a passive virtual paradigm since an intransitive that becomes a neo-deponent must be equipped with a passive subparadigm.

6.4.2 *Variation and virtual paradigms*

In Flobert's vast survey of the history of deponent verbs, he reserves a special place for what he terms 'variants déponents'. For some authors a lexeme is deponent; for other authors of the same period the lexeme is regular. Sometimes there is variation within the same author. Examples of the variant *fabrico*/*fabricor* 'carve, manufacture' are given below, both from the same period.

(44)	i-i,	qui	sign-a	fabrica-ntur
	pro-NOM.PL	wh.NOM.PL	statue -ACC.PL	make-3PL.PRS.PASS (=ACT)
	'those who carve statues'		(Cicero, *De Officiis*; Stage III)	

(45)	Hunc	crater-a	fabricav-erat	Alcon
	this.ACC.SG	bowl-ACC.SG	make-3SG.PST.PRF.ACT	Alcon.NOM.SG
	'Alcon made this bowl'		(Ovid, *Metamorphoses*; Stage III)	

For us this type of variation is naturally captured as switching from inheriting the first-order default link that syntactic and morphological paradigms are equivalent (*fabrico*) to overriding it (*fabricor*).

6.4.3 *Deponency in Greek*

In the spirit of Flobert, a somewhat shorter survey of the history of Greek deponents, specifically transitive deponents is offered by Lavidas and Papangeli (2007). The time periods are Ancient Greek (800–300 BC) > Hellenistic Greek (300 BC – sixth century AD) > Early Medieval Greek (sixth–eleventh century AD) > Late Medieval Greek (twelfth–fifteenth century AD) > Modern Greek (AD 1453 – present[19]). We find similarities with Flobert's story for Latin. In sum there are deponents that take up an active paradigm at one of the post-Classical periods, Flobert's 'activations'. Lavidas and Papangeli do not mention passivations. Unlike Latin there is also a class of verbs that is deponent in Ancient Greek and remains deponent in Modern Greek. One such lexeme is the verb 'fight': Ancient Greek *max-omai* (mediopassive) > Modern Greek *max-ome* (mediopassive).[20] But like Latin there is a class of neo-deponents. A nice example is the lexeme for 'desire', shown in the (very) Modern Greek sentence about ice-cream in (46) (Lavidas and Papangeli 2007: 107):

(46)

	i	egkios	ligureftike	pagoto
	the	pregnant.NOM.SG	desire.3SG.PST.MEDIOPASS (=ACT)	ice-cream.ACC.SG

'The pregnant woman desired an ice cream.'

It would appear that historical deponency can be subjected to a paradigmatic realignment analysis for Greek, just as for Latin.

6.4.4 *Before deponency*

Latin activation and passivation as well as Greek activation involve the reassignment of the status of an item's morphological paradigm, from virtual to real. In the case of neo-deponents, the reassignment works the other way: the change is passive forms being used for active functions, which means the active paradigm is being 'relegated' to virtual status. Paradigm status – virtual or real – is a function of what a lexical entry is doing with the first-order default: inheriting or overriding it. We end by briefly considering how our defaults/overrides model would accommodate the stage that leads to deponency in the first place.

Recall from Chapter 5, Section 5.5 that the argument that deponents are not really instances of mismatch is based on functionally middle deponent verbs like *morior* 'die' and *nascor* 'be born'. The r-morphology was originally a marker of middle voice, so in this historic context there is no motivation for a paradigm to be realigned if it is not actually misaligned. However, newer deponents like *hortor* have truly misaligned paradigms. To accommodate emergent deponency, our model would have to distinguish the 'middle' deponent types like *morior* from the non-middle. The innovation that triggers deponency as true mismatch is the emergence of the passive voice. This is through a functional extension of the r-morphology, and we could represent it as the path equation in (47).

(47) `<syn passive> == "<mor middle>"`

The r-morphology will be contained in the inflectional hierarchy and inherited by all lexical entries. For middle lexical entries like *morior*, `<mor middle>` is the value of the path `<syn middle>`, shown in (48).

(48) `<syn middle> == "<mor middle>"`

We would have to ensure that grammatical middle lined up with semantic middle, and we could do this through evaluable paths, similar to how we account for the correspondence between grammatical and semantic animacy for Russian nouns as outlined in Chapter 3, Section 3.1.3. So (48) would be restricted to *morior, nascor* and other middle verbs with r-morphology. Likewise, we would want non-subject affected verbs to be able to inherit (47). The middle morphology will be available to these items as a virtual paradigm, values inherited from the morphological hierarchy only. We would then see passive morphology as the initial mismatch where a passive syntactic paradigm is linked to a middle morphological paradigm. A subsequent stage where grammatical middle is lost would be expressed by removing (48). This would mean middle morphology is not relevant for any lexemes, as middle is no longer a grammatical feature. However, middle morphology has a kind of indirect relevance in that its realization is the target of a referral by a path expressing a feature that does have currency, the passive voice (47). Because of the loss of the middle, the middle morphology is reanalysed as passive morphology, so concomitant with the removal of (48) is the modification of (47) as (49).

(49) `<syn passive> == "<mor passive>"`

Once we have arrived at this stage, 'true' deponents like *hortor* can emerge by redirecting the path `<syn active>` to the target of the referral in (49), `"<mor passive>"`.

This model would express the distinction between deponent *morior* and deponent *hortor* – the former a product of inheriting from (48) at a prior stage when it was available, and the latter a product of inheriting from the stage where (47) has been modified to (49). In such a model, nothing stops *morior* from having a virtual active paradigm, as it inherits morphological active values from the morphological hierarchy; so in principle, it is subject to activation in the same way as all other deponents.

6.5 Concluding remarks

In this chapter we have provided further evidence for autonomous morphology by claiming that a specific type of paradigmatic restructuring, realignment, is based on a product of pure morphology, virtual paradigms. These objects do not have synchronic relevance to syntax but may have diachronic relevance, which is the case in the regularization of Latin deponents where they are called into the service of syntax by the same levelling pressures that account for paradigmatic restructuring in general. A virtual paradigm is based on the notion that lexemes contain two paradigms: a set of function/form associations that are used for lexical insertion, the syntactic paradigm; and a set of function/form functions that are the direct product of realizational rules, the morphological paradigm. In Network Morphology these are values inherited from the lexemic hierarchy and the morphological hierarchy, respectively, such that lexical entries have two sets of theorems, one for `<syn>` paths and another for `<mor>` paths. By default the two paradigms are the same, as stated in the universal paradigm linkage default. In Network Morphology this default is the first order default that `<syn> == "<mor>"`. But as a default, the link is subject to override. Deponents are the effect of overriding the default as discussed in Chapter 5. Because Network Morphology assumes a featural interface with syntax, non-equivalence between the morphological and syntactic paradigms is not problematic: syntax is blind to the formal properties of the word-forms. We have shown that the default can be reset by overriding the override and inheriting the exceptional case default, a move made possible by a lexical entry's virtual paradigm. The idea of potential forms hiding in the system awaiting actualization is close to Saussure's view of analogical levelling, as observed in Anderson (1992: 365–8):

> It is a mistake to suppose that the generative process occurs only at the moment when new creation emerges: its elements are already given. Any word I improvise…already exists potentially in the language… Its actualisation in speech is an insignificant fact in comparison with the possibility of forming it. (Saussure 1915, part [227])[21]

7 *Derivation*

7.0 Introduction

Up until now we have been looking at Network Morphology treatments of distinctly inflectional phenomena. As a framework for word structure more generally, we end by considering how Network Morphology treats the relationship between a deriving lexeme, or *base*, and its derivatives. Recall from Chapter 1, Section 1.3.3 that an option available for autonomous morphology is submodularity, separating within morphology an inflectional and a derivational module. Network Morphology takes this option by supplying a hierarchy orthogonal to the lexemic hierarchy in addition to the morphological hierarchy. This is shown graphically in Figure 7.1, a representation of the relation between the Russian base *č′itat′* 'read' and its derivative *č′itatel′* 'reader'.

Here the derivative lexical entry is inheriting from two sources, a node lexical entry which is its base and a node representing generalizations about nouns derived from verbs marked by the suffix *-tel′* and carrying the meaning 'person who X-es', labelled WFR (word-formation rule). The first source of inheritance is a node from the lexemic hierarchy, and the second from the *derivational* hierarchy.

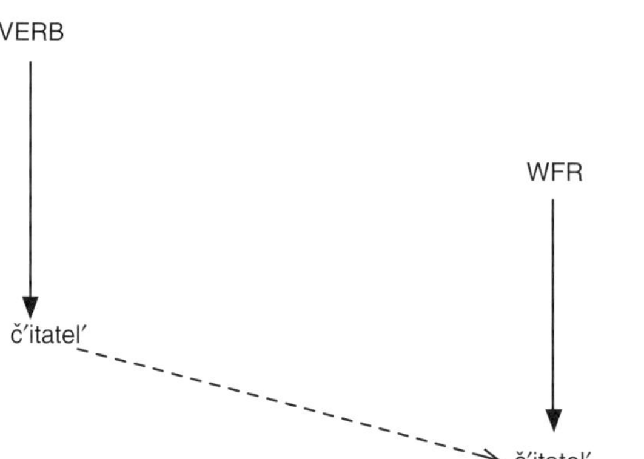

Figure 7.1 *A base and its derivative in Network Morphology*

In this chapter we show how such an approach to derivation goes some way in accounting for the distinctions between inflection and derivation that were summarized in Chapter 1, Section 1.3.3. The distinctions are repeated here in (1).

(1)	Parameter	Inflection	Derivation
1.	Purpose	build the form of a lexeme required by a given syntactic context	build a new lexeme from an existing lexeme
2.	Syntactic determinism	determined by syntax	not determined by syntax
3.	Obligatoriness	function is obligatory	function is not obligatory
4.	Productivity	fully productive	not fully productive
5.	Transparency	transparent	not always transparent
6.	Base inheritance	all base features are inherited	base features that are inherited are limited
7.	Exponence order	after derivational exponent; closes word	before inflectional exponent; need not close word

Parameter 1 falls out from the way Network Morphology characterizes a derivative lexeme, as we shall see: the result of inheriting from another lexical entry which is a node that is already part of the lexemic hierarchy, and from a WFR node. Regarding parameters 2 and 3, morphosyntactic features are expressed as `<syn>` paths placed in the lexemic hierarchy that refer to `<mor>` paths. And as we have seen in previous chapters, the `<mor>` path values are declared in the morphological (= inflectional) hierarchy. In this way Network Morphology can separate functional differences between inflection and derivation: only inflectional functions are expressed as `<syn>` paths. Their obligatoriness is expressed by the fact that we require `<syn>` paths for them. Parameters 5 and 6 concern inheritance and so are naturally expressed in an inheritance-based approach. Parameter 7 is due to the WFR node carrying instructions about how to form the stem of a derived word, namely the stem of its base lexeme plus exponent of derivational function. The new complex stem is subsequently used in equations in the morphological hierarchy, such as `<mor sg dat> == "<stem>" u`. Finally, parameter 4 is expressed by the possibility of overriding the facts that are otherwise inherited from the base lexical entry and from the WFR. Different specifications of the override express the full range of lack of productivity found within derivation.

In Section 7.1 we discuss derivation as specifically lexeme-formation, where the derived lexeme differs from its base at any or all levels of lexical representation: syntactic, semantic, phonological and morphological. Changes at these levels are brought about by inheriting from a WFR node which encodes syntactic, semantic, phonological and morphological level facts. In Section 7.2 we show how the traditional category-changing, conversion, transposition and category-preserving classes of derivation can be expressed as the interplay of inheritance from the base lexical entry node and inheritance from a WFR node, as graphed in Figure 7.1. In Section 7.3 we discuss affix/exponent competition in derivational morphology and demonstrate how it is resolved in Network Morphology by an approach to derivation that makes use of the Pāṇinian principle and base-driven affix selection. Such an approach is reserved for productive derivation only. Semi-productivity, the topic of Section 7.4, is expressed as either lexical items inheriting from less productive WFR nodes that in turn inherit the productive pattern but override in specific ways; or lexical entries that inherit directly from a productive pattern but override certain aspects of it.

7.1 Derivation as lexeme-formation

As an inferential–realizational theory, Network Morphology treats derivation differently from compounding. The *-tel´* element in *čítatel´* is an exponent of a derivational function, such as 'personal noun', and is introduced by a rule of word-formation. By contrast, in the Russian compound lexeme *divankrovat´* 'sofa bed', the *krovat´* element is another lexeme. In derivation, the meaning of the complex is deduced from the meaning of the base and the rule that introduces a formal modification to it, i.e. concatenating *-tel´* to the right edge. In compounding, meaning of the complex word is incrementally built up from the meanings of the elements: *divan* 'sofa' plus *krovat´* 'bed' yields 'sofa bed'.[1] In wholesale lexical-incremental theories, all word structure is treated like compounding. The only difference between derivation and compounding is the status of the morpheme: in compounding it is free, and in derivation it is bound. The implication of such an approach is that derivational semantics based on bound morphemes, and lexical semantics based on free morphemes are non-distinct. This is the claim made in recent work by Lieber (2004, 2007, 2009). For example, the bare semantics of the words *chef* and *author* and the affix *-er* found in *player* (roughly equivalent to *-tel´*) are the same (Lieber 2004: 37)[2]. The semantics of the free morpheme base and the bound morpheme affix are integrated in the derivation of the complex item. The schema for the derivative *driver* is given in (2), taken from Lieber (2004: 55).

(2) [+material, dynamic ([$_i$], [+dynamic ([$_i$], [ ])])]

The affix's representation is [+material, dynamic], i.e. something both concrete and process. It serves as a predicate of the base verb's representation [+dynamic ([ ], [ ])], itself a process predicate taking agent and theme arguments. The 'agentive noun' reading of *driver* is through direct composition of the two representations, yielding the process noun reading, and coindexing to yield the more specific *agentive* process noun. The agentive reading comes from coindexing the affix's (R) argument with the agent argument of the base so that both form a single referential unit. For *employee*, the affix *-ee* would have the same representation as *-er* but coindex the second (theme) argument of the base to denote a patient/theme process noun (Lieber 2009: 82)[3].

In Network Morphology derivational word-formation is not the result of assembling morphemes as Saussurean signs, rather it is building a new lexeme from an existing lexeme, as licensed by rule. So word-formation is really rule-based *lexeme-formation*. Inheritance plays a key role, as the function/form mapping represented by the derivative lexeme is the result of inheriting the function/form mapping that the base lexeme constitutes along with its modification, a set of instruction(s) provided by the WFR. In what follows we briefly consider word-formation as lexeme-formation. We then show in the following section how various kinds of derivational relatedness can be expressed as the interplay of inheritance from the base lexical entry node and inheritance from the WFR node.

As discussed in Chapters 1 and 2, Network Morphology lexical entries represent lexemes. These are the minimal linguistic sign, a locus of parallel information types, namely phonological, syntactic, semantic and morphological. As a leaf node in a set of interconnected inheritance hierarchies, a lexeme in Network Morphology is partially specified and filled out by inheritance from the network. We gave the lexeme schema for *zakon* 'law' in Chapter 1 (39). Here in (3) is the schema for the base verb *č´itat´* and its derivative *č´itatel´*.

(3)

Č´ITAT´		Č´ITATEL´
syntactic level syn cat = V args = 2 (NP_NP)		*syntactic level* syn cat = N
semantic level 'read'	>	*semantic level* 'person who reads' sem sex = male

phonological level	*phonological level*
stem 1 = /č´it-/	–
stem 2 = /č´ita-/	/č´ita-tel´/
morphological level	*morphological level*
mor class = V_I	mor class = N_I

In (3) the > symbol indicates that the relation between these lexemes is derivational in nature. The derivational relation can be characterized by the activity / lack of activity at a given level of description. At the syntactic level, there is a category change from (transitive) V to N. At the semantic level, there is a modification of the base's semantics, broadly from 'X' to 'person who Xes'. More formally we could express this as λx [person (x) & read (x)]. Then at the formal level, the base's second stem is modified by the addition of the string of segments /tel´/ to the right edge, i.e. modified by suffixation. In principle, stem modification could result from prefixation, suffixation, infixation, vowel/consonant alternation, or suprasegmental operations. Finally, the inflectional pattern of exponence is a change at the morphological level from a specific conjugation class (V_1) to a specific declensional class (N_I).

We represent the derivational relation in Network Morphology as the inheritance between base and derivative lexical entries, given in (4).[4]

(4) a. Č'itat':

```
    <> == VERB
    <gloss> == read
    <conjugation_class> == V_I:<mor>
    <root all> == č'it
    <stem 2> == <root all> a⁵
    <valence> == 2.
```

b. Č'itatel':

```
    <> == NOUN
    <base> == "Č'itat':<>"
    <gloss> == <base gloss> person
    <stem> == <base stem 2> tel'
    <sem sex> == male.
```

Changes at the semantic and phonological level are actually modifications: inheriting facts from the base lexical entry and altering them in some way. These base facts that are subject to modification are inherited through the second equation in (4b). By default all path:value facts available at `Č'itat'` are inherited by `Č'itatel'` as an extension of the path `<base>`. Such base facts are clearly indicated in the derivative's theorems, shown in (5).

(5)
```
Č'itatel':<base syn cat> = v.
Č'itatel':<base gloss> = read.
Č'itatel':<base root all> = č'it.
Č'itatel':<base stem 2> = č'it a.
...
```

Change at the semantic level is a matter of specifying an operation over the `<base gloss>` fact which is available at `Č'itatel'` through inheritance (equation 2 in (5)). This amounts to adding some semantic feature value, here encoded as 'person', to the value of `<base gloss>`. The result will be a complex value: `<gloss> = read person`. We refine this rather crude semantic representation later on, but the principle of adding a value to a value inherited from the base is our main point here. In similar fashion, phonological-level change is inheritance and modification, expressed by the fourth equation in (4b). This time the value of `<base stem 2>` is accessed (equation 4 in (5)) and concatenated with an atom representing the suffix *–tel´*, resulting in `<stem> = č'itatel'`.

Change at the syntactic level in (3), from verb to noun, is expressed by changing the source of inheritance from the node VERB in (4a) to NOUN in (4b) in the lexemic hierarchy, nodes that hold `<syn cat>` facts. In this case what has been inherited by the derivative, the first equation in (5), is substituted for some other value. We can draw a distinction between change in the derivative that is the result of a straight substitution – syntactic-level change – and change that is the result of inheriting from the base and modifying in some way what has been inherited – semantic and phonological-level change.

So far we have only considered the relation between base and derivative, viewed in Network Morphology as inheritance by a derivative lexical entry node from a base lexical entry node. But in Figure 7.1 we saw that there was a second source of inheritance, the WFR node. The full specification of a derivative lexical entry is inheritance from both sources. As motivation for the WFR node, consider the NM representation of the derivative *p´isatel´* 'writer' in (6).

(6)
```
Pisatel':
  <> == NOUN
  <base> == "P'isat':<>"
  <gloss> == <base gloss> person
  <stem> == <base stem 2> tel'
  <sem sex> == male.
```

Most of the equations in (6) are identical to those found at `Č'itatel'` (4b), suggesting a pattern that can be abstracted and stated at a higher node. Word-formation as lexeme-formation assumes a means of handling this kind of redundancy by treating it as the output of some rule. The predictable information residing in a derivative lexeme is abstracted to a redundancy rule that operates over a class of lexemes which are complex in the same way. In this way the class of lexemes can be underspecified, and the missing structure 'filled in' by rule. An early version of lexical redundancy rules for derivationally complex lexemes is found in Jackendoff (1975). Such rules '…designate as redundant that information in a lexical entry which is predictable by the existence of a related lexeme' (Jackendoff 1975: 643). The redundant and predictable information can be syntactic, semantic and phonological and so covers all three levels of description of the underspecified lexical entry. Such lexical redundancy rules were developed as generative WFRs in Aronoff (1976), and most fully described in Anderson (1992: ch. 7). They are assumed in most derivational accounts where the lexeme is the minimal sign, in other words where word-formation is strictly lexeme-formation.

There are many derivatives of *-tel´* besides *č´itatel´* and *p´isatel´*. Some of them are listed in (7) along with their bases.

(7)

Base	Gloss	Derivative, Nom	Acc	Gen	Gloss
č´itat´	'read'	č´itatel´	č´itatel´a	č´itatel´a	'reader'
p´isat´	'write'	p´isatel´	p´isatel´a	p´isatel´a	'writer'
grab´it´	'steal'	grab´itel´	grab´itel´a	grab´itel´a	'thief'
xran´it´	'guard'	xran´itel´	xran´itel´a	xran´itel´a	'custodian'
terzat´	'torment'	terzatel´	terzatel´a	terzatel´a	'tormentor'
podžigat´	'set on fire'	podžigatel´	podžigatel´a	podžigatel´a	'arsonist'
zaušat´	'abuse'	zaušatel´	zaušatel´a	zaušatel´a	'abuser'

A WFR could be used to hold the facts which these items share and, thus, reduce the redundancy. Shared facts include the stem ending in *-tel´*, the syntactic category noun and the broad meaning 'person who Xes'. WFRs for lexeme-formation have a structure parallel to the lexemes over which they generalize, namely a phonological, syntactic and semantic level of description. The shared facts can be distributed across the levels as in (8).

(8) Base > *-tel´* WFR > Derivative

syntactic level
syn cat = N
semantic level
'person who [base sem]'
(implied: {+animate,+male})
phonological level
[base stem 2] -tel´

Other facts that the derivatives in (7) share are that they are male animates and belong to the same declensional class, a fact we can infer from the exponents being used to realize the nominative, accusative and genitive singular cases (third to fifth columns in (7)). Russian Declension 1 animates were discussed in Chapter 2; see (44) in Section 2.2.7. But we do not need to include these additional facts in the WFR, as they are implied by what is already there. As we showed in Chapter 3, Section 3.1.3, semantic animacy implies syntactic animacy, expressed by the genitive/accusative syncretism. And the fact 'person who Xes' placed at the WFR's semantic level of description implies semantic animacy. More specifically it implies *male* animates: in Chapter 3, Section 3.1.3 we showed the correlation between male semantics and Declension 1 (example 44).

A WFR such as the one proposed in (8) allows for underspecified derivative lexemes. In Network Morphology these are more parsimonious versions of the lexical entries given in (4b) and (6). Their full specification comes from inheriting facts from both the base lexical entry and a WFR node. The derivatives *č´itatel´* and *p´isatel´* are given new representations in (9) and (10).

(9)
```
Č'itatel':
  <> == WFR_TEL'
  <base> == "Č'itat':<>".
```

(10)
```
P'isatel':
  <> == WFR_TEL'
  <base> == "P'isat':<>".
```

As well as from their respective base lexical entries, both items inherit from the node `WFR_TEL'`, representing the WFR in (8). The node is situated in the derivational hierarchy and is represented in (11).

(11)
```
WFR_TEL':
  <> == NOUN
  <gloss> == λx [ <sem feature> (x) & "<base gloss>" (x) ]
  <sem feature> == person
  <stem> == "<base stem 2>" tel'.
```

Lexical entries inheriting from this node will inherit change in syntactic category via the first equation, modification in the semantics through the second and third equations, and phonological modification through the last equation. Semantic modification is expressed by concatenating the value for `<sem feature>` locally specified as `person` with the value of `<base gloss>` to yield the desired representation λx [person (x) & read (x)]. WFR nodes are distinguished by the syntactic category node from which they inherit in the lexemic hierarchy, the value of the path `<sem feature>` and the value of the path `<stem>`. This expresses the fact that distinctions between WFRs are based on distinctions at different levels of lexical description.

What's missing from the WFR is redundant information about declensional class and animacy. As we said, this is implied by the semantic feature 'person'. We modify the Russian inflection theory discussed in Chapter 3 by adding an interdependency node SEM_SEX which determines semantic sex based on derivational semantic features.

(12)
```
SEM_SEX:
  <person> == male
  <female> == female
  <> == undifferentiated.
```

The second equation is for the derivation of female nouns. For example, *p'isatel'* has the [+female] correspondent *p'isatel'n'ica*. The third equation expresses the default that any other kind of derivation results in a sex undifferentiated noun. Example (13) is a modification of the NOUN node from the lexemic hierarchy which we saw in Chapter 3, Section 3.1.3.

(13)
```
NOUN:
  <> == NOMINAL
  <syn cat> == n
  <sem feature> == [+material]
  <declensional_class> == DECLENSION:< "<sem sex>" >
  <syn gender> == GENDER:< "<sem sex>" >
  <syn animacy> == "<sem animacy>"
  <sem animacy> == ANIMACY:< "<sem sex>" >
  %<sem sex> == undifferentiated
  <sem sex> == SEM_SEX:<"<sem feature>">
  ...
```

As can be seen from the last two equations, we have altered the theory by replacing the default about `<sem sex>` with an evaluable path, thereby allowing a lexical entry's derived semantic feature to play a part in determining semantic sex. Recall from Chapter 3, Section 3.1.3 that we express semantic sex determining animacy and declensional class by evaluation at the interdependency nodes DECLENSION and ANIMACY, equations 4 and 7. These nodes are repeated here for convenience.

(14)
```
DECLENSION:
  <male> == N_I:<mor>
  <female> == N_II:<mor>
  <undifferentiated> == "<mor formal gender>".
```

```
GENDER:
  <male> == masc
  <female> == fem
  <undifferentiated> == "<mor formal gender>".

ANIMACY:
  <> == animate
  <undifferentiated> == inanimate.
```

Some theorems of the lexical entry `Č'itatel'` are given in (15). Values are inherited from the base lexical entry in the lexemic hierarchy (equations 1 to 3), the `WFR_PERSON` node in the derivational hierarchy (equations 4 to 7), indirectly from interdependency nodes in the lexemic hierarchy (equations 8 and 9) and indirectly from `N_I` in the inflectional hierarchy by virtue of the `DECLENSION` interdependency node in (14) (equations 10 and 11).

(15)

```
Č'itatel':<base syn cat> = v.
Č'itatel':<base gloss> = read.
Č'itatel':<base stem> = č'it a.
Č'itatel':<syn cat> = n.
Č'itatel':<gloss> = λx [ person (x) & read (x) ].
Č'itatel':<sem feature> = person.
Č'itatel':<stem> = č'it a tel'.
Č'itatel':<syn gender> = masc.
Č'itatel':<syn animacy> = animate.
Č'itatel':<mor sg nom> = č'it a tel'.
Č'itatel':<mor sg acc> = č'it a tel' ^ a.
...
```

7.2 Inheritance-based derivational relatedness

The inheritance-based approach to derivational relatedness that Network Morphology assumes is not novel in itself. In an interesting paper, Deo (2007) argues that the component of Pāṇini's Sanskrit grammar that handles nominal derivation, the taddhita section of the *Sūtrapāthaṭha*, is an extensive default inheritance hierarchy. Inheritance hierarchy accounts of German nominal derivation are provided by Krieger and Nerbonne (1993), who aim to demonstrate that derivation in the HPSG lexicon is more naturally and efficiently expressed through feature-structure schemas that generalize over classes of derivatives than lexical rules, which in HPSG are operators over feature structures. They illustrate with German derivatives in *-bar*, roughly equivalent to English *-able* adjectives, for example *faxbar* 'faxable'. Riehemann (1998) develops the schema for *-bar* which, like the WFR in (11), has a semantic, syntactic and phonological level of description from which underspecified members of the class of *-bar* derivatives inherit. The partial feature structure of the schema showing the levels of description is given in (16).

(16)

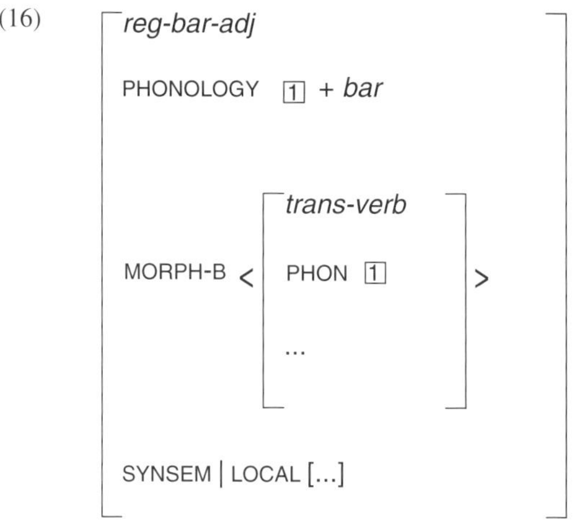

The embedded feature structure MORPH-B carries base information ('morphological base'), including the stem, encoded as the value of the feature PHON. The phonological level of description is the concatenation of the base's stem and the string *bar*, i.e. `"<base stem>" bar` in a Network Morphology version. The feature MORPH-B also contains the condition that the base lexeme be a transitive verb, as well as other conditions not shown here. We return to base conditions in Section 7.3.

Booij (2005, 2009) has proposed a construction grammar approach to morphology where the generalizations about a class of derivatives is represented as a schema or template that serves as the root node in an inheritance hierarchy, analogous to the constructional idioms that are the objects of enquiry in construction grammar (Kay 1997; Goldberg 2006). The word-formation template for derivatives such as *baker*, *writer* and *player* in Construction Morphology is shown in (17), based on Booij (2005: 124).

(17) $[[x]_X\ y]_Y$

|

$[[x]_V\ er]_N$ 'one who V's'

|

$[[bak]_V\ er]_N$

⋮

$[bake]_V$

The template encodes phonological information represented by the *x* and *y* variables and syntactic category information (X, Y). The second node in the hierarchy is similar to the WFR proposed for *-tel´* nouns in (11), an abstraction of a class of derivatives. It states that the class shares noun as syntactic category, has the semantics 'one who Vs' and the affix *-er*. Moreover, all the bases of the items in this class are verbs. The derivative *baker* multiply inherits from the word-formation template and the lexical item *bake*. (We have modified Booij's graph with the dashed line to indicate a second source of inheritance for the derivative.)

Booij's approach shows that a WFR in a declarative, hierarchical setting is better viewed as a schema or template. In Network Morphology such templates generalize over lexemes, accounting specifically for lexeme-formation, unlike Construction Morphology which assumes that the morpheme is the minimal sign.[6] So from this point, we will use the term *lexeme-formation template* (LFT) for our account. In (17) the highest level of abstraction is linearization information (prefix/suffix). The root node expresses the fact that an affix is added to the right edge. In other words, *-er* derivation is a kind of suffixation. We can incorporate a linearization generalization into our analysis by replacing the equation `<stem> == "<base stem 2>" tel'` with `<stem> == "<base stem>" "<deriv affix>"` and then defining `<deriv affix>` as inheriting `tel'`, as shown in (18).

(18)
```
LFT_PERSON:
  <> == NOUN
  <gloss> == λx [ <sem feature> (x) & "<base gloss>" (x) ]
  <sem feature> == person
  <stem> == "<base stem 2>" "<deriv affix>"
  <deriv affix> == tel'.
```

Most nominal derivation in Russian is in fact suffixation, so we could go further by adding a SUFFIXATION node that contains the fourth equation and then point the path `<stem>` to it for inheritance. Other LFTs would share suffixation by similarly inheriting from SUFFIXATION.

We could think of canonical derivation as the situation where the derivative lexeme is distinguished from the base lexeme at every level of lexemic description: it has a new syntactic category, a different meaning, a different stem and a different inflectional class. So (18) is an example of a canonical LFT where inheritance from the LFT is *maximal*. This is another way of viewing parameter 6 in (1), which states that derivation is distinguished from inflection by limiting the extent of inheritance from the base. The more a derivative can be characterized as whatever its base is, the less new information must be coming from the LFT, and the less maximal the LFT is. Within a language's system of derivation, we should provide for the possibility that classes of derivatives may or may not be canonical. The nature of the departure from the canon could then be used to characterize a given class. Spencer (2005) makes the link between canonical derivation viewed in this way and the canonical correspondence among syntactic, semantic and morphological properties: the *principle of the morpholexically coherent lexicon* (2005: 101). So the syntactic property 'noun' corresponds to semantic property 'thing' (based on Jackendoff's 1990 semantic primitives for syntactic categories), and 'thing' corresponds to noun inflection, as does 'noun'. Canonical derivation implies changes at all levels of lexical representation as a kind of harmonization effect. If the change is, say, to noun then the semantics needs to change to 'thing', and the item has to inflect according to a noun's pattern of inflection.

For the class of nouns in (7), there is (a) inheritance from the base lexeme at the phonological and semantic levels and (b) inheritance from the LFT at *all* levels, with the effect that what is inherited from the base is altered. Example (19) presents the canonical situation.

(19)

	Source of inheritance	
Lexemic level	Base	LFT
syntactic	X	✓
semantic	✓	✓
phonological	✓	✓
morphological	X	✓

When both sources of inheritance are brought into play, along with the four levels of description, there are in principle multiple ways in which a class of derivatives can be non-canonical. We can imagine a good number of variations in the distribution of ticks and crosses given in (19). This number is, however, constrained by a bi-conditional implication at the syntactic level due to the syntactic category coming from the LFT or the base, but not both. So a cross for the base at this level implies a tick for the LFT. Moreover, inheritance from the base at the semantic and phonological levels is obligatory for there to be a base–derivative relation. Two items that do not share both basic form and meaning are not *morphologically* related, though by sharing one of these they may enter into other lexical relations, for example homonymy, synonymy, hyponymy, etc. Cases of unproductive derivational relatedness can be characterized as overriding the inheritance of the semantic level, resulting in lack of transparency, but this is a question of productivity not canonicity, and it is important to keep these two notions distinct. The upshot is that the ticks in the Base column in (19) are fixed. With this in mind, we briefly look at non-canonical derivation cases characterized by what is being inherited and from where.

7.2.1 Conversion

In the first non-canonical case, inheritance from the base follows the canonical pattern in (19) but inheritance from the LFT represents a departure at the phonological level. This is shown in (20) with a cross at the phonological/LFT intersection.

(20)

	Source of inheritance	
Lexemic level	Base	LFT
syntactic	X	✓
semantic	✓	✓
phonological	✓	X
morphological	X	✓

The schema in (20) represents cases of conversion. An example from Russian is the qualitative adjective *dobr-ij* 'kind', which is derived from the Declension IV noun *dobr-o* (Tixonov 1985). The LFT responsible can be represented as in (21).

(21)
```
LFT_QUAL_ADJ:
  <> == ADJ
  <gloss> == λx [ <sem feature> (x, "<base gloss>" ]
  <sem feature> == possess_quality_of.
```

Conversion is expressed by saying nothing about the path `<stem>`. Instead, we invoke Paradigm Function Morphology's Identity Function Default (Stump 2001: 53), which was introduced in Chapter 2, Section 2.3.1 for underspecification and Russian stress, and in Chapter 3, Section 3.1.1 for Kokota possessive marking. This is a high-level default that nothing *phonological* happens in a morphological operation. Here it is expressed as a series of path equations at the lexemic hierarchy root node, LEXEME.

(22)
```
LEXEME:
  <stem> == "<base stem>"
  <base stem> == "<root all>"
  ...
```

The first equation defines a lexical entry's stem as being whatever the root of its base is, by default. This is the identity function default. The second equation ensures that there will be a value for underived lexical entries, which have no base lexical entry to inherit from. Theorems for the lexeme *dobrij* are given in (23).

(23)
```
Dobrij:<syn cat> = adj.
Dobrij:<gloss> = λx [ possess_quality_of (x, good_deed ) ].
Dobrij:<sem feature> = possess_quality_of.
Dobrij:<stem> = dobr.
Dobrij:<base stem> == dobr
Dobrij:<mor sg nom> = dobr ^i ^j.
...
```

The fourth and fifth equations show identity between `Dobrij`'s stem and the stem of its base lexeme.

Since semantic- and syntactic-level inheritance from the LFT still takes place in conversion, lack of exponent can be associated with a range of semantic and syntactic features. Mel'čuk (2006: 304) gives a variety of English conversion examples. One class is characterized by change in syntactic category to verb, and the meaning 'submit Y to the action of X for which X is designed or intended'. Examples include *bomb* (N) > *bomb* (V), *saw* (N) > *saw* (V), and *hammer* (N) > *hammer* (V). For another class the syntactic change is to noun, and the semantic change 'one who Xes': *gossip* (V) > *gossip* (N), *cheat* (V) > *cheat* (N). The LFT that is responsible here therefore must enter into competition with the more productive *-er* LFT. For yet another class, the semantics is 'a unit of X', and Noun is the derived syntactic category: *kiss* (V) > *kiss* (N). Finally, valence-changing derivation in English can also be due to conversion. Mel'čuk derives causative *burn* (Vt) from *burn* (Vi).[7]

It should be noted in the Russian example that although there is no LFT inheritance at the phonological level, the resulting derivative is nonetheless morphologically distinct according to its pattern of inflections: the base inflects like a verb and the derivative like a noun. In other words, there is morphological harmony. Likewise, in the English examples, the derivative takes plural exponent *-s*, in contrast to the base. In this sense conversion is the least *non-canonical* type of derivational relatedness.

7.2.2 *Transposition*

The second non-canonical class involves lack of semantic-level inheritance from the LFT, denoted by a cross at the LFT/semantics intersection in (24). With respect to all other lines of inheritance, this class is canonical.

(24)

	Source of inheritance	
Lexemic level	Base	LFT
syntactic	X	✓
semantic	✓	X
phonological	✓	✓
morphological	X	✓

Nominalizations are an example of this class. In Russian, verbs productively derive action/event nouns in *-k* and *-en´ij*. Examples given in Bredenkamp, Sadler and Spencer (1998) include *pobel´it´* 'whitewash' > *pobelka* 'whitewashing', *per´ip´isat´* 'copy' > *per´ip´iska* 'copying', *razrušit´* 'destroy' > *razrušen´ijo* 'destroying/destruction', *rešit´* 'decide' > *rešen´ijo* 'deciding, decision'. These are analysed as simple transpositions from the verb category to the noun category, where the default-event verb semantics is retained without modification (see Spencer 2005: 95). So, for example, we can propose an LFT for nominalizations as in (25).

(25)
```
LFT_NOMINALIZATION:
  <> == NOUN
  <gloss> == "<base sem feature>" "<base gloss>"
             <sem feature>
  <stem> == SUFFIXATION
  <deriv affix> == enij
  <declensional_class> == N_IV:<mor>.
```

The second equation expresses the retention of semantics that characterizes transposition. If we assume a default primitive feature 'event' for verbs (see Jackendoff 1990), this can be stated as a fact at VERB and will be inherited by the base lexical entry, for example the lexical entry for *rešit´*. The LFT takes this as a value and combines it with the base lexical entry's gloss value to yield the semantic representation. So nothing new is provided by the LFT itself – semantics comes from the base. However, the full representation requires a semantic value that does come from the LFT. This is the default semantic property associated with a noun, namely 'thing', expressed as the last path in equation 2's RHS. By inheriting from NOUN, the LFT will inherit this default semantic property. This expresses the fact that a nominalization, though semantically an event, is nonetheless a thing (Spencer 2005: 106): 'a nominalization is the name of whatever kind of thing the base denotes … an event nominalization is the name of an event'. Syntactic-, phonological- and morphological-level facts all come from the LFT (equations 1, 4, 5 and 6, respectively).[8]

Transposition is less canonical than conversion because the semantic properties do not line up with the syntactic and morphological properties: an event ends up syntactically and morphologically a noun. Spencer (2005) observes that nominalizations can show 'different degrees of noun- or verb-hood'. In Chapter 1, Section 1.2.2, we looked at the nominalization *upravlen´ijo* derived from the verb *uprav´it´* 'govern' and showed how the verb's case assignment properties are inherited by the derivative. So the verb assigns instrumental case to its internal argument, and this assignment persists as a derived noun. The example we gave is repeated here as (26).

(26) V russk-om jazyk-e vstreča-et-sja
in Russian-SG.PREP language-SG.PREP meet-3SG-REFL
upravl-eni-e tvoritel´n-ym padež-om
govern-NMLZ-SG.NOM instrumental-SG.INS case-SG.INS
'In Russian you get government of the instrumental case.'

In our inheritance model, a greater degree of verb-hood amounts to more facts being inherited from the base, here the syntactic property of instrumental case assignment. Allowing this property to get through results in less canonical derivation according to parameter 6 in (1). We could use the equation `<syn case_assign> == "<base syn case_assign>"` to express greater degree of verb-hood as even more inheritance from the base *uprav´it´*.

7.2.3 *Category-preserving derivation*

The final class of non-canonical derivational relatedness that we consider is the more extreme version of *upravlen´ijo*, where all syntactic-level facts are inherited from the base rather than the LFT. In terms of parameter 6, this is the situation where derivation begins to look like inflection.

(27)

	Source of inheritance	
Lexemic level	Base	LFT
syntactic	✓	X
semantic	✓	✓
phonological	✓	✓
morphological	X	✓

Back in Chapter 1, Section 1.3.3 we showed how in Russian expressive derivation all syntactic facts are inherited from the base, including syntactic gender. So the Declension IV augmentative *dom´išč´o* that is derived from Declension I *dom* house inherits syntactic class and gender from its base despite change to an inflectional class associated with another gender (neuter). This is shown again in (28).

(28) gromadn-ij rižʹ-ij dom-išč´-o
huge-SG.M rust-SG.M house(M)-AUG-SG

Category-preserving derivation is the term for the inheritance profile shown in (27): despite a change brought about by inheritance at the semantic, phonological and morphological levels, the derivative remains the same at the syntactic level. This level is inherited from the base rather than the LFT, describing precisely the nature of its non-canonical behaviour. Category-preserving derivation can be represented as in (29), a node from which any LFT node that is characterized as category-preserving may inherit, for example augmentation and diminutivization (30) (e.g. *rabotka* from *rabota* 'work').

(29)
```
LFT_CAT_PRESERVING:
  <> == LEXEME
  <syn> == "<base syn>"
  <gloss> == λx ["<sem feature>" (x) & "<base gloss>"
             (x)]
  <stem> == SUFFIXATION.
```

(30)
a.
```
LFT_AUGMENTATIVE:
  <> == LFT_CAT_PRESERVING
  <sem feature> == big
  <deriv affix> == 'išč'
  <declensional_class> == N_IV:<mor>.
```
b.
```
LFT_DIMINUTIVE:
  <> == LFT_CAT_PRESERVING
  <sem feature> == small
  <deriv affix> == k
  <declensional_class> == N_II:<mor>.
```

In (29) the second equation expresses the profile of this kind of derivation – all paths that extend <syn> inherit whatever values matching paths have at the base lexical entry. This will include <syn cat>, <syn gender> and <syn sem feature> (see above). The third equation expresses a default subsective semantics associated with category-preserving derivation where denotation of [[X] Y] is a subset of X (Stump 1991: 702).[9] The last equation is there to express the generalization that category-preserving derivation is by default marked by some suffix. Example (30) shows how two different LFTs share all these properties of category-preserving derivation by means of inheritance from common node LFT_CAT_PRESERVING. So despite specifying Declension IV for augmentatives (30a), the syntactic gender will be inherited from the base due to (29), thereby creating a potential dissociation between the derivative's gender and its inflectional class (30a, equation 4), as in *dom´ išč´-o.*

Stump (1991; 1993; 2001: ch. 4) proposes that what marks out category-preserving derivation is the fact that it yields headed derivational expressions, parallel to endocentric compounds. The base heads the derivationally complex expression. So in *dom´iščo* the base *dom* is the head: [[*dom*$_{\text{head}}$] ´ *išč*]. As such, *dom*'s syntactic properties determine those of the whole expression. The subsective semantics associated with this kind of derivation is a function of its headedness. He further suggests that a subtype of category-preserving derivation allows not only the base's morphosyntactic properties to be those of the expression as a whole, but also its purely morphological properties, for example pattern of inflection, to persist. Inflection in such cases is marked on the head rather than the edge of the expression, as in all other products of derivation. Evidence of head-marking category-preserving derivation occurs when inflection appears inside derivation, a case of non-canonical derivation according to parameter 7 in (1). In Chapter 1, Section 1.3.3, we gave an example of such a case, the Shughni plural diminutive for 'baby goats'. The example is repeated in (31).

(31)	čost	wam	gujbuc-en-ik=en	dis	maỹʒůnǰ-idi
	appear.PST	her.OBL	babygoat-PL-EXPR=3PL	very	hungry-INTENS

'The dear little kids appeared very hungry to her.'

In (31) we see the effect of plural marking on the head of [[*gujbuc*] *ik*] because the diminutive category-preserving rule in Shughni happens to be the head-marking type. Essentially *-ik* is being attached to the plural word-form *gujbuc-en*, so *-ik* suffixation takes a word-form as its input and specifies a word-form as its output, i.e. it is a 'word-word' rule. This property of the rule is stated in the Head-Application Principle.

(32) *Head-Application Principle* (Stump 2005b: 67)
When stem *d* arises from stem *b* through the application of a word-word rule *r* then for each cell <*b*, σ> in *b*'s paradigm, if <*b*, σ> has realization *x*, then the corresponding cell <*d*, σ> in *d*'s paradigm has realization *r*(*x*).

So the cell <*gujbuc*, {NUM:PL}> realized as *gujbucen* in the base lexeme's paradigm will be that found in the derivative lexeme's paradigm.

We represent headmarking as a subtype of category-preserving derivation by means of inheritance (33).

(33)
```
LFT_HEAD_MARKING:
  <> == LFT_CAT_PRESERVING
  <mor> == "<base mor>" "<deriv affix>".
```

The first equation expresses head marking as a kind of category-preserving derivation by inheriting from the category-preserving node (29). The second equation expresses the Head-Application Principle. Any path that extends `<mor>`, i.e. a cell in the inflectional paradigm of the lexical entry inheriting from this node, inherits the value of that same path extension that belongs to the base lexical entry. Concatenated to this value is the affix marking the derivation, *-ik* in the Shughni example. If Shughni diminutive derivation is expressed by the node in (34), the theorems show that inflection is inside derivation (35).

(34)
```
LFT_DIMINUTIVE:
  <> == LFT_HEAD_MARKING
  <sem feature> == small
  <deriv affix> == ik.
```

(35)
```
Guǰbucik:<syn cat> = n.
Guǰbucik:<syn sem feature> = thing.
Guǰbucik:<gloss> = small baby_goat.
Guǰbucik:<sem feature> = small.
Guǰbucik:<mor sg> = guǰbuc ik.
Guǰbucik:<mor pl> = guǰbuc en ik.
```

Head-marking category-preserving derivation accounts for the non-canonical exponent order in the Shughni example. Looking at it the other way, the Shughni exponent ordering is evidence of head marking. But it is not always clear whether we are dealing with head marking since exponent order is only relevant when both the inflectional and derivational are suffixes, or both are prefixes. Stump shows that Sanskrit verb prefixation must be head marking category-preserving derivation because of what happens in the third-singular imperfect when an augment attaches to the left of the stem. So *car-* derives *abhi-car-* whose infinitive is suffixal: *abhicarati*. Here there is no formal evidence for head-marking. But in the third-singular imperfect, an inflectional prefix is used and appears inside the derivational prefix: *abhy-a-carat* (Stump 2001: 97). Russian prefixation typically marks category-preserving derivation. For verbs it is clear that we are dealing with head marking since non-regularity in the base paradigm is seen in the derivative paradigm (see Brown 1998c: 220). The past-tense singular masculine of *idti* 'go' is suppletive *šel*; and the past-tense singular masculine of derived *prijti* is *prišel*. Prefixes are also used to derive adjectives from adjectives, for example *gramotnij* 'literate' derives *negramotnij* 'illiterate'. There are two analyses of negative adjective derivation: either the LFT that introduces the prefix also introduces the adjectival inflectional morphology, analogous to the LFTs for augmentatives and diminutives in (30), or the morphology is inherited from the base as an instance of head marking. We will assume the prefixation itself is an indicator of head marking in Russian. To express this we reverse the path descriptors posited for Shughni in (33) for a parallel Russian `LFT_HEAD_MARKING` node: `<mor> == "<deriv affix>" "<base mor>"`. Both adjectival and verbal prefixal LFTs will inherit from such a node. The LFT that accounts for *negramotnij* is given in (36). Since prefixation in Russian is the default linearization for category-preserving derivation, we can change the fourth equation in (29) to `<stem> == PREFIXATION`, which (36) will then inherit.

(36)
```
LFT_NEG_ADJ:
  <> == LFT_HEAD_MARKING
  <gloss> == λx <sem feature> ["<base gloss>" (x) ]
  <sem feature> == ¬
  <deriv affix> == n.
```

The LFTs described up to this point generalize over classes of items which are all derived in the same affix. But we already saw that nominalizations can be expressed by at least two affixes (*rešen´ijo, pobelka*). And back in Chapter 1, we showed that *-k* is not the only marker of diminutives: they can be in *-ik*, as in *dom´ik* 'house (dim)'and *-(e)c* as in *zoloteco* 'gold (dim)'. An inferential–realizational approach provides for a one-to-many mapping of function and form. In the next section, we look at how there can be competition amongst affixes to express a given function, and how the competition is resolved.

7.3 Resolving affix competition

The category-changing LFT in (18) accounts for a class of personal noun derivatives that are all derived in the suffix *-tel´*, a small set of which we gave in (7). But there are many other formal means of deriving personal nouns. For example, the 1980 Academy Grammar lists about fifty.[10] Example (37) is a sample of the different affixes available in Russian to express personal noun derivation.

(37)

Affix	Derivative		Base	
Productive				
-tel´	*grab´itel´*	'thief'	*grab´it´*	'steal'
-n´ik	*vestn´ik*	'herald'	*vest´*	'news'
-´ik	*frontov´ik*	'front-line soldier'	*frontovoj*	'front-line'
-ec	*skupec*	'skinflint'	*skupoj*	'stingy'
-´ist	*traktor´ist*	'tractor driver'	*traktor*	'tractor'
-šč´ik	*betonšč´ik*	'concrete worker'	*beton*	'concrete'

Less productive				
-ak	*ribak*	fisherman	*riba*	'fish'
-ač	*trubač*	trumpeter	*truba*	'trumpet'
-an	*vel´ikan*	giant	*vel´ikij*	'huge'
-´ar	*ovčar*	shepherd	*ovca*	'sheep'
-un	*begun*	runner	*begat´*	'run'

We have separated out those affixes considered 'productive'.[11] We will return to the various senses derivational morphologists attach to the term productive in Section 7.4, as they have important implications for a Network Morphology approach to derivation. But for present purposes, we will say that they are the affixes still used to coin new words, that the words derived in them are compositional and thus semantically transparent, and that each affix has a large number of lexemes derived in it, whereas not all of these properties are true for the second set of affixes. In the spirit of inferential–realizational morphology, we resolve productive affix competition by relating affixes paradigmatically and allowing the Pāṇinian principle to play a role in their selection. We assume a single function, broadly 'personal noun', containing more than one realization possibility, along with the information needed to determine the correct realization for a given base. So our personal noun LFT will be updated with a set of affixes licensed by properties of the base lexeme.

Such an approach entails constraining the way base lexemes interact with an LFT in two ways. First the lexemes which derive personal nouns in one particular affix must be exhaustively selected by the LFT to undergo a particular rule of exponence. And second the LFT must stop the same rule of exponence from applying to those lexemes that use another affix to realize the 'personal noun' function. Many models of derivation view these constraints as various types of *restriction* or *condition* that can be laid on a base lexeme's properties that, if met, allow the lexeme to undergo a specific role of exponence (e.g. Aronoff 1976; Anderson 1992; Plag 2003)[12]. These conditions can be broadly categorized as syntactic, semantic and formal (phonological/morphological), depending on what level of lexical representation is relevant. For example, the choice of affix may depend on the base's syntactic category. Deriving personal nouns in *-tel´* is usual when the base is a verb, and when its argument structure has an NP first argument and an NP second argument. Derivation in *-tel´*, therefore, has *syntactic conditions* attached to it that select all bases of the type `<syn cat> = v, <syn valence> = 2`. At the same time, it filters out all bases with different values for these syntactic features. Incorporating conditions such as these into the LFT allows for a paradigmatic relation amongst more than one affix relating to one function.[13] Amongst the productive affixes given in (37), we can find similar selectional preferences such that no affixation process overlaps with another in its set of bases. In fact we can think of it the other way around: this complementary distribution of affixes over bases is suggestive of their productivity. In this section we present an overview of the different conditions that an LFT can lay on a base, illustrating with the productive affixes in (37) as well as with others for adjectival derivation. We will use these short sketches of a fragment of the Russian derivational system to gradually build up the Network Morphology representation of the personal noun LFT for Russian.

7.3.1 Syntactic conditions

The first three affixes in (37) *-tel´*, *-n´ik* and *-´ik* are complementarily distributed across verb, adjective and noun bases, respectively. Examples demonstrating this syntax-based distribution are given in (38).

(38)

Base type		Personal noun	
Verb bases			
č´itat´	'read'	*č´itatel´*	'reader'
p´isat´	'write'	*p´isatel´*	'writer'
grab´it´	'steal'	*grab´itel´*	'thief'
xran´it´	'guard'	*xran´itel´*	'custodian'
Noun bases			
bariš	'profit'	*barišn´ik*	'profiteer'
izmena	'betrayal'	*izmenn´ik*	'traitor'
kleveta	'scandal'	*klevetn´ik*	'slanderer'
skit	'monastery'	*skitn´ik*	'monk'
sokol	'falcon'	*sokol´n´ik*	'falconer'
vest´	'herald'	*vestn´ik*	'herald'
Adjective bases			
gorlovoj	'throat'	*gorlov´ik*	'throat specialist'
pravovoj	'legal'	*pravov´ik*	'jurist'
krovnij	'blood'	*krovn´ik*	'blood relative'
sezonnij	'seasonal'	*sezonn´ik*	'seasonal worker'
serebr´anij	'silver'	*serebr´an´ik*	'silversmith'
neft´anoj	'oil'	*neft´an´ik*	'oil worker'

To capture syntactically determined operations for personal noun derivation, we update the LFT node for personal nouns by introducing a dependency on the phonological-level fact, i.e. the affix to be inherited. All other aspects remain the same. The updated LFT is shown in (39).

(39)

```
LFT_PERSON:
  <> == NOUN
  <gloss> == λx [ <sem feature> (x) & "<base gloss>" (x) ]
  <sem feature> == person
  <stem> == SUFFIXATION
  <deriv affix> == LFT_PERSON_AFFIX:
  <"<base syn cat>" "<base syn valence>">.

LFT_PERSON_AFFIX:
  <v 2> == tel'
  <n 1> == nik
  <adj 1> == ik.
```

The last equation expresses a syntactic condition as `<deriv affix>`, inheriting its value through an evaluable path containing syntactic category and valence values. Resolution is at a newly introduced `LFT_PERSON_AFFIX` interdependency node.

7.3.2 Formal conditions

Syntactic conditions give a complementarity between three types of suffixation in example (37), but Russian has (at least) three additional suffixes for productive personal noun formation. In addition to syntactic properties, to determine choice of affix we can use a base lexeme's formal properties. We have seen that the suffix *-´ik* is used for adjectival bases, but so too is the suffix *-ec*, as shown in (40).

(40)

Base type		Personal noun	
Adjectival bases			
podlij	'ignoble'	*podlec*	'scoundrel'
skupoj	'stingy'	*skupec*	'skinflint'
znakomij	'familiar'	*znakomec*	'acquaintance'
upr´amij	'obstinate'	*upr´amec*	'obstinate person'
slepoj	'blind'	*slepec*	'blind person'
mudrij	'wise'	*mudrec*	'wise person'
sčastl´ivij	'lucky'	*sčastl´ivec*	'lucky person'
len´ivij	'lazy'	*len´ivec*	'lazy bones'
lub´imij	'favourite'	*lub´imec*	'favourite person'
č´ornij	'black'	*č´ornec*	'monk'

The syntactic category of the base provides a way of discriminating among *-tel´*, *-n´ik* and the pair *-´ik/-ec*. To decide between the members of the pair, we need something more than syntactic category. When we compare the *-ec* derivatives in example (40) with the *-´ik* derivatives in example (38), we can attempt to deduce two non-overlapping environments that involve bases' formal properties. The bases that select *-´ik* end in /v/ or /n/ (*gorlovoj*, *krovnij*, *neft´anij*); *-ec* is selected by bases other than those ending /v/ or /n/. In other words, *-ec* represents the Elsewhere Condition.[14]

This analysis is not quite right though. The derivative *č´ornec* 'monk', the last item in (40), ends in the segment /n/ yet selects *-ec* instead of *-´ik*. Likewise, *sčastl´ivij* 'lucky' and *len´ivij* 'lazy' are both bases that select *-ec* despite ending in /v/. The paradigmatic situation is maintained, however, when we recognize that *-ik* is selected on morphological rather than purely phonological grounds. All the bases in (38) are themselves derived in the affixes *-n* or *-ov*. The suffix *-´ik* is restricted to bases derived in these affixes. As *č´ornij*, *sčastl´ivij* and *len´ivij* are either underived or derived in an affix other than *-n* and *-ov*, their environments do not overlap. The personal noun LFT is further updated to incorporate a morphologically based formal condition on the selection of affixes when the base is specifically an adjective (41).

(41)
```
LFT_PERSON_AFFIX:
  <v 2> == tel'
  <n 1> == nik
  % <adj 1> == ik
  <adj 1> == LFT_PERSON_AFFIX_DEADJ:
             <"<base deriv affix>">.

LFT_PERSON_AFFIX_DEADJ:
  <ov> == ik
  <n> == <ov>
  <> == ec.
```

In the last equation of the first node, the evaluable path expresses the fact that the base's derivational affix is used to determine the affix of the query lexical entry (the derivative). In the second node, we see that if this value is the affix *-ov* or *-n*, then *-´ik* is used; otherwise *-ec*.

When a base is adjectival, affix selection is dependent upon a portion of the form of this lexeme's base, in particular that part that corresponds to the affix inherited by a different LFT. Such an approach does raise a theoretical concern: formal conditions that target the morphological portion of the stem break the Bracket Erasure Convention (BEC) (Kiparsky 1982: 11; 1983: 3), which states that 'morphological … processes cannot be sensitive to internal structure'. But there are plenty of examples like the deadjectival person noun case showing there must be some access to internal structure. In a seminal work on lexeme-based derivational rules in English, Aronoff

(1976: 53) uses *morphological* conditions to explain English derivatives in *-ity* selecting bases in *-al* and *-ic*, for example *electric* > *electricity*, *modal* > *modality*. Dutch female personal noun formation also seems sensitive to the affixation of the base where the choice between two productive operations, *-ster* affixation and *-e* affixation, is determined by whether or not the base's stem includes the suffix *-aar* or *-ier*, in which case *-ster* used, or something else, in which case *-e*. So *handelaar*, *herbergier* > *handelaarster* 'merchant', *herbergierster* 'innkeeper'; but *gids*, *leerling* > *gidse* 'guide', *leerlinge* 'pupil' (van Marle 1985: 218–28; Booij 2002: 102; 2005: 119). When language users are confronted with a derivationally complex word, they can interpret it through a morphological parse which isolates the stem from how it is modified. Morphological parsing can therefore also be performed on the base to determine the appropriate morphological operation to derive a new word. A more relaxed version of the BEC which still makes the lexical integrity point behind the BEC is the Adjacency Constraint (Siegel 1977: 192), where access to the word's internal structure is limited to that part of the structure introduced by an immediately preceding rule of word-formation. This constraint is expressed in our account by the path `"<base deriv affix>"` in (41), a value of the lexical entry's *immediate* base.

The morphological level can be used as a determiner of affix in another way. In Chapter 1, Section 1.2.1, we showed how for Russian diminutives choice of affix depends on properties of the base. At first blush it looks as if it is the gender that is significant since the generalization is that masculines derive diminutives in *-ʹik*, for example *dom* 'house' > *domʹik*; feminines use *-k*, for example *rabota* 'work' > *rabotka*; and neuters *-c*, as in *zoloto* 'gold' > *zolotce*. However, there are a number of nouns like *dʹadʹa* 'uncle' which, though masculine, belong to the feminine-associated Declension II. Crucially these select the *-k* affix rather than *-ʹik*, so *dʹadka* and not **dʹadʹik*. For diminutive affix selection, it must therefore be declensional class that determines the affix, a purely morphological property. This information is available as a fourth level of lexical representation for every lexeme. The updated diminutive LFT with rival affixes determined by the base's inflectional class is given in (42).

(42)
```
LFT_DIMINUTIVE:
  <> == LFT_CAT_PRESERVING
  <sem feature> == small
  <deriv affix> == LFT_DIM_AFFIX:<"<base mor formal
                   gender>">
  <declensional_class> == LFT_DIM_CLASS:
                          <"<base mor formal gender>">.
```

```
LFT_DIM_AFFIX:
  <fem> == k
  <neut> == c
  <masc> == ik.

LFT_DIM_CLASS:
  <fem> == N_II:<mor>
  <neut> == N_IV:<mor>
  <masc> == N_I:<mor>.
```

The third equation of the first node expresses affix selection being dependent on declensional class, albeit indirectly. What is actually being used is the value of the base's *formal* gender, a purely morphological feature whose value is determined by inflectional class membership. Each inflectional class node in the morphological hierarchy contains this value. Recall that formal gender was used in the account of Russian inflection in Chapter 3, Section 3.1.3 to determine the (syntactic) gender of a noun, thereby expressing the strong association between inflectional class and gender (see specifically example (52)). The last equation in the first node expresses the association between the base's declensional class (formal gender) and the declensional class the derivative ends up in (last node), so that a morphological level fact is essentially being used for two purposes.[15]

7.3.3 Semantic conditions

We end our discussion on affix competition with semantically determined affix selection. Relational adjectives are derived in a number of affixes, the productive ones being *-ov*, *-sk* and *-n*. Examples in *-ov* and *-n* were given in (38). We give a few more examples in (43) along with adjectives in *-sk*.

(43)

Derivative		Base	
sezonnij	'seasonal'	*sezon*	'season'
krovnij	'blood'	*krov´*	'blood'
parusnij	'sail'	*parus*	'sail'
serdečnij	'heart, cordial'	*serdce*	'heart'
kn´ižnij	'book, bookish'	*kn´iga*	'book'
gramotnij	'literate'	*gramota*	'literacy'
vkusnij	'tasty'	*vkus*	'taste'
gorlovoj	'throat'	*gorlo*	'throat'
šumovoj	'sonic'	*šuma*	'noise'
apel´s´inovoj	'orange'	*apel´s´in*	'orange'
beregovoj	'coastal'	*bereg*	'coast'
slonovij	'elephant'	*slon*	'elephant'
vkusovoj	'gustatory'	*vkus*	'taste'

avtorskij	'author'	*avtor*	'author'
advokatskij	'advocate'	*advokat*	'advocate'
uč´itel´skij	'teacher'	*uč´itel´*	'teacher'
ribackij	'fisherman'	*ribak*	'fisherman'
Kanadskij	'Canadian'	*Kanada*	'Canada'
Kievskij	'Kievan'	*Kiev*	'Kiev'

The *-sk* class of bases denotes either a person or a geopolitical entity. The *-ov* class is more heterogeneous. An LFT for relational adjectives incorporating semantically based affix selection is given in (44).

(44)
```
LFT_REL_ADJ:
  <> == ADJ
  <gloss> == λx [ <sem feature> (x, "<base gloss>") ]
  <sem feature> == related_to
  <stem> == SUFFIXATION
  <deriv affix> == LFT_REL_ADJ_AFFIX:<"<base sem
                    feature>">.

LFT_REL_ADJ_AFFIX:
  <person> == sk
  <geo_political> == <person>
  <> == ov.
```

The last equation in the first node expresses the dependency on a base's semantic feature. The second node expresses the association between *-sk* and the class of base which denotes person or geopolitical entity. The suffix *-ov* is the elsewhere case.

The LFT in (44) does not account for the very large class of adjectives in *-n*, such as *sezon* 'season' > *sezonnij* 'seasonal'. Like the *-ov* class, the *-n* class is heterogeneous. But we cannot give elsewhere status to both. It turns out that these affixes are not actually in competition if we examine the broad semantics of members of the *-n* class. Some like *sezonnij* are relational adjectives, and some are qualitative adjectives, such as *gramotnij* 'literate'. The LFT responsible for *-n*-derived adjectives is underspecified for whether its output is a relational or qualitative adjective. This is information that must therefore be lexically specified. For some adjectives the context decides the interpretation. For example, *serdečnij* from *serdce* 'heart' can mean either 'cordial' (qualitative) or 'heart related, cardiac' (relational) as in *serdečnij bolezn´* 'heart disease' (see Townsend 1975: 215–16 for discussion of *-n*-derived adjectives). To capture these properties, we set up a semantically neutral adjective LFT, shown in (45). The semantic level of derivatives inheriting from this node is filled in by lexically specifying the appropriate inheritance of the gloss path value, either from the relational or qualitative LFT node.

(45)
```
LFT_ADJ:
  <> == ADJ
  <stem> == SUFFIXATION
  <deriv affix> == n.

Sezonnij:
  <> == LFT_ADJ
  <base> == "Sezon:<base>"
  <gloss> == LFT_REL_ADJ.
```

When there is more than one rival affix available to realize a particular derivational function, the base's properties can be accessed to resolve the competition. We have updated our LFTs to incorporate this sensitivity to the base. In this way we are able to account for affix competition through a paradigmatic relation between affixes that is partially determined by the Pāṇinian principle. The effect is morphological blocking where affixation type α, by simply applying, blocks the possibility of affixation type β (see, for example, Kiparsky 2005). Of course, this approach is limited to strictly productive affixes. In (37) we listed a number of less productive affixes. These do not enter into a paradigmatic relation with the productive affixes or with each other. In the next section, we address the broader issue of productivity and show how a default inheritance-based approach to derivation naturally handles non-productivity in its full range of senses.

7.4 Productivity

Derivational productivity carries with it (at least) three different senses, following Corbin (1987: 176).[16] The use of an affix should be viewed as productive not only because many items are found with it but also because of its full participation in the language's lexeme-formation system. A type frequency comparison of *-ec* and *-n´ik* from Zaliznjak's (1977) dictionary reveals that *-n´ik* with 856 types has a higher frequency-based productivity than *-ec* with 544 types. But given the right syntactic and formal conditions, a lexeme will be derived in *-ec* and not *-n´ik*, and from this system-based viewpoint they are equally productive. We will distinguish frequency-based productivity (*profitable* productivity in Corbin) from system-based productivity (*available* productivity in Corbin). The LFTs described above account for system-based productive affixes in Russian, some of which have a higher frequency-based productivity than others. There may of course be a correlation between the manner in which an affixation process participates in the system and its frequency-based productivity. For example, fewer conditions on the base might imply a larger class of bases that are available for the given affix. This is essentially the claim in Booij (1977: 5). In our account of adjective derivation, the elsewhere case *-ov* should derive more lexemes than *-sk* since the latter contains a semantic condition. Again using Zaliznjak, we can get some sense of whether this kind of correlation stands. We in fact find that in this instance the more restricted affixation has higher frequency-based productivity: there are 1,387 types in *-ov* and getting close to three times as many in *-sk*, 3,280. At the same time when we compare two affixes with an equal number of conditions, for example *-n´ik* and *-tel´*, we get nothing like parity in their type frequencies. Zaliznjak lists 2,045 nouns in *-tel´* and 856 in *-n´ik*.[17] While degree of specification on inputs seems to have no bearing on frequency-based productivity, it may be a different story for output specification. We showed how the adjective-deriving suffix *-n* is semantically underspecified, since both qualitative and relational adjectives are derived in this suffix. The number of *-n* types in Zaliznjak is 10,815, far outweighing any other adjective-deriving affix.

As well as system-based and frequency-based productivity, Corbin gives a third sense of the word, degree of semantic transparency (*regularity* productivity). An item may be productive on the transparency scale while having low system- and frequency-based productivity. The items we listed in (37) as less productive, for example *-ak* as in *ribak* 'fisherman' and *-ač* as in *trubač* 'trumpeter', are nonetheless transparently productive. Though they do not enter into the condition-based affixation system, they are straightforwardly interpreted as being formally and semantically related to a base lexeme in the stem *rib-* and *trub-*, respectively, and having the derived semantics associated with the person LFT. Though these suffixes may no longer coin new personal nouns, they still encode a personal-noun-derivative lexeme. A better distinction than productive versus less productive would be generatively *and* analytically productive (system-based productive) as distinct from analytically productive *only* (transparently productive).

The default/overrides machinery in Network Morphology is ideal for teasing out the transparently productive only from the non-productive altogether. In the former we want the nature of the inheritance to differ marginally from the system-based productive cases. The way in which facts about derivational semantics, syntactic class, animacy, gender, and declensional class are acquired does not distinguish *ribak* 'fisherman' and the like from what we were calling 'productive' lexemes. What does distinguish them is a single override, a phonological level fact about the affix used. Even the linearization generalization, another phonological-level fact, gets inherited just as with the most productive cases (*-ak* is a suffix). Transparent-only productivity is expressed as inheritance from the person LFT node, but a lexically specified override of the path `<deriv affix>`. Since *-ak* is used for over fifty nouns (based on Zaliznjak), the alternative affixation is represented as a node situated *under* the more general LFT from which it inherits, overriding for a single path. We therefore represent *ribak* as belonging to a subregular class of items whose subregularity is made explicit.

(46)
```
LFT_PERSON_AK:
  <> == LFT_PERSON
  <deriv affix> == ak.
```

We express the contrast between transparently productive only cases and those which are not transparent by introducing a semantic-level override for the latter. In Russian the verb *dv´igat´* 'move' derives *dv´igatel´*. But the semantics of the derivative is unpredictable: it is not 'person who moves' but 'engine'. Formally and syntactically, the derivative belongs to the class of *-tel´* items. Semantically, it is at odds with members of its class. In our inheritance-based account, it inherits syntactic, phonological- and morphological-level information from the person LFT but overrides at the semantic level. The lexical entry for *dv´igatel´* is given in (47).

(47)
```
Dv'igatel':
  <> == LFT_PERSON
  <base> == "Dv'igat':<>"
  <syn animacy> == inanimate
  <gloss> == engine.
```

In addition to overriding the gloss path, the lexical entry has also to override the animacy fact, an implication that is inherited from the person LFT (recall our discussion in Section 7.1).

What we have shown in (47) is actually a mismatch between derivational function and the semantics of the lexical entry. There is of course a strong tendency for such a mismatch amongst the products of derivative lexical entries as they are subject to semantic drift, explaining the parameter 5 setting in (1) that distinguishes inflection from derivation: inflection is always transparent, derivation is *not always* transparent. This is naturally captured in our defaults system. We could go further and capture shifts in transparency by allowing items like *dv´igatel´* to inherit the transparent semantics as a kind of virtual interpretation. Just as we had virtual and actual paradigms existing side by side in our deponency account, we could have virtual and actual interpretations coexisting, where the former is inherited from the network. This would require a minor modification of our theory: replacing the paths `<sem feature>` and `<gloss>` at an LFT with the paths `<deriv sem feature>` and

`<deriv gloss>` allowing for a semantics specific to derivation. We then could add as a high-level default the association of derived and non-derived semantics: `<sem feature> == "<deriv sem feature>"`, and `<gloss> == "<deriv gloss>"`. We would situate these equations at the LEXEME node in the lexemic hierarchy. Given these modifications, the theorems of the lexical entry for *dv´igatel´* will contain an actual gloss and a virtual gloss (48).

(48)
```
Dv'igatel':<gloss> = engine.
Dv'igatel':<deriv gloss> = λx [ person (x) & move (x) ].
Dv'igatel':<stem> = dviga tel'.
...
```

In the nineteenth-century dictionary by Dal´ (1880), the entry *dv´igatel´* has the meaning corresponding to the value of `<deriv gloss>` in (48). The item is perfectly transparent according to Dal´, and even forms a female counterpart *dv´igatel´n´ica*. A lexical entry representing the earlier gloss has the theorem in (49), where the lexical entry inherits from the LFT without any overriding.

(49)
```
Dv'igatel'_ Dal':<gloss> = λx [ person (x) & move (x) ].
Dv'igatel'_ Dal':<deriv gloss> =
                λx [ person (x) & move (x) ].
Dv'igatel'_ Dal':<stem> = dviga tel'.
...
```

The difference between (48) and (49) is that in (48) there is a mismatch between the actual semantics and the derived semantics, expressed as distinct values for `<gloss>` and `<deriv gloss>`.

We have shown how our account distinguishes unproductive items such as *dv´igatel´* from the productive, and further discriminates amongst the latter between items that display frequency-based, system-based and transparent-only productive behaviour. Defaults play a central role in expressing these distinctions just as they do in teasing apart different types of inflectional non-regularity. For non-regularity we proposed a classification based on the nature of a lexical entry's relation to the network of inheritable facts. We can do the same with cases of productivity. System-based productive items, a subset of which will have frequency-based productivity, inherit from the network in the same way as inflectionally regular lexical entries. Transparent-only productive items are parallel to network-directed non-regulars in that the lexical entry specifies an override, but the alternative value is retrieved from a node which is in a hierarchical relation with the highest-level node in the network. This is the situation of the *-ak* affixation node inheriting from the person LFT node. Unproductive items behave similarly to lexically listed non-regulars since the override is specified in the lexical entry, and the alternative value is also lexically specified, in our example above for semantic-level information.

7.5 Concluding remarks on derivational morphology in Network Morphology

There are different ways of approaching derivational morphology. A morpheme-based approach, such as lexical morphology or more recently Lieber's framework (2004), is bottom up: the meaning and selectional properties of affix lexical entries are considered, and derivation is the result of building larger constituents from smaller so that in principle there is no distinction between derivation and compounding. A top-down approach assumes derivational functions, analogous to morphosyntactic features. Word-formation rules, in the spirit of Anderson (1992) or lexical redundancy rules following Jackendoff (1975), associate derivational function with an exponent of that function. Classification of derivational processes may revolve around the phonological reflex of derivation – specific affixes. This is what Kastovsky (2005: 108) discusses as the *Wortbildungsmodell* in the word-formation studies tradition. On the other hand, classification may be based on derivational functions or categories, the *Wortbildungstyp*. This approach dominates the Slavic tradition (see, for example, Vinogradov 1960; Gvozdev 1961; Šanskij 1975; Švedova *et al.* 1980).[18] Szymanek (1988) and Beard (1995) are different proposals of what these derivational categories might be. In our account we are after a classification similar to the second by assuming derivational functions. It is a different classification, however, since the emphasis is on the nature of the relation between derivative lexeme and its base lexeme where the relation is expressed by inheritance. Both the *source* of inheritance and its *content* are factors. Inheritance is from the base lexeme and a node storing the redundant information that characterizes a particular class of derivatives. And it can involve syntactic-, semantic-, phonological- and morphological-level facts. The interplay of the source and content properties of inheritance yields the four broad derivational-relatedness classes: category-changing, conversion, transposition and category-preserving derivation.[19] It also provides for the possibility of hybrid classes, for example a transposition that has no phonological reflex, i.e. a conversion/transposition hybrid.[20]

We have shown that derivational-relatedness can be linked to canonicity, where category-changing derivation is the canonical class since change from base to derivative is observable at every level of representation expressed as maximal inheritance from the LFT. Other classes represent various departures from the canonical situation and are precisely expressed as what the exact deviations in source and content inheritance are. In this way we can account for some of the parameters used to distinguish inflection and derivation. Parameters 1 and 2 characterize the purpose of derivation as building new lexemes, assuming maximal differentiation from the related existing lexeme. This is why category-changing derivation is canonical derivation. And what follows is that in the canonical case, the inheritance of base features is limited, parameter 6. Parameter 7, exponence of derivation inside exponence of inflection, falls out from parameter 1 since derivational exponents build stems of new lexemes, which are then subject to inflection, to create their paradigms. One canonical departure is inheriting too much from the base – category-preserving derivation. This can lead to head marking where, as well as morphosyntactic features, a base's paradigm is being inherited. This non-canonical situation results in inflection inside derivation, since the base acts as a head, and it is the head that is being inflected.

Our derivational-relatedness approach is realizational; therefore, it assumes realizational rules which we recast as lexeme-formation templates expressed as nodes in the hierarchy of derivational information. We showed how these nodes hold generalizations about the changes that a particular derivation produces, as well as regulating the selection of affixes that can be used to mark the changes. Instances of derivation vary in the manner in which they interact with the lexeme-formation system, and we have shown how this variation corresponds to different senses of derivational productivity.

Derivational morphology throws up many challenges for morphological theory, and a single chapter on the Network Morphology approach is bound to be limited in stating the full problem space, let alone the solution space. Our aim was to show that inheritance and defaults can play an extremely important role within the solution space, and that a framework based on these notions has some clear advantages in accounting for derivational morphology and its interaction with the rest of the grammar.

8 *Conclusion*

8.0 Taking stock

Our starting point was the view that morphology constitutes a linguistic system which cannot be reduced to the principles of syntax or phonology, a position held by other leading theories such as Paradigm Function Morphology and A-morphous Morphology. Our goal was to account for the different types of morphological autonomy, using the notion of lexeme as part of a network as the basis for the investigation. Our approach distinguishes between rules and the route by which those rules may be inherited. This simultaneous combination of rule-like and list-like behaviour, we argue, is a particular property of morphological systems.

8.1 Autonomous morphology

While morphology may not play a major role in some languages, for others it contributes an additional systematic layer in its own right. We illustrated in Chapter 3 how the inheritance structure associated with the parts of speech in the lexemic hierarchy may be sufficient to deal with morphology which closely meshes with the requirements of syntax. Network Morphology provides a mechanism for moving from autonomous to straightforward morphology, so that it is possible to account both for the simple instances, as well as those where the relationship between words and syntax is complex. In so doing we also demonstrated, with an implemented account, that the mechanisms we have put in place can deal with at least some subset of clitics and other affixation which appears to be distributed according to principles associated with phrases.

Network Morphology makes a distinction between the classes defined for syntax, in the lexemic hierarchy, and a separate morphological hierarchy which provides the minimal set of rules necessary to realize the forms required by syntax. Even beyond this, Network Morphology can break down the rule system into recognizable layers (which are language specific). One example we discussed was the stress system of Russian nominals (Chapter 2), where the patterns of stress cannot be accounted for in purely phonological terms and fully inflected forms of words are the product of accessing the information from isolatable hierarchies defining stress patterns and affixal morphology. For both of these subcomponents there is partial autonomy, in that the stress patterns are not restricted to one inflectional class, and the inflectional classes are not restricted to one pattern. This highlights that it is more than just a matter of considering the relationship between parts of speech and morphological classes. The morphology may actually be the result of more complex layering, and being able to treat this complexity in terms of layering of hierarchies presents us with degrees of morphological complexity which can be a point of typological contrast between languages which are otherwise very closely related, as noted in Chapter 2.

In Chapter 3 we investigated the autonomy associated with inflectional classes, which provide more forms than are needed by syntax. We suggested that defaults are required for inflectional classes, even though it is logically possible that there might be none, and that these defaults are naturally associated with parts of speech. In contrast with inflectional classes, syncretism (Chapter 4) involves the morphology failing to make distinctions which are relevant for syntax. The least dramatic kind of syncretism is where the feature structure assumed for the syntax can be used to characterize the syncretism. The attribute ordering we introduced in Chapter 2 can account for the straightforward examples where distinctions of one feature, such as gender, are lost in the presence of others, such as case or number. Network Morphology differs from other inferential–realizational frameworks in emphasizing the interplay of attribute ordering with other constructs to capture the differences between the language-specific and the cross-linguistically more prevalent patterns of syncretism, which we saw in Chapter 4. We also argued that these mechanisms, such as generalized referral, can account for a whole spectrum of related phenomena. In particular, they provide a ready account of deponency (Chapter 5), where morphology involves the use of forms normally associated with an opposing function to the one for which they are used. These mismatches involve feature slippage of some kind: either the morphology is inert to a distinction which exists in syntax, or the syntactic function contrasts with the morphological form.

Pure morphology, such as inflectional-class affiliation, theme vowels and stem indexes (morphomes), is a different kind of autonomy. The kind of syncretism which is neither directional nor involves natural classes requires such pure morphological features and is evidence for this different kind of autonomy. Within Network Morphology these can either be used to describe the properties of stems or to address particular nodes within the morphological hierarchy, a typical function of inflectional class features.

The distinction between the lexemic hierarchy and the morphological hierarchy in Network Morphology brings with it the potential for virtual paradigms. The inheritance links between the lexemic hierarchy and the morphological hierarchy allow for the possibility that paradigmatic contrasts inherent within the morphological hierarchy (and used by many lexemes) can be activated as part of historical change for those lexemes which have previously not accessed them (Chapter 6). This activation is associated with the distinction between exceptional and normal case defaults (Chapter 2). Change is not just a matter of rules, but also a matter of the interaction between rules and individual lexemes. This may involve a switch back to a higher default, such as happens with the exceptional case default, where a subregular item resorts to the more general pattern. Furthermore, because paths define paradigms in Network Morphology, the change can also be seen in terms of switching at a particular point so that a particular part of the paradigm changes to follow the default pattern. In deponency, for example, identifying the root of the paradigm in terms of the distinction between active and passive means that this identifies whole slabs of information, as opposed to being limited to just one cell in the paradigm.

8.2 Rules and defaults in morphology

Great emphasis has been placed on the role of inheritance and the different notions of default within Network Morphology (underspecification, override by class, the exceptional and normal case defaults). The sharing of morphology between inflectional classes is a matter of inheritance, and so inflection-class features for certain languages, such as Russian, can actually be replaced by nodes for the particular inflectional classes, with sharing of the morphology potentially generalized beyond the particular parts of speech (as we saw in Chapter 3). This allows us to isolate default realizations to which many lexemes will have access in the normal case, and others will access as exceptional case defaults.

Defaults are a core notion for linguistic morphology. Given the differing degrees of regularity and subregularity within the system, they are a natural way of treating morphology. While it is based on the notion of rule, a key property of morphology within the Network Morphology framework is that the rules are part of an inheritance network which contains generalizations distributed across this network. The often posited difference between rules and listing under this framework is seen as an artefactual distinction, because the rules apply throughout different domains, potentially applying to all lexemes, but also, in virtue of the system of defaults and overrides, all the way down to individual lexemes. The use of constructs such as the exceptional case default and the normal case default (introduced in Chapter 2) allows the exceptional items to have access to the more general rules, with some degree of specification in the lexical entries. This property of Network Morphology means that we can see the resort to more general rules in part as an emergent property of lexemes, a property which also aligns with the historical analysis based on virtual paradigms.

We also saw how derivation could be accounted for in terms of the interconnectedness of a network, this time with the rules allowing one set of lexemes to be derived from another (Chapter 7). As with inflection, information is located across the network, coming from nodes representing the deriving lexeme and a redundancy rule specific to lexeme-formation, what we termed a lexeme-formation template. The different ways in which the network is accessed for derivational information characterize the different types of word-formation, category changing, category preserving, conversion and transposition, as well as the sense of productivity at play for a given derivational situation.

The key advantages of Network Morphology are that we can observe different degrees of regularity in the inheritance network and observe that one class of item partially belongs to another class within a *hierarchical* relation. The notion of default introduced in this framework is therefore a *cascaded* notion, and contrasts significantly with the categorical distinction made between defaults on the one hand and 'pure' irregularity/exceptionality on the other. Irregularity is a matter of degree, but is also constrained by the provision of exceptional case default mechanisms. While Network Morphology can account for defaults based on underspecification which more readily reflect cross-linguistic tendencies, the use of class overrides and the normal case and exceptional case default allow us to contrast these more general properties with language-specific systematicity.

8.3 Consequences

Network Morphology, as a default inheritance-based approach, is particularly promising for developing linguistic typology further, because, on the one hand it does not require a categorical distinction between the active rule system and the exceptions, and on the other we can place the less general patterns at different positions in the network. Typological tendencies, such as the relation between number and gender, can be expressed by placing constraints on the order of attributes expressing these features. And we can make a distinction between typological constraints in the full morphological model, and constraints in the morphological analysis. However, these constraints represent important cross-linguistic tendencies which are subject to exception and can be combined with language-specific systematicity. We saw, for example, an interplay between underspecification and referrals in our treatment of syncretism. We argue that an adequate framework for morphology has to take these different types of element into account and map the limits of the interaction, rather than attempt to wish away these distinctions in order to support a very limited and, ultimately, ill-defined notion of what it means to be constrained.

The observation and classification of different types of autonomous morphology is an important issue for typology, and the Node Elimination principle (Chapter 2) allows us to move from the complex systems which interest morphologists to a straightforward mapping between syntax and morphology. The existence of both stem-indexing and inflectional classes, as well as other systematic layers within morphology, as different kinds of autonomy, suggests further interactions. For example, on the one hand we may have just instances where autonomous stems exist and these are partially matched with morphosyntax.

While language-specific systematicity is rife in morphological systems, we can still observe the interaction of lexemes and rules – beyond the artefactual rule–list distinction – and this is bound up with the key theoretical notions of normal case and exceptional case defaults. On the one hand, there is a rule which applies normally, and this is subject to varying degrees of exception, but in the last resort we may find an item we expect to belong to a subregular type reverting to the more general pattern.

8.4 Importance of implementation for morphological theory

The analyses we present have been implemented and tested to see that they do indeed make predictions in line with the observable facts. We consider this to be an important standard to observe in morphological theory. We can isolate particular rules within the morphological network to determine their contribution, but ultimately the interconnected nature of morphological knowledge means that we need implementation to make sure that our theoretical claims actually work. The solution to one particularly interesting problem should not detract from the more general cases in the language. This is why we have implemented and tested our analyses. This allows us to claim that our arguments about morphology have external validity. Implementation in this way will allow for improvement and evaluation, and it should be seen as a prerequisite for work on morphological theory.

Notes

1 Options in constructing a morphological framework

1 These Shughni examples are taken from Hippisley and Stump's field notes. The transcription used for Pamiri follows the Iranianist tradition. Some glyphs are also found in IPA, though they do not necessarily have the same value. For good descriptions of the Shughni verbal system, see Payne (1980) and Dodyxudoeva (1988).

2 We adopt the notation commonly found in unification grammar where features are given in { }, with the colon delimiting the feature (on the left) from its value (on the right). The 'grouping' defined by the cell is the unification of these two features, i.e. {NUM:SG, PER:1}.

3 'The paradigm is a set of morphological contrasts that a given class of lexemes can make.' We will also use the term *inflectional class* to refer to a class of lexemes that share similar morphological contrasts. The term *declensional class* (or declension) is used when the inflectional class is nominal, and the term *conjugational class* when the inflectional class is verbal.

4 However, note that pronoun doubling could count as a syntactic analog of multiple exponence (Matthew Baerman, personal communication). See, for example, subject pronoun doubling in the Flemish dialect of Lapscheure (Haegeman 2005).

5 The transcription system used for Russian here and throughout is outlined on pp. xx–xxii.

6 We call this case *prepositional* following the Russian tradition, but it is also known as the *locative*.

7 Some nouns fall outside the four classes. A more detailed discussion of Russian noun inflection is presented in Chapter 3.

8 Also not shown here is the generalization that Declension I nouns whose stem-final consonant is morphologically soft will use *-ej* as an exponent of genitive plural. The plural stem *l′ud′-* ends in a palatal /d/, which makes it count as morphologically soft. Its genitive plural is *l′udej*.

9 The stem *-in-* alternates with *-ir-* in certain morphological contexts.

10 Compare Ackema's (1995) X-bar treatment of word structure.

11 Essentially, specifier is the default assignment of a non-head word piece (Stump 1993: 486).

12 See the discussion in Stump (2001) for the contrast between an inferential–realizational as opposed to a lexical–incremental approach to word structure.

13 Gregory Stump, personal communication.

14 See discussion in Hippisley (1996).
15 Textual Russian examples are given in transliteration (as opposed to transcription), see pp. xx–xxii.
16 See Stump (2001: ch. 1), who draws on Zwicky (1992: 356), for a full discussion of these two interface options.
17 Examples (21) and (22) come courtesy of Marina Chumakina.
18 For a textbook treatment of concomitant NP movement in passives, see Carnie (2007).
19 The strikeout expresses a silent copy, in accordance with the copy theory of movement.
20 The list to which Williams is referring is that presented in Harley and Noyer (1999: 3); the item on the list that implies a rejection of lexical hypothesis is number 4: 'Syntactic hierarchical structure all the way down.' For a more recent discussion of Distributed Morphology's anti-lexicalist stance, see Embick and Noyer (2007: 289–92).
21 This exponent taxonomy is presented and discussed in Harley and Noyer (1999: 3).
22 They also look at case-marking properties of verbs before and after movement, for example *drive trucks* versus *driver of trucks* where *-er* has moved to be adjacent to the VP head which now licenses a different case.
23 This observation has its origins in Cattell (1976) and Huang (1982). It falls out from GPSG's theory of unbounded dependencies (Gazdar, Klein, Pullum and Sag 1985).
24 For inheritance and lexical knowledge representation see, for example, Touretzky (1986), Flickinger (1987), Daelemans (1992) and Sowa (2000).
25 The features differ in type, though Lieber's model constrains them to being solely semantic features. We explore conditions on bases in Chapter 7, the Network Morphology approach to derivation.
26 See also Stump (2005b) for a recent discussion of the issues surrounding distinctions between inflection and derivation.
27 Stump (2010: 517) contrasts Network Morphology with Paradigm Function Morphology in how these default/override relations are expressed. In Network Morphology 'these relations are regulated by their position in default-inheritance hierarchies; in Paradigm Function Morphology they are regulated by the Pāṇini Determinism Hypothesis.'

2 A framework for morphological defaults

1 Verbs of the *hit* type end in an alveolar plosive. The identity can be interpreted as arising either from suppression of the suffix or from suffixation of a less regular /t/ or /d/ which cannot be realized because doubled consonants are prohibited in English (Huddleston and Pullum *et al.* 2002: 1601). (The relevant chapter on inflectional morphology in Huddleston and Pullum's *Cambridge Grammar of the English Language* was prepared in collaboration with Frank Palmer.)
2 We have already presented the Russian declensional classes in Chapter 1 and do so again in this chapter in (29).

3 In Brown *et al.* (1996) the attribute used was `index`, but here we have used `stress_index`, as it is more informative for the reader.

4 We have based this default on Lieber's (2004) analysis of lexical semantics and morphology in English and the claim that the vast majority of simplex nouns lack the processual flavour associated with the [+dynamic] feature.

5 For work on German using DATR see Bleiching, Drexel and Gibbon (1996) and Cahill and Gazdar (1997, 1999). Bleiching *et al.*, discuss noun syncretism, and Cahill and Gazdar use DATR to formulate their analysis of adjectives, determiners, pronouns and nouns.

6 Carstairs (1984) talks of plural being a trigger for gender syncretism. Given our constraints, it is not so much an issue of the feature value (i.e. plural), as the feature itself (i.e. number) which brings about an asymmetry in behaviour across the values, in whatever way this is manifested.

7 This does not detract from the significant challenges phenomena such as these pose, of course. In the Arabic example, for instance, one challenge is the role of clauses versus NPs in the formulation of the syntactic constraint (as discussed in LeTourneau 2003).

8 In these paths we have omitted aspect, using non-past and past. But the argument would still hold if we treated aspect as inflectional and had paths such as `<mor impf pres>`, `<mor perf fut>` and so on.

9 The affixal exponence in Russian declensional classes does not attain the complexity of other affixal systems (see Blevins 2006: 545). However, the contribution of morphologically determined stress in Russian and its interaction with affixal exponence (as in the genitive plural) contributes significantly to its complexity. Strictly speaking, if we wish to gauge the complexity in terms of full word-forms, the stress patterns must be factored in, thereby increasing the number of classes significantly. As our analysis of the stress system and affixal exponence is implemented, it demonstrates that the relative complexity observable in the full forms can readily be accounted for as a network of realization rules.

10 The data are based on information in Brown *et al.* (1996) which was itself compiled on the basis of data from Ilola and Mustajoki (1989) and the electronic version of Zaliznjak (1977). Similar information can be found in Zaliznjak (1967: 172–3) and Halle (1970: 174).

11 Pattern C stress is treated as something akin to heteroclisis in that it is analysed as a combination of pattern A in the singular and pattern B in the plural. According to the analysis presented here, the plural of pattern B is determined by the generalization that the plural has the same value as the singular (by having ending stress in the case of pattern B). Pattern C shares pattern B's value for plural stress, but its stress value in the singular differs from the plural, so its ending stress in the plural is not the product of the default generalization that the plural is the same as the singular. The RHS `<stress sg>` is not quoted, and therefore the generalization that stress in the plural is the same as the singular is true for the local context at `STRESS_B`, but not the global context. We introduce the concepts of local and global context in the next section.

12 In Brown *et al.* (1996) and Brown (1998a) the quotation marks were also referred to as indirection markers.

13 A node need not be specified, of course, as the evaluable path could involve inheritance from the context specific to the node at which the statement is made, or from the global context.

14 This segmentation is, of course, a kind of subanalysis, in the sense of Müller (2008). Müller (2008: 203) rightly identifies an important issue related to subanalysis in his discussion of Baerman *et al.*'s (2005) work on inflectional syncretism. Baerman *et al.* (2005) argued that it is best to look at the word level for evidence of syncretism, while the analyses they provide make reference to form elements which are parts of words. As Müller indicates, this is an issue which arises from the relationship of typology to morphological theory. It can also be thought of in terms of evidence versus analysis. Some subanalyses can be built on identities which could just be due to accident. We reduce the chances of this if we look at the whole word level or provide other evidence of systematicity. In the case of (49), the argument relies on the fact that this pattern holds across the whole nominal lexicon and that it can be repeated for the instrumental plural.

15 The situation is more complex than represented here, as the avoidance register rules differ from those of the ordinary language, but this does not make a material difference to the points being made. See Evans *et al.* (2002:148–52) for details.

16 The brolga belongs to the crane family.

17 Przepiórkowski (2003) provides a fairly comprehensive HPSG account in which the five basic genders of Mańczak (1956) are given an additional hierarchical structure which accounts for different patterns of agreement. Our purpose here is to demonstrate that the distinctions we have applied earlier can readily be used to analyse what is known to be a particularly challenging gender system.

18 We thank Magdalena Fiałkowska for her intuitions on these examples.

19 Earlier in this chapter, we discussed animacy in Russian. Although the information stored at the `NOUN` node is similar for the two languages, crucial parts of the inheritance work differently.

20 As argued here, the treatment of both of these phenomena involves a switch to follow the exceptional case default for `<syn animacy>`, while the lexeme's value for `<sem animacy>` remains unchanged. Evidence to support this differentiation comes from pronoun agreement, as these may reflect the semantic value, rather than the syntactic. We assume that in the case of personification of animals in fairy tales the nouns are best treated as involving a change in the specification of `<sem animacy>` to `person` because of the substantive differences in the semantics and their potential status as proper names.

21 This is normally true, but there are exceptions. The noun *babsztyl* 'hag', for example, is treated as an animate noun of masculine gender (see Rappaport 2010: 170). This noun is obviously pejorative in meaning. As we argue, masculine is the exceptional case default gender, so it fits into the system of defaults we elaborate here. We have already argued that the value it has for subgender, namely animate, is the default value for subgender.

22 The noun itself also has a different form in the nominative plural which reflects this distinction.

23 Although we have not provided the evidence here, feminine nouns denoting persons also need to be assigned the syntactic subgender value `person`, as this plays

a role in Polish for resolution rules in conjoined phrases (see Corbett 1991: 285 and Brown 1998a for discussion). Relevant examples can be found in Doroszewski (1962: 237) and Zieniukowa (1981: 81). In our implementation, lexical entries for nouns denoting female humans must specify that the semantic animacy is `person`. Nouns with female human denotation will inherit `person` as the normal case default for syntactic animacy, because, by default, syntactic animacy is the same as semantic animacy, an equation at the `NOUN` level, given in (77).

24 Choice depends on declensional class membership.

25 We assume that morphological classes of this type cannot be used as 'islands of reliability' in the sense of Albright (2002), as they are the declarative locations for the generalizations which are learned by a system such as Albright's.

3 Inflectional classes

1 The fragment associated with this analysis, including the treatment of the syntax, can be found on the website accompanying this book.

2 The third-person pronouns have different stress from the adjectives, and the patterning of their stems may differ, but this information can readily be expressed in the lexical entries or at the `PRONOUN` node in the lexemic hierarchy.

3 In relation to nouns, we have left out of consideration hybrids and other items where the agreement patterns may vary (see Corbett 1991). Similarly, for adjectives there is a recognizable group, discussed by Spencer (2002), which denotes people and functions as nouns. As argued by Spencer, these share properties with third-person pronouns. In our terms this means that they require a value for `<syn gender>` which is either inherited on the basis of generalizations about their semantics or specified in the lexical entry. An example is *bol'noj* 'medical patient (male)' / *bol'naja* 'medical patient (female)', based on the adjective *bol'noj* 'sick'.

4 For the genitive plural, the nature of the choice of alternants has to be the same for there to be overlap for the purposes of counting. This is true of `N_II` and `N_IV`, which both alternate between no exponent and *-ej* (see also Brown and Hippisley 1994).

5 The bare stem is the overall default for words, as discussed in Chapter 2, Section 2.3.1. The node `MOR_NOMINAL` inherits this from `MOR_WORD`.

6 Declension III inherits this exponent from Declension II by an orthogonal network relation. This is why it is specified at both. The actual rule of exponence is specified at `N_II`, and the node `N_III` refers to it for the genitive singular.

7 The palatoalveolar sounds /š/ and /ž/ in Russian are functionally soft, even though on phonological grounds they should no longer count as such. In contrast, the sound /j/ functions as a hard consonant (Reformatskij 1975: 85), even though we would expect it to be soft.

8 The four–class approach is also associated with Karcevskij (1932). Attempts to generalize about morphological structure by positing fewer than four inflectional classes usually group together under one class the lexemes which are divided between Declensions I and IV in the four-class approach. The approach based on three classes is the most common (some examples are Vinogradov, Istrina and Barxudarov 1953; Isačenko 1968; Gabka 1975; Barnetová *et al.* 1979; Garde 1980;

Švedova *et al.*1980; and Halle 1990). The three-class approach usually groups Declensions I and IV together and treats Declensions II and III as separate. Two other approaches to the question of structure sharing between Russian nouns have two declensions. That of Zaliznjak (1967: 205–7) groups Declensions I, II and IV together and treats III as separate. Stankiewicz (1978: 666–7) treats Declensions I, III and IV together and II as separate. The point to note from all of the approaches based on three or fewer classes is that I and IV always occur together.

9 This way of treating the indeclinables differs from that introduced in Fraser and Corbett (1995: 132), who had an additional declensional class (class `N_V`) for this purpose.

10 For the distinction between global and local contexts for inheritance, see Chapter 2, Section 2.2.7.

4 Syncretism

1 The three properties follow the wording of Baerman, Brown and Corbett (2005: 2), except that there the result of the failure to make the distinction is characterized as a 'mismatch'. We reserve the term 'mismatch' for the more extreme instances which are either deponent or deponent-like, as explained in Chapter 1, Section 1.2.1. As we shall argue later, the Dalabon syncretisms have deponent-like properties.

2 Under the definition in (1), because syntactic relevance is criterial, the sharing of exponents across inflectional classes is a qualitatively different phenomenon from syncretism. Müller (2004, 2008: 214), on the other hand, places such sharing within the remit of syncretism.

3 This case is required with the prepositions *pr′i* 'at', *v* 'in', *na* 'on' and *o* 'about' in modern Contemporary Standard Russian.

4 As Declension I nouns have a form uniquely associated with the genitive singular, the identities between the nominative plural forms and the genitive singular forms in Declensions II, III and IV are no barrier to establishing a unique distribution for that form. (Furthermore, subsets of lexemes belonging to these classes distinguish genitive singular and nominative plural through their stress patterns.)

5 The RHS of some of the equations have been set out over two lines. The quoted path `"<stress pronoun>"` is used to place the stress on the final syllable of the exponent for third-person pronouns. This is undefined for adjectives, so will not appear for them. They will take the value associated with `"<stress sg>"`, if their lexical entry associates them with the required stress pattern. The path `"<mor vowel sg>"`, which appears in the RHS of a number of equations in (8), is /o/. This contrasts with the theme vowel /i/ used in the plural for adjectives. Additional points of note are that the singular dative feminine is inherited orthogonally from the `MOR_NOUN` node, and the noun declensional class node `N_II` is the orthogonal inheritance source for the singular instrumental feminine. The former involves inheritance of the referral of singular dative to singular prepositional at `MOR_NOUN` and extends this with the gender feature `fem`. Its ultimate effect is to say that the form of the singular dative feminine is the same as the form of the singular prepositional feminine (also defined at `MOR_ADJ`). This is an orthogonal

inheritance example of generalized referrals, which we discuss in Section 4.4. The LHS paths at noun nodes lack gender features, but the value will be inherited from the equations where the LHS has the most specific matching paths (i.e. `<mor sg dat>` and `<mor sg inst>`).

6 We can contrast overdifferentiation, where a formal difference is correlated with a syntactic distribution, with overabundance, where two or more forms realize the same cell of a paradigm. A new syntactic distribution, of course, entails a new cell in the paradigm. For discussion of overabundance in Italian see Thornton (2011). Stolz (2008) discusses a similar phenomenon in Welsh where a significant number of lexemes have a choice of plurals.

7 This amounts to the claim that we expect phenomena such as defectiveness or syncretism either to occur in patterns which are morphology-specific (i.e. morphomic) or in patterns which reflect morphosyntactic feature structure, such as suggested in Chapter 2, Section 2.2.3. So if number is ordered before case for nouns, it is more likely that we can pick out a natural class on the basis of number alone, but not possible to pick out a natural class on the basis of case alone.

8 The forms of the definite here are given without the article *ʾal-*. This syncretism is treated in Fischer (1997: 195) as an oblique case. The evidence for the syncretism is the existence of separate genitive and accusative case distinctions in the singular.

9 Slovene presents other examples which could readily be treated as referrals. Indeed, Perlmutter and Orešnik's (1973: 420) 'prediction' rule for the accusative in Slovene is an example from the earlier generative tradition of a referral-like generalization.

10 These would be as referrals where the case syncretism is limited to a particular number, namely dual.

11 More information on the morphological template of the Dalabon verb can be found in Evans, Fletcher and Ross (2008: 95).

12 As the Dalabon verb has subject and object agreement, we use an angled bracket in our abbreviations of the two arguments. For instance, the abbreviation 2SG > 3SG means that a second-person singular subject acts on a third-person singular object. An abbreviation 2 > 3 means that a second-person subject of any number acts on a third-person object of any number.

13 It should be noted that this relationship between the dual and plural transitive prefixes on the one hand, and the dual and plural intransitive prefixes on the other, is also reflected in the prefix inventory of Wunderlich (2001: 236), where the transitive prefixes add the feature value [+lr] ('there is a lower role') to the feature combinations of the intransitive prefixes.

14 Within Dalabon kinship classification, as with other Australian languages, there is a distinction between 'harmonic' and 'disharmonic' kin relations. Dalabon has special inflectional markers for reference to kin who are in a 'disharmonic' relation.

15 Wunderlich (2001: 248) says that 'no assumption of a person hierarchy… proves successful' for Dalabon. However, (22) is a truth independent of any formal analysis. The difference must lie in how one chooses to interpret it. If, for example, one assumes that the form of 2SG > 1SG would otherwise be **dah-*, and the form of 2PL > 1SG **nulah-*, then the referrals, by creating syncretism of second with third or first with third, avoid syncretism of objects in the presence of higher-animacy subjects. In Wunderlich's morpheme-based approach, the forms which would be generated

in the absence of additional representational mechanisms would be **ngah dah* and **ngah nulah*, because the first prefix can fill any first-person slot. In our approach **ngah-* cannot occur in either cell, because it is marked as a first singular transitive subject. Our analysis is surface-true, as *ngah-* never occurs as an object.

16 We use lower-case `a`, `s` and `o` to represent the relations transitive subject, intransitive subject and object, respectively. This is based on the convention in Dixon (1994: xxii, 6) of using upper-case A, S and O for these relations. We have used lower-case, as this is standard practice for DATR attributes.

5 Morphological mismatch and extended deponency

1 We follow Aronoff's (1992b) analysis of the four Latin verb conjugations as a function of one of four theme vowels available to build a Latin stem.

2 Perfect passive is realized periphrastically: the past participle marked for gender and number agreement together with a form of *esse* 'be'.

3 Actually *ferō* displays an additional override in that some of its word-forms are based on the root rather than the first stem. This and other details of our Latin theory are given on the accompanying website.

4 Kennedy (1962: 90) claims that the imperfect forms of *incipiō* 'begin' are used to stand in for the defective cells. A reviewer has pointed out that at an earlier stage of Latin the lexeme was not defective, having for example present first-person singular *coepio*. In Network Morphology paradigmatic change can be expressed as the appearance of an override, in this case `<syn active imperfective> == undefined`. It can equally be expressed as the removal of an override, i.e. regularization, which we show in the next chapter is the case for deponents.

5 As pointed out by a reviewer, a deponent lexeme used in the ablative absolute construction, which requires a participle form, can have a passive interpretation. For example, deponent *adipiscor* 'obtain' in the phrase *adepta aliqua re* is passive, 'after something having been obtained'. So here passive morphology corresponds to passive syntax.

6 Transcription conventions for Archi have changed since 1977. We are grateful to Marina Chumakina for helping with the updates.

7 Marina Chumakina first identified a subclass of Archi nodes as displaying extended deponency behaviour. We are grateful for the observation.

8 One view is that the *-r mediopassive is actually a dialectal feature of 'Proto-Italo-Celtic', as it is absent in Sanskrit and Greek, for example. But this view has been seriously challenged by the existence of -r in Tocharian and Anatolian (Andrew Byrd, personal communication). The claim is that the *-r was replaced by active marker *-i in Indo-Iranian, Greek, Germanic and Albanian (see discussion in Fortson 2004: 85–7).

9 Baerman attributes the translation to Yonge (1856).

6 Defaults and paradigmatic restructuring: diachronic deponency

1 The basic alternant is [s]. Verner's Law gives *[s] > *[z] for the stem in the past plural and past participle cells of the paradigm, where voiceless fricatives become

voiced between two vowels, as long as the first is unstressed. This *[z] is then subject to rhotacism, a change found in Western Germanic only, yielding [r]. In the present cell the *[s] changes to [z] due to OE intervocalic voicing, a process that occurs after Verner's Law had run its course (Fortson 2004: 303).

2 Following our investigation of Pushkin's oeuvre using Vinogradov's (1954) concordance.

3 Based on Arlotto (1972: 132–4).

4 Another possibility is to conceive a disorganized paradigm where Category A is realized by a pattern of exponence normally associated with Category B, while at the same time Category B uses a pattern of exponence normally associated with Category A, a symmetrical misalignment. Such cases do exist and are presented in detail in Baerman (2007a) as 'morphological reversals'.

5 The verb *consolor* 'console' is a deponent.

6 Translation from Nixon (1924).

7 Again, these examples are taken from Flobert's excellent survey of deponent verbs. Flobert tends to give the verb form only, together with source. For clarity we have supplied the sentence context and our own translation unless otherwise stated. Here Flobert's source is Lodge (1901–33), a concordance of Plautus' complete set of plays.

8 Translation from Walker (1957).

9 Translation from Nixon (1924).

10 Translation from Nixon (1924).

11 This default hierarchy approach to historical development is worked out in detail in Hippisley and Gazdar (1999) for the colour lexicon of the Slavonic family.

12 The *-um* is ordinarily an exponent of neuter singular agreement, so here must be an instance of Corbett's (1991: 159) 'neutral' agreement marker.

13 Translation from Nixon (1924).

14 Stump adapts the term 'exploratory expression', used as a principle of syntactic change (Harris and Campbell 1995), to this particular means of morphological change.

15 Translation from Nixon (1924).

16 *continebatur* and *continebantur* in some manuscripts.

17 Bonnet (1968: 411).

18 'One cannot accept at face value the usual explanation that deponents are falling into disuse in the spoken language. This is doubly false: vulgarisms are not a one-way street, for there are vulgar deponents.'

19 I.e. modern period starts from the fall of Constantinople.

20 Lavidas and Papangeli (2007: 117).

21 English translation Harris (1983: 164–5).

7 Derivation

With special thanks to Greg Stump for a careful reading of an earlier version of this chapter, and for advice on the lambda abstraction representations used here.

1 Of course this mechanism for interpretation does not take into account the fact that the relationship between elements in a compound can be of different kinds. See

Bauer (2009) and Scalise and Bisetto (2009) for a classification of the relations between a compound word's elements.

2 Lieber's ontology is based on Jackendoff's (1990) Lexical Conceptual Structures.

3 For *-ee* an additional base restriction is required, namely that the first argument must be sentient and volitional.

4 There is no morphological information recorded in the derivative in (4b) because inflectional class is implied by 'male', as discussed in Chapter 3, Section 3.1.3.

5 The formation of the second stem is subject to generalization, not shown here.

6 Booij (2005) is an argument in favour of derivation and compounding being structurally similar to one another, as it is argued that it makes most sense to assign affix derived words a morphological constituent structure (2005: 122); this echoes Lieber's *lexical* approach to derivation.

7 This is controversial. Haspelmath in his study of morphological valence alternation pairs treats such cases as non-directed 'labile' alternation (1993: 92). For arguments against treating any transitivity alternation as derivational, see Beard (1995: 178–90), and for the counterarguments see Spencer (2005: 115).

8 An alternative derived semantic representation for *destruction* and the like is Nom(destroy´) where Nom is a semantic function applied to a verb's meaning to produce noun meanings. So we could change the second equation in (25) to `<gloss> == nom("<base gloss>")` (Gregory Stump, personal communication).

9 Strictly speaking, a non-intersective interpretation is required here since diminutive is a dimension of size (see, for example, Chierchia and McConnell-Ginet 2000: 248–9). So we could replace the equation with `<gloss> == λx ["<sem feature>" ("<base gloss>") (x)]` for expressives that are specifically diminutive and augmentative.

10 All of these appear in Cubberley's (1994) investigation into word-formation affixation as covered in the 1980 Academy Grammar.

11 Roughly following Townsend (1975) and Cubberley (1994).

12 For detailed discussion on word-formation conditions, see Rainer (2005); for a good summary see Scalise and Guevara (2005: 159–60).

13 This has been proposed in Van Marle (1985) for Dutch personal nouns.

14 Van Marle (1985) invokes the Elsewhere Condition in his paradigmatic presentation of Dutch personal noun affixation.

15 For details of how pure morphology interacts with affix and declensional class selection in Russian expressive morphology, see Hippisley (1996) and the references there.

16 For a detailed discussion of derivational productivity, see Bauer (2001); and for the history of the concept of productivity, including Corbin's contribution, see Bauer (2005).

17 These counts are of animate nouns. Both affixes can also derive inanimate instrument nouns, and such items were excluded.

18 This is the approach taken by Marchand (1960) for English.

19 This higher level of classification finds its way into the Russian derivational tradition, for example Uluxanov (1979).

20 Such possibilities are explored in Hippisley (2009).

References

Ackema, Peter. 1995. Syntax below zero. PhD dissertation, Utrecht University.

Ackema, Peter and Ad Neeleman. 2004. *Beyond morphology: interface conditions on word formation*. Oxford University Press.

2007. Morphology ≠ syntax. In Gillian Ramchand and Charles Reiss (eds.), *The Oxford handbook of linguistic interfaces*, 325–52. Oxford University Press.

Ackerman, Farrell and Gregory T. Stump. 2004. Paradigms and periphrastic expression: a study in realization-based lexicalism. In Louisa Sadler and Andrew Spencer (eds.), *Projecting morphology*, 111–57. Stanford: CSLI Publications.

Ackerman, Farrell, James P. Blevins and Robert Malouf. 2009. Parts and wholes: implicative patterns in inflectional paradigms. In James P. Blevins and Juliette Blevins (eds.), *Analogy in grammar: form and acquisition*, 54–82. Oxford University Press.

Aikhenvald, Alexandra Y. and R. M. W. Dixon. 1998. Dependencies between grammatical systems. *Language* 74, 56–80.

Albright, Adam. 2002. Islands of reliability for regular morphology: evidence from Italian. *Language* 78, 684–709.

Anderson, Stephen R. 1985. Typological distinctions in word formation. In Timothy Shopen (ed.), *Language typology and syntactic description,* vol. III: *Grammatical categories and the lexicon*, 30–56. Cambridge University Press.

1992. *A-morphous morphology.* Cambridge University Press.

2005. *Aspects of the theory of clitics*. Oxford University Press.

Anderson, Stephen R., Lea Brown, Alice Gaby and Jacqueline Lecarme. 2006. Life on the edge: there's morphology there after all! *Lingue e linguaggio* 5, 33–48.

Arlotto, Anthony. 1972. *Introduction to historical linguistics*. Boston: Houghton Mifflin.

Aronoff, Mark. 1976. *Word formation in generative grammar*. Cambridge, MA: MIT Press.

1992a. Noun classes in Arapesh. In Geert Booij and Jaap van Marle (eds.), *Yearbook of Morphology 1991*, 21–32. Dordrecht: Kluwer.

1992b. Stems in Latin verbal morphology. In Mark Aronoff (ed.), *Morphology now*, 5–32. Albany, NY: State University of New York Press.

1994. *Morphology by itself: stems and inflectional classes*. Cambridge, MA: MIT Press.

Asher, R. E. 1985. *Tamil*. London: Croom Helm.

Baerman, Matthew. 2002. Kashmiri. *The Surrey Syncretism Database*. www.smg.surrey.ac.uk/Syncretism/examples/Kashmiri/nounpro2.pdf. Last accessed 5 May 2010.

2006a. Chukchi. *The Cross-linguistic Database for Deponency*. www.smg.surrey.ac.uk/deponency/WALS/Chukchi.htm. Last accessed 5 May 2010.

2006b. Latin. *The Typological Database for Deponency*. www.smg.surrey.ac.uk/deponency/Examples/Latin.htm. Last accessed 5 May 2010.

2006c. Archi. *The Typological Database for Deponency*. www.smg.surrey.ac.uk/deponency/Examples/Archi.htm. Last accessed 5 May 2010.

2007a. Morphological reversals. *Journal of Linguistics* 43.1, 33–61.

2007b. Morphological typology of deponency. In Baerman *et al*. (eds.), 1–19.

2008. Historical observations on defectiveness: the first singular non-past. *Russian Linguistics* 37 (1), 81–97.

Baerman, Matthew, Dunstan Brown and Greville G. Corbett. 2002. *The Surrey Syncretism Database*. www.smg.surrey.ac.uk/syncretism/index.aspx. Last accessed 5 May 2010.

2005. *The syntax–morphology interface: a study of syncretism*. Cambridge University Press.

Baerman, Matthew and Greville G. Corbett. 2010. Introduction. In Baerman, Corbett and Brown (eds.), 1–18.

Baerman, Matthew, Greville G. Corbett, Dunstan Brown and Andrew Hippisley (eds.). 2007. *Deponency and morphological mismatches*. Oxford University Press.

Baerman, Matthew, Greville G. Corbett and Dunstan Brown (eds.). 2010. *Defective paradigms: missing forms and what they tell us*. Oxford: British Academy and Oxford University Press.

Baker, Mark. 1985. The mirror principle and morphosyntactic explanation. *Linguistic Inquiry* 16, 373–416.

1988. *Incorporation: a theory of grammatical function changing*. University of Chicago Press.

Baldi, Philip. 1976. Remarks on the Latin r-form. *Zeitschrift für Vergleichende Sprachforschung* 90, 222–57.

Baltin, Mark and Chris Collins (eds.). 2007. *The handbook of contemporary syntactic theory*. Oxford: Blackwell.

Barnetová, V. *et al*. 1979. *Russkaja grammatika,* vol. I. Prague: Academia Praha.

Bauer, Laurie. 1990. Be-heading the word. *Journal of Linguistics* 26, 1–31.

2001. *Morphological productivity*. Cambridge University Press.

2005. Productivity: theories. In Štekauer and Lieber (eds.), 315–34.

2009. Typology of compounds. In Rochelle Lieber and Pavol Štekauer (eds.), *The Oxford handbook of compounding*, 343–56. Oxford University Press.

Beard, Robert. 1995. *Lexeme-morpheme base morphology: a general theory of inflection and word formation*. Albany, NY: State University of New York Press.

1998. Derivation. In Andrew Spencer and Arnold Zwicky (eds.), *Handbook of morphology*, 44–65. Oxford: Blackwell.

Bleiching, Doris, Guido Drexel and Dafydd Gibbon. 1996. Ein Synkretismusmodell für die deutsche Morphologie. In Dafydd Gibbon (ed.), *Natural language processing and speech technology: results of the third KONVENS conference, Bielefeld*, 237–48. Berlin: Mouton de Gruyter.

Blevins, James P. 2006. Word-based morphology. *Journal of Linguistics* 42, 531–73.

Bobaljik, Jonathan David. 2002. Syncretism without paradigms: remarks on Williams. 1981. In Geert Booij and Jaap van Marle (eds.), *Yearbook of Morphology 2001*, 53–85. Dordrecht: Kluwer.

Bonami, Olivier and Gilles Boyé. 2006. Deriving inflectional irregularity. In Stefan Müller (ed.), *Proceedings of the 13th International Conference on HPSG, Varna, 24–27 July 2006*, 360–81. Stanford: CSLI Publications.

Bonnet, Max. 1968. *Le Latin de Grégoire de Tours*. 2nd edn. Hildesheim: Georg Olms.

Booij, Geert. 1977. *Dutch morphology. a study of word formation in generative grammar*. Dordrecht: Foris.

1996. Inherent versus contextual inflection and the split morphology hypothesis. In Geert Booij and Jaap Van Marle (eds.), *Yearbook of Morphology*, 1–16. Dordrecht: Kluwer.

2002. *The morphology of Dutch*. Oxford University Press.

2005. Compounding and derivation: evidence for construction morphology. In Wolfgang Dressler, Dieter Kastovsky, Oskar Pfeiffer and Franz Rainer (eds.), *Morphology and its demarcations: selected papers from the 11th Morphology Meeting, Vienna, February 2004*, 109–32. Amsterdam: John Benjamins.

2009. Compounding and Construction Morphology. In Rochelle Lieber and Pavol Štekauer (eds.), *The Oxford handbook of compounding*, 201–16. Oxford University Press.

Boyé, Gilles and Patricia Cabredo Hofherr. 2010. Defectiveness in French and Spanish verbs. In Baerman, Corbett and Brown (eds.), 35–52.

Bredenkamp, Andrew, Louisa Sadler and Andrew Spencer. 1998. Investigating argument structure: the Russian nominalization database. In John Nerbonne (ed.), *Linguistic Databases*, 137–60. Stanford: CSLI Publications.

Brown, Dunstan. 1998a. Defining ‘subgender’: virile and devirilized nouns in Polish. *Lingua* 104, 187–233.

1998b. From the general to the exceptional: a network morphology account of Russian nominal inflection. PhD dissertation, University of Surrey.

1998c. Stem indexing and morphonological selection in the Russian verb. In Ray Fabri, Albert Ortmann and Teresa Parodi (eds.), *Models of inflection*, 196–221. Tübingen: Niemeyer.

2001. Constructing a typological database for inflectional morphology: the SMG database for syncretism. In Steven Bird, Peter Buneman and Mark Liberman (eds.), *Proceedings of the IRCS workshop on linguistic databases, Institute for Research in Cognitive Science, University of Pennsylvania, December 11–13, 2001*, 56–64.

2007. Peripheral functions and overdifferentiation: the Russian second locative. *Russian Linguistics* 31, 61–76.

Brown, Dunstan and Andrew Hippisley. 1994. Conflict in Russian genitive plural assignment: a solution represented in DATR. *Journal of Slavic Linguistics* 34, 48–76.

Brown, Dunstan, Greville G. Corbett, Norman M. Fraser, Andrew Hippisley and Alan Timberlake. 1996. Russian noun stress and Network Morphology. *Linguistics* 34, 53–107.

Brown, Dunstan, Carole Tiberius and Greville G. Corbett. 2004. Inflectional syncretism and corpora. Paper presented at the *Fifth International Workshop on Linguistically Interpreted Corpora (LINC-04)*. Twentieth International Conference on Computational Linguistics. Geneva, Switzerland. 29 August 2004. Paper available at www.coli.uni-sb.de/linc04/brown.pdf.

2007. The alignment of form and function: corpus-based evidence from Russian. *International Journal of Corpus Linguistics* 12.4, 511–34.

Brown, Dunstan, Carole Tiberius, Marina Chumakina, Greville Corbett and Alexander Krasovitsky. 2009. Databases designed for investigating specific phenomena. In Marin Everaert, Simon Musgrave and Alexis Dimitriadis (eds.), *The use of databases in cross-linguistic studies*, 117–54. Berlin and New York: Mouton de Gruyter.

Browne, Wayles. 1993. Serbo-Croat. In Bernard Comrie and Greville G. Corbett (eds.), *The Slavonic languages*, 306–87. London and New York: Routledge.

Bybee, Joan. 1985. *Morphology: a study of the relation between meaning and form.* Amsterdam: John Benjamins.

Bybee, Joan, Revere Perkins and William Pagliuca. 1994. *The evolution of grammar.* Chicago and London: University of Chicago Press.

Cahill, Lynne and Gerald Gazdar. 1997. The inflectional phonology of German adjectives, determiners, and pronouns. *Linguistics* 35, 211–45.

1999. German noun inflection. *Journal of Linguistics* 35, 1–42.

Carnie, Andrew. 2007. *Syntax: a generative introduction.* 2nd edn. Oxford: Blackwell.

Carstairs, Andrew. 1983. Paradigm economy. *Journal of Linguistics* 19, 115–28.

1984. Outlines of a constraint on syncretism. *Folia Linguistica* 18, 73–85.

Carstairs-McCarthy, Andrew. 1992. *Current morphology.* London: Routledge.

1994. Inflection classes, gender, and the principle of contrast. *Language* 70, 737–88.

Cattell, R. 1976. Constraints on movement rules. *Language* 52, 18–50.

Černyx, P. Ja. 1953. *Jazyk Uloženija 1649 Goda: voprosy orfografii, fonetiki i morfologii v svjazi s istoriej Uložennoj knigi.* Moscow: Izdatel′stvo Akademii nauk SSSR.

Chierchia, Gennaro and Sally McConnell-Ginet. 2000. *Meaning and grammar: an introduction to semantics.* Cambridge, MA: MIT Press.

Chumakina, Marina, Andrew Hippisley and Greville Corbett. 2004. Istoričeskie izmenenija v russkoj leksike: slučaj čeredujuščegosja suppletivizma [Historical changes in the Russian lexicon: alternating suppletion]. *Russian Linguistics* 28, 281–315.

Comrie, Bernard. 1991. Form and function in identifying cases. In Frans Plank (ed.), *Paradigms: the economy of inflection*, 41–55. Berlin and New York: Mouton de Gruyter.

Corbett, Greville G. 1980. Animacy in Russian and other Slavonic languages: where syntax and semantics fail to match. In Catherine V. Chvany and Richard D. Brecht (eds.), *Morphosyntax in Slavic*, 43–61. Columbus, OH: Slavica.

1982. Gender in Russian: an account of gender specification and its relationship to declension. *Russian Linguistics* 6, 197–232.

1991. *Gender.* Cambridge University Press.

2000. *Number.* Cambridge University Press.

2006. *Agreement.* Cambridge University Press.

2007. Deponency, syncretism and what lies between. In Baerman *et al.* (eds.), 21–44.

2009. Canonical inflection classes. In Fabio F. Montermini, Gilles Boyé and Jesse Tseng (eds.), *Selected proceedings of the Sixth Decembrettes: morphology in Bordeaux*, 1–11. Somerville, MA: Cascadilla Proceedings Project.

Forthcoming. Canonical morphosyntactic features. In Dunstan Brown, Greville G. Corbett and Marina Chumakina (eds.), *Canonical morphology and syntax*. Oxford University Press.

Corbett, Greville G. and Matthew Baerman. 2006. Prolegomena to a typology of morphological features. *Morphology* 16, 231–46.

Corbett, Greville G. and Norman Fraser. 1993. Network Morphology: a DATR account of Russian nominal inflection. *Journal of Linguistics* 29, 113–42.

1997. Vyčislitel/naja lingvistika i tipologija [Computational linguistics meets typology]. *Vestnik Moskovskogo Universiteta. Serija 9. Filologija*, 122–40.

Corbin, Danielle. 1987. *Morphologie dérivationelle et structuration du lexique* (2 vols.). Tübingen: Niemeyer.

Cubberley, Paul. 1994. *Handbook of Russian affixes*. Columbus, OH: Slavica.

Daelemans, W., K. de Smedt and G. Gazdar. 1992. Inheritance in natural language processing. *Computational Linguistics* 18, 205–18.

Dal′, Vladimir. 1880. *Tolkovyj slovar′ velikorusskago jazyka,* vol I. Moscow and St Petersburg: M. O. Vol′f.

Deo, Ashwini. 2007. Derivational morphology in inheritance-based lexica: insights from Pāṇini. *Lingua* 117, 175–201.

Dixon, R. M. W. 1994. *Ergativity*. Cambridge University Press.

Dodyxudoeva, Lelja R. 1988. *Šugnanskij glagol v istoričeskom osveščenii.* Dušanbe: Akademija Nauk Tadžiskoj SSR.

Donohue, Mark. 2001. Animacy, class and gender in Burmeso. In Andrew Pawley, Malcolm Ross and Darrell Tryon (eds.), *The boy from Bundaberg: studies in Melanesian linguistics in honour of Tom Dutton*, 97–115. Canberra: Pacific Linguistics.

Doroszewski, Witold. 1962. *O kulturę słowa: Poradnik językowy.* Warsaw: PIW.

Dressler, Wolfgang U., Marianne Kilani-Schoch, Natalia Gagarina, Lina Pestal and Markus Pöchtrager. 2006. On the typology of inflection class systems. *Folia Linguistica* 40, 1–2, 51–74.

Embick, David and Alec Marantz. 2008. Architecture and blocking. *Linguistic Inquiry* 39.1, 1–53.

Embick, David and Rolf Noyer. 2001. Movement operations after syntax. *Linguistic Inquiry* 32.4, 555–95.

2007. Distributed morphology and the syntax–morphology interface. In Gillian Ramchand and Charles Reiss (eds.), *The Oxford handbook of linguistic interfaces*, 289–324. Oxford University Press.

Ernout, Alfred. 1945. *Morphologie historique du Latin*. Paris: Klincksiek.

Ernout, Alfred and François Thomas. 1953. *Syntaxe Latine*. 2nd edn. Paris: Klincksieck.

Evans, Nicholas. 1997. Head classes and agreement classes in the Mayali dialect chain. In Mark Harvey and Nicholas Reid (eds.), *Nominal classification in aboriginal Australia*, 105–46. Amsterdam: John Benjamins.

2004. *Bininj Gun-wok: a pan-dialectal grammar of Mayali, Kunwinjku and Kune*. Canberra: Pacific Linguistics.

Evans, Nicholas, Dunstan Brown and Greville G. Corbett. 1998. Emu divorce: a unified account of gender and noun class assignment in Mayali. In M. C. Gruber, D.

Higgins, K. Olson and T. Wysocki (eds.), *Proceedings of the 34th annual meeting of the Chicago Linguistic Society*, 127–42 . Chicago: CLS.

2001. Dalabon pronominal prefixes and the typology of syncretism: a Network Morphology analysis. In Geert Booij and Jaap van Marle (eds.), *Yearbook of Morphology 2000*, 187–232. Dordrecht: Kluwer.

2002. The semantics of gender in Mayali: partially parallel systems and formal implementation. *Language* 78, 111–55.

Evans, Nicholas, Janet Fletcher and Belinda Ross. 2008. Big words, small phrases: mismatches between pause units and the polysynthetic word in Dalabon. *Linguistics* 46, 89–129.

Evans, Roger and Gerald Gazdar. 1996. DATR: a language for lexical knowledge representation. *Computational Linguistics* 22.2, 167–216.

Evans, Roger, Gerald Gazdar and Lionel Moser. 1993. Prioritised multiple inheritance in DATR. In Ted Briscoe, Ann Copestake and Valeria de Paiva (eds.), *Inheritance, defaults and the lexicon*, 38–46. Cambridge University Press.

Fedjanina, Nina A. 1976. *Udarenie v sovremennom russkom jazyke*. Moscow: Russkij jazyk.

Finkel, Raphael and Gregory Stump. 2007. Principal parts and morphological typology. *Morphology* 17, 39–75.

Fischer, Wolfdietrich. 1997. Classical Arabic. In Robert Hetzron (ed.), *The Semitic languages*, 187–219. London: Routledge.

Flickinger, Daniel. 1987. Lexical rules in the hierarchical lexicon. PhD dissertation, Stanford University.

Flobert, Pierre. 1975. *Les verbes déponents Latins des origines* à *Charlemagne*. Paris: Les Belles Lettres.

Fortson, Benjamin W. 2004. *Indo-European language and culture: an introduction*. Oxford: Blackwell.

Fortune, Reo F. 1942. *Arapesh*. (Publications of the American Ethnological Society 19.) New York: J. J. Augustin.

Frank, Wright Jay. 1999. Nuer noun morphology. MA thesis, State University of New York, Buffalo.

Fraser, Norman M. and Greville G. Corbett. 1995. Gender, animacy and declensional class assignment: a unified account for Russian. In Geert Booij and Jaap van Marle (eds.), *Yearbook of Morphology 1994*, 123–50. Dordrecht: Kluwer.

1997. Defaults in Arapesh. *Lingua* 103, 25–57.

Gabka, K. 1975. *Die russische Sprache der Gegenwart*, vol. II. Düsseldorf: Brücken-Verlag.

Garde, P. 1980. *Grammaire russe*. Paris: Institut d'études slaves. (Collection de grammaires de l'Institut d'études slaves, VII, I.)

Gazdar, Gerald, Ewan Klein, Geoffrey Pullum and Ivan Sag. 1985. *Generalized phrase structure grammar*. Cambridge, MA: Harvard University Press.

Gerdts, Donna B. 1998. Incorporation. In Arnold Zwicky and Andrew Spencer (eds.), *The handbook of morphology*, 84–100. Oxford: Blackwell.

Goldberg, Adele. 2006. *Constructions at work: the nature of generalization in language*. Oxford University Press.

Goldsmith, John and Jeremy O'Brien. 2006. Learning inflectional classes. *Language Learning and Development* 2, 219–50.

Greenberg, Joseph H. 1963. Some universals of grammar with particular reference to the order of meaningful elements. In Joseph H. Greenberg (ed.), *Universals of language*, 73–113. Cambridge, MA: MIT Press.

Gvozdev, A. N. 1961. *Sovremennij russkij jazyk.* Moscow: Prosveščenie.

Haegeman, Liliane. 2005. Verdubbeling van subjectpronomina in de Zuide-Nederlandse dialecten: een reactie uit Lapscheure. *Taal en Tongval* 56, 119–59.

Halle, Morris. 1970. A note on the accentual patterns of the Russian nominal declension. In Roman Jakobson and Shigeo Kawamoto (eds.), *Studies in general and oriental linguistics*, 167–74. Tokyo: TEC.

1990. An approach to morphology. *NELS, BLSA Twentieth Annual Meeting*, 151–84. University of Massachusetts, Amherst.

Halle, Morris and Alec Marantz. 1993. Distributed morphology and the pieces of inflection. In K. Hale and S. J. Keyser (eds.), *The view from Building 20: essays in linguistics in honor of Sylvain Bromberger*, 111–76. Cambridge, MA: MIT Press.

Hansson, Gunnar O. 2007. Productive syncretism in Saami inflectional morphology. In Ida Toivonen and Diane Nelson (eds.), *Saami linguistics*, 91–135. Amsterdam: John Benjamins.

Harley, Heidi. 1994. Hug a tree: deriving the morphosyntactic feature hierarchy. In Andrew Carnie and Heidi Harley (eds.), *MIT Working Papers in Linguistics 21*, 275–80. Cambridge, MA: MIT Press.

Harley, Heidi and Rolf Noyer. 1999. Distributed morphology. *Glot International* 4.4, 3–9.

Harris, Alice and Lyle Campbell. 1995. *Historical syntax in cross-linguistic perspective.* Cambridge University Press.

Harris, Roy (trans.). 1983. *Course in general linguistics.* [*Cours de linguistique générale* by F. de Saussure.] London: Duckworth.

Haspelmath, Martin. 1993. More on the typology of inchoative/causative verb alternations. In Bernard Comrie and Maria Polinsky (eds.), *Causatives and Transitivity*, 87–120. Amsterdam: John Benjamins.

2002. *Understanding morphology*. London: Arnold.

Heath, Jeffrey. 1991. Pragmatic disguise in pronominal-affix paradigms. In Frans Plank (ed.), *Paradigms: the economy of inflection*, 75–89. Berlin: Mouton de Gruyter.

1998. Pragmatic skewing in 1 <-> 2 pronominal combinations in Native American languages. *International Journal of American Linguistics* 64, 83–104.

Hippisley, Andrew. 1996. Russian expressive derivation: a Network Morphology account. *Slavonic and East European Review* 74.2, 201–22.

1997. Declarative derivation. PhD dissertation, University of Surrey.

1998. Indexed stems and Russian word formation: a Network Morphology account of Russian personal nouns. *Linguistics* 36, 1039–124.

2001. Word formation rules in a default inheritance framework: a network account of Russian personal nouns. In Geert Booij and Jaap van Marle (eds.), *Yearbook of morphology 1999*, 221–61. Dordrecht: Kluwer.

2007. Declarative deponency: a Network Morphology account of morphological mismatches. In Baerman *et al.* (eds.), 145–74.

2009. Towards a declarative definition of derivational relatedness: an orthogonal multiple inheritance approach to word-formation typology. Paper read at *Universals and Typology in Word-Formation*, Šafárik University, Košice, Slovakia, August 2009.

2010a. Paradigmatic realignment and morphological change: diachronic deponency in Network Morphology. In Franz Rainer *et al.* (eds.), *Variation and change in morphology*, 107–27. Amsterdam: John Benjamins.

2010b. A declarative approach to language change: regularization as realignment. In Max Bane, Juan José Bueno Holle, Thomas Grano, April Lynn Grotberg and Yaron McNabb (eds.), *Proceedings of the* 44th *annual meeting of the Chicago Linguistic Society,* 261–75. Chicago: CLS.

Hippisley, Andrew and Gerald Gazdar. 1999. Inheritance hierarchies and historical reconstruction: towards a history of Slavonic colour terms. In Sabrina Billings, John Boyle and Aaron Griffith (eds.), *Proceedings of the 35th annual of the Chicago Linguistic Society*, vol. I, 125–40. Chicago: CLS.

Hippisley, Andrew, Marina Chumakina, Greville G. Corbett and Dunstan Brown. 2004. Suppletion: frequency, categories and distribution of stems. *Studies in Language* 28.2, 389–421.

Hjelmslev, Louis. 1943. *Omkring sprogteoriens grundlæggelse.* Copenhagen: Ejnar Munksgaard.

1961. *Prolegomena to a theory of language*. Trans. of Hjelmslev 1943. Madison, WI: University of Wisconsin Press.

Hock, Hans Henrich. 1986. *Principles of historical linguistics*. The Hague: Mouton.

Hualde, Jose Ignacio and Jon Ortiz de Urbina (eds.). 2003. *A grammar of Basque*. Berlin and New York: Mouton de Gruyter.

Huang, Cheng-Teh J. 1982. Logical relations in Chinese and the theory of grammar. PhD dissertation, MIT.

Huddleston, Rodney and Pullum, Geoffrey K. *et al.* 2002. *The Cambridge grammar of the English language*. Cambridge University Press.

Huntley, David. 1980. The evolution of genitive-accusative animate and personal nouns in Slavic dialects. In Jacek Fisiak (ed.), *Historical morphology*, 189–212. The Hague, Paris and New York: Mouton.

Ilola, Eeva and Arto Mustajoki. 1989. *Report on Russian morphology as it appears in Zaliznyak's grammatical dictionary*. (Slavica Helsingiensia 7.) Department of Slavonic Languages, University of Helsinki.

Isačenko, A. V. 1968. *Die russische Sprache der Gegenwart*, vol. I. Halle: Max Niemeyer Verlag.

Jackendoff, Ray. 1975. Morphological and semantic regularities in the lexicon. *Language* 51, 639–71.

1990. *Semantic structures*. Cambridge, MA: MIT Press.

Jakobi, Angelika. 1990. *A Fur grammar: phonology, morphophonology, and morphology*. Hamburg: Helmut Buske.

Karcevskij, S. 1932. Sur la structure du substantif russe. *Charisteria Guilelmo Mathesio quinquagenario: a discipulis et circuli linguistici pragensis sodalibus oblata*, 65–73. Prague: Cercle linguistique de Prague.

Kastovsky, Dieter. 2005. Hans Marchand and the Marchandeans. In Štekauer and Lieber (eds.), 99–124.

Kay, Paul. 1997. Construction Grammar. In Paul Kay (ed.), *Words and the grammar of context,* 123–32. Stanford: CSLI Publications.

Kemmer, Suzanne. 1993. *The middle voice*. Amsterdam: John Benjamins.

Kennedy, Benjamin. 1962. *Revised Latin primer*. Harlow: Longman.

Kibrik, Aleksandr E. 1977a. *Opyt strukturnogo opisanija Arčinskogo jazyka,* vol. II: Taksonomičeskaja grammatika. (Publikacii otdelenija strukturnoj i prikladnoj lingvistiki 12.) Moscow: Izdatel´stvo Moskovskogo Universiteta.

1977b. *Arčinskij jazyk: teksty i slovar´*. Moscow: Izdatel´stvo Moskovskogo Universiteta.

Kiparsky, Paul. 1982. Lexical morphology and phonology. In In-Seok Yang (ed.), *Linguistics in the morning calm: selected papers from SICOL-1981*, 3–91. Seoul: Hanshin Publishing.

1983. Word formation and the lexicon. In Frances Ingemann (ed.), *Proceedings of the 1982 Mid-American Linguistics Conference*, 3–29. University of Kansas.

2005. Blocking and periphrasis in inflectional paradigms. In Geert Booij and Jaap van Marle (eds.), *Yearbook of Morphology 2004*, 113–35. Dordrecht: Kluwer.

Kiparsky, Valentin. 1967. *Russische historische Grammatik,* vol. II: *Die Entwicklung des Formensystems*. Heidelberg: Carl Winter.

Klavans, Judith. 1985. The independence of syntax and phonology in cliticization. *Language* 61, 94–120.

Klenin, Emily. 1983. *Animacy in Russian: a new interpretation*. Columbus, OH: Slavica.

Kotyczka, Josef. 1980. *Kurze polnische Sprachlehre.* Berlin: Volk und Wissen.

Krieger, Hans Ulrich and John Nerbonne. 1993. Feature-based inheritance networks for computational lexicons. In Ted Briscoe, Ann Copestake and Valeria de Paiva (eds.), *Inheritance, defaults and the lexicon*, 90–136. Cambridge University Press.

Kuhn, Jonas. 2007. Interfaces in constraint-based theories of grammar. In Gillian Ramchand and Charles Reiss (eds.), *The Oxford handbook of linguistic interfaces*, 613–50. Oxford University Press.

Kühner, Raphael. 1955. *Ausführliche Grammatik der Lateinischen Sprache* (revised by Andreas Thierfelder). Hamburg: Hahn.

Ladd, D. Robert, Bert Remijsen and Caguor Adong Manyang. 2009. On the distinction between regular and irregular inflectional morphology: evidence from Dinka. *Language* 85, 659–70.

Lavidas, Nikolaos and Dimitra Papangeli. 2007. Deponency in the diachrony of Greek. In Baerman *et al.* (eds.), 97–26.

LeTourneau, Mark S. 2003. Interpretability, feature strength, and impoverished agreement in Arabic. In Dilworth B. Parkinson and Samira Farwaneh (eds.), *Perspectives on Arabic linguistics XV*, 85–134. Amsterdam: John Benjamins.

Lieber, Rochelle. 1992. *Deconstructing morphology.* University of Chicago Press.

2000. Internal structure of words. In G. Booij, C. Lehmann and J. Mugdan (eds.), *Morphology: an international handbook on inflection and word formation*, 404–16. Berlin: Mouton de Gruyter.

2004. *Morphology and lexical semantics*. Cambridge University Press.

2007. The category of roots and the roots of categories: what we learn from selection in derivation. *Morphology* 16, 247–72.

2009. A lexical semantic approach to compounding. In Rochelle Lieber and Pavol Štekauer (eds.), *The Oxford handbook of compounding*, 78–104.Oxford University Press.

Lodge, Gonzalez. 1901–33. *Lexicon Plautinum,* vols. I-II. Leipzig. Reprinted 1962, Hildesheim: Olms.

Luís, Ana and Spencer, Andrew. 2005. A paradigm function account of 'mesoclisis' in European Portuguese. In Geert Booij and Jaap Van Marle (eds.), *Yearbook of Morphology 2004*, 177–228. Dordrecht: Kluwer.

Maiden, Martin. 2002. Sound change, morphemic structure and the rise of suppletion in the Romance verb. Paper presented at the Surrey Linguistics Circle, University of Surrey.

2004. When lexemes become allomorphs: on the genesis of suppletion. *Folia Linguistica* 38, 227–56.

Maiden, Martin and Paul O'Neill. 2010. On morphomic defectiveness: evidence from the Romance languages of the Iberian peninsula. In Baerman, Corbett and Brown (eds.), 103–24.

Mańczak, Witold. 1956. Ile jest rodzajów w polskim? *Język Polski* 36.2, 116–21.

Marchand, Hans. 1960. *The categories and types of present-day English word-formation.* Wiesbaden: Harassowitz.

Matthews, Peter H. 1972. *Inflectional morphology*. Cambridge University Press.

2007. How safe are our analyses? In Baerman *et al.* (eds.), 297–316.

Matthews, William Kleesmann. 1960. *Russian historical grammar*. University of London, Athlone Press.

McMahon, April. 1994. *Understanding language change*. Cambridge University Press.

Mel'čuk, Igor. 2006. *Aspects of the theory of morphology*. Berlin: Mouton de Gruyter.

Meyer, Peter. 1994. Grammatical categories and the methodology of linguistics. Review of W. Andries van Helden, *Concept formation between morphology and syntax. Russian Linguistics* 18, 341–77.

Miller, Philip H. 1992. *Clitics and constituents in phrase structure grammar*. New York: Garland.

Mithun, Marianne. 1984. The evolution of noun incorporation. *Language* 60, 847–94.

Mithun, Marianne and Greville G. Corbett. 1999. The effect of noun incorporation on argument structure. In Lunella Mereu (ed.), *Boundaries of morphology and syntax*, 49–71. Amsterdam: John Benjamins.

Mofu, Suriel Semuel. 2008. Biak morphosyntax. PhD dissertation, Oxford University.

Müller, Gereon. 2004. On decomposing inflection class features: syncretism in Russian noun inflection. In Gereon Müller, Lutz Gunkel and Gisela Zifonun (eds.), *Explorations in nominal inflection*, 189–227. Berlin: Mouton de Gruyter.

2008. Review of Matthew Baerman, Dunstan Brown and Greville G. Corbett, *The syntax–morphology interface: a study of syncretism. Word Structure* 1, 199–232.

Nixon, Paul. 1924. *Plautus* (5 vols.). Cambridge, MA: Harvard University Press.

Noyer, Rolf. 1997. *Features, positions and affixes in autonomous morphological structure.* New York: Garland.

1998. Impoverishment theory and morphosyntactic markedness. In Steven G. Lapointe, Diane K. Brentari and Patrick M. Farrell (eds.), *Morphology and its relation to phonology and syntax*, 264–85. Stanford: CSLI Publications.

Palmer, Bill. 2009. *Kokota grammar: Oceanic Linguistics Special Publication*. Honolulu: University of Hawai'i Press.

Palmer, Bill and Dunstan Brown. 2007. Heads in Oceanic indirect possession. *Oceanic Linguistics* 46, 199–209.

Payne, John. 1980. The decay of ergativity in Pamir languages. *Lingua* 51, 147–86.

Perlmutter, David M. and Janez Orešnik. 1973. Language-particular rules and explanation in syntax. In Stephen R. Anderson and Paul Kiparsky (eds.), *A festschrift for Morris Halle*, 419–59. New York: Holt, Rinehart and Winston.

Plag, Ingo. 2002. The role of selectional restrictions, phonotactics, and parsing in constraining suffix ordering in English. In Geert Booij and Jaap Van Marle (eds.), *Yearbook of Morphology 2001*, 285–314. Dordrecht: Kluwer.

2003. *Word-formation in English*. Cambridge University Press.

Plag, Ingo and Harald Baayen. 2009. Suffix ordering and morphological processing. *Language* 85, 109–52.

Plank, Frans. 1994. Inflection and derivation. In R. Asher (ed.), *Encyclopedia of language and linguistics*, vol. III., 1671–8. Oxford: Pergamon Press.

Plank, Frans and Wolfgang Schellinger. 1997. The uneven distribution of genders over numbers: Greenberg's Nos. 37 and 45. *Linguistic Typology* 1, 53–101.

Priestly, T. M. S. 1993. Slovene. In Bernard Comrie and Greville G. Corbett (eds.), *The Slavonic languages*, 388–454. London: Routledge.

Przepiórkowski, Adam. 2003. A hierarchy of Polish genders. In Piotr Bański and Adam Przepiórkowski (eds.), *Generative linguistics in Poland: morphosyntactic investigations*, 109–22. Warsaw: Instytut Podstaw Informatyki PAN.

Rainer, Franz. 2005. Constraints on productivity. In Štekauer and Lieber (eds.), 335–52.

Rappaport, Gilbert C. 2010. The grammaticalization of the category *masculine personal* in West Slavic. In Björn Hansen and Jasmina Grković (eds.), *Diachronic Slavic syntax: gradual changes in focus, Wiener Slawistischer Almanach Sonderband* 74, 169–80. Munich, Berlin and Vienna: Verlag Otto Sagner.

Redkin, V. A. 1971. *Akcentologija sovremennogo russkogo literaturnogo jazyka: posobie dlja učitelej*. Moscow: Prosveščenie.

Reformatskij, A. A. 1975. Fonemy jot i 'i' v russkom jazyke. In A. Reformatskij (ed.), *Fonologičeskie ètjudy*, 74–96. Moscow: Nauka.

Riehemann, Suzanne. 1998. Type-based derivational morphology. *Journal of Comparative Germanic Linguistics* 2, 49–77.

Roberts, Ian. 2007. Head movement. In Baltin and Collins (eds.), 113–47.

Ross, Malcolm. 2005. Pronouns as a preliminary diagnostic for grouping Papuan languages. In Andrew Pawley, Robert Attenborough, Robin Hide and Jack Golson (eds.), *Papuan pasts: cultural, linguistic and biological histories of Papuan-speaking peoples*, 15–66. Canberra: Pacific Linguistics.

Sag, Ivan A., Thomas Wasow and Emily M. Bender (eds.). 2003. *Syntactic theory: a formal introduction*. Stanford: CSLI Publications.

Saloni, Zygmunt. 1988. O tzw. formach nieosobowych męskoosobowych we współczesnej polszczyźnie. *Biuletyn Polskiego towarzystwa jezykoznawczego* 41, 155–66.

Samvelian, Pollet. 2007. A (phrasal) affix analysis of the Persian ezafe. *Journal of Linguistics* 43, 605–45.

Šanskij, N. M. 1975. *Russkij jazyk. Leksika. Slovoobrazovanie.* Moscow: Prosveščenie.

Sapir, Edward. 1911. The problem of incorporation in American languages. *American Anthropologist* 13, 250–82.

Saussure, Ferdinand de. 1915. *Cours de linguistique générale*. Paris: Payot.

Scalise, Sergio and Emiliano Guevara. 2005. The lexicalist approach to word-formation and the notion of the lexicon. In Štekauer and Lieber (eds.), 147–88.

Scalise, Sergio and Antonietta Bisetto. 2009. The classification of compounds. In Rochelle Lieber and Pavol Štekauer (eds.), *The Oxford handbook of compounding*, 34–53. Oxford University Press.

Schmitz, Leonhard. 2004. *Grammar of the Latin language*. New York: Hippocrene. First published 1851 by Lea & Blanchard.

Selkirk, Elizabeth. 1982. *The syntax of words*. Cambridge, MA: MIT Press.

Siegel, Dorothy. 1977. The adjacency constraint and the theory of morphology. In M. J. Stein (ed.), *Proceedings of the 8th Annual Meeting of the North-Eastern Linguistics Society*, 189–97. Amherst: University of Massachusetts.

Skorik, Pjotr Ja. 1977. *Grammatika čukotskogo jazyka (Čast' 2: Glagol, Narečie, Služebnie Slova)*. Leningrad: Nauka.

Smith-Stark, T. Cedric. 1974. The plurality split. In M. W. L. Galy, R. A. Fox and A. Brucks (eds.), *Proceedings of the 10th annual meeting of the Chicago Linguistic Society*, 657–71. Chicago: CLS.

Sowa, John F. 2000. *Knowledge representation: logical, philosophical, and computational foundations*. Pacific Grove, CA: Brooks Cole Publishing Co.

Spencer, Andrew. 1991. *Morphological theory*. Oxford: Blackwell.

1993. Review of Rochelle Lieber, *Deconstructing morphology*. *Language* 69, 580–7.

2000a. Agreement morphology in Chukotkan. In Wolfgang U. Dressler, Oskar E. Pfeiffer, Markus Pöchtrager and John R. Rennison (eds.), *Morphological Analysis in Comparison*, 191–222. Amsterdam and Philadelphia: John Benjamins.

2000b. Morphology and syntax. In Geert Booij, Christian Lehmann and Joachim Mugdan (eds.), *Morphology: an international handbook on inflection and word formation*, 312–35. Berlin: Mouton de Gruyter.

2002. Gender as an inflectional category. *Journal of Linguistics* 38, 279–312.

2004. Morphology – an overview of central concepts. In Louisa Sadler and Andrew Spencer (eds.), *Projecting Morphology*, 67–110. Stanford: CSLI Publications.

2005. Towards a typology of 'mixed categories'. In C. Orhan Orgun and Peter Sells (eds.), *Morphology and the web of grammar: essays in memory of Steven G. Lapointe*, 95–138. Stanford: CSLI Publications.

Sridhar, S. N. 1990. *Kannada.* London and New York: Routledge.

Stang, Christian S. 1952. *La langue du livre 'Učenie i xitrost' ratnago stroenija pexotnyx" ljudej' 1647*. Oslo: Norske Videnskaps-Akademi.

Stankiewicz, Edward. 1978. The inflection of Serbo-Croatian substantives and their genitive plural endings. In H. Birnbaum (ed.), *American contributions to the Eighth International Congress of Slavists,* vol I: *Linguistics and Poetics*, 666–81. Columbus, OH: Slavicas.

Steinhauer, Hein. 1985. Number in Biak; counterevidence to two alleged language universals. *Bijdragen tot de Taal-, Land- en Volkenkunde* 141, 462–85.

Štekauer, Pavol and Rochelle Lieber (eds.). 2005. *Handbook of word-formation*. Dordrecht: Springer.

Stewart, Thomas and Gregory Stump. 2007. Paradigm function morphology and the morphology–syntax interface. In Gillian Ramchand and Charles Reiss (eds.), *The Oxford handbook of linguistic interfaces*, 383–421. Oxford University Press.

Stolz, Thomas. 2008. Kymrische Ausnahmen order walisische Regeln? Was die substantivische Pluralvariation uns lehrt. In Cornelia Stroh and Aina Urdze (eds.), *Morphologische Irregularität: neue Ansätze, Sichtweisen und Daten*, 111–50. Bochum: Universitätsverlag Dr. N. Brockmeyer.

Strecker, Karl. 1929. *Einführung in das Mittellatein*. Berlin: Weodmann.

Stump, Gregory T. 1990. Breton inflection and the split morphology hypothesis. In R. Hendrick (ed.), *The syntax of the modern Celtic languages*, 97–119. San Diego: Academic Press.

1991. A paradigm-based theory of morphosemantic mismatches. *Language* 67, 675–725.

1993. Review of Rochelle Lieber, *Deconstructing morphology*. *Journal of Linguistics* 29, 485–90.

1998. Inflection. In Andrew Spencer and Arnold Zwicky (eds.), *The handbook of morphology*, 13–43. Oxford: Blackwell.

2001. *Inflectional morphology: a theory of paradigm structure*. Cambridge University Press.

2002. Morphological and syntactic paradigms: arguments for a theory of paradigm linkage. In Geert Booij and Jaap van Marle (eds.), *Yearbook of Morphology 2001*, 147–80. Dordrecht: Kluwer.

2005a. Rules about paradigms. In C. Orhan Orgun and Peter Sells (eds.), *Morphology and the web of grammar: essays in memory of Steven G. Lapointe*, 49–82. Stanford: CSLI Publications.

2005b. Word-formation and inflectional morphology. In Štekauer and Lieber (eds.), 49–72.

2006. Heteroclisis and paradigm linkage. *Language* 82, 279–322.

2010. Morphology. In Patrick Hogan (ed.), *The Cambridge encyclopedia of the language sciences*, 515–19. Cambridge University Press.

Švedova, N. Ju (ed.). 1984. *Slovar' russkogo jazyka S.I. Ožegova*. Moscow: Russkij Jazyk.

Švedova, N. Ju., N. D. Artunjunova, A. V. Bondarko, Val. Vas. Ivanov, V. V. Lopatin, I. S. Uluxanov and F. P. Filin. 1980. *Russkaja grammatika*, vol. I. Moscow: AN SSSR.

Szymanek, Bogdan. 1988. *Categories and categorization in morphology*. Lublin: Catholic University Press.

Thorndahl, W. 1974. *Genetivens og lokativens -y/-ю-endelser i Russiske middelaldertekster. (med Tysk resumé)*. Copenhagen: Rosenkilde og Baggers Forlag.

Thornton, Anna. 2011. Overabundance (multiple forms realizing the same cell): a non-canonical phenomenon in Italian verb morphology. In Maria Goldbach, Marc-Olivier Hinzelin, Martin Maiden and John Charles Smith (eds.), *Morphological autonomy: Perspectives from Romance inflectional morphology*. Oxford University Press.

Timberlake, Alan. 1993. Russian. In Bernard Comrie and Greville G. Corbett (eds.), *The Slavonic languages*, 827–86. London: Routledge.

2004. *A reference grammar of Russian.* Cambridge University Press.

Tixonov, A. N. 1985. *Slovoobrazovatel´nyj slovar´ russkogo jazyka.* Moscow: Russkij Jazyk.

Tokarski, Jan. 1993. *Schematyczny indeks a tergo polskich form wyrazowych. Opracowanie i redakcja: Zygmunt Saloni.* Warsaw: Wydawnictwo Naukowe PWN.

Tosco, Mauro. 2001. *The Dhaasanac language*. Cologne: Rüdiger Köppe.

Touretzky, D. 1986. *The mathematics of inheritance systems*. London: Pitman.

Townsend, Charles. 1975. *Russian word-formation*. Columbus, OH: Slavica.

Trask, Robert Lawrence. 1997. *A student's dictionary of language and linguistics.* London: Arnold.

Tseng, Jesse. 2003. Phrasal affixes and French morphosyntax. In Gerald Penn, Gerhard Jäger, Paola Monachesi and Shuly Wintner (eds.), *Proceedings of Formal Grammar 2003*, 177–88. Stanford: CSLI Publications.

Uluxanov, I. C. 1979. Slovoobrazovatel´nye otnošenija meždu častjami reči. *Voprosy jazykoznanija* 28.4, 101–10.

Unbegaun, B. O. 1935. *La langue russe au XVIe siècle (1500–1550),* vol. I: *La flexion des noms*. Paris.

1969. Les anciens russes vus par eux-memes. *Selected papers on Russian and Slavonic Philology*, 272–86. Oxford: Clarendon Press.

Uspensky, Boris A. 1965. *Strukturnaja tipologija jazykov*. Moscow: Nauka.

van den Heuvel, Wilco. 2006. *Biak: description of an Austronesian language of Papua.* Utrecht: LOT.

van Helden, W. Andries. 1993. *Case and gender: concept formation between morphology and syntax* (2 vols.). Amsterdam: Rodopi.

van Marle, Jaap. 1985. *On the paradigmatic dimension of morphological productivity.* Dordrecht: Foris.

Vasmer, Maks. 1986. *Ètimologičeskij slovar´ russkogo jazyka*, ed. and trans. O. N. Trubačev. 2nd edn. Moscow: Progress.

Vinogradov, V. V 1960. *Grammatika russkogo jazyka,* vol 1: *Fonetika i morfologija.* Moscow: Nauka.

(ed.). 1954. *Slovar´ jazyka Puškina*. Moscow: Gosudarstvennoe izdatel'stvo inostrannyx i nastsional'nyx slovarej.

Vinogradov, V. V., Istrina, E. S. and S. G. Barxudarov (eds.). 1953. *Grammatika russkogo jazyka,* vol. L: *Fonetika i morfologija*. Moscow: AN SSSR.

Walker, G. S. M. (ed.). 1957. *Sancti Columbani opera*. Dublin Institute for Advanced Studies.

Wertz, C. A. 1977. The number of genders in Polish. *Canadian Slavonic Papers* 19, 50–63.

Williams, Edwin. 1981. On the notions 'lexically related' and 'head of word'. *Linguistic Inquiry* 12, 245–74.

2007. Dumping lexicalism. In Gillian Ramchand and Charles Reiss (eds.), *The Oxford handbook of linguistic interfaces*, 353–81. Oxford University Press.

Worth, Dean S. 1966. On the stem/ending boundary in Slavic indeclinables. *Zbornik za Filologiju i Lingvistiku* 9, 11–16.

Wunderlich, Dieter. 2001. A correspondence-theoretic analysis of Dalabon transitive paradigms. In Geert Booij and Jaap van Marle (eds.), *Yearbook of Morphology 2000*, 233–52. Dordrecht: Kluwer.

Wunderlich, Dieter and Ray Fabri. 1995. Minimalist morphology: an approach to inflection. *Zeitschrift für Sprachwissenschaft* 14, 236–94.

Wurzel, Wolfgang U. 1984. *Flexionsmorphologie und Natürlichkeit*. Berlin: Akademie-Verlag.

Xu, Zheng, Mark Aronoff and Frank Anshen. 2007. Deponency in Latin. In Baerman *et al.* (eds.), 127–44.

Yonge, C. D. (trans.). 1856. *The Orations of Marcus Tullius Cicero*. London: Henry G. Bohn.

Zaliznjak, Andrej A. 1967. *Russkoe imennoe slovoizmenenie*. Moscow: Nauka.

1973. O ponimanii termina 'padež' v lingvističeskix opisanijax. In Andrej A. Zaliznjak (ed.), *Problemy grammatičeskogo modelirovanija*, 53–87. Moscow: Nauka.

1977. *Grammatičeskij slovar' russkogo jazyka*. Moscow: Russkij jazyk.

Zieniukowa, Jadwiga. 1981. *Rodzaj męski osobowy we współczesnych językach zachodniosłowiańskich*. Wrocław: Zakład Narodowy im. Ossolińskich, Wydawnictwo Polskiej Akademii Nauk.

Žukova, Alevtina N. 1972. *Grammatika korjakskogo jazyka: fonetika, morfologija*. Leningrad: Nauka.

Zwicky, Arnold. 1985a. Heads. *Journal of Linguistics* 21, 1–29.

1985b. How to describe inflection. In Mary Niepokuj, Mary Van Clay, Vassiliki Nikiforidou and Deborah Feder (eds.), *Proceedings of the eleventh annual meeting of the Berkeley Linguistics Society*, 372–86. Berkeley Linguistics Society.

1992. Some choices in the theory of morphology. In R. D. Levine (ed.), *Formal grammar: theory and implementation*, 327–71. Oxford University Press.

1993. Heads, bases and functors. In Norman Fraser and Greville G. Corbett (eds.), *Heads in grammatical theory*, 292–315. Cambridge University Press.

1996. Syntax and phonology. In K. Brown and J. Miller (eds.), *Concise encyclopedia of syntactic theories*, 300–5. Oxford: Elsevier Science.

Index of languages

Arabic, Classical (Afroasiatic, Semitic), 165
Arabic, Modern (Afroasiatic, Semitic), 19, 63
Arapesh (Torricelli), 96
Archi (Nakh-Daghestanian, Lezgic), 16, 188, 189, 192–3, 209–17

Basque (Isolate), 9
Biak (Austronesian, South Halmahera-West New Guinea), 62
Bininj Gun-wok (Gunwinyguan), 88, 90–6, 105–6, 191
Breton (Indo-European, Celtic), 9
Burmeso (East Bird's Head-Santani, Burmeso), 147–8

Chukchi (Chukotko-Kamchatkan), 11, 29, 179, 189

Dalabon (Gunwinyguan), 47, 61, 152, 169, 170–80, 185
Dhaasanac (Afroasiatic, Cushitic), 152, 173, 180–4
Dinka (Nilo-Saharan, Nilotic), 148
Dutch (Indo-European, Germanic), 19, 28, 40, 274, 289, 298

English (Indo-European, Germanic), 20, 23, 27, 38, 44, 114, 115, 154, 158, 263, 273, 290, 291, 298
English, Old (Indo-European, Germanic), 223, 224, 225, 263, 274, 290, 298

Finnish (Uralic, Finnic), 8
Flemish, Lapscheure dialect, *see* Dutch
Fur (Nilo-Saharan, Fur), 62, 112

German (Indo-European, Germanic), 60, 258, 291

Greek (Indo-European, Greek), 193, 245–6, 296
Greek, Ancient, *see* Greek
Greek, Modern, *see* Greek

Kannada (Dravidian), 163
Kashmiri (Indo-European, Dardic), 163–4
Kokota (Austronesian, Oceanic, Northwest Solomonic), 118, 122, 138, 262
Koryak (Chukotko-Kamchatkan), 60–1, 179

Latin (Indo-European, Italic), 13–14, 15–16, 24, 108–9, 111, 124, 159–60, 186–9, 194–209, 217–19, 225–8, 229, 230, 231–43, 244–5, 296

Mansi (Uralic, Mansi), 21–2
Mayali, *see* Bininj Gun-wok
Mohawk (Iroquoian, Northern Iroquoian), 27

Nahuatl (Uto-Aztecan, Aztec), 20
Ngiyambaa (Pama-Nyungan), 189
Nuer (Nilo-Saharan, Nilotic), 148

Old English, *see* English, Old
Old Russian, *see* Russian

Polish (Indo-European, Slavonic), 81, 96–105, 109, 162, 224, 293
Portuguese (Indo-European, Italic), 117

Russian (Indo-European, Slavonic), 4–6, 8, 14–15, 20, 24, 30–3, 34, 39–40, 47–50, 51, 55–7, 58–60, 63–6, 67–90, 112, 113, 123, 124, 125–31, 135–9, 142, 143, 149, 153–9, 160–2, 223–4, 249, 251, 257, 260, 262, 264, 268–70, 271–81

Saami, North (Uralic, Sami), 180
Sanskrit (Indo-European, Indic), 258, 268, 296
Serbian/Croatian/Bosnian (Indo-European, Slavonic), 18
Shughni (Indo-European, Iranian), 1, 9, 20, 38, 39, 267–9, 289
Slovene (Indo-European, Slavonic), 167–9, 295
Somali (Afroasiatic, Cushitic), 19

Tamil (Dravidian), 163
Tsakhur (Nakh-Daghestanian, Lezgic), 165
Turkish (Altaic, Turkic), 24

Index of names

Ackema, Peter, 18, 19, 28
Ackerman, Farrell, 12, 41, 112
Aikhenvald, Alexandra Y., 160
Albright, Adam, 293
Anderson, Stephen R., 6, 17, 43, 117, 248, 255, 270, 281
Anshen, Frank, 217
Arlotto, Anthony, 297
Aronoff, Mark, 7, 15, 96, 181, 217, 239, 255, 270, 273, 296
Asher, R. E., 163

Baayen, Harald, 34
Baerman, Matthew, 16–18, 33, 40, 60, 62, 65, 85, 130, 148, 151, 154–6, 160, 161, 163–5, 170, 181, 184, 187, 188–9, 192, 193, 202, 209, 218, 292, 294, 296, 297
Baker, Mark, 22
Baldi, Philip, 217
Baltin, Mark, 29
Bauer, Laurie, 12, 298
Beard, Robert, 12, 281, 298
Bender, Emily M., 35
Bisetto, Antonietta, 298
Bleiching, Doris, 291
Blevins, James, 112, 291
Bobaljik, Jonathan David, 169, 179
Bonami, Olivier, 35
Bonnet, Max, 231, 244, 297
Booij, Geert, 62, 259, 260, 274, 278, 298
Boyé, Giles, 35, 161
Bredenkamp, Andrew, 264
Brown, Dunstan, 9, 53, 58–9, 60, 62, 66, 68, 74, 87, 99, 103–5, 118–19, 130, 131, 133, 137, 161, 164, 170, 171, 188, 268, 291, 293, 294
Brown, Lea, 117
Browne, Wayles, 18
Bybee, Joan, 40, 63, 64, 175

Byrd, Andrew, 296

Cabredo Hofherr, Patricia, 161
Cahill, Lynne, 291
Campbell, Lyle, 297
Carnie, Andrew, 290
Carstairs-McCarthy, Andrew, 111, 112, 124, 160, 291
Cattell, R., 290
Černyx, P. Ja., 59
Chierchia, Gennaro, 298
Chumakina, Marina, 9, 16, 164, 223, 290, 296
Collins, Chris, 29
Comrie, Bernard, 152, 155
Corbett, Greville G., 4, 5, 9, 14, 16, 18–19, 26, 27, 33, 40, 51–2, 53, 60, 62–3, 81, 87, 96, 113, 130, 134, 135, 138–39, 142, 147, 161, 163–4, 167, 168, 171, 185, 187–8, 193, 223, 238, 243, 244, 293, 294, 297
Corbin, Danielle, 277, 278, 298
Cubberley, Paul, 298

Daelemans, W., 36, 290
Dal′, Vladimir, 280
de Smedt, K., 36
Deo, Ashwini, 258
Dixon, R. M. W., 160, 296
Dodyxudoeva, Lelja R., 289
Donohue, Mark, 147
Doroszewski, Witold, 293
Dressler, Wolfgang, 149
Drexel, Guido, 291

Embick, David, 21, 23, 35, 290
Ernout, Alfred, 202, 218, 231, 244
Evans, Nicholas, 87, 88, 91, 92, 96, 147, 170, 171, 173, 174, 292, 295
Evans, Roger, 36, 41, 45

Fabri, Ray, 160, 175
Fedjanina, Nina A., 71
Finkel, Raphael, 112
Fischer, Wolfdietrich, 165, 295
Fletcher, Janet, 295
Flickinger, Daniel, 36, 290
Flobert, Pierre, 202, 217, 218, 222, 231, 232, 233, 234, 236, 238, 239, 241, 242, 244, 245, 297
Fortson, Benjamin W., 296, 297
Fortune, Reo, 96
Frank, Wright Jay, 148
Fraser, Norman, 31, 51, 52, 53, 96, 134, 135, 139, 167, 168, 294

Gabka, K., 293
Gaby, Alice, 117
Gagarina, Natalia, 149
Garde, P., 293
Gazdar, Gerald, 36, 41, 45, 290, 291, 297
Gerdts, Donna, 20
Gibbon, Dafydd, 291
Goldberg, Adele, 259
Goldsmith, John, 111
Greenberg, Joseph H., 60, 62, 160
Guevara, Emiliano, 298
Gvozdev, A. N., 281

Haegeman, Liliane, 289
Halle, Morris, 20, 24, 73, 179, 291, 294
Hansson, Gunnar O., 180
Harley, Heidi, 21, 35, 290
Harris, Alice, 297
Harris, Roy, 297
Haspelmath, Martin, 8, 298
Heath, Jeffrey, 174
Hippisley, Andrew, 9, 16, 53, 133, 137, 188, 223, 289, 290, 293, 297, 298
Hjelmslev, Louis, 159
Hock, Hans Henrich, 223
Hualde, Jose, 9
Huang, Cheng-Teh J., 290
Huddleston, Rodney, 44, 290
Huntley, David, 102

Ilola, Eeva, 291
Isačenko, A. V., 293
Istrina, E. S., 293

Jackendoff, Ray, 255, 261, 264, 281, 298
Jakobi, Angelika, 62

Kastovsky, Dieter, 281
Kay, Paul, 259
Kemmer, Suzanne, 217
Kennedy, Benjamin, 194, 202, 296
Kibrik, Aleksandr E., 209
Kilani-Schoch, Marianne, 149
Kiparsky, Paul, 273, 277
Kiparsky, Valentin, 59
Klavans, Judith, 117
Klein, Ewan, 290
Klenin, Emily, 81
Kotyczka, Josef, 162
Krasovitsky, Alexander, 164
Krieger, Hans Ulrich, 258
Kuhn, Jonas, 17
Kühner, Raphael, 202, 218

Ladd, Robert D., 148
Lavidas, Nikolaos, 245, 297
Lecarme, Jacqueline, 117
LeTourneau, Mark S., 291
Lieber, Rochelle, 2, 9–12, 17, 21, 22, 34, 210, 251, 252, 281, 290, 291, 298
Lodge, Gonzalez, 231, 297
Luís, Ana, 117

Maiden, Martin, 16, 161
Malouf, Robert, 112
Mańczak, Witold, 292
Manyang, Caguor Adong, 148
Marantz, Alec, 20, 23, 24, 35, 179
Marchand, Hans, 298
Matthews, Peter H., 51, 217
Matthews, William Kleesmann, 59
McConnell-Ginet, Sally, 298
McMahon, April, 223
Mel'čuk, Igor, 263
Meyer, Peter, 152
Miller, Philip H., 117
Mithun, Marianne, 20, 26, 27
Mofu, Suriel Semuel, 62
Moser, Lionel, 36
Müller, Gereon, 173, 292, 294
Mustajoki, Arto, 291

Neeleman, Ad, 18, 19, 28
Nerbonne, John, 258
Nixon, Paul, 109, 186, 297
Noyer, Rolf, 21, 23, 24, 35, 159, 168, 175, 290

O'Brien, Jeremy, 111
O'Neill, Paul, 161
Orešnik, Janez, 295
Oritz de Urbin, Jon, 9

Pagliuca, William, 175
Palmer, Bill, 118, 119
Palmer, Frank, 290
Papangeli, Dimitra, 245, 297
Payne, John, 289
Perkins, Revere, 175
Perlmutter, David M., 295
Pestal, Lina, 149
Plag, Ingo, 34, 270
Plank, Frans, 38, 62
Pöchtrager, Markus, 149
Priestly, T. M. S., 168, 169
Przepiórkowski, Adam, 292
Pullum, Geoffrey, 44, 290

Rainer, Franz, 298
Rappaport, Gilbert C., 104, 292
Redkin, V. A., 71
Reformatskij, A., 293
Remijsen, Bert, 148
Riehemann, Suzanne, 258
Roberts, Ian, 22
Ross, Belinda, 295
Ross, Malcolm, 147

Sadler, Louisa, 264
Sag, Ivan A., 35, 290
Saloni, Zygmunt, 102
Samvelian, Pollet, 117
Šanskij, N. M., 281
Sapir, Edward, 20
Saussure, Ferdinand de, 248
Scalise, Sergio, 21, 298
Schellinger, Wolfgang, 62
Schmitz, Leonhard, 242
Selkirk, Elizabeth, 10
Siegel, Dorothy, 274
Skorik, Pjotr Ja, 11, 189
Smith-Stark, T. Cedric, 163
Sowa, John F., 290
Spencer, Andrew, 3, 8–10, 11, 29, 151, 179, 189, 262, 264, 265, 293, 298
Sridhar, S. N., 163
Stang, Christian S., 59
Stankiewicz, Edward, 294
Steinhauer, Hein, 62
Stewart, Thomas, 228, 229
Stolz, Thomas, 295
Strecker, Karl, 231, 244
Stump, Gregory T., 7, 9, 11–12, 34, 37, 38, 41, 51, 57, 108, 112, 147, 152, 169, 228–29, 262, 266–8, 289, 290, 297, 298
Švedova, N. Ju., 159, 161, 281, 294
Szymanek, Bogdan, 281

Thomas, François, 202, 218
Thorndahl, W., 59
Tiberius, Carole, 130, 164
Timberlake, Alan, xx, 53
Tixonov, A. N., 262
Tokarski, Jan, 162
Tosco, Mauro, 180, 181
Touretzky, D., 36, 290
Townsend, Charles, 276
Trask, Robert Lawrence, 151
Tseng, Jesse, 117

Uluxanov, I. C., 298
Unbegaun, B. O., 59, 224
Uspensky, Boris A., 60

van den Heuvel, Wilco, 62
van Helden, W. Andries, 152
van Marle, Jaap, 274
Vasmer, Maks, 224
Vinogradov, V. V., 281, 293

Wasow, Thomas, 35
Wertz, C. A., 102
Williams, Edwin, 10, 17, 21, 25, 26, 35, 290
Worth, Dean S., 139
Wunderlich, Dieter, 160, 175, 179, 295
Wurzel, Wolfgang, 112

Xu, Zheng, 217, 218

Zaliznjak, Andrej A., 71, 72, 81, 88, 152, 161, 278, 279, 291, 294
Zieniukowa, Jadwiga, 293
Žukova, Alevtina N., 60
Zwicky, Arnold M., 12, 13, 17, 18, 19, 37, 38, 39, 108, 152, 290

Index of subjects

activation of a deponent verb,
    see regularization and deponency
Adjacency Constraint, 274
affix competition, 34, 269–77
agglutination, *see* radical agglutination
agreement
  canonical, 19
  controller, 19, 127, 128–9, 218, 242
  'partial', 40, 63
  'reduced', 19, 63
  resolution, 18
  target, 18, 61, 86, 91, 97, 100, 103, 128–9, 132, 142, 155, 156, 161, 218, 242, 247, 273
alignment and diachronic deponency, 219, 221–6, 235, 247
allomorphy (inflectional), 9, 112, 198, 209
A-morphous Morphology, 6, 283
analogical levelling and extension, 223, 248
animacy
  semantic, 47, 80–2, 90, 101, 143, 144, 246, 256
  syntactic, 47, 80–2, 101–3, 143, 144, 256
attribute ordering, 45, 54, 57–64, 66, 68, 85–6, 110, 112, 129, 157, 162, 174, 175, 184, 284; *see also* feature, and ordering
augmentative derivation, *see* expressive derivation
autonomy (morphological)
  and incorporation, 26–7
  and movement effects, 28–9
  different types of, 45, 55–7, 69, 107–10, 151, 283–5, 287

blocking, *see* morphological blocking
Bracket Erasure Convention (BEC), 273

case
  and gender, 62, 64
  and number, 47, 49, 51, 53, 58, 59, 60, 61, 72, 85, 88–90, 106, 112, 129, 148, 157, 161, 166, 168, 192
category-changing derivation, *see* derivational relation
category-preserving derivation, *see* derivational relation
clitic, 20, 39, 116–18, 122, 150, 170, 175, 176, 177–8, 283
component, *see* interface
compound, 8, 10–11, 12, 20, 27, 28, 43, 251, 267, 281, 297, 298
conditions, *see* derivational conditions
conjugation, 189, 194, 195, 196–201, 202, 205, 221, 253
conjugational class, 64, 195, 197, 200, 202, 226, 235–8
construction grammar, 259
Construction Morphology, 259, 260
controller, *see* agreement, controller
conversion, *see* derivational relation
cumulation, *see* radical agglutination

DATR
  attribute, 49, 57
  discussion of, 6, 41
  empty path, 54, 57, 69, 75, 76, 82, 102, 158
  equation, 48, 49
  evaluable path, 82–3, 95, 101, 114, 133, 137, 139, 142, 143, 144, 182, 183, 199, 246, 257, 272, 273
  LHS, 49, 53, 57, 67, 69, 77, 78, 83, 85, 93, 101, 102, 131, 133, 142, 195, 207
  node, 46–7
  path, 49, 232

DATR (*cont.*)
  path extension, 84–6, 152, 157, 159, 161, 162, 167, 169, 172, 212, 268
  RHS, 49, 50, 53, 78, 80, 81, 115, 122, 139, 142, 144, 195, 222, 264, 291, 294
  subpath, 57, 66–7, 84, 157, 195, 196, 203, 211, 212, 220
declension
  and gender, 51, 52, 99, 103, 138, 139, 143, 144, 159, 160
  assignment of, 139–42
  class, 4, 32, 51–4, 57, 58, 59, 69–80, 81, 84, 88–90, 97, 99, 103, 109, 122–44, 157, 253, 256, 257, 274, 275, 278, *see also* inflectional class
default, *see also* Pāṇinian Determinism
  default inference, 34, 35, 84, 86, 151, 152, 155, 156–67, 169, 170, 180–4, 203
  default inheritance, 6, 30–5, 36, 45, 51, 53, 55, 116, 258
  exceptional case default, 45, 46, 84, 86–106, 113, 184, 188, 191, 192, 203, 207, 208, 220, 222, 235, 240, 248, 285–7
  levels or orders of default, 190–3, 195, 202–9, 213, 214, 216, 220, 221, 231, 235, 245, 246, 248
  normal case default, 84, 86–106, 187, 191, 285, 286
defective, defectiveness, 40, 161, 162, 189, 192, 193, 200, 201, 204, 208–9, 215, 218, 225, 228, 231, 238, 239, 241, 242, 243, 295, 296
deponency
  and attribute ordering, 188, 196, 211, 220
  and generalized referral, 108, 284
  canonical, 185, 193, 208
  extended deponency, 43, 188–94, 209–13, 216
  form and function default properties of, 188–9, 192
  neo-deponency, 244–5, 246
  properties of, 186–94, 201–2, 221–6
  semi-deponency, 191, 193, 201, 205–8, 216, 220
derivation
  canonical, 37, 39, 260, 261, 262, 265, 267, 282
  derivational hierarchy, 37, 249, 256, 258
  vs. inflection, 37–40
derivational conditions, 271–7
derivational relation
  and canonical derivation, *see* derivation, canonical
  category-changing as type of, 10, 281, 282
  category-preserving as type of, 265–9, 281, 282
  conversion as type of, 251, 262–3, 265, 281, 286
  discussion of, 253
  transposition as type of, 251, 263–5
diachrony and deponency, 221–48
diminutive, *see* expressive derivation
dissociation (function and form)
  different types of, 13–19, 22–5, 29, 36, 43, 53, 107, 108, 144, 146, 151, 153, 186, 187, 267
Distributed Morphology, 19–29, 35, 169

edge feature, 117–18, 119–22, 251, 253, 260, 267
Elsewhere Condition, 34, 273
entropy, 112
equation, *see* DATR, equation
evaluable path, *see* DATR, evaluable path
exceptional case default, *see* default, exceptional case default
exceptionality, *see* regular/regularity, and exceptionality
exhaustiveness, 63–4
exponence
  multiple, 3
  ordering of, *see* attribute ordering
  rule of, 7, 73, 125, 126, 270, 293
expressive derivation, 14, 39, 265, 266, 268
extended deponency, *see* deponency, extended deponency
extension, *see* DATR, path extension

facts (morphological), 5, 35
feature
  and attribute, 57, 58, 61, 63, 64
  and morphology–syntax interface, 16, 17, 63, 117, 219, 229, 248
  and ordering, 67, 162, 164, 165, 169; *see also* attribute ordering
  combination of, 41, 196
  geometry and syncretism, 35, 162
  morphological, 14, 17, 29, 50, 73, 109–10, 211, 275, 285

morphosyntactic, 3, 7, 12, 14, 16, 17, 21, 41, 46, 49, 53, 57, 63, 65, 71, 85, 88, 108–9, 114, 116, 117, 118, 151, 152, 154, 156, 157, 158, 160, 187, 190, 201, 211, 219, 229, 250, 281, 282, 295
semantic, 210, 254, 257, 276, 290
Feature Interaction Paradox, 164
formalism
and DATR, *see* DATR
frequency
and patterns of syncretism, 166
and productivity, 277–81; *see also* productivity, different senses of
and Russian case, 130
and stress patterns in Russian, 74, 278
full morphological model, 45–50, 61, 62, 67, 102, 141, 157, 176, 181, 287
function–form, *see* meaning–form

gender
and adjectives, 51, 65, 68, 85, 86, 103, 123, 127–30, 134, 156, 157, 161, 164, 166
and animacy, 47, 88, 90, 97, 98, 139, 142, 143, 144, 163
and pronouns, 61, 85, 99, 103, 123, 127, 128–9, 161, 166
formal assignment, 51, 52, 92, 95, 103, 105, 128, 142, 143, 275
formal gender, 143, 144, 258, 275
semantic assignment, 51, 52, 53, 90, 92, 103, 105, 140, 142, 163
structured gender, 99, 103
subgender, 96, 97–105
generalization
and inheritance, *see* inheritance
and location of, 1, 21, 54, 111, 160, 207
Generalization Violation, 131, 133, 136
generalized referral, *see* deponency, and generalized referral; syncretism, and generalized referral

head
and movement, 23, 25, 28
complex head, 23, 24, 28
marking, 40, 122, 267, 268, 269, 282
Head-Application Principle, 267, 268
heteroclisis, 35, 193, 214, 228
heuristic
majority default, *see* Majority Default (heuristic)
rules of referral beat rules of exponence, *see* referral
hierarchy
derivational, *see* derivation, derivational hierarchy
lexemic, 36, 45, 54–7, 69, 70, 82, 107, 111, 113, 116, 119, 121, 122, 123, 124, 125, 135, 138, 139–44, 145, 187, 190, 195, 210, 211, 226, 230, 248, 249, 250, 254, 256, 257, 258, 262, 280, 283, 285
morphological, 36, 45, 57, 69, 70, 76, 78, 79, 80, 107, 108, 109, 111–49, 157, 160, 190, 202, 211, 226–31, 235, 247, 248, 249, 250, 275, 283, 285
hierarchy relations, 31, 54–7, 75, 76, 79, 80, 85, 131, 158, 280, 286
homonymy
and defectiveness, 192, 193, 215, 240
and syncretism, 9
HPSG, 35, 258

Identity Function Default, 84, 122, 131, 177, 262, 263
incorporation
and morphological autonomy, *see* autonomy (morphological), and incorporation
incremental morphology, 12, 17, 21, 22, 251
index
and morphome, 15, 16, 161, 180–4, 196, 198, 200, 284
indices, 54, 80, 109, 111, 152
inferential–realizational morphology, 6, 7, 12, 41, 42, 51, 53, 54, 58, 60, 80, 84, 94, 117, 126, 160, 229, 251, 269, 270, 284
inflection
canonical, 37, 113–14
vs. derivation, 37–40
inflectional class, 5, 7, 9, 13, 14–16, 17, 18, 29, 30–3, 35, 36, 39, 42, 45, 70, 111–50, 187, 190, 195, 198, 233, 235, 256, 260, 266, 267, 274, 275, 283–5, 287, *see also* declension; conjugation
canonical, 5, 113, 138, 147, 148
inflectional proximity (of classes), 131, 134–5, 138
inheritance
default, *see* default, default inheritance
global (context for), 80–2, 139

inheritance (*cont.*)
local (context for), 80–2, 139, 183
monotonic, 33, 35, 149
multiple, 6, 35–7, 42, 69
interdependency node (type of node in a network), 139–40, 144, 257, 258, 272, *see also* DATR, evaluable path
interface
morphology and syntax, 17, 42, 186, *see also* feature, and morphology–syntax interface
and principle of morphology-free syntax, 17, 18, 42, 142, 187
and principle of syntax-free morphology, 17, 18, 42, 63, 117, 122

lambda abstraction, *see* semantic level of lexeme
lexeme, 6–13, 45–57, 69–83
lexeme-formation, 251–8, 277
lexeme-formation template (LFT), 260–82, 286
lexemic hierarchy, *see* hierarchy, lexemic
lexical entry, 1, 3, 7, 9, 10, 21, 22, 23, 32, 34, 35, 39, 52, 53, 69, 75, 82, 83, 84, 93, 94, 100, 101, 106, 115, 139, 140–1, 182, 195–9, 200, 203, 204, 206, 208, 211, 212, 213, 214, 215, 222, 226, 234, 235, 237, 246, 248, 249, 250, 251, 252, 253, 254, 255, 256, 257, 258, 263, 264, 266, 268, 273, 274, 279, 280
lexical knowledge representation language, *see* DATR
lexical redundancy rule, 255, 281
lexical specification
different degrees of, 80, 87, 96, 101
lexicalist hypothesis, 25, 26
lexical–realizational morphology, 21
LHS, *see* DATR, LHS

Majority Default (heuristic), 125, 131, 136
mandatory inheritance, *see* inheritance, monotonic
meaning–form
association, 3, 10, 217
canonical function/form mapping, 117, 187
dissociation, *see* radical agglutination; dissociation (function and form)
mediopassive, 245
middle
and origin of Latin passives, 217–19, 246–7
Mirror Principle, 22, 23, 26
misalignment and diachronic deponency, 36, 219
mismatch
and derivation, 279–81, *see also* dissociation
modularity in morphology and inflection/derivation distinction, 37–40
monotonic, *see* inheritance, monotonic
morpheme
in Distributed Morphology, *see* Distributed Morphology
morpheme-based morphology, 10, 12, 20, 21, 22, 51, 281
morpholexically coherent lexicon, principle of, 261
morphological analysis, 45–9, 50, 53, 61, 66, 83, 85, 287
morphological blocking, 277
morphological change and deponency, 225, 232, 241, 244, 246
morphological hierarchy, *see* hierarchy, morphological
morphological paradigm, as opposed to syntactic, *see* paradigm linkage
morphological projection, 107, 114, 115, 116, 124, 125, 145, *see also* autonomy (morphological)
morphology-free syntax, *see* interface
morphome, *see* index, and morphome
morphosyntactic feature, *see* feature, morphosyntactic
morphotactics, 2, 3, 10, 116
multiple exponence, *see* exponence, multiple

network
network relations, 54, 55, 69, 73, 74, 79, 80, 124, 133
neutralization, *see* syncretism
No Blur Principle, 112
node, *see* DATR, node
Node Elimination, 108, 113, 114, 115, 119, 122, 145–6, 287
nominalization, 264–5, 269
nominals, 55, 63, 75, 77, 78, 79, 80, 84, 85, 86, 113, 123, 127, 128, 133, 137, 139, 152, 154, 161, 165, 167, 169, 284
number
and case, *see* case, and number

and gender, 19, 46, 61, 64, 65, 68, 147, 162, 163, 195, 287

obligatoriness, 37, 250
ordering of attributes in a DATR path, *see* attribute ordering
ordering of features, *see* attribute ordering; feature, and ordering
orthogonality
  and hierarchies cohabiting a network, 42
  and multiple inheritance, 35–7, 42
overdifferentiation, 158, 159
Overextended Ancestor Prohibition, 85, 86, 112, 128, 161

Pāṇini and competition, 22, 34, 35, 179, 191, 251, 270, 277
Pāṇinian Determinism, 34, 35, 83
paradigm
  paradigm relations, 151
  paradigm signature, 40, 45, 46, 68, 148
  paradigm splits, 40, 45, 66, 68, 161, 191
  virtual paradigm, 221, 222, 226–31, 243–5, 247, 248, 285, 286
Paradigm Economy, 111, 112
Paradigm Function Morphology (PFM), 7, 169, 228, 229, 283
paradigm linkage, universal default rule of, 228, 229, 230, 231, 243, 248
paradigmatic realignment, *see* realignment and diachronic deponency
paradigmatic restructuring and deponency, 221, 222–6
partial agreement, *see* agreement, 'partial'
passivation of a deponent verb, *see* regularization and deponency
path, *see* DATR, path
periphrasis, 20, 175
person
  as a value of animacy, 97, 102, 103
  implied by animacy, 256, 257, 279
phonological level of a lexeme, 7, 12, 38, 41, 70, 223, 252–7, 258, 260, 261, 262, 263, 264, 266, 270, 271, 278, 279, 281
phonology, 38, 69, 109, 110, 223
possession hosts, 119, 121
possessive adjective, 14, 15, 127
principal parts, 112, 148
productivity
  and defaults, 106–7
  different senses of, 37, 38, 250, 262, 271, 281, 282, 286

radical agglutination, 7–10, 17, 41
  deviations
    cumulation, 8, 9, 24
    extended exponence, 8, 9
    meaningless morphs, 8, 9, 10
    zero morphs, 8, 9, 24
realignment and diachronic deponency, 219, 220, 221–2, 225–6, 231, 234, 235, 240, 241, 243, 246, 247
realization
  and rule, 41, 90, 122, 151, 172, 189, 229, 230, 231, 247, 282
referral
  referral-based syncretism, 131, 148, 167–9, 180
  rules of referral beat rules of exponence, 126, 136, 138, 147
regular/regularity
  and exceptionality, 44, 87, 90, 94, 96, 286
  degrees of, 5, 34, 35, 42, 43, 86, 94, 113, 187, 188, 189, 190, 194, 199–201, 203, 208, 217, 219, 220, 228, 231, 244, 268, 279, 280, 285, 286, 287
  semi-regularity, 5–6, 33, 34
regularization and deponency, 234–43, 246, 247, 248, 285
relevance, 63, 64
RHS, *see* DATR, RHS
rules, morphology as, 45, 46, 50, 285, 286

seamless-web morphology, 19–29, 42
semantic level of lexeme, 7, 253, 254, 255, 256, 261, 262, 263, 270, 276, 279, 281
semantics
  and derivation, 11, 251, 253, 266, 267, 275–7, 278–81
  and morphosyntax-relevant features, *see* feature, morphosyntactic
semi-productivity, *see* productivity, different senses of
signature, *see* paradigm, paradigm signature
stem
  and Archi nouns, 209–13
  and indexing, *see* index, and morphome

stem (*cont.*)
  and Latin conjugation, 16, 195, 199–201
  and paradigmatic restructuring, 222–6
  and theme vowels, *see* theme vowel
  formation, 197, 200, 202, 209, 211, 212
stress
  hierarchy, 74–80
  morphological vs. phonological, 70–80
sub-path, *see* DATR, sub-path
suppletion, 9, 16, 215, 216, 223
syncretism
  and generalized referral, 108, 170–5, 180
  by default inference, 156–67, 180–4
  by indexing, 167, 180–4
  by referral, 167–9, 180
  canonical, 154, 155, 156, 244
  Set Theoretic School definition of, 152
syntactic determinism, 37, 250
syntactic paradigm, as opposed to morphological, *see* paradigm linkage
syntax of words, 3, 10–12
syntax-free morphology, *see* interface

target, *see* agreement, target
theme vowel, 15, 16, 17, 24, 84, 111, 132, 187, 197, 198–9, 284
theorem
  and full morphological model, 46, 48
transparency
  and productivity, 37, 112, 262, 278, 280; *see also* productivity, different senses of
transposition, *see* derivational relation

underspecification
  and default inference, *see* default, default inference
  and syncretism, 157, 168, 170–5, 178, 179, 180, 181, 183, 184
uninflectedness, 65, 154, 155, 156, 158, 159, 162

variation
  and deponency, 196, 219, 245
virtual paradigm, *see* paradigm, virtual paradigm
voice attraction, 218–19

word-formation rule (WFR), 239, 249–51, 254–7, 258, 260, 274, 281
word-syntax, *see* syntax of words
Wortbildungsmodell of derivation, 281
Wortbildungstyp, 281